Labour and Sustainable Development

LABOUR AND SUSTAINABLE DEVELOPMENT

M. S. GUPTA
M.Com., Ph.D.
Department of Commerce
R.K.D. College, (Magadh University), Patna
Bihar, (India)

SERIALS PUBLICATIONS
NEW DELHI (INDIA)

First Published – 2009

ISBN: 978-81-8387-206-5

Published by

SERIALS PUBLICATIONS
4830/24, Prahlad Street, Ansari Road
Darya Ganj, New Delhi-110002 (India)
Phone : 23245225 Fax : 91-11-23272135
E-mail: serials@satyam.net.in

CONTENTS

SECTION-IV

Agricultural Labour: Some Iusses

PREFACE

Labour plays a dual role in rural development as both the beneficiary and a major productive resource of development. The structure, size, quality or type, spatial distribution of the labour force can be important in affecting national aggregate supply potential and national development. Most developing countries are characterized by a rapidly growing population and labour force. Absorbing the growing labour force in productive employment is one of the principal challenges of development. Much of this labour force is absorbed in traditional agriculture while an increasing number of people seek employment in non-farm activities. The majority of population in developing countries live in the rural areas, which are often described as the home of the impoverished people engaged in agriculture.

Hence, labour still continues to be the central issue of analysis and policy-making in developing countries because a large portion of the population in these countries cannot find employment or earn a decent living. The conditions of many people in the rural areas of many parts of the world including India have occupied centre stage in development for about more than five decades. The conditions in terms of social, economic, political, organizational and health largely end up as gloomy. While enormous resources and visible efforts have been invested over the years to address the unbalanced development against the rural sector, wide disparities still exist between the urban and rural sectors.

I would like to place on record our deep appreciation and gratitude to all the contributors from different parts of the world for time and effort that they have put into preparing their contributions.

I feel highly privileged to express my profound regard and heartfelt indebtedness to Dr. Alakh N. Sharma, Institute for Human Development, New Delhi; Dr. N.K. Choudhary, Professor and Head, Department of Economics, Patna University, Patna and Dr. Asha Singh, Professor and Head, Department of Economics, Magadh Mahila College, Patna University, Patna for their help and encouragement in my academic pursuits. I express my sincere regards to Dr. S.B. Rai, Principal, R.K.D. College, Patna for encouraging me to complete this academic work. I am also thankful to Dr. T.K. Shandilya, Department of Economics, College of Commerce, Patna for help by way of good discussion over the present issue.

I am thankful to all my colleagues, friends and relatives who helped me directly or indirectly in finalizing the manuscript. I also appreciate the support of my wife, Manju Sahu and children, Mallika Aishwarya and Kumar Manorath for preparation of the manuscript and achieve this milestone.

Lastly, I appreciate the enthusiasm and efforts of Mr. S.K. Jha of M/s Serials Publications, New Delhi for publishing this work in present form within minimum possible time with such a professional approach.

M. S. Gupta
Patna (Bihar), INDIA

LIST OF CONTRIBUTORS

Angela Dziedzom Akorsu, Doctoral Programme Member, Manchester Business School, University of Manchester, UK.

Asha Singh, Professor and Head, Department of Economics, Magadh Mahila College (Patna University), Patna.

Bipin Kumar, Head, Department of Economics, R.R.S. College (Magadh University), Mokama.

C. Muthuraja, Faculty Member, P.G. Department of Economics, The American College, Madurai 625 002 (Tamil Nadu).

Clement A Tisdell, Emeritus Professor of Economics, The School of Economics, University of Queensland, Brisbane, QLD, 4072. Australia.

Jane Kabubo-Mariara, Senior Lecturer, School of Economics, University of Nairobi, Nairobi, Kenya.

John Victor Mensah, Senior Research Fellow, Centre for Development Studies, University of Cape Coast, Ghana.

Krishna Kant Jha, Faculty Member, P.G. Department of Commerce, C.M. College, Darbhanga.

Kuldip Kaur, Reader, Punjab School of Economics, GNDU, Amritsar.

Kwabena Barima Antwi, Lecturer, Department of Geography and Tourism, University of Cape Coast, Ghana.

M.S. Gupta, Department of Commerce, R.K.D. College (Magadh University), Patna 800 020.

Mahesh Chandra Prasad, Senior Lecturer, Department of Applied Economics and Commerce, Patna University, Patna-800005.

Mamata Swain, Professor & Head, North Orissa University, Baripada, Orissa.

Maneet Gill, Research Scholar, Punjab School of Economics, GNDU, Amritsar.

Md. Reyazuddin, Reader in Commerce, Vanijya Mahavidyalaya, Patna University, Patna.

Motsomi Marobela, Department of Management, University of Botswana.

Nilufar Jahan, Economist , Australian Bureau of Agricultural and Resource Economics, Canberra, Australia.

Patrick Kwashie Akorsu, Lecturer, School of Business, University of Cape Coast, Ghana.

Pelotshweu T. Moepeng, Research Fellow, Botswana Institute of Development Policy Analysis, P/Bag BR 0029 Gaborone, Botswana.

Pushpa Sinha, Department of Economics, Patna Women's College (Patna University), Patna.

Ratna Mitra, Department of Economics, Patna Women's College (Patna University), Patna.

Tapan Kumar Shandilya, Department of Economics, College of Commerce (Magadh University), Patna.

SECTION-I

LABOUR AND DEVELOPMENT

1

LABOUR: A BENEFICIARY OR VICTIM OF RURAL DEVELOPMENT IN GHANA?

John Victor Mensah & Kwabena Barima Antwi

INTRODUCTION

Labour plays a dual role in rural development as both the beneficiary and a major productive resource of development. It is the contribution to productive activity made by the workforce both by manually and intellectually (Pass *et al,* 1993: 298). Labour is one of the four main factors of production, the others being natural resources (land), capital and entrepreneurship. Labour force may be distinguished from 'work force' but the terms may be used interchangeably. Labour force represents the total number of workers available for employment in a country and comprises those people working as employees, the self employed and unemployed. Work force is the people who work in an industry or a firm, considered as a group. The labour force, together with the capital stock, determines a country's aggregate supply potential. The structure, size, quality or type, spatial distribution of the labour force can be important in affecting national aggregate supply potential and national development. For example, a country with a predominantly young labour force will tend to find it easier to train workers in the changing skills needed to take advantage of emerging technologies. It also has implications for the nature of aggregate demand.

The level of reward (wages, salaries and profits) received by rural workers, to a large extent, depends on the level and strategy of rural development-be it technocratic, reformist and radical[1]. For example, in the capitalist economy the reward level is largely determined by the forces of demand for and supply of labour so skilled and unskilled workers earn different wages. Workers may also benefit from the services and facilities put in place by the rural development programmes such as improved technology, credit, land reforms, road, market, potable water, health services, schools and information supply. Where rural development is a failure, labour may be a victim of the negative change, thereby exacerbating the gap between rural and urban sectors.

Most developing countries are characterised by a rapidly growing population and labour force. Absorbing the growing labour force in productive employment is one of the principal challenges of development. Much of this labour force is absorbed in traditional agriculture while an increasing number of people seek employment in non-farm activities. The majority of populations in the developing countries live in the rural areas, which are often described as the home of the impoverished people engaged in agriculture. While it is true that most rural people are poor, there are some comparatively wealthy landowners, as well as people engaged in a wide range activities of activities such as manufacturing, processing, trading and services. Some members of rural communities may even have income levels and life-styles comparable with those of the wealthiest urban dwellers (Dixon, 1990).

Agriculture is the main economic activity in the rural sector in most developing countries and land remains the core basis of wealth and political power. Evidence shows that there is in general an inverse relationship between the proportion of people living in rural areas and per capita gross domestic product (Dixon, 1990). In the developing countries, the proportion of the total population living in rural areas is usually much greater than in the developed countries. Apart from the city states of Hong Kong and Singapore, some Latin American countries have a low proportion of the population in rural areas for their level of development. In the 1980s, sub-Saharan African countries had about 90 per cent of their population living in rural areas (World Bank, 1988).

However, in almost all developing countries, there is a very substantial reduction in the proportion of people living in rural areas. Between 1990 and 2000, Africa experienced high urbanization of annual growth rate of 8.1 per cent. Even though Africa is less urbanised region it has the fastest demographic growth rate. About two thirds of the population live in poor environment with no sanitation, water, electricity, transportation or adequate health care services. Africa's urbanisation processes are distinct within the context of weak state institutional capacity, low economic growth and weak civil society organisations (Urban Management Programme, 2004). While the proportion of the population living in rural areas has declined, the number has continued to increase (Dixon, 1990).

In Ghana in 1960, the Greater Accra Region, the hub of national industrialisation programme had a gross value added per capita of 176 Ghana pounds compared to the Ashanti and Western regions (second highest) with 68 Ghana pounds, and northern Ghana with 30 Ghana pounds. Mensah (1981) corroborated the disparities in the distribution of socio-economic facilities in Ghana, 1960-1980.

Assefa (1980) and Ewusi (1984), based on 1974/75 household survey in Ghana, observed that the rural sector was slightly worse off than the national profile of income distribution. The lower 20% of the rural sector received 6% of income as against the national lower 20% that received an average of 7.1% while the upper 20% of the rural sector received slightly more (45.5%) than the national upper 20% average (45%).

Assefa (1980) noted that, the urban sector with only 33% of the total population accounted for 45% of total national expenditure in 1974/75. Both per capita rural and urban expenditures in real terms declined over the period: 1961- 1975. The fall was more with the average rural income resulting in the widening of rural-urban income gap. According to Ewusi (1984), income distribution within the rural sector appeared slightly better than that of the urban sector. In the urban sector, the lowest decile received 1.5% of income compared to their rural counterparts that received 1.8% of income. In 1974/75, the computed values of Gini coefficient for the nation, the rural sector and the urban sector were 0.3664, 0.3762 and 0.4024 respectively. As a rule of thumb, a Gini coefficient of less than 0.5 depicts a low income inequality while that of greater than 0.5 shows high income inequality.

Ghana Statistical Service (1995) indicates that poverty in the rural areas is higher than the national average. A larger proportion of the poor is concentrated in the savannah area. The poorest area in Ghana is the rural savannah, followed by the rural coastal, urban savannah and rural forest. Thus, poverty is a rural phenomenon in Ghana.

The need to reduce rural poverty and rural-urban disparity necessitated many governments in independent developing countries including Ghana to incorporate rural development into their national and international programmes. Based on secondary data through library research, this chapter examines the link between labour and rural development programmes in Ghana. It discusses whether labour is a beneficiary or victim of rural development programmes. It argues that though poverty levels are declining in recent years, poverty is still a rural phenomenon and therefore needs policy reforms, and monitoring and evaluation.

The chapter is organised into eight sections. The next section presents the theoretical perspectives of labour. Defining the rural sector is the focus of the third section while section four discusses the threat to traditional societies and rural production. Section five deals with the meaning of rural development. The link between labour and rural development in Ghana is discussed in the sixth section. Sections seven discusses the assessment, achievements and lessons while the last section presents the conclusions.

THEORETICAL PERSPECTIVES OF LABOUR

The study of labour is influenced by four main schools of thought namely neo-classical, Keynesian, institutional and radical approaches (Thomas, 1991). The neo-classical perspective focuses on the rather abstract study of the demand and supply sides of labour markets at the micro level. The demand side analysis is strongly embedded in the marginal productivity approach, which reflects the behaviour of profit-maximising entrepreneurs within highly competitive market structures. The supply-side analysis is based on individual preferences between work and leisure or between work and investment in human capital. In this way, one obtains a coherent analytical framework that yields seemingly precise outcomes for wage structures and employment levels.

After World War II, the Keynesian analysis complemented the micro-economic neo-classical analysis. The Keynesian perspective focused on macroeconomics and gave unemployment a central role in its analysis. It identified various types of unemployment: structural, cyclical, seasonal and frictional. The Keynesian analysis asserted that the neo-classical approach of relying on the market in the determination of wages did not hold in a world where a limited effective demand would cause involuntary unemployment. The neo-classical approach has survived in principle with modifications from macro-insights.

The institutional school deals with the main actors in the labour market: trade unions, employers and the government. The central theme focuses on the in-depth analysis of bargaining processes between these actors. The outcomes are the details of payment conditions and the legalities of work contract. This school assigns an important role to the government as a mediator in conflicts and as an intervening force through its education, manpower and social policies. Ample *prima facie* evidence exists about the weak, unprotected, unorganised and low skilled nature of work with small-scale industries (SSIs), and therefore unemployment in SSIs forms one of the sub-markets of the labour market (Thomas, 1991).

The radical school is based on the Marxist hypothesis that capital owners exploit workers. This approach tends to examine the wider societal relations of power inequalities in the specific markets and their institutional underpinnings. The radical view on exploitation, discrimination and income inequalities offers a broader scope for application to the developing countries where unemployment is pervasive. It sets out primarily to reveal the underlying power structures that have an overriding impact on all markets and institutions.

The four approaches have generated different research methods in terms of the objects of analysis, the research questions and the techniques applied. The neo-classical approach tends to concentrate on demand-supply analysis for work and labour; the Keynesian approach emphasises unemployment issues; the institutional approach tends to examine the actors in the labour market and collective bargaining; and the radical approach focuses on class differences on the supply side and the control of labour in the context of national power relationships on the demand side. Even though there are some very good scientific and political reasons why these paradigms are different, the study of labour should combine the elements of different approaches (Magnum and Philips, 1988; Thomas, 1991).

Employment creation and conditions of work through viable investment activities are important in setting national objectives. The level of employment is a basic measure of economic well-being of a nation or sector. Increasing unemployment is a major concern to all citizens because of its social consequences and costs to both individuals and society while improvement in the employment situation is a source for hope in the future. Conditions of work deal with issues such as reward systems, working environment, hours of work, and procedures of resolving disputes.

A typical developing country could be represented by a three-tier employment structure, consisting of an urban formal sector, an urban informal sector, and rural economy. The urban labour market (both formal and informal sectors) is likely to pay higher wages than the rural labour market. This wage differential is partly explained by the fact that urbanites have to pay higher prices for food and housing than rural residents, and they are often compelled to buy commodities (water, fuel, materials) that are obtainable virtually free in rural areas. Evidence shows that most urban residents, even recent rural-urban migrants, are better off than all but the wealthiest rural residents (Gillis *et al.*, 1996).

Depending on the amount of population pressure and the prevailing pattern of land tenure, some rural people are forced to depend on wage employment because they have no land to farm or not enough to support their families. These agricultural labourers make up the very lowest income stratum in low income countries. In the rural areas, there are other farmers who engage in small-scale non-farm activities to provide important supplements to agricultural income.

DEFINING THE RURAL SECTOR

The definition of 'rural', like that of 'urban', is the subject of much debate. In many cases, the division between rural and urban is a highly artificial one and tends to defy universal acceptance. Urban centres generally operate as the transmitters of change to the rural areas. In recent years, the degree of urban-rural interaction has increased dramatically. The development of communications and commercialisation has resulted in the distinctiveness of rural areas being broken down. Aspects of urban life and global events now impinge directly on most rural communities in the developing countries (Dixon, 1990). High levels of geographical and occupational migration (temporary and permanent) are major influences on bringing rural and urban areas closer together in terms of their characteristics.

In Ghana, every settlement with a population of less than 5,000 is officially regarded as rural while that with a population of 5,000 or more is an urban. However, the distinction between rural and urban should include their functions and the principal occupations of the inhabitants. If the majority of the inhabitants are engaged in occupations like agriculture or timber exploitation, then the settlement is rural, but if the predominant occupations are industrial, commercial, administrative, or cultural (i.e. not directly related to the land), then the settlement is urban. An urban area is usually where rural people buy their tools and seek for services, and send their children for higher education (Dickson and Benneh, 1970).

THREAT TO TRADITIONAL SOCIETIES AND RURAL PRODUCTION

Traditional rural societies have evolved agricultural systems in which limited technology is applied to enable the needs of subsistence and limited exchange to be sustained over long periods of time. Traditional systems are capable of adapting to population growth, the introduction of new crops and techniques, and to a degree of commercialisation. However, there are limits to the ability of traditional systems to cope with rapid externally induced change. For example, agricultural systems in the developing countries have come increasingly under pressure as they have been incorporated into the global economy. Incorporation has destroyed or disrupted established mechanisms for coping with harvest failure, population growth, and the need for surplus production. The process of incorporation and establishment of production for the market generally involved the breakdown of localised subsistence production and the creation of a dependence on cash income from crop sales. The farmers involved have to adopt a more risky agricultural strategy. A successful subsistence harvest normally means that there will be sufficient food for the community. In contrast, a bumper cash-crop harvest carries no such guarantee but may result in low prices and insufficient income to purchase necessities. The contemporary problems facing the rural sector and people can be fully understood only in the context of how they developed.

Under colonial rule, the establishment of production for the market, fixed cash, rent, taxes and wage labour, all set in motion a process of differentiation. Land could be sold or taken by landlords and moneylenders in default of payment. Small farmers in some cases lost their land and became landless labourers, while large farmers, merchants, moneylenders, and landlords acquired land. Colonial agricultural policy was aimed at facilitating the development of commercial production, which sometimes did not conform to the local situation.

Incorporation of colonial land and labour into the world market was the establishment of plantation economies, which developed from the early seventeenth century to produce a range of tropical and sub-tropical crops, using slave labour (Potter *et al*, 2004). During the eighteenth and nineteenth centuries over nine million Africans were transported to the Americas, principally to produce sugar. This gave way to the employment of wage labour in some cases even before the abolition of slavery, because it was more productive and more profitable.

Many of the plantation companies became the core of current multinational agribusiness corporations. Between 1911 and 1930 Lever Brothers (now Unilever) established oil palm plantations in what are now Ghana, Democratic Republic of Congo, Nigeria, Gabon, and Cameroon. In 1926, Firestone purchased over 30,000 hectares of land at US$1 in Liberia to establish the world's largest rubber plantation.

The end of colonial period resulted in a general reduction of foreign ownership of plantations. Some were taken over by local concerns and others broken up into smallholder operations. Multinational agribusinesses have moved increasingly into control over marketing, processing, and supply of seeds, fertilisers, machinery, and other inputs. They have also been attracted to developing countries to take advantages of cheap land and labour to produce a variety of new products such as meat, fruit, vegetables and fresh flowers for developed countries. Smallholder developments frequently followed plantation development, in many cases acting as an 'expansion tank' for variation in demand. Private ownership of land and sometimes land colonisation schemes were important in smallholder development (Dixon, 1990; Potter *et al*, 2004).

Rural poverty is extremely complex and subject to various explanations. Most contemporary explanations can be grouped under socio-economic or environmental factors. The socio-economic approach (also known as political economy) relates the root cause of poverty to the skewed distribution of wealth and power in society. The commercialisation and incorporation of rural economies set in motion a process of inequality. According to Myrdal (1957), the interplay of market economic forces is usually more likely to increase, rather than decrease, regional inequalities. Neoclassical theory postulates that inequality is inherent in the capital system. For capitalism to be maintained as a socio-economic system there must be the accumulation of physical capital, and it is solely the capitalists, a small group of entrepreneurs, who engage in capital accumulation (Canterbury, 2005: 858).

Poverty could also be seen as self-inflicted. Individuals, families, and communities are poor due to idleness, drunkenness, unwise expenditure, incompetence and ignorance. Rural poverty is a result of processes which concentrate power and resources. These processes operate at all scales, from the international to the local. Processes operating at the local scale then reinforce the national and international ones. For example, if the international price of cocoa falls, then the national wholesale price falls as a result, and merchants pass the loss down the chain. The smallest and least powerful merchants and farmers lose most.

The environmental school focuses on shortage of resources, poor environmental conditions, and degradation of the environment. The relationship between poor environment and poverty is complex and has given rise to various interpretations (Hansen, 1992; Sachs, 2005). Poverty, as a factor of environmental degradation, is closely tied to population. Chambers (1994:3) notes that "higher population increases poverty, poverty leads to higher population, poverty is bad for the environment, increased population is bad for the environment and environmental deterioration contributes to poverty". Most of the impoverished rural communities are found in the poorest environments in sub-Saharan Africa, India and Bangladesh. Nevertheless many writers do not fall neatly into either of these two groups.

Poverty and inequality have the tendency to create tension among a population as the poor perceive the rich to be living their affluent lives through the sweat of the poor. It is also easy to create conditions where the poor are denied participation in many activities and access to resources because they are unable to pay for them.

The need to reduce poverty and inequality consequently became incorporated into national and international programmes. The next section looks at the concept of rural development.

RURAL DEVELOPMENT

'Rural development' is subject to various definitions and phrases. The World Bank (1975) notes that rural development is a strategy designed to improve the economic and social life of the rural poor. It involves extending the benefits of development to the poorest among those seeking a livelihood in the rural areas. The rural poor include small-scale farmers, tenants and the landless. This definition reflects how views of development have changed since the early 1970s. During the 1950s and 1960s development policies centred on growth maximisation, where the poor were expected to gain from the 'trickle down' of the benefits resulting from overall rapid growth. By the late 1960s, however, it was realised that rapid growth was characterised by a widened gap between the poor and the rich (Dixon, 1990).

During the early 1970s such terms as 'redistribution with growth' or 'growth with justice' appeared and rural development has become more broadly based. Besides, many governments and development partners (e.g. the World Bank and UNDP) stressed the need for 'integrated rural development' schemes to raise agricultural productivity and improve nutrition as well as improving rural healthcare, education, transport and marketing. Schumacher (1973) emphasised the need for transfer of appropriate technology from the rich to poor countries to improve the productivity of labour.

According to Mabogunje (1980), rural development is concerned with the improvement in the living standards of low income population living in rural areas on a self sustaining basis through transforming the socio-spatial structures. He emphasised the broad based, comprehensive and transforming nature of rural development. Todaro (1994) observes that rural development is integrated and a broad spectrum of activities encompassing small-scale agricultural progress and non-farm businesses to improve living standards. Even though agriculture is an obvious choice for concentration in programmes of rural development, the other sectors have to complement agricultural development. Thus, rural development is different from agricultural development.

Rural development refers to all those activities that affect the well-being of rural population including the provision of basic needs such as food and the development of human capital in the country side through education programmes. It concentrates on problems that have a direct bearing on raising agricultural production and farmers' incomes (Gillis *et al.*, 1996: 423).

Even though rural development has taken different forms in many parts of the world, the strategies may be grouped under three broad categories: technocratic, reformist, and radical as shown in Table 1. Most developing countries have adopted policies with strong technocratic elements. The main objective is to increase productivity, particularly in agriculture, which is the essence of Green Revolution. The criticism of such an approach is that it retains the structures that perpetuate inequalities of incomes and access to resources. This approach is often justified on two grounds: first, maximising agricultural growth; and second, the

Table 1
Major Types of Rural Development

Development strategy	*Objectives*	*Major beneficiaries*	*Dominant form of tenure*	*Ideology*	*Representative countries*
Technocratic	Increase output	Landowning elite	Large private and corporate farms, plantations, latifundia, various tenancy systems	Capitalist	Philippines, Brazil, Ivory Coast
Reformist	Redistribute income (and wealth); increase output	Middle peasants, 'progressive' farmers	Family farms; co-operatives	Nationalist	Mexico, Egypt
Radical	Social change; redistribute political power; wealth; and output	Small peasants and landless labourers	Collectives; communes; state farms	Socialist	Vietnam, China, Cuba, Algeria

Source: Griffen (1974: 204)

redistribution of resources would be costly and politically unacceptable.

Radical strategies focus on fundamental social change which rejects capitalism and attempts to construct some form of socialism. The revolutionary approach is based on the acceptance of the structural causes of poverty. Elimination of poverty must be the removal of the processes that perpetuate it.

The reformist approaches are essentially a compromise between the technocratic and radical types of change. Such policies take a variety of forms but in essence they involve attempts to redistribute power, income, and access to resources. In practice, the underlying structures are left largely intact. The various strategies reflect different views of the causes of rural poverty.

LABOUR AND RURAL DEVELOPMENT IN GHANA

The colonial exploitation of resources in Ghana (then the Gold Coast) not only hastened the collapse of the traditional rural structures but also distorted certain basic relationships in the society. The economy of the country became monetised such that traditional factors of production including labour were easily converted into commodities that could be exchanged in a self regulating market. For example, land acquisition and alienation became rife with the new production process. Land alienation and the rise of "progressive wealth farmer" led to the growth of inequalities among farming communities. By 1930, a small group of wealthy farmers in the Gold Coast were already responsible for a disproportionately large amount of the cocoa shipped from the colony (Frimpong-Ansah, 1996).

To ensure that production was sustained for the greater benefits of colonial exploitation, an integration plan to enhance capitalist accumulation was developed. The plan was based on the creation of an appropriate spatial order in which the peripheral rural areas were linked first to the colonial capital in the country. Hence transportation network and the urban system formed the two main elements of colonial penetration. Some highways and bridges, the seaport and railways network were constructed. Social facilities like schools, colleges, hospitals, telecommunications and water systems were established and concentrated in few towns such as Accra, Kumasi and Sekondi-Takoradi that formed "the golden triangle" (Brown, 1986).

During the pre-independence era (1945-57), the open colonial system underwent substantial modifications, the core of which focused on the expansion of the public sector and the gradual transfer of political if not economic power. The developmental state of Nkrumah undertook an aggressive policy of social inclusion through massive investment in human capital formation through the provision of free compulsory basic education, which fed into the tertiary education sector with science and technology as the anchor All these attempts were change the space economy of the period which had established a market centre-periphery pattern. The centre included the cocoa, mineral, timber export sector and coastal port towns. The periphery referred mainly to the labour reserve for the export sector (Songsore, 1979; Brown, 1986).

The dualism in the economy called for rural development that could be seen as the "rescue" strategy to supply the visible missing links needed to improve productivity and income; to supply basic socio-economic needs (e.g. schools, markets, clinics, water, and roads); create employment; and reduce rural-urban migration.

Ghana's development since independence in 1957 has witnessed a number of strategies of rural development. The rural development policies and programmes in post-independence Ghana are as follows:

1. Seven-Year Development Plan (1963/64-1969/70).
2. Youth and Rural Development Programme (1969-72).
3. Operation Feed Your-Self (1974-1978).
4. Economic Reforms (1983-1988).

5. Decentralisation policy as proxy for rural development (1988-to date).
6. Poverty Reduction Strategies
   - Ghana Poverty Reduction Strategy (GPRS I–2002-2005)
   - Growth and Poverty Reduction Strategy (GPRS II–2006-2009).

Seven-Year Development Plan (1963/64–1969)

Immediately after independence a socialist euphoria defined national development policy whose rural dimension saw a collective approach to rural transformation in agriculture, infrastructure and social services. The mass of peasants would be transformed into a national agricultural workforce to produce mass agricultural commodities to feed the nation. The Nkrumah government established the Workers Brigade, state farms and the food production and distributing companies, all of which formed part of programme for agricultural modernisation. The agricultural improvement programme was also tied to employment creation. The government also pursue a policy of import substitution industrialisation, which aimed at promoting rapid economic development. It was built on the rationale that industrialisation would quick start backward linkage effects with the local space economy as a way of addressing rural-urban disparities.

Even though the policies might be well intentioned they were less complementary. The implementation outcomes of the strategy exacerbated rural-urban disparities by:

- Increasing urban unemployment and deepening variation in income levels between the urban and rural areas;
- Allowing industrial products to enjoy high degree of protection locally because they could not compete with imported commodities. The situation somehow discouraged agricultural expansion;

- Causing foreign exchange shortages as a result of increased imports of raw materials for industries since strong backward linkages could not be established;
- Promoting low technology transfer because the strategy was based on capital intensive technology; and
- Encouraging a tendency toward a primate city configuration.

The plan though essentially directed at industrialisation rather than rural development, recognised the political nature of these social and economic decisions. Nkrumah's programme was halted when his government was overthrown by a military coup d'etat in 1966.

Youth and Rural Development Programme (1969-72)

This era of liberalism, in which the rural development challenge was part of the process of private investments catalysed by the development of rural infrastructure to open market, allowed commodities to move free into markets. It was a period that witnessed a more private sector approach in rural development but heavily and systematically backed by huge public investments in rural infrastructure to enable the rural private sector to emerge.

The Youth and Rural Development programme was formulated in the Second Republic under Dr. K. A. Busia in 1969. The Policy of Youth and Rural Development recognised the need to establish a new basis for rural prosperity. The main aim of the policy was to educate rural people and bring their outlook, opportunities and standards of living closer to those of urban dwellers. This could be achieved through productivity drives, the establishment of rural industries, and by means of education.

The eight main thrust of the policy were:

1. Adult education for rural development;
2. Identification of ways to commercialise all forms of production in rural areas;

3. Intensification of productivity drives with the aim of increasing efficiency and raising income level;
4. Finding new ways of thrift and finance for all rural areas;
5. Industrialisation of the countryside;
6. Improvement of transport and communication in the rural areas;
7. Impressing that investment could not be made without increase in the incomes of rural people; and
8. Investing government grant-in-aid in profit making enterprises and projects.

The main problems that accompanied the policy implementation were related to:

1. Accomplishing education of rural people for economic and social changes;
2. Inadequate funds to support general economic changes in the rural areas;
3. Integrating and sustaining the interests of youth (12-25 years) with those of adults;
4. Integrating and balancing the interests of those in the rural areas with those of the people in the urban areas;
5. Difficulties encountered in finding ways and means of integrating the activities of the existing Workers' Brigade with national economic activities.

The recognition of the need to integrate the interests of those in the rural areas with those of the people in the urban centres and to make standards of life of rural people comparable to those of city dwellers indicates that the policy was directed towards an integrated approach to rural development (Dorvlo, 1979; Brown, 1986).

Operation Feed Yourself (1974–1978/9)

The Acheampong government, after successful military takeover of power in January 1972, embarked on two programmes related to food and industrial raw material production, namely, "Operation Feed Yourself" and "Operation Feed Your Industries" in 1974. These programmes were embarked upon at the period when many countries were practising Green Revolution, which is the application of science and technology to Third World agriculture. The programmes encouraged Ghanaians to increase agricultural production to meet their household food requirements and generate enough to feed the agro-based industries. People were also encouraged to farm their backyards, especially those in the urban areas. The era marked a process of economic nationalism which saw mobilisation of human and financial resources towards Green Revolution and led to a massive investment in rural infrastructure such as feeder roads, irrigation facilities and rural housing.

The idea of growth centres was discussed in the 5 year development plan of 1975. It sought to ensure that policies which encouraged the dispersal of industries favoured the growth of smaller settlements in the rural areas. In that plan, a number of regional capitals received various face lifts to enable them act as secondary "magnets" for rural migrants streaming down to the primate centres. The establishment of Regional Development Corporations in all the political administrative areas was a purposeful thought to bring the needed balance in local and national development.

The first two years of the military regime (1972 and 1973) witnessed increased agricultural output. The economy, however, began to deteriorate steadily throughout the rest of the 1970s, largely as a result of poor domestic policies, economic mismanagement, corruption, and adverse external terms of trade shocks, particularly oil prices. High inflation, massive unemployment, large budget deficits, balance of payment deficits, continuous devaluation of the national currency (cedi) and drought made life unbearable for both the rural and urban dwellers. The most observable outcome of the policy failure was the exodus of Ghanaians (skilled and unskilled) to both developed and developing countries for greener pastures. By the end of the 1970s, there was enough evidence that efforts at rural development had not generated commensurate gains. Between 1978 and 1981, there were three military regimes that contributed to the virtual collapse of the Ghanaian economy with tremendous hardships to the people.

Economic Reforms (1983-1988)

The persistent economic decline of the late 1970s and the early 1980s necessitated the government of Provisional National Defence Council (PNDC) to adopt of the World Bank's prescribed economic recovery programme (ERP) in 1983. The prolonged period of stabilisation, in which the fundamentals of survival and coping mechanisms saw the neglect of rural development in favour of structural adjustment programme (SAP). The economic recovery policies led to improved performance in the economy with an average gross domestic product (GDP) growth of 5 per cent per annum between 1983 and 1992 while inflation dropped from 123 per cent in 1983 to 10 per cent in 1992 but the growth could not be sustained. During the implementation of SAP, the Programme of Action to Mitigate the Social Costs of Adjustment (PAMSCAD) was introduced in 1986 to help the poor and vulnerable groups who had suffered most to adjust to the economic reforms. However, results from Ghana Living Standards Survey (GLSS) 1, 2 and 3 undertaken between 1987 and 1992 by Ghana Statistical Service indicated a decline in welfare nation wide including the rural sector.

Decentralisation Policy as proxy for Rural Development (1988- to date)

Decentralisation refers to transfer of power and means to the grassroots to create opportunities for localities to develop faster than under centralisation. It puts emphasis on growth-with-equity policies with the realisation that development is a complex that cannot be planned and controlled from the centre (Cheema and Rondinelli, 1983). Ghana's sustained efforts at rural development through decentralisation began in 1988 with the enactment of PNDC Law 207, 1988 and further broadened by the Local Government Act 462 of 1993, after the coming into force of the Fourth Republican Constitution.

Decentralisation seeks to give the people the responsibility of managing their own affairs and also to strike a balance in the exercise of actual power between the State and local communities. It is a means of rural self-determination, which aims at "growth with equity". Almost two decades of practising decentralisation policy, more districts have been created in the country, from 110 in 1988 to 138 in 2004 and 166 in 2007. The idea is to bring governance to the doorsteps of the people. In the process, some rural communities have become district capitals and zonal capitals with some basic infrastructure and services provided. For example, to support the decentralisation policy, the government has been implementing rural electrification programme to provide energy from the national grid to all district capitals and settlements within a 20 kilometre radius of the district capitals. This energy provision has the potential of giving impetus to rural small-scale enterprises and to create employment (Mensah, 2000). Ghanaians' access to electricity (55 per cent) is the highest in sub-Saharan African Africa outside South Africa (World Bank, 2007).

The decentralisation process also has some employment opportunities within the local government structures for the people. Most of the rural people are often employed as unskilled labour with low wages on either temporary or permanent basis. Others are employed in various capacities by community-based or non-governmental organisations operating in the district.

The Metropolitan, Municipal and District Assemblies (MMDAs) are the highest political, administrative, planning and financial authorities in the respective districts charged with the responsibility of overall development. It must be noted that the District sub-structures have their problems such as inadequate infrastructure, logistics, funds, and motivated staff and councillors (Actionaid Ghana, 2002). The Local Government elections of

1998 led to the establishment of Unit Committees, Urban/Town and Area Councils, but their full operationalisation has remained rather elusive, after three such elections.

Two approaches to Ghana's decentralisation over the last two decades are devolution (transferring power and authority to MMDAs) and de-concentration (moving personnel and creating new offices from the centre to the districts). Despite the sustained effort towards decentralisation as a means for rural development, there are a number challenges. These include over reliance of the MMDAs on central government transfers and less of internally generated funds; low remuneration for staff; inadequate logistics; and ineffective performance of local government sub-structures.

Since 1995, the National Development Planning Commission (NDPC) has been preparing guidelines for District Assemblies to formulate their Medium-Term Development Plans. These are to enhance participation of all stakeholders in the district planning process. The implementation of the participatory process still needs improvement (Mensah, 2005).

Poverty Reduction Strategies

The inception of two rounds of poverty reduction strategies: Ghana Poverty Reduction Strategy (GPRS I–2002-2005) and Growth and Poverty Reduction Strategy (GPRS II–2006–2009) represent quite a different policy perspective to rural development. The GPRS process in essence re-asserted the centrality of the central government and its affiliates [Ministries, Departments and Agencies (MDAs)] in directing rural development. In implementing the GPRS 1, most of the resources that were released to support accelerated rural development [the Heavily Indebted Poor Countries (HIPC funds)] went primarily through the MDAs rather than the MMDAs.

The GPRS II clearly indicates a framework towards a more decisive process of centrally economic and social transformation. The foreword of the GPRS II document notes that "... we have symbolically changed the name of the programme from the 'Ghana

Poverty Reduction Strategy' (GPRS I) to the 'Growth and Poverty Reduction Strategy' (GPRS II) – the same initials, GRPS, but with a fundamentally different focus and content. The implications of this change for rural transformation have been manifested in the priorities selected for each of the three pillars of the GPRS II namely, private sector led growth, human resource development, and good governance and civic responsibility.

The results of these developmental shifts have been:

1. A strong private sector philosophy in selective development of growth poles and sectors–e.g. cassava, textiles, oil palm, sorghum to feed the growing agro-industrial consumer market, both domestically and internationally;
2. An increase in the use of mechanised means of production and a shift away from peasant-based agriculture; and
3. Re-emergence of central planning and implementing MDAs and the establishment of new initiatives aimed at directing socio-economic transformation centrally.

Some people have argued that both GPRS I and II have given little or no focus on rural development but rather there is a section on urban development, housing and slum upgrading/ urban regeneration. However, the central goal of the GPRS has been growth and poverty reduction, which would ultimately be beneficial to rural dweller. It should be noted that the GPRS complements the decentralisation process towards poverty reduction and rural development as they were being implemented simultaneously.

ASSESSMENT, ACHIEVEMENTS AND LESSONS LEARNT IN GHANA

As noted by Dixon (1990), determining how successful rural development programmes have been is quite a difficult task. The assessment procedures of both national and international development agencies have been widely criticised because very often people with vested interest conduct reviews to show that the programmes are successful. An alternative is to examine the rural poverty trends.

Rural poverty trends in Ghana is quite complex. The measurement problems are coupled with difficulty of obtaining comparable data over time. Even if the more optimistic views on the reductions in the proportions of rural poor are accepted, the number of poor people might not have declined. While some studies indicate a decline in the number of people below the poverty line, the degree of polarisation might well have increased.

Rural development programmes in the late 1960s and 1970s were generally not successful due to political instability and economic mismanagement. Household data covering 1974/75 shows that income was fairly distributed but a considerable number of Ghanaians lived below the poverty line, ranging from 62 per cent to 20 per cent depending on the poverty line assumed (Baffoe, 1992). The economic cries in the 1970s contributed exodus of Ghanaians for greener pastures. In early 1983, over a million of Ghanaians were expelled from Nigeria amidst drought in the West African sub-region, which made life extremely difficult. The situation compelled the government to adopt economic reforms prescribed by the Bretton Woods institutions.

Using Forster, Greer and Thorbecke Poverty Index, Mensah and Acheampong (2005) observed that poverty worsened during the period of economic reforms (1988-1998) and was more widespread in the rural sector than in the urban sector. The results were consistent with the general perception and literature that SAP impacted negatively on income distribution and poverty in developing countries. The removal of agricultural subsidies, introduction of "cash and carry" system in the health care sector, and retrenchment of about 60,000 workers from the civil service by 1989 made life much harder for the rural people. It is well known that in Ghana, many civil servants send remittances to their rural relatives to supplement their living. The average standard of living in Ghana fell by 5 per cent between 1987 and 1989 but increased sharply by 15 per cent (Ghana Statistical Service, 1995).

The incidence of national poverty declined from 52 per cent in 1991/92 to 40 per cent in 1998/1999, given the upper poverty line of 900,000 (Ghana Statistical Service, 2000).

ISSER (2004) explains why a greater number of people in the informal sector are below the poverty line. Most poor people are food crop and export farmers whose farming activities are organised on an informal basis. For example, using the upper poverty line, 59.4 per cent of food crop farmers (representing 58.1 per cent of the total poor population) as against only 9.5 per cent of wage employees in both public and private jobs were poor in 1998/99. This is mainly due to the human capital endowment of wage employees, which gives them access to employment and higher income opportunities. Also, the implicit public policy of keeping the minimum wage above the poverty threshold has benefited wage employees.

The incidence of poverty declined over the past decade. Poverty levels declined from 39.5 per cent in 1995 to 28.5 per cent in 2005 (using lower poverty line of 700,000 cedis). About 750,000 people in 2,014 communities have gained access to new or improved water supplies and sanitation systems. However, most of the poverty reduction was concentrated in the forest region (both urban and rural) while the Northern Savannah region, which was already by far the poorest of the ecological zones, appears to have been left behind in the national poverty reduction trend. While the rural savannah areas accounted for 25 per cent of the population in 2006, it accounted for just over 50 per cent of the poor (Ghana Statistical Service, 2007).

With regard to non-farm activities that complement farm incomes, Mensah (2004; 2006) observes that urban small-scale firms have significantly higher profits than their rural counterparts in the Central Region of Ghana. Low profits and inefficiency result in the firms' inability to offer better conditions of service for their workers.

The preceding results suggest that poverty is declining but it still exists in Ghana, especially among the rural people. Even though the recent rural development programmes are having positive impacts on the people, more efforts and clearer strategies are still needed to remove rural poverty for accelerated national development. The difference in working conditions (e.g. income levels, labour market segmentation, and legal protection) between urban and rural labour still persists. Rural employment is often characterised by no formal contracts, limited regular pay, low remuneration, and no social protection. These have interconnections with the four theoretical perspectives of labour explained above.

Various lessons could be learnt from the preceding discussions. First, the various rural development programmes in Ghana had good intentions but most of them did not receive enough time for implementation due to political instability from military coup makers. Second, external shocks such as oil price hikes and declining price of primary commodity exports hindered the positive impacts of the programmes. Third, economic mismanagement and corruption also contributed to impede the full realisation of the objectives of rural development programmes.

The implications are that first, all stakeholders including the government, private sector and civil society as well as the international community should encourage democratic principles, good governance, prudence economic management, investment, and human resource development. Second, the developed countries should practise fair trade with the developing countries within the neo-liberal global system, and respect national sovereignty as encouraged by the United Nations and international law.

CONCLUSION

Successive governments in Ghana have undertaken rural development programmes with the goal of eliminating the disparity between rural and urban economies. The post independence programme had a radical strategy with socialist ideology. Since then the strategies have been largely technocratic with capitalist ideology. Full implementation of the programmes prior to the 1980s was largely impeded by frequent military coups, economic mismanagement and unfair international trade relations. The recent rural development programmes, not free from the challenges of globalisation and unfair international trade relations, have shown modest success as manifested by declining poverty levels. However, inequalities between the urban labour and its rural counterparts still persist. The rural economy is still dominated by agriculture and unorganised labour characterised by no formal contacts, low and irregular incomes and limited social protection. Northern Ghana continues to top the poverty indicators with long periods of inactivity, thereby compelling the youth to migrate to southern Ghana in search for non existent jobs. Indeed, many of the youth survive under very difficult and dangerous conditions. Both internal stakeholders and international development partners need to work in a concerted effort to make labour a productive factor and beneficiary of rural development programmes. Ghana should position itself strategically to utilise the opportunities associated with globalisation.

Notes

1. These strategies are explained later in the paper.

References

Actionaid Ghana (2002), *Local Governance Performance: Case Study of Five Districts of Ghana,* Buck Press Ltd., Accra.

Assefa, B. (1980), *Poverty, Inequality and Stagnation: The Ghanaian Experience*, ILO, Geneva.

Baffoe, J. K. (1992), "Income Distribution and Poverty Profile in Ghana 1987-88", *African Development Review*, Vol. 4, No. 1, pp. 1-29.

Brown, C. K. (ed.) (1986), *Rural Development in Ghana*, Ghana Universities Press, Accra.

Canterbury, D. (2005), "Globalization, Inequality, and Growth in the Caribbean", *Canadian Journal of Development Studies*, Vol. XXVI, No. 2, pp. 847-866.

Chambers, R. (1994), "The Poor and the Environment: Whose Reality Counts?", Paper Presented at the Conference on Poverty Reduction and Development

Cooperation, Centre for Development Research, Copenhagen, 23-24 February 1994.

Cheema, G. S. and Rondinelli, D. A. (1983), *Decentralisation and Development: Policy Implementation in Developing Countries,* Sage Publications, London.

Dickson, K. B. and Benneh, G. (1970), *A New Geography of Ghana*, Longman Group Ltd., London.

Dixon, C. (1990), *Rural Development in the Third World,* Routledge, London.

Dorvlo, L. K. T. (1979), *Integrated Approach to Rural Development–An Interpretation: A Critical Examination of Some Policy Issues arising from Ghana's Youth and Rural Development Programme*, E.P. Church Press Ltd., Ho.

Ewusi, K. (1984), "The Dimensions and Characteristics of Rural Poverty in Ghana", *Technical Publication*, No. 42, ISSER, Legon.

Frimpong-Ansah, J. H. (1996), *Flexibility and Responsiveness in the Ghanaian Economy: Reflections on Post-Decline Atrophy Syndrome*, Ghana Academy of Arts and Sciençes, Hartfield.

Ghana Statistical Service (1995), *The Pattern of Poverty in Ghana 1988-1992: A Case Study Based on the Ghana Living Standards Survey*, Commercial Associates Ltd., Accra.

Ghana Statistical Service (2000), *Poverty Trends in Ghana in the 1990's,* Ghana Statistical Service, Accra.

Ghana Statistical Service (2007), *Ghana Living Standards Survey*, Ghana Statistical Service, Accra.

Gillis, M., Perkins, D. H., Roemer, M. and Snodgrass, D. R. (1996), *Economics of Development*, W. W. Norton and Company, New York.

Griffen, K. (1974), *The Political Economy of Agrarian Change*, Macmillan, London.

Hansen, S. (1992) 'Population and the Environment', *African Development Review,* Vol. 4, No. 2, pp. 118-164.

Institute of Statistical, Social and Economic Research (ISSER) (2004), *The State of the Ghanaian Economy in 2003*, ISSER, University of Ghana, Legon.

Mabogunje, A.L. (1980), *The Development Process: A Spatial Perspective*, Hutchinson, London.

Mensah, J. V. (2000), *Small-Scale Industries in Ghana's Economic Development: Comparative Economic Efficiency of Rural and Urban Small-Scale Industries in the Central Region,* unpublished PhD Thesis, Development and Project Planning Centre, University of Bradford.

Mensah, J. V. (2004), 'The Profits of Urban and Rural Small-Scale Industries in Ghana: Evidence from the Central Region', *The Global Journal of Finance and Economics*, Vol. 1, No. 2, pp. 227-248.

Mensah, J. V. (2005), "Problems of District Medium-Term Development Plan Implementation in Ghana: The Way Forward", *International Development Planning Review*, Vol. 27, No. 2, pp. 245-270.

Mensah, J. V. and Acheampong, I. K. (2005), "Economic Reforms, Inequality and Poverty in Ghana" in V. B. Jugale (ed.), *Poverty, Globalisation and Human Development*, Serials Publications, New Delhi, pp. 71-104.

Mensah, J. V. (2006), "Labour and Employment of Small-scale Industries in Ghana: Empirical Evidence from the Central Region", *The Global Journal of Finance and Economics*, Vol. 3, No. 1, pp. 39-61.

Mensah, M. (1981), *Regional Inequalities: the Distribution of Socio-economic Facilities*, unpublished MSc. Thesis, University of Wales, Swansea.

Myrdal, G. (1957), *Rich Lands and Poor*, Harper and Row, New York.

Pass, C., Lowes, B. and Davies, L. (1993), *Collins Dictionary of Economics*, Harper Collins Publishers, Glasgow.

Potter, R. B., Binns, T., Elliott, J., Smith, D. (2004), *Geographies of Development*, Pearson/Prentice Hall, London and New York.

Sachs, J. (2005), *The End of Poverty: How We can Make it Happen in Our Lifetime*, Penguin Books, London.

Schumacher, E. F. (1973), *Small is Beautiful: A Study of Economics as if People Mattered*, Blond and Briggs Ltd., Abacus, London.

Songsore, J. (1979), "Structural Crisis", *ISS Occasional papers*, GAA/FES No.71, ISS, The Hague.

Todaro, M. P. (1994), *Economic Development* (5th Edition) Longman Group Limited, New York.

Urban Management Programme (2004), *Presentation of Urban Management Programme*, Internet 26/8/04.

World Bank (1975), *Rural Development Sector Policy Paper*, World Bank, Washington D.C.

World Bank (1988), *World Development Report*, Oxford University Press, Oxford.

World Bank (2007), *www.worldbank.org* March 2007.

2

ASSOCIATIONS BETWEEN POVERTY AND SOCIO-ECONOMIC VARIABLES IN A TYPICAL TSWANA RURAL VILLAGE: NEW INSIGHTS

Pelotshweu T. Moepeng & Clement A. Tisdell

INTRODUCTION

The incidence of poverty in rural Botswana is a major concern and latest reports suggest it is on the rise while it is declining for urban areas (Central Statistics Office Botswana 2004; Tumelo 2004). There is limited information about factors associated with the incidence of rural poverty in Tswana villages and in this article, we aim to identify significant socio-economic variables that are associated with the occurrence of poverty in a typical Tswana village. Available empirical data for these variables from our case study are mostly (but not entirely) qualitative. Because qualitative data are categorical observations, they have no numerical (quantitative) meaning because no arithmetic calculations, such as the mean, are permissible (Selvanathan *et al.* 2000).

The socio-economic variables related to the incidence of poverty in the selected village in Botswana, Nshakazhagwe, are the following attributes associated with the household heads in this village: (1) their age, (2) level of education, (3) gender, (4) the number of sources of income of the household head, (5) whether the household head is engaged in wage employment, (6) whether the household head receives private or government income transfers, (7) whether or not heads are involved in conducting a home business, and (8) whether or not they obtain income from sales of livestock, crops or natural resources.

The results are based on a survey conducted in Nshakazhogwe village of all households in 2005 by the first listed author. The article begins with an outline of the survey procedure adopted and a discussion of methods used to organize the data. These are followed by cross-tabulations of the various socio-economic variables of the heads of household and the incidence of poverty. In addition, Pearson Chi-square tests are conducted to determine the statistical difference of the socio-economic variables of heads of household and the occurrence of poverty in the village. It should be noted that the analysis is cross sectional and considers the influence of each of the selected socio-economic variables independently. The analyses of associations are, therefore, of a partial nature.

SURVEY PROCEDURE AND METHOD OF ANALYSIS USED FOR THE CASE STUDY

Description and Choice of Case Study

Nshakazhogwe village in the northeast region of Botswana was chosen from a selected cluster of 8 villages in the region with a population range of 1000 to 2000. Nshakazhogwe's population of 1700 falls in this range (Central Statistics Office Botswana 2001). The national average age of the household head in rural areas is 49.1 years (Central Statistics Office Botswana 2004) and in Nshakazhogwe the average age of the household head of 56 years. Although this statistic is somewhat higher than the national average, it is close. In Nshakazhogwe, the proportion of heads of household with primary education or less is 80 per cent which is comparable to 83 per cent of the heads of household in rural areas having primary education or less (Central Statistics Office

Botswana 2004). These characteristics suggest that this village is typical of a rural Tswana village.

Most Tswana villages are located next to rivers which are commonly used by poor households to water livestock. Nshakazhogwe is next to Shashe River and its economy relies on the river system for both human and livestock watering. Crop production and natural resource harvesting form part of the traditional village livelihood systems in the rural areas of Botswana (BIDPA 2001; Watson and Dlamini 1999). Nshakazhogwe was purposively chosen as a case study because it had a population that was large enough for statistical validity of the results.

Timing of Study, Sample Selection and Data Collection

The case study survey was undertaken from September to November 2005. This period is favourable for study interviews in rural Tswana villages because it is just after harvest time and before the annual seasonal rainfall. Therefore, most heads of households were available for interviews. Personal interviews were conducted as the most appropriate method of data collection because household lists were inadequate. Therefore, mail questionnaires in the area were not practical. One typical cluster as a case study was used because the geographical area of interest covered, more than 150km by 90km area, is wide and the limited funds and time for this research allowed this choice only.

A village map, also used by the Central Statistics Office of Botswana, which divides the village into six enumeration areas was used to guide household interviews for this study. The household was the sampling unit. The head of household was the main person interviewed. All households in one enumeration area were contacted before commencing interviews in the next enumeration area. A total of 330 households were contacted and interviewed out of 366 eligible households in the village. It was found that 34 houses were vacant and their owners could not be interviewed, and 1 questionnaire had missing information. There were 29 institutional housing units at a secondary school and 10 institutional housing units at the local primary school that were not contacted and interviewed. Households in institutional houses were not included as is the norm in most household interviews in developing countries (Deaton 1997).

Limitations of the Interview Method

The interview method is very costly. As a result, the budget considerations enabled the selection of only one village which might raise questions about its representativeness. However, given that all the Tswana villages have similar language, population sizes ranging between 1200 and 1900, similar infrastructure background, the same resource base and climate, the selection of one village can be considered adequately representative. Except, for villages in western Botswana, all the characteristics of the selected village are similar to all the rural villages of Botswana making it a typical Tswana rural village.

Data Collection and Reliability

The study used four research assistants, with previous experience in 2004 Agricultural Census project of the Central Statistics Office. They were between 21 to 25 years of age. Two were females and two were males. Two research assistants came from the area and this reduced the language barrier problems. The inclusion of locals in the research team increased the participation rate, and the reliability and validity of information received. The first listed author was the principal researcher and translated the questionnaire into Setswana, the national language, which was used for asking questions in the field. Enumerators translated and recorded answers in English. The principal researcher trained and supervised the enumerators and was present in the village throughout the survey period and also carried out household interviews. In addition, the principal researcher accompanied each enumerator at the beginning of the survey to ensure that questions were correctly asked and understood. Any queries and clarifications were answered as they arose in the field.

Research Permit, Ethical Standards and Non-response

A research permit was secured from the Ministry of Finance and Development Planning, Botswana which facilitated research team introductions in the study village. Interviewers assured respondents of the anonymity (confidentiality) of their answers and interviewers also asked for the consent of the respondent to the interview, which had to be confirmed by a signature of the respondent on the consent form provided by the enumerator. Prior to the full scale study, a 3 day pilot study was carried out in Makaleng village in the North East administrative district. Feedback from the pilot study helped to improve questionnaire design and indicated that the subject of the questionnaire was attractive to respondents. The problem of non-response was small because of an attractive and easy to understand questionnaire, the timing of the study before the rainy season, the use of experienced enumerators, paying visits to respondents 7 days of the week, including weekends and the role of various relevant gatekeepers.

Coding, Data Entry and Storage

A coding sheet was developed according to each section of the questionnaire providing both a code for the answer and a label and coding was completed in the field. Where the answer was not stated, a Code 9 or 99 was assigned.

Interpreting the Implications of the Data Obtained and Analysis

The interpretation of the households interview results in Nshakazhogwe village are considered to be a random cluster sample of a larger population; namely all households in rural Botswana. This interpretation enables theories of statistical inference to apply because one is using the whole village as a sample of all villages in rural Botswana. Data entry and storage were done in the field immediately after coding, using a Census and Survey Processing System (CSPro) software package and an SPSS software was applied for analysis.

A review of the economic theory and poverty literature suggests that in rural Botswana, the most relevant objective methods to determine the extent of rural poverty are the cost of basic needs (CBN) method, which is also used by the Botswana Central Statistics Office (CSO) to determine the national poverty rate. In this study, a CBN method for determining the poverty rate was applied using all individuals in the study, where equivalence scale method was used. The results of this survey will be summarised by cross tabulating these. A chi-square goodness of fit was chosen to test the significance of an association between the incidence of poverty attributes and socio-economic variables of household heads in rural areas. This test is relevant because the case study sample size of 330 is large and results are reliable because all the expected frequencies were more than five. Given the hypothesis of this paper, a random variable associated with a cross tabulation of n households assuming a selected attribute of household head, in an r by k contingency table has a chi-square distribution with (r-1)(k-1) degrees of freedom. The null hypothesis of no association is rejected for large absolute discrepancies between observed and expected numbers (Newbold 1995).

LIFE-CYCLE OF POVERTY: INCIDENCE OF POVERTY AND AGE OF HOUSEHOLD HEAD

The relationship between the age group of a household head and the incidence of poverty is displayed in Figure 1. Figure 1 shows that the incidence of relative poverty in Nshakazhogwe village rises sharply from less than 3 per cent for those in the age group 20-29 years to 21 per cent for age group 30-39 years and then declines slightly to 20 per cent for those aged 40-49 years. A high incidence of poverty in the latter age groups could be because there are very limited opportunities for employment in the rural villages of Botswana. Even when there are employment opportunities, they are likely to be in traditional agriculture which is not covered by Botswana's minimum wage legislation and usually pays below minimum wages (Ministry of Finance and

Development Planning 2002). Household heads in the age group 30-49 years of age usually have a higher number of dependants than those in other groups because they are raising their children. Therefore, requirements of these groups for support of growing children might explain the high rates of the incidence poverty as they are also faced with poor agricultural prospects and few employment opportunities.

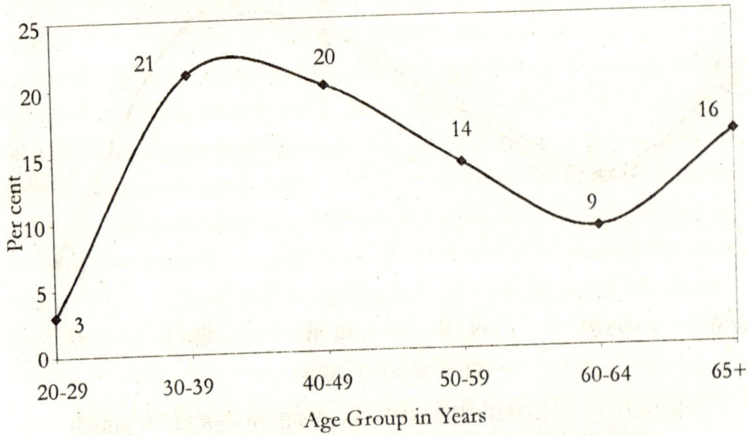

Figure 1 : Relative Incidence of Household Poverty by Age Group of Household Head in Nshakazhogwe Village 2004

A further factor that contributes to the high incidence of poverty amongst household heads aged 30-49 years is that they are not normally in receipt of private remittances or state income transfers. Their offspring are mainly too young to migrate and send remittances. Although this also applies to those aged 20-29, they are very likely to have fewer dependants and may obtain work more easily because of their superior physical strength.

As illustrated in Figure 1 the incidence of poverty falls in Nshakazhogwe to 14 per cent for age group 50-59 years and further to 9 per cent for 60-64 years age group. This observed decline of the incidence of poverty in Nshakazhogwe as the age of household heads increases, coincides with an increase in the age of their offspring. Most of the children of household heads in this group have completed their school education and many have migrated to non-rural areas where they find jobs. Households that have sent some of their members as out-migrants are more likely to benefit from remittances in the form of income transfers which are likely to increase the income of household heads who remain in rural areas. This reduces those incidences of poverty. Thus, a reduction in their dependency ratio and a rise in the level of private remittances received by these household heads aged 50-60 years help to explain their comparatively low incidence of poverty compared to other age groups. In addition, many will have had a chance to save and accumulate productive assets and establish social contacts that could add to their income. Furthermore, they are likely to have accumulated a significant amount of knowledge and experience which would be favourable to their economic prospects.

Figure 1 further shows that the relative incidence of poverty rises to 16 per cent for age group 65 years and above. An increase in the incidence of poverty as the household head is aged 65 years and above could indicate that sources of income decline sharply in that age group because the flow of income stops when individuals retire from active employment or they cannot work easily. In addition, in this age group, farming activities become limited because individuals are no longer able to do hard work. Also in this age group widowhood increases. In this village case study, about 70 per cent of heads of household were in widowhood which has negative implications for incoming income as most of these individuals were female. This implies that their husbands, who were likely breadwinners, had died. Although the incidence of poverty among the heads of household in 65 years and above age group is higher than for age groups 50-59 years and 60-65 years, it is much lower than for age groups 30-39 years and 40-49 years. A lower incidence of poverty among the age group of 65 years and above could be a result of the impact of the old age pension scheme in Botswana and the role of private transfers which might not be available for heads of household in younger age groups. But it is likely that private transfers for this age group would have tapered off compared to the 50-64 year old group. This is because their offspring are likely to have increasing need to take care of their own children and are less able to make transfers to parents.

INCIDENCE OF POVERTY AND THE EDUCATIONAL STATUS OF HOUSEHOLD HEADS

Rather surprisingly the incidence of poverty in this rural village tends to rise with the level of education of the household head. The relationship is graphed in Figure 2 which is based on Table 1. There is hardly any difference between the incidence of poverty experienced by household heads with no schooling (27.5%) and that experienced by household heads with only primary level

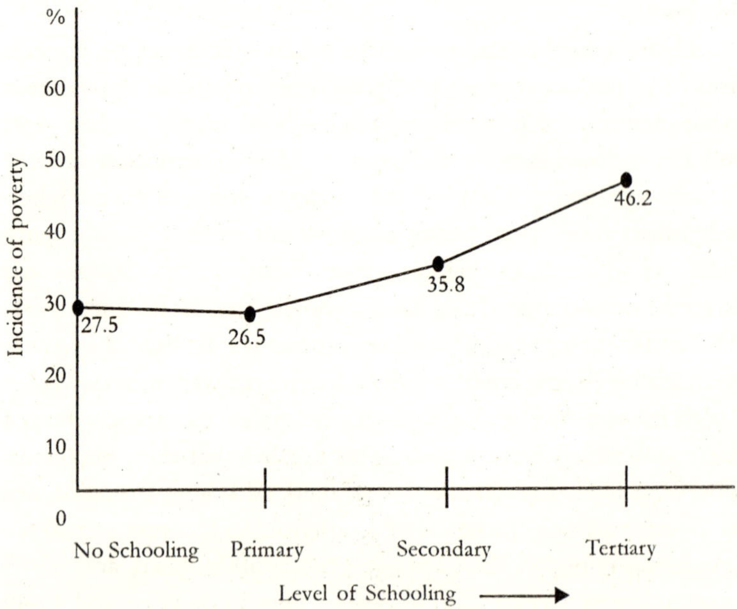

Figure 2: Relative Incidence of Household Poverty by Educational Status of Household Heads in Nshakazhogwe, 2005

schooling. The incidence rises substantially to 35.8% for those household heads who have completed secondary school education and to 46.2% for those completing tertiary education. Therefore, in this village, a positive relationship appears to exist between the incidence of poverty of household heads and their level of educational attainment. Usually, economists predict the reverse relationship. See for example, Bardhan and Udry (1999) and Schultz (1988).

The reasons for this perverse relationship may be several. First, there are few employments or occupational positions in rural villages, such as Nshakazhogwe, that call for other than basic education. For those who remain in the village, there may be a low or negative return on education beyond the primary school level. On the other hand, those who migrate from the village to non-rural areas may obtain a positive return on increased education and have a lower risk of being in poverty. It may also be that those how have more education and remain in the village are less enterprising or able than those who leave. Some sorting may occur. Furthermore, there are also other factors influencing the incidence of poverty apart from the level of educational attainment of the household head. For example, most of those with tertiary education in the village are retired and this may increase their susceptibility to poverty. While the impacts of these other factors require further investigation (compare Stern, 1991) we cannot dismiss the hypotheses that obtaining education beyond primary level is not very effective in reducing the incidence of poverty amongst those who do not migrate from the village or if they migrate, return to it.

Table 1 provides a detailed cross tabulation of the incidence of poverty in the village in relation to the educational attainment of household heads. The Chi-square test reveals that the differences in incidence of poverty of those with no schooling or primary schooling compared to that for household heads with secondary or tertiary education is not statistically significant ($\alpha > 0.10$) (Table 1).

Table 1
Cross-tabulation of the Poverty Status of Household Heads and their Educational Status, Nshakazhogwe, 2005

Education Status of Household Head		*Household Head Poverty Status*		
		Not Poor	*Poor*	*Total*
No School	Count	50	19	69
	% within Education Status of Household Head	72.5%	27.5%	100.0%
	% within Poverty Status of Head	21.4%	19.8%	20.9%
Primary	Count	143	52	195
	% within Education Status of Household Head	73.3%	26.7%	100.0%
	% within Poverty Status of Head	61.1%	54.2%	59.1%
Secondary	Count	34	19	53
	% within Education Status of Household Head	64.2%	35.8%	100.0%
	% within Poverty Status of Head	14.5%	19.8%	16.1%
Tertiary	Count	7	6	13
	% within Education Status of Household Head	53.8%	46.2%	100.0%
	% within Poverty Status of Head	3.0%	6.3%	3.9%
Total	Count	234	96	330
	% within Education Status of Household Head	70.9%	29.1%	100.0%
	% within Poverty Status of Head	100.0%	100.0%	100.0%

Chi-Square Tests

	Value	*df*	*Asymp. Sig. (2-sided)*
Pearson Chi-Square	3.645(a)	3	.302
N of Valid Cases	330		

a 1 cells (12.5%) have expected count less than 5. The minimum expected count is 3.78.

GENDER OF HOUSEHOLD HEAD AND POVERTY

Table 2 is a cross tabulation of the incidence of poverty and the gender of the heads of household. The results show that 31.3 per cent of all male heads of household were poor whereas 28 per cent of all female heads of household were poor. The results of a Pearson Chi-square statistical test show that gender is not significantly associated with the incidence of poverty in Nshakazhogwe village (Table 2). In particular, the incidence of poverty is slightly higher in male headed households than in female headed households. This could be because income transfers play a major role in household income, and female headed households are more likely to receive income transfers than male heads of household.

Table 2
Cross tabulation of Household Poverty Status and Gender of Household Head

Gender		*Household Head Poverty Status*		
		Not Poor	*Poor*	*Total*
Male	Count	77	35	112
	% within Gender	68.8%	31.3%	100.0%
	% within Household Head Poverty Status	32.9%	36.5%	33.9%
Female	Count	157	61	218
	% within Gender	72.0%	28.0%	100.0%
	% within Household Head Poverty Status	67.1%	63.5%	66.1%
Total	Count	234	96	330
	% within Gender	70.9%	29.1%	100.0%
	% within Household Head Poverty Status	100.0%	100.0%	100.0%

Chi-Square Tests

	Value	*df*	*Asymp. Sig. (2-sided)*
Pearson Chi-Square	.383(b)	1	.536
N of Valid Cases	330		

a Computed only for a 2x2 table

b 0 cells (.0%) have expected count less than 5. The minimum expected count is 32.58.

ASSOCIATION OF NUMBER OF SOURCES OF INCOME OF HOUSEHOLD HEAD WITH THE OCCURRENCE OF POVERTY

Figure 3 shows the distribution of the incidence of poverty among heads of household by the number of income sources that they depend on for their livelihood. Poor heads of household tend to rely more on one source of income (41 per cent) than is the case with the not poor heads of household in this case study village (27 per cent). This characteristic of the rural poor in Botswana is not consistent with empirical observations that poor agrarian households often diversify their activities with the hope that bad fortune in one activity will be compensated by good fortune in another–a livelihood strategy that is a form of self-insurance (Dasgupta 1993). Even though 42 per cent of poor households depend on two sources of income, very few of the poor household (17 per cent) compared to the not poor households (48 per cent) depend on more than two sources of income.

Table 3 shows the percentage of the household heads that are poor for each of the number of sources of income. It shows

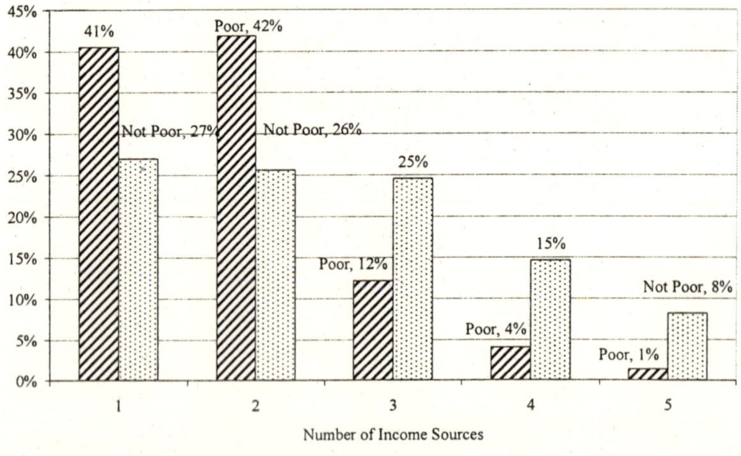

Figure 3: The Distribution of Poor and Not Poor Households by Poverty Status by Number of Sources of Income

that poor household heads constitute 28 per cent and 42 per cent of households that use one source and two sources of income respectively. Overall, the proportion of households that use one source or two sources of income is 70 per cent. This observation supports our earlier observation that income sources for the poor households in Botswana are not widely diversified. Poor heads of household that have 3 or more sources of income constitute 30 per cent of all households.

Table 3
Number of Sources of Income by Percentage of the Poor

No of Income Sources	*Total Number of Households*	*% of Poor Households*	*Cumulative %*
1	92	28	28
2	138	42	70
3	63	19	89
4	33	10	99
5	4	1	100
	330	100	

WAGE EMPLOYMENT AND POVERTY

Table 4 is a cross tabulation of the incidence of poverty and the employment status of the heads of household. The results in Table 4 show that 29 per cent of household heads that were not employed were poor and 29.2 per cent of household heads that were employed were also poor. In addition, 44 per cent of heads of household that are not poor compared to 43.8 per cent of heads are poor were not employed. The results of a Person Chi-square statistical test are not significant (Table 4) and show that the there is no association between the incidence of poverty in Nshakazhogwe and the employment status of the head of household. The role of transfers from members of some households as out migrants employed elsewhere and government welfare programmes might play a major role in explaining this result.

Table 4
Cross Tabulation of Household Poverty Status and Employment Status of Household Head

Employment Status of Household Head		*Household Head Poverty Status*		
		Not Poor	*Poor*	*Total*
Not-employed	Count	103	42	145
	% within Employment	71.0%	29.0%	100.0%
	% within Household Head Poverty Status	44.0%	43.8%	43.9%
Employed	Count	131	54	185
	% within Employment	70.8%	29.2%	100.0%
	% within Household Head Poverty Status	56.0%	56.3%	56.1%
Total	Count	234	96	330
	% within Employment	70.9%	29.1%	100.0%
	% within Household Head Poverty Status	100.0%	100.0%	100.0%

Chi-square

	Value	*df*	*Asymp. Sig. (2-sided)*
Pearson Chi-Square	.002(b)	1	.965
N of Valid Cases	330		

a Computed only for a 2x2 table

b 0 cells (.0%) have expected count less than 5. The minimum expected count is 42.18.

INCOME TRANSFERS AND POVERTY

Income transfers are an important source of income in rural Botswana (BIDPA 2001). Table 5 displays the results of a cross tabulation of the incidence of poverty and the whether the heads of household receive private transfers. Overall, 53.9 per cent of all households in Nshakazhogwe received private transfers. In particular, these results show that 53.4 per cent of heads of household that are not poor compared to 55.2 per cent of poor households receive private transfers. These results also indicate that the proportion of heads of household that did not receive private transfers who are poor is 28.3 per cent compared to 29.8 per cent poor heads of household among those that received private transfers. The results of a Pearson Chi-square test are not statistically significant ($\alpha > 0.10$) (Table 5). Therefore there is no association between the relative frequency of private transfers and the incidence of poverty. Given the importance of transfers, this suggests that the incidence of poverty would be much higher if these transfers were not made.

Table 5
Cross Tabulation of Household Poverty Status and the Frequency of Private Transfers to Household Heads in Nshakazhogwe

Private Transfers		*Household Head Poverty Status*		
		Not Poor	*Poor*	*Total*
Did not-receive	Count	109	43	152
	% within Private Transfers	71.7%	28.3%	100.0%
	% within Household Head Poverty Status	46.6%	44.8%	46.1%
Received	Count	125	53	178
	% within Private Transfers	70.2%	29.8%	100.0%
	% within Household Head Poverty Status	53.4%	55.2%	53.9%
Total	Count	234	96	330
	% within Private Transfers	70.9%	29.1%	100.0%
	% within Household Head Poverty Status	100.0%	100.0%	100.0%

Chi-Square Tests

	Value	*df*	*Asymp. Sig. (2-sided)*
Pearson Chi-Square	.088(b)	1	.767
N of Valid Cases	330		

a Computed only for a 2x2 table

b 0 cells (.0%) have expected count less than 5. The minimum expected count is 44.22.

Table 6 displays the results of a cross tabulation of the incidence of poverty and whether the heads of household receive government transfers. The total proportion of households that receive government transfers in Nshakazhogwe is 45.5 per cent. Specifically, these results show that 47.4 per cent of heads of household that are not poor compared to 40.6 per cent of heads of household that are poor received government transfers. Almost 41 per cent of poor heads of household received government transfers whereas, around 59 per cent of heads of poor household

Table 6
Cross Tabulation of Household Poverty Status and Government Transfers Received

Govt. Transfers		*Household Head Poverty Status*		
		Not Poor	*Poor*	*Total*
Did not-receive	Count	123	57	180
	% within Govt Transfers	68.3%	31.7%	100.0%
	% within Household Head Poverty Status	52.6%	59.4%	54.5%
Received	Count	111	39	150
	% within Govt Transfers	74.0%	26.0%	100.0%
	% within Household Head Poverty Status	47.4%	40.6%	45.5%
Total	Count	234	96	330
	% within Govt Transfers	70.9%	29.1%	100.0%
	% within Household Head Poverty Status	100.0%	100.0%	100.0%

Chi-Square Tests

	Value	*df*	*Asymp. Sig. (2-sided)*
Pearson Chi-Square	1.274 (b)	1	.259
N of Valid Cases	330		

a Computed only for a 2x2 table

b 0 cells (.0%) have expected count less than 5. The minimum expected count is 43.64.

did not. The results of the Pearson Chi-square tests are not statistically significant (Table 6). Whilst the differences in Table 6 are not statistically significant, the poor less frequently received government transfers in this village than the non-poor. This suggests some problems in the target efficiency of the welfare safety net. Therefore, further investigations are required to improve the targeting of government safety nets to ensure that more of those who receive them are poor rather than the not poor. However, just what proportion of those receiving government transfers would be poor or not poor in their absence is not known.

HOME BUSINESSES AND POVERTY INCIDENCE

The results of a cross tabulation of the incidence of poverty and whether the heads of household operated a home business are shown in Table 7. These results show that 16.7 per cent of poor heads of household compared to 13.7 per cent of non-poor heads of household operated a home business. The results also indicate that 33.3 per cent of those heads of household who operated a home business were poor whereas only 28.4 per cent of heads of household who do not operate a home business were poor. The Pearson Chi-square tests are not statistically significant (α>0.10) as shown in Table 7. In this instance, even though the difference between the poor and non poor is not statistically significant in this village a slightly higher proportion of those operating home business are likely to be poor compared with those that do not. A plausible explanation for this observation is that the poor are likely to have no skills that they can offer to find better paying job opportunities, and therefore are likely to venture into traditional beer home brewing for sale in their homes or operate mini-convenience grocery shops in their homes.

AGRICULTURAL PURSUITS (LIVESTOCK, CROPS AND NATURAL RESOURCES) AND POVERTY INCIDENCE

In this section, we analyze the association between three dominant traditional agricultural pursuits as sources of livelihood in rural Botswana and the incidence of poverty in Nshakazhogwe.

Table 7
Cross Tabulation of the Incidence of Household Poverty and whether or not Heads of Households Heads Operate a Home Business

Home business		*Household Head Poverty Status*		
		Not Poor	*Poor*	*Total*
No	Count	202	80	282
	% without Home businesses	71.6%	28.4%	100.0%
	% within Household Head Poverty Status	86.3%	83.3%	85.5%
Yes	Count	32	16	48
	% within Home business	66.7%	33.3%	100.0%
	% within Household Head Poverty Status	13.7%	16.7%	14.5%
Total	Count	234	96	330
	% of all	70.9%	29.1%	100.0%
	% within Household Head Poverty Status	100.0%	100.0%	100.0%

Chi-Square Tests

	Value	*df*	*Asymp. Sig. (2-sided)*
Pearson Chi-Square	.490(b)	1	.484
N of Valid Cases	330		

a Computed only for a 2x2 table

b 0 cells (.0%) have expected count less than 5. The minimum expected count is 13.96.

Table 8 displays the results of a cross tabulation of the incidence of poverty and the dependence of heads of household on livestock sales and the Pearson chi-square test results. These results show that 26.4 per cent of all households in Nshakazhogwe benefited from livestock sales. Of those who had livestock sales, 31.3% were poor. Only 24.2% of those who did not have livestock sales were poor.

A Pearson chi-square test revealed that the differences in these results are not statistically significant ($\alpha>0.10$). Therefore, there was not a statistically significant difference between the percentage of the poor having livestock sales and those without such sales.

Table 8
Cross Tabulation of Incidence of Poverty of Household Heads whether or not they had Livestock Sales

Livestock Sales		*Household Head Poverty Status*		
		Not Poor	*Poor*	*Total*
No	Count	177	66	243
	% those without Livestock Sales	72.8%	27.2%	100.0%
	% within Household Head Poverty Status	75.6%	68.8%	73.6%
Yes	Count	57	30	87
	% those with Livestock Sales	65.5%	34.5%	100.0%
	% within Household Head Poverty Status	24.4%	31.3%	26.4%
Total	Count	234	96	330
	% of all	70.9%	29.1%	100.0%
	% within Household Head Poverty Status	100.0%	100.0%	100.0%

Chi-Square Tests

	Value	*df*	*Asymp. Sig. (2-sided)*
Pearson Chi-Square	1.665(b)	1	.197
N of Valid Cases	330		

a Computed only for a 2x2 table.
b 0 cells (.0%) have expected count less than 5. The minimum expected count is 25.31.

However, the data do not reveal information about the amount of income received from livestock sales by individual households. Therefore, more information is required for further comparison of benefits of different households who sell livestock. Thus, it is suggested that future research should seek the actual number of livestock sales and value of livestock sales by individual owners in rural areas. Such data will be useful to measure the extent of income from communal land.

Table 9 provides a cross-tabulation of whether or not household heads had crop sales and the incidence of poverty. The results show that 8.8 per cent of all heads of household in this village had crops sales. The relative proportion of poor heads of household that benefited from crop sales is 10.5 per cent compared to 8.1 per cent of non-poor heads of households. Of all the heads of households that benefited from crop sales, 34.5 per cent were poor. A Pearson Chi-square test shows that these results are not statistically significant (Table 9). Although the difference of the relative proportion of heads of household that benefited from crop sales is not statistically significant, those who sold crops were more frequently poor. Crop production in Botswana results in low returns because of recurring droughts

Table 9
Cross Tabulation of Incidence of Poverty and Heads of Household Benefits from Crop Sales

Crop Sales		*Household Head Poverty Status*		
		Not Poor	*Poor*	*Total*
No	Count	215	85	300
	% those without Crop Sales	71.7%	28.3%	100.0%
	% within Household Head Poverty Status	91.9%	89.5%	91.2%
Yes	Count	19	10	29
	% those with Crop Sales	65.5%	34.5%	100.0%
	% within Household Head Poverty Status	8.1%	10.5%	8.8%
Total	Count	234	95	329
	% of All	71.1%	28.9%	100.0%
	% within Household Head Poverty Status	100.0%	100.0%	100.0%

Chi-Square Tests

	Value	*df*	*Asymp. Sig. (2-sided)*
Pearson Chi-Square	.487(b)	1	.485
N of Valid Cases	329		

a Computed only for a 2x2 table

b 0 cells (.0%) have expected count less than 5. The minimum expected count is 8.37.

which are associated with a high risk crop failure. In addition, the opportunity cost of migration to modern sector jobs by young able bodied people results in the loss of net income from labour based agricultural production such as crop production. Further research is recommended to consider the per capita benefits from crop sales by income status of a household in rural areas of Botswana.

Table 10 depicts a cross tabulation of the incidence of poverty and whether heads of household benefit from the sale of harvested natural resources. Table 10 shows that 8.2 per cent of all heads of household, in this village case study benefit from the sale of harvested natural resources. The relative proportion of poor heads of household that benefit from the sale of harvested natural resources is 7.3 per cent while it is 8.5 per cent of non-poor heads of household. However, the poor heads of household are 25.9 per cent of all heads of households that benefit from the sale of natural resources. A Pearson Chi-square test results show the differences between poor and non-poor households are not statistically significant ($\alpha>0.10$). However, in practice, the relative involvement of the non-poor in harvesting natural resources is slightly higher than for the poor. Even though, this study did not measure the extent to which each household harvested the natural resources, observations during the case study suggest that the per capita harvesting of natural resources is higher for not poor households than is the case for poor households. This happens because high income households that harvest natural resources use hired labour to harvest natural resource such as grass cutting for thatch, firewood harvesting and river sand harvesting for sale using movable capital such as tractors and trucks to transport these resources from the communal areas to the market place. Conversely, the poor households used natural resources for subsistence and relied on wheelbarrows for their transport. Therefore, further research might be conducted to determine the extent of natural resource harvesting in relation to the level of income of households. Such research would provide relevant information about natural resource harvesting, environmental problems and the incidence of poverty.

Table 10
Cross Tabulation of Household Head Poverty and the Dependence of Heads of Household on Harvested Natural Resources Sales

Sale of Harvested Natural Resource		*Household Head Poverty Status*		
		Not Poor	*Poor*	*Total*
No	Count	214	89	303
	% those without Natural Resource Harvest	70.6%	29.4%	100.0%
	% within Household Head Poverty Status	91.5%	92.7%	91.8%
Yes	Count	20	7	27
	% those with Natural Resource Harvest	74.1%	25.9%	100.0%
	% within Household Head Poverty Status	8.5%	7.3%	8.2%
Total	Count	234	96	330
	% of all	70.9%	29.1%	100.0%
	% within Household Head Poverty Status	100.0%	100.0%	100.0%

Chi-Square Tests

	Value	*df*	*Asymp. Sig. (2-sided)*
Pearson Chi-Square	.143(b)	1	.706
N of Valid Cases	330		

a Computed only for a 2x2 table
b 0 cells (.0%) have expected count less than 5. The minimum expected count is 7.85.

CONCLUDING COMMENTS

Although the results of this analysis should be interpreted cautiously, they reveal that for the typical rural village selected for the case study, the incidence of poverty tends to be highest at two stages in the life-cycle of village household heads. It is highest for the age group 30-49 years of age and has another (but lower) peak for those who are 65 years of age or older. Reasons were suggested for the pattern observed but more study is desirable to identify fully the reasons for the high level of poverty amongst village household heads in the 30-49 age group. An 'unusual' association was found between the level of education of household heads and the incidence of their poverty. Contrary to that commonly predicted, the incidence of poverty of household heads tended to rise with their level of education, although the association was not statistically significant. Several factors seem to explain this result. First, there are few opportunities for utilizing other than basic education in rural villagers. While economic gains are likely in non-rural areas from greater education, opportunities for this gain are limited for educated persons who remain in their rural village. Second, the results are to some extent influenced by the age structure of household heads. Further study of the reasons for this possible 'perverse' relationship and for the lack of statistical significance of education as a factor affecting the incidence of poverty is desirable.

There was not a statistically significant difference in the incidence of poverty of female heads of households compared to male heads of households. In fact, the incidence was slightly lower for female head of households than for male heads of households. This contrasts with findings from other countries– usually the evidence of poverty is found to be higher in female headed households than male headed ones. One of the reasons may be that female heads in Tswana rural villages benefit to a greater extent and more frequently from remittances than male heads.

It was also observed that the evidence of poverty in this rural village tends to fall as the number of sources of income of the family head increase. Conversely, the fewer the sources of income, the more likely is the family had to be in poverty. Reasons for this were suggested but further investigation .would be worthwhile.

In this rural village, whether or not the household head had wage employment did not significantly affect the incidence of poverty. The reason for this seems to be that a large number of household heads depend on other sources of income such as income transfers, that is private remittance, and government welfare payments. It was found, however, that a substantial number of the poor failed to obtain private remittances or government transfers. The reasons for this need investigation and the magnitudes of the transfers would help to further extend the analyses. Although the analysis indicates that there is no statistically significant relationship between the receipt of income transfers and the incidence of poverty of household heads, this does not mean that these transfers did not reduce the incidence of poverty. This is because the incidence of poverty in this study is measured after the transfers are made. There is little doubt that transfers of income kept the incidence of poverty in this village lower than it would otherwise be in the absence of the transfers. The impact of the transfers on the incidence of poverty in rural villages should be studied further.

Whether or not the household head has a small home business, sold livestock, sold crops or sold natural resources was not significantly associated with the incidence of poverty of household head in the village. However, only a small proportion of the villagers engaged in these rural pursuits.

By considering individual socio-economic variables one at a time, it has been possible to establish associations between some of these and the incidence of poverty of household heads in a typical Tswana rural village. In other cases, no statistically significant relationships were found to exist. However, the occurrence of poverty is often associated with several variables and so relationships involving multiple variables should be considered in further analysis. Nevertheless, this study has managed to highlight relationships that are worthy of further consideration and which in some cases, are at variance with existing findings in the literature. Some of these differences may be due to the particular structure of Botswana's rural community in relation to the general nature of society in Botswana.

References

Bardhan, P. and Udry, C. (1999), *Development Microeconomics*, Oxford University Press, Oxford.

BIDPA (2001), *Consultancy on the Review of the Rural Development Policy*, Ministry of Finance and Development Planning, Gaborone, Botswana.

Central Statistics Office Botswana (2001), *Population and Housing Census*, Central Statistics Office, Gaborone.

Central Statistics Office Botswana (2004), *Household Income and Expenditure Survey 2002/03*, Government Printer, Gaborone.

Central Statistics Office, Botswana (2004), *Gini Coefficient in Botswana*, Government Printer, Gaborone.

Dasgupta, P. (1993), *An Inquiry into Well-being and Destitution*, Clarendon Press, Oxford.

Deaton, A. (1997), *The Analysis of Household Surveys–A Microeconomic Approach to Development Policy*, World Bank, London.

Fidzani, N. H. (2001), *Property Rights and Their Effects on the Livestock Sector in Botswana*, Goteborg; Goteborg University.

Lucas, R. E. B. and Stark, O. (1985), 'Motivations to Remit: Evidence from Botswana', *Journal of Political Economy*, Vol. 93, No. 5, pp. 901-18.

Ministry of Finance and Development Planning (2002), *Revised National Policy for Rural Development*, Government Printer, Gaborone.

Newbold, P. (1995), *Statistics for Business and Economics*, Prentice Hall, New Jersey.

Regmi, G. and Tisdell, C. A. (2002), 'Remitting Behavior of Nepalese Rural-to-Urban Migrants: Implications for Theory and Policy', *The Journal of Development Studies*, Vol. 38, No. 76-94.

Schultz, T. P. (1988), 'Education Investments and Returns', in H. Chenery and T. N. Srinivasan (eds), *Handbook of Development Economics*, Amsterdam.

Selvanathan, A., Selvanathan, S., Keller, G. and Warrack, B. (2000) *Australian Business Statistics*, Nelson Thompson, Melbourne.

Stern, M. J. (1991) 'Poverty and the Life Cycle, 1940-1960', *Journal of Social History*, Vol. 24, No. 3, pp. 521-40.

Taylor, J. E. and Martin, P. L. (2001) 'Human Capital: Migration and Rural Population Change', in B. L. Gardner and G. C. Rausser (eds), *Handbook of Agricultural Economics*, Elsevier, Amsterdam.

Tumelo, S. (2004), *16th December 2004 Press Release of the Results of "The Household Income and Expenditure Survey (HIES)", "Literacy Survey" and "Botswana Aids Impact Survey II (BAIS II)"*, Central Statistics Office, viewed 20 March 2006, *<http://www.cso.gov.bw/>*.

Watson, H. K. and Dlamini, T. B. (1999), *An Assessment of the Sustainability of the Utilisation of Savanna Products in Botswana*, Department of Geography and Environmental Studies, University of Durban Westville, Durban.

Wikan, G. (2006), 'Cash, Crops and Cattle. A Study of Rural Livelihoods in Botswana', Hedmark College, Norway. Report No. 7, July.

3

LABOUR RELATIONS IN BOTSWANA'S SMALL BUSINESSES—REAL EMPLOYMENT OR DISGUISED UNEMPLOYMENT?

Motsomi Marobela

INTRODUCTION

This study examines critically the claims of the relative importance of the small business sector in economic development. Specifically, it challenges the prevailing dominate view that they provide employment, especially in the context of African economy like Botswana. In doing this, an attempt is made to situate the debate within the larger socio-economic domain. It is argued that labour relations in a small businesses is wanting, hence the issue of employment generation should be assessed in relation to the conditions of workers in small firms. It is contended that the vulnerability of these workers is made worse by the labour laws which do not guarantee decent employment.

CONTEXT OF LABOUR RELATIONS

Harman (1989) argues that it is important to place any discussion of labour relations in a broader political and economic context where it is rooted. This applies to research on small businesses labour relations as well because they don't exist in isolation. They are interwoven in the aggregate economy from which the political, economic and social relations influence their operations (Gerry, 1979). A common but mistaken approach in the study of small businesses often ignores this connection and therefore the tendency to reduce their problems to the micro level. But as Gerry (1979:6) asserts there are 'complex set of relations between the components of a socio-economic formation which impact on small businesses.

This complexity is mirrored in the development of Botswana's economy. Over the last three decades, Botswana has witnessed significant economic growth (Limi, 2006). For example, in 2006, Botswana foreign reserves were P48 billion-$ billion, with total foreign assets estimated at P76 billion (Bank of Botswana, 2006). It is such enormous wealth that has led to the characterisation of Botswana as an upper middle income country. However this unprecedented economic performance is challengeable in two respects, its contradictory development is revealed in terms of higher unemployment and poverty. As Siphambe (2007) argues Botswana is not an exceptional case when assessed from employment growth. It is fair to argue that the same argument applies to the level of poverty (See BIDPA, 1997). Though for many years, there has been phenomenal economic boom and this has been accompanied by a jobless growth.

According to government statistics (Republic of Botswana 2004) which are seen as an underestimate, the overall rate of unemployment in the country is about 24 per cent. Furthermore, the country's proportion of people living below $1 a day is 268, 298, constituting about 20 per cent of the (Republic of Botswana, 2004) people from an estimated population of 1.7 million inhabitants. These figures reflect uneven development in Botswana economy which undermines a lot of what is said about Botswana's good governance and economic successes. This study argues that a common feature of Botswana which is normally ignored the increasing unemployment. More significantly Botswana has experienced a notable amount of inequality (Good, 2002; Bond,

2006; UNDP, 2007) despite its notable economic progress. It is from this background that we see the desperate need for jobs pushing ordinary people to start small businesses to cope with bad living conditions arising from the failure of the economy to create better jobs. This dynamic between economic growth and unemployment is not unique to Botswana but prevalent in other African countries, for example South Africa is one such case. Indeed, it is a global phenomenon that typifies capitalist development and the crisis of unemployment and underdevelopment.

It is from this background the role SMMEs contribution to employment should be seen, that is, the need to recognise the emergence of small businesses as largely a result of the failure of the mainstream economy to provide jobs for the poor. Consequently, I argue that it is not enough to celebrate SMMEs as agents of job creation. What is critical is the nature of the jobs that they provide and the resultant income to meet of worker's welfare. In other words, it is the quality of jobs that matters most not the quantity.

METHODOLOGY

Capps (1993) argues that a broad approach to the study of small businesses allows for a more rigorous methodology that goes beyond appearance. In this respect, Trepo and de Geuser (2003) model, the Socio-Economic Approach to Management (SEAM) is useful. Inferring from SEAM, three dimensions are important in assessing the management of capitalist labour relations: contradictions, conflict and complexity. I believe such a perspective is in line with a "dialectical view" of management (See. Nord 1974, Benson 1977) or perhaps what Adcroft, et al (2004) describe as the 'revolutionary school of management'. The premise of this school of thought flows from the view that before we consider problems of labour relations in small businesses, it is essential to explain first the nature of small business in relation to the mode of production. In this case the Capitalist Mode of Production (CPM) is important.

Labour relations emerged as an attempt by the bourgeoisies to protect workers from capitalist exploitation. Marx (1973) saw the relation of labour and capital as marked by antagonistic interests. This conflict arises because of a class relationship between capital and labour. In a capitalist mode of production the relations of production are exploitative because capitalists appropriate surplus value which belongs to labour as its own profit. Without doubt contemporary work organisation is underpinned by the same conflict of class interests. These antagonistic interests define and shape the nature of work and with it industrial relations in a capitalist society.

To interrogate the complex process of changes in the Botswana's economy leading to the rise of small businesses and the ways in which government attempts to support them in terms of policy development and programmes. Critical realist philosophy is used to help, provide insight and context to the issues. Fleetwood, (2004) argues that critical realism offers a better alternative in the study of management and organisation because of its emphasis on ontology–a theory of being. According to Archer, (1995) realism investigates phenomenon from ontological depth. That means investigation has to go beyond appearance in order to explain the conceptual and structural processes behind labour relations. This deeper articulation of phenomenon comes from realists view reality as stratified and emergent and hence, the need to provide explanation to the events and experiences from observed data. Such an account of reality requires conceptualisation of the economic system as comprising socioeconomic structures and mechanisms and the relations amongst different forces. It also means that we have to acknowledge that managing organisations is not a smooth process but a constant struggle of the interactions, transformation and contradiction of diverse agents at different levels of the economy system.

This context is important in understanding the relationship between the development of Botswana's capitalism and the crisis of unemployment, hence the adoption of neoliberal reforms in the public corporations to create business for the private sector which is generally expected to provide more employment and alleviate poverty. A casc study of small businesses contracted by the University of Botswana is examined following the adoption of privatisation policy. Based on interviews with workers from three small companies doing catering, cleaning, gardening and security. Critical realism provides an important exposition that connects the changes from political and economic process and their relation with the university structures, mechanisms and powers, which promote privatisation and outsourcing of work and unintentionally result in bad employment practices for workers.

APPROACHES TO LABOUR RELATIONS

There are three main approaches to the study labour relations: unitary, pluralist and the Marxist perspective (Bendix 1992). For the purpose of this study, we focus on the unitary paradigm because Botswana's labour laws have tended to be unitary inclined. According to Salamon (2000), a unitarist's perspective is premised on the view that all parties in an organisation pursue a common goal and have shared values. Moreover, it relies on managerial prerogative to ensure that there is organisational congruence. Consequently, any conflict is discouraged as it is deemed destructive. Trade unions are not tolerated as they are seen to have a propensity to cause strikes which may render the organisation dysfunctional.

In Botswana the labour laws are framed to suit the unitary perspective because such an environment suits political stability which is crucial for business. This is significant in light of the fact that Botswana is a highly mineral dependent economy. Therefore labour laws that are likely to promote industrial conflict will upset the business interests but will also challenge the state, which is a major partner in the diamond sector. The 2004 Debswana miner's strike which was declared illegal is a classical example of the close relation between government and the mining sector. Botswana is the world largest exporter of diamonds (Siphambe, 2007) and diamonds remain a principal source of revenue for the country (Bank of Botswana, 2006).

The managerial prerogative is inherently entrenched in the Botswana labour laws–the Trade Dispute Act, the Trade Union and Employers Organisation Act and the Employment Act. These pieces of legislation are pro-business. Hence when there is dispute or worker's grievances the state through the Ministry of Labour and Home Affairs, invariably exercises unilateral power which is derived from the labour laws. For example, the right to strike and to unionise and associate freely has been a source of discontent for the labour unions. Only recently government has attempted to move towards a somewhat pluralistic direction albeit without pressure from both national labour movement and international agencies such as the International Labour Organisation (ILO). For instance, the establishment of the Industrial Court in 1992 and the ratification of the ILO core conventions in 1997 on Freedom of Association and the Right to Organise. However, it has taken many years since the ratification for government only moved the amendments in 2005-2006 parliamentary session (Siphambe, 2007). Although these are positive steps these rights remain meaningless as long as the labour laws are formulated in a way that makes difficult for workers to seek quick redress because of unnecessarily long procedures which are meant to deliberately frustrate their course.

With respect to small businesses, the situation is rather bad for most of its workers as there is hardly any employment protection at all. Most of the workers in Small, Micro and Medium Enterprises (SMMEs) face diverse difficulties. They suffer abuse from employers, work under hazardous conditions and are denied basic rights like leave and minimum wage. This happens mostly because unlike large businesses, small enterprises are not per se subjected to government labour legislation (Rempel, 1993). Moreover, one constraining factor is that small business workers are hardly unionised. The absence of such protective mechanisms for employees, therefore allows management to go beyond normative exploitation and control typical in labour process studies.

But even if the labour laws were to apply as well to small businesses things would still not be better because as suggested earlier Botswana government Labour Laws are oppressive as expression of the maintenance of the national economy and also serve the country's agenda to attract Foreign Direct Investment. Citing the World Bank research, de Jonge (2004) has noted that there seems to be link between labour market flexibility and FDI. Overall, it is the general crisis of capitalist accumulation which is based on exploitation of labour.

Developing countries such as Botswana are far away from industrialising because the capitalist system subordinates them to the periphery. That means they remain part of an important process in the supply chain of accumulation. As the main providers of cheap raw material and consumers of expensive finished products from industrialized countries, they cannot use their rich resources to create jobs. Hence mass unemployment is one such problem that forces ordinary people in developing countries to start petty production in small business for subsistence. In terms of neoclassical economics lack of employment means the supply of labour is high, compelling the price or wages to go down. It is this macro-economic failure that makes the unemployed people to tolerate the pain of working merely to survive.

GLOBALISATION, COMPETITIVENESS AND EXPLOITATION OF LABOUR

The ever changing geopolitical environment is shaping labour relations in general and small businesses, in particular. The integration of developing countries into the mainstream global economic system is often hailed as a good opportunity that brings foreign investment and job creation. In reality research points out that in fact such integration creates more problems than solutions because it occurs in an even plate. Though on the surface the rhetoric of global village and markets appears to be good news in reality, there are negative effects from globalised economy particularly for the developing world. Marx (1976) had long foreseen the global nature of the capitalist system, and its attendant problems which stem from the crisis of accumulation and competition. Today this trajectory is much more advanced and pronounced than Marx envisaged. This global transformation has profound implications for the labour market, the costs for ordinary workers are characterised by what Bloch (1998) refers as an "assault on the labour market".

As Marx has suggested under conditions where you have a "reserve army of workers" like in Botswana, the situation has the propensity to drive wage labour so cheap to the point of reducing a worker to a pauper. As free market orthodoxy creates destructive competition the effects of what has been described as "cut-throat competition" have been harsh for labour. Capitalist globalisation has pushed the small businesses to margins and thus to avoid perishing these petty producers are forced to resort to the most crude employment practices. In order to survive and avoid closure the small businesses owner has two choices. The least route is to self-exploit themselves and family members. The common alternative which makes business sense is to take advantage of the prevailing labour market situation. That is, to employ cheap labour and pass the net effects of market failure to the employees who under harsh living conditions have no choice but to take what comes to make ends meet.

Like other countries, Botswana is integrated in the global capitalist economy, where companies are supposedly free to enter and operate business anywhere. In fact, Botswana is viewed as ahead of other African countries in terms of globalisation to the extent that it has been singled out by the World Economic Forum as the most globalised economy in Africa:

> Botswana has retained its number one position in Africa as the 'most globalised' country on the continent. The announcement was made by the Carnegie Endowment for International Peace through its Foreign Policy magazine

during a ceremony in Washington DC marking the release of its fourth annual Globalisation Index. *(http://www.gov.bw/cgi-bin/news.cgi?d=20040227)*. See also *(http://www.weforum.org)*

To qualify for such a stature, the neoliberal globalisation requires developing countries to remove of protectionist barriers and open the economy to the global markets. In this respect, Botswana has done well by conforming to the World Trade Organisation demands of economic liberalisation. But as Weeks (2001) argues these reforms comes at a cost to the developing world. According to Weeks, countries that have embraced globalisation policies such as liberalisation, privatisation, deregulation have actually faired badly. And these are mainly from sub Saharan region. Callinicos (2003) opines with this view when he states that neo-liberalism has failed to either bring growth or reduce poverty and inequality. Instead, the main beneficiaries of globalisation are the rich countries that benefit from unfair trade and competition imposed by developing countries (See Stiglitz, 2002).

Global changes that sought to transform the public sector through reforms such as productivity and labour market flexibility have come with other negative dynamics which have made workers lives vulnerable. For example, the quest for costs minimization and enhancing the role of private sector participation in the economy has been accompanied by a call for empowerment by contracting out, outsourcing and privatisation of jobs by public corporations. In addition, liberalisation of the labour laws that encourage flexible work practices that seeks the most from exploiting labour are now pervasive. The result is even more disappointing for workers. Thus, most of the decent jobs have been destroyed through retrenchment and those that accompany these reforms have been poor quality jobs that fail to give decent pay, particularly in the small business sector. Moreover, the new work values that come with the neo-liberal globalisation have serious implications for labour relations in small businesses that benefit from contracted work. Without trade unions and inadequate legislation many of the small business en ployees remain exposed to abuse by the employers.

Breaking down the frontiers of trade brings intense competition which mainly serves the multi-nationals from the North. Government of Botswana, which has instituted wide ranging reforms aimed at liberalising the economy, acknowledges this dilemma when they observe, "Perhaps the most fundamental and pervasive change has been the gradual opening of the economy of Botswana and the Southern African region to the pressures of international competition (Republic of Botswana, 1997:149).

This global imperative is also recognised in the latest government plan period—National Development Plan 9, which takes as its theme "development through competitiveness in the global markets". While globalisation is seen by some as a positive phenomenon that has propelled economic development and offered opportunities for companies to partake in the enlarged market for prosperity in reality there have been enormous problems that militate against small businesses. Lack of capital, access to modern technology and unskilled labour are some of the issues that impeded their competitiveness. These problems serve as barriers that hinder them to penetrate global markets.

With respect to labour, globalisation has come with a new management spin which have sorted to reduce the demand for labour whilst increasing the profitability of firms. Perhaps this goes to support Callinicos's, (2003) argument that globalisation has increased wage labourers worldwide. But this comes with misery to the workers as he asserts that their exploitation is central to the functioning of the capitalist system. That means the working conditions of ordinary workers have not improved but worsened as capitalist amass more profits Klein, (2000). The question is, to what extent does the dichotomy between profits and wages affect small businesses employees? In order to understand the prospects and limits of small businesses, it is crucial to situate them within the global context. The advent of globalisation has brought in new challenges and problems for the small business and with that shaped the way they organise to survive the harsh competition of the globalised economy.

IMPACT OF SMALL BUSINESS ON THE FORMAL ECONOMY

There is no doubt that small businesses appeal to a number of people as a form of sustenance. It is also generally accepted that small businesses play a central role in the economy. Hence, the predominant view in the discourse which suggests that small businesses play a crucial role in the economic development especially with regard to employment creation (Birch, 1979; Hull, 1986; Murphy, 1996; Ebner, 2005). This view is also prevalent in the discourse of small businesses in Botswana. Thus for example, Rempel 1993; Briscoe 1995; Molapisi, 1997 all acknowledge the critical role played by small businesses in Botswana's development.

Governments worldwide also recognize the small businesses as crucial in development because they are assumed to be the main employment generators. In Botswana, the government policy paper on SMMEs gives a picture on the extent which small businesses contribute to the economy as noted:

> Although official statistics on SMMEs are lacking in Botswana, the Task Force has estimated that there are approximately 56 300 such businesses currently operating in Botswana, employing 125 000 people, including business owners. Based on the 1996 study on the Role of Small and Medium Enterprises (SMEs) in Botswana (Newell, 1996), the SME sector's contribution to GDP was estimated at 30-45%, while that of large firms was at 38-48% of GDP. SMEs would account for 50% of formal employment. It is a proven fact that job creation is one of the most important contributions made by SMMEs (Republic of Botswana, 1999:3).

Moreover, the Government of Botswana, economic and public policy is informed by this position (c.f. Industrial Development Policy; National Development Plan 8 and 9; Privatization Policy 2000; Vision 2016). The development of various policies support initiatives and programmes such as Financial Assistance Policy

(FAP), Citizen Economic Development Agency (CEDA), Local Enterprise Agency (ILEA), which targets small enterprises bear testimony to this. According to government paper No. 1 of 1998 (Industrial Development Policy for Botswana), the policy will seek to address among other things the issue of employment creation. In addition, the government policy on SMMEs has identified economic diversification and employment creation as one of the objectives. Not surprisingly, as the two are the main problems of the economy.

Like in other countries, small businesses are arguably the biggest employer and many people depend on them for a subsistence to make a livelihood. The question that comes to mind is what type of employment are they generating? This is a pertinent question which is normally swept under the carpet by proponents of employment generation. As Atkinson and Storey (1994) rightly posit, the issue is "quality as opposed to quantity of employment". Therefore, it matters what type of value is accrued from such employment. Ideally wages are supposed to help workers to meet the basic essentials of life. But as argued, low wages are a general feature of SMMEs in many countries and this makes it difficult for workers to afford a decent standard of living. Hence, this kind of employment has been questioned because of its sub-standard rewards. That is why, some have labelled this type of employment "disguised unemployment" (Gerry, 1979; Perkins, *et al.* 2001).

Although it is acknowledged that small businesses play a significant role, for instance such as provision of survival jobs and helping to avail some essential services and goods which the formal businesses might not be interested in because of low profits. However, in many respects small businesses are lacking when it comes to labour rights. Compensation of these problems often happens at the cost of upholding workers rights. Therefore the belief that small businesses are the largest in the economic sector and create more employment is somehow flawed or not sustainable taking into account that most of the SMMEs, conditions of work are not in accordance with the basic minimum standards decency expected in the workplace. Even where the minimum wages are stipulated, they still fall far short of meeting the basic needs of life. This gives credence to the notion that most of the small businesses in developing countries are formed as a response to the harsh realities of life:

> The problems in life which confront people on the way to reaching their goals are poverty, inability to support and educate children, small business, poor housing, no transport, no formal work, and customers who don't pay debts. Lack of money was the main issue in all these. The way to overcome these problems and reach the goals is through money and business. (Alexander, *et al* 1983:9).

Though this study dates back to two decades however, the issues raised then are still pertinent today. A decade later after this observation Rempel *et al* (1993) found that "the problems of employment creation, income distribution and poverty alleviation are common to most low and middle income countries Botswana is no exception".

Today these hurdles are still prevalent and in fact more widespread and pushing many people to seek refuge in starting some form of business. The creation of the National Strategy for Poverty Reduction by government (Mogae, 2003) is evidence that unemployment is a serious in Botswana. More concretely, the government conservative figures of 2002/3 Household Income and Expenditure Survey (HIES) reveal that national unemployment rate is around 24 per cent *(http://www.sco.gov.bw/html/household/hies3.html)*. Though, the latest government figures suggest that unemployment has dropped to 19 per cent HIES (2004), still the situation on the ground does not show any improvement. In fact, life is becoming difficult for most of the workers who are paid minuscule wages. There is a also a contradiction here because while on the one hand, the government statistics show an increase in employment, on the other, Bank of Botswana figures points to a decline in employment (Bank of Botswana, 2006).

With close to half of the population living below the poverty datum line (Hanson, 2003; UNDP, 2005), many people are desperate and struggling to survive in the rich Botswana. For instance, according to the Minister of Finance and Development Planning, Baledzi Gaolathe in 2005, 60 000 Batswana were employed by government under public works programme called, Namola Leuba (Poverty alleviation). This is a lot given the fact that Botswana's population is just under 2 million and the country has over $5.1 billion in foreign reserves *(http://en.wikipedia.org/wiki/Botswana).*

LABOUR RELATIONS IN SMALL BUSINESSES- ISSUES AND PERSPECTIVES

Rainbird (1991) has argued that the offshoot of small businesses is linked to the developments taking place in bigger firms. Central to this assertion is the crisis of competition within these larger firms and the need to adopt cost effective measures to sustain profitability. This crisis is expressed in the changes occurring in the labour market where more flexible work practices are being adopted by competing firms. One of these practices is subcontracting work to small firms. Though on the surface it would appear as if subcontracting is meant to empower small operators, in fact, it is primarily a cost saving strategy that pushes the problem down to the small operator. Ultimately, the real victim is the small business employee who has to make do with a lower payment:

> Evidence that subcontracting reduces labour costs for larger companies is provided by the study by Evans and Lewis (1989) of the construction industry. Contractors quoted typical savings of between 20 and 30 per cent in subcontractor's tender prices over those based on their own direct labour. The same applies when the self-employed themselves subcontract, drawing on casual or self-employed labour. Therefore, the outcome of the growth of self-employment is a reduction in labour costs. On these grounds, it could be argued that self employment constitutes a form of disguised wage labour. It is true that in the short term

> self-employment may raise income and lead to capital accumulation in some cases. But such growth of petty capital is achieved only self-exploitation and depression of labour costs. This strategy of labour intensification allows few resources for productivity-enhancing investment and leaves the self-employed able to compete only with each other, and not with more profitable, higher-productivity capitals. To define them as capitalists entrepreneurs is therefore highly misleading (Rainbird, 1991: 214).

The tendency to restructure and resort to exploitation of wage labour in small businesses is encouraged mostly by labour market flexibility adopted by governments. Research on small business practices shows that most of them operate in an unregulated environment. Although in some cases labour laws may exist but they do not go far enough to protect workers rights. The pursuit of flexible labour markets that encourage temporary and casual work is one such example that has sought to do away with restrictive labour laws. In addition, the informal character of small business also makes it difficult to enforce labour laws because their vastness makes it is difficult to regulate their behaviour.

In Botswana, implementation of labour laws is a huge problem. In practice, such legislation is not effective at all as small firm owners are not aware or ignore the labour laws. A number of factors are responsible for this. The major one being the political will to effect measures that will ensure compliance. But the nature of small businesses also means that some of them will close up if they are subjected to comply with the minimum standards of proving decent work. This tolerance of crude exploitation goes together with the flawed ideology of employment creation. The fact that some have called this employment "disguised unemployment" is not without reason. As I have pointed out the crisis of the jobless economy leaves many people desperate for employment which formally is not there. The role played by such petty micro businesses is therefore significant in as far as they serve as buffer zones that absorb and hide the problem of employment. The recognition of small businesses as creators of jobs therefore leads those companies which are in a position to pay well to take advantage of implementation bottlenecks such as lack of labour officer's inspections to free ride on the back of the ordinary worker and disregard even the most basic human rights.

Recruitment

In the case of small business organisations, there are no formal systems in place to recruit workers. Normally, employment follows informal recruitment methods. The most common being done by word of mouth. If there is a vacancy, employees are asked to recommend people they know. Small businesses will not waste money advertising in the media because a high unemployment rate ensures disposable labour anytime. Therefore, the nature of the jobs are such that most of the them do not require skilled labour and hence, they do not really require prior training or formal training once employed. On employment, a worker does not sign the contract of employment. Some work for over three years without any paper that shows that they are in fact employed by the company. Even in the developed countries like Britain, formal means of recruitment, training and pay and grievance handling were found to be absent in the small businesses, except at supervisory level (Matlay, 2002). The lack of records is a serious problem because without any documentation it is difficult to demand your rights. Added to that there is confusion because workers really do not know their status, that is, whether they are still temporary or have been employed on permanent basis. For the employer, this informality appears to suit their needs. Without any prove they can always shift the blame to the employee.

Pay and Conditions of Service

Even when it comes to the sensitive issue of wages, there are no records kept. The contract of employment is verbal and so are the wages and conditions of work. A worker is just told "you will get this much a month and that is it". At the end of the month, the supervisor hands over to each worker some brown envelope.

This is when a worker starts to ask questions by going back to the beginning of the month. Counting the number of days worked including Saturday which is treated as a normal day. The figures then reveal that if one gets a lump sum, it must be based on hours worked a day. So adding back and forth and using simple arithmetic an ordinary worker divides the salary lump sum with the days worked. This then helps to figure the daily rate and from the daily he or she can tell the hourly entitlement for an hour working a full day of eight hours. It is at this point that things don't add up. Because what the poor worker gets is below the prescribed minimum wage. But the employer has a way out, as he can simply say this what we agreed on, it is up to you take it or leave it. Does an ordinary worker have a chance? The case study shows that yes indeed workers do fight back exploitation even though they are aware that they risk everything. This especially applies to those workers still classified as temporary and casual workers. This category of workers is normally paid below the minimum wage. Their temporary status can be extended for many years against the law which says after a year they should be employed as full time workers. If there have a dispute and take it up with labour officers they risk expulsion because government officers are seen to be corrupt and working together with employers. One worker for example was told "the doors are open and many people are ready to take you job". This was when she asked her supervisor about working on holiday and her transfer from temporary to permanent. When they do intervene, the Department of Labour give the employer up to three months to respond to the dispute. This creates disillusionment to temporary workers because when the three months period elapses some of them may have already lost employment.

Work Organisation and Trade Unions

As stated earlier Botswana labour laws are essentially unitary in character. For a long time they have been anti–union and therefore oppressive not only to big businesses employees but also to small business workers. The neoliberal employment practices vigorously defend the interests of the employer. Flexible work can be so broad as to encompass part-time, casual work, temporary work. This gives space to employers to abuse workers because lack of legislation to protect workers against oppression and exploitation. For example, the trade dispute act requires two thirds of the workers to be members to form a union. Also a problem is the size, structure and management of small businesses. Since they employ a few people, it is easy for management or owners to ruthlessly punish those who complain. The work atmosphere does not promote trade unionism. Matlay (2002) for example, in his study of industrial relations in Britain found that on a few micro-businesses recognised unions. It could be argued that lack of protection means such workers are vulnerable because without a trade union they have no collective bargaining. Hence management by fear is prevalent. With this kind of work set up it becomes so easy for people to get fired. The absence of trade unions is a great disadvantage to employees of small businesses because they face the worst working conditions. As Bolle (1997) notes, 'unions quite simply oppose this form of employment which they consider precarious'. Another dimension to this is that the poor wages they get make it difficult to affiliate to Manual workers union because from what they are paid they cannot afford to pay trade union monthly subscription fees.

Family Management and Control

Studies have shown that the family dynamic is central to the successes or failure of SMMEs. SMMEs success is sometimes a result of the fact that the owner-manager is always around hence it is easy to exercise control. Another critical factor is the dependence on family members for cheap labour. Thus kids and relatives can always offer assistance rewarded in kind. This family connection is seen as boosting the level of commitment to the company. In addition it is identified as critical factor to enforcing crude management practices. A family member who manages is more inclined to protect the family business at all cost. Therefore it is not uncommon to find strict work conditions imposed on workers. Workers can be fired for late coming or absenteeism irrespective of whether they are mitigating circumstances such as illness. This complex interrelation between management and family is illustrated below in what Hatten (2003) calls overlapping perspectives.

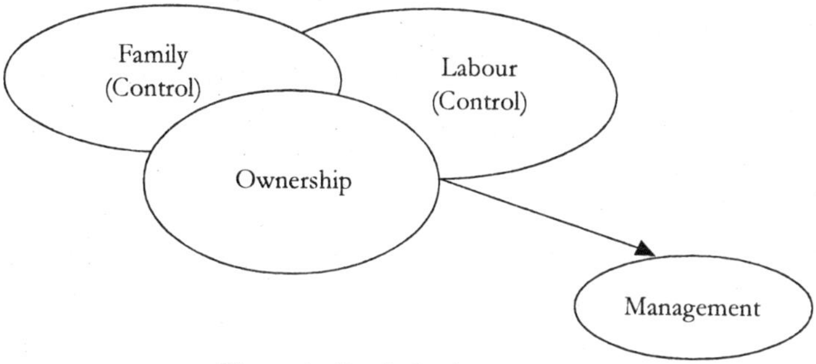

Figure 1 : Family Business Dynamic

While there is widespread recognition of the centrality of the family to performance however the interaction between family and business is not always put from the workers standpoint. The economic motive is normally emphasised at great disadvantage to the ordinary worker who suffer a lot from family management which imposes strict adherence to rules and long hours of work which are not concomitant with payment. In one of the businesses the manager was the wife and the husband-owner working elsewhere on a fulltime basis. Her financial dependence and emotional attachment to the business blinded her to see her workers human beings. Workers wages will be deducted for no reason and women denied maternity leave. They worked to the very last days of birth and have to quickly come back to work shortly after birth because if they take the three months maternity leave prescribed by law they will lose their jobs.

In another case the owner-manager spent most of his time concerned with his Moraka (Cattle-post). Therefore less attention was given to the business. He was not concerned about workers grievances, and money that was supposed to improve workers welfare was used to fund the cattle project. This happened despite the fact that he was getting a good amount from outsourced cleaning of which value came from the labour which was uncared for.

Social Welfare and Benefits

Small businesses workers enjoy very little welfare benefits. As we have seen they hardly take rest as they normally work six days a week. Most of the women workers are not allowed maternity leave. Compared with medium to large businesses which offer retirement benefits like pension and gratuity workers SMMEs do not enjoy these benefits. Though employees may be legally entitled to these benefits, the law has for a long time allowed room for abuse of the workers by the employers. This often happens when a worker is about the reach the fifth year and entitled to claim gratuity. Unscrupulous employers will find a pretext of dismissing them by framing flimsy excuses that eventually result in dismissals and a worker offered a one month salary or so, in lieu of notice. Hence, the employer can evade the financial obligation of paying for five years of continual service. Such unfair dismissals have been widely reported to the department of labour and the Industrial Court. Small business workers work on the weekends, on average six days a week. flexible/temporary and part-time work has rendered weekend's normal days, not optional as they used to be. That means most of their time is taken by companies at great cost to the family. When do they find time to spend with the loved ones?

But when there is neither protection nor decent pay at work people are forced to do what they don't like. A report on the ILO conference on the informal economy concluded:

> The conference adopted conclusions of the committee on the informal economy which among other things, identified

> the need to extend decent work for all workers, irrespective of where they work. The committee also concluded that legislation was an important instrument to address the issues of recognition and protection of workers and employers in the informal sector. It was concluded that Governments had the responsibility to provide an enabling framework at national and local levels to support representational rights. SADC Employment and Labour Sector conference 18-23rd February 2002, cited in Department of Labour and Social Security Eighteenth Annual Report 2002:58.

According to the Department of Labour and Social Security annual reports of 2001 to 2003 respectively, the major causes of disputes in Botswana as failure to pay wages, failure to pay notice, failure to pay leave and unfair dismissals respectively. It worth noting that this problem is continuous since in three consecutive reports covering the years 2001-3 all identify this pattern.

Employment Survival

Poverty and unemployment in Botswana put the lives of many people at risk. The lack alternatives in the formal sector to provide employment, forces people to take the most precarious jobs which put them in a vulnerable situation in terms of job security. People work in order to survive. In a capitalist economy, mass unemployment is a typical feature of this economic system. In a way the abundant pool of labour supply furthers the interests of capitalists because it drives wages down. In addition, to cope with stiff competition they restructure and outsource or contract out to reduce labour costs. For small businesses it pushes them to create survival jobs. As other scholars have rightly argued the worthiness of such employment is not sustainable. And indeed, given bad employment practices the small businesses are not at all about real credible employment that offers decent pay. Because they don't help workers to meet the basics of life, they are, at best survival jobs for the poor. The absence of social security for the unemployed in Botswana leaves people with no other alternative of survival except to take bad jobs which resemble slave work.

Commitment and Motivation

As argued, the level of pay and conditions of work are horrible in small businesses. But for an employee to work to his or her best ability he or she must be satisfied to some extent, at least the income must be able to meet physiological needs (Maslow, 1954). The absence of both intrinsic and extrinsic rewards in SMMEs is problematic because it leads to lower commitment to the job. Without any real incentives to offer and lack of job satisfaction, managerial coercion becomes the only option for inducing positive behaviour and high productivity. Such coercion measures are real and serious as failure to comply can mean loss of work. Additionally, punitive sanctions are a common phenomenon in small business. Mechanisms such as paying late and cutting a high an arbitrary amount for asceticism were reported by workers. However, it must be stated that motivation and lack of commitment is a general problem for businesses irrespective of size. And as suggested earlier it is a characteristic of capitalist work. Marx (1961) exposition on the dialectic that comes with capitalism is useful in understanding why motivation is an inbuilt problem. Conflicting interests of labour and capital causes this friction. The capitalist wants more profits and to realise them he or she cheapens the cost of labour, hence lower reward is seen as exploitation by the workers and it is this that breeds resistance. Workers appear to go with Vroom's (1964) 'valency theory', because the job does not offer any attractive outcome, so they do what is commonly referred by ordinary workers in Botswana, as go lekanya tiro le madi (equating work/effort with money).

CONCLUSION

The importance of small businesses and their impact on economy development has received increasing attention. This study sought to explore the issue of economic contribution of small businesses in terms labour relations. That is, employment practices and workers rights. In doing this I have attempted to link the role of small businesses in relation to wider issues of economic development. I have argued that conceptualising SMMEs, as if they exist in isolation from the wider socioeconomic environment is problematic because it ignores the impact of these forces in shaping policy and consequently their employment practices.

Such impact is suggested to come with global changes, specifically the advent of neo-liberal ideology and its thrust on the need for policy orientation in line with the free market orthodoxy as the best system that can bring economic development and prosperity. But sadly, the opposite seems to be true. A case, Botswana's economic success is counter posed with its unequal distribution of wealth reflective in poverty and unemployment. As a result many people resort to starting small businesses. However, most of these petty traders do not offer sustainable and decent employment. Hence, it is doubtful whether SMMEs really contribute significantly to employment creation and economic development. The concentration of government on businesses has made it to ignore basic human rights of the majority of workers. There is need for a revamp of Botswana labour Laws in favour of a new fairer legislation (Employment Act and Trade Union Act) that protects small scale workers from rampant exploitation and abuses by the employers. Issues of job insecurity, bad working conditions, low wages and workplace democracy deserve urgent attention. Such an act should recognise worker representation not necessarily through union presence. For small businesses informal structures like work committees, could go along way in giving workers a voice.

References

Alexander, E. (*et al*, 1983), '*Informal Sector Business in Four Botswana Communities*', Gaborone: Ministry of Finance and Development Planning: Ministry of Local Government and Lands.

Adcroft, A., Willis, R. and Clarke-Hill (2004), '*A European Perspective on the Revolutionary School of Management*', *European Business Review*, Vol. 16, pp. 248-266.

Archer, M. (1995), '*Realist Social Theory: The Morphogenetic Approach*', Cambridge: Cambridge University Press.

Arthur, C. J. (1986), *'Dialectics of Labour: Marx and His Relation to Hegel',* Oxford: Blackwell.

Bank of Botswana (2006), Annual Report, Gaborone: Bank of Botswana.

Bendix, S. (1992), *'Industrial Relations in South Africa'.* Cape Town: Juta and Co.

Benson, K. J. (1979), *'Organizations: A Dialectical View', Administrative Science Quarterly,* Vol. 22, pp. 1-21.

Birch, D. L. (1979), *'The Job Generation Process ',* MIT Project on Neighbourhood and Regional Change, Cambridge: Mass.

Bolle, P. (1997), *'Part-time Work: Solution or Trap?* International Labour Review, Vol. 136, pp. 557-579.

Bond, P. (2006), *'Looting Africa: The Economics of Exploitation'.* Pietermaritzburg: University of Kwazulu-Natal Press.

Bloch, B. (1998), *'Globalisation's Assault on the Labour Market: a German Perspective'. European Business Review,* Vol. 98, pp. 13-24

Briscoe, A. (1995), *'Small Business Support in Botswana',* Gaborone: Morula Press, 1995.

—— (2005), *'Labour Survey',* Gaborone: Morula Press.

Callinicos, A. (2003), *An Anti-Capitalist Manifesto',* Cambridge: Polity.

Capps, G. (1993), *'Small Enterprise Promotion in Botswana. Autonomous Self Employment versus Disguised Wage Labour'.* Bachelor of Science Economics Degree Dissertation.

de Jonge, A. (2004), *'Human Rights and Human Welfare',* Vol. 4, pp. 107-118.

Ebner, A. (2005), 'Entrepreneurship and Economic Development: From Classical Political Economy to Economic Sociology', *Journal of European Studies,* Vol. 32, pp. 256-274.

Fleetwood, S. (2004). 'An Ontology for Organisation and Management Studies', in S. Fleetwood and S. Ackroyd (eds.) *Critical Realist Applications in Organisation and Management Studies,* London: Routledge.

Gaolathe, B. (2006), Budget Speech, Gaborone: Government Printer.

Gerry, C. (1979), *'Poverty in Employment: A Political Economy of Petty Commodity Production in Dakar',* Senegal, Unpublished PhD Thesis. School of Economic Studies. University of Leeds.

Good, K. (2002), *'The Liberal Model and Africa: Elites against Democracy',* New York: Palgrave.

Hanson, L. (2003), *'Botswana Through the Eyes of the Outsider',* Monitor, Gaborone: Dikgang Publishing House.

Hatten, S. T. (2003), '*Small Business Management*', New York: Houghton Mifflin Company.

Hyman, R. (1989), '*The Political Economy of Industrial Relations*', London: Macmillan Press.

Hull, G. (1986), '*A Small Business Agenda. Trends in a Global Economy*', Boston: University Press of America.

Klein, N. (2000), *No Logo*', London: Flamingo.

Limi, A. (2006), 'Did Botswana Escape from the Resource Curse'? IMF Working Paper, WP/706/138

Matlay, R. (2002), 'Industrial Relations in SME Sector of the British Economy: An Empirical Perspective', *Journal of Small Business and Enterprise Developmentm,* Vol. 9, pp. 307-318.

Maslow, A. (1954), '*Motivation and Personality*', New York: Harper and Row.

Marx, K. (1973), '*Grundrisse*', London: Penguin Books.

——— (1976), '*Capital, Vol.3*', Harmondsworth: Penguin Books.

——— (1961), 'Karl Marx: *Selected Writings in Sociology and Social Philosophy*', in T. Bottomore, and Rubel, M. (eds.) Harmondsworth: Penguin Books.

Mogae, F. G. (2003), '*State of the Nation Address to the First Meeting of the Fifth Session of the Eighth Parliament*', Gaborone: Government Printer.

Molapisi, D. (1997), '*Poverty Assessment and Poverty Alleviation in Botswana*'. Gaborone: BIDPA.

Murphy, M. (1996), '*Small Business Management*', London: Pitman.

Nord, R. W. (1974), 'The Failure of Current Applied Behavioral Science- A Marxian Perspective', *Journal of Applied Behavioural Science*, Vol. 10, p 61-78.

Perkins, H. D. (2001), '*Economics of Development*', New York: Norton & Company.

Trepo, G. and de Geuser, F. (2003), 'Managing the Unmanageable. How Can SEAM Give Back to Employees and Work Situations their Anthropological Original Substance'? *Journal of Organisational Change Management,* Vol. 16, p. 99-106.

Rainbird, H. (1991), 'The Self Employed: Small Entrepreneurs or Disguised Wage Labour'? In A. Pollert, (ed.), *Farewell To Flexibility*, Oxford: Blackwell.

Republic of Botswana (1997), '*National Development Plan 8 & 9*', Ministry of Finance and Development Planning, Gaborone: Government Printer.

Republic of Botswana (1999), Ministry of Commerce and Industry, Policy on Small and Medium and Micro Enterprises in Botswana. Gaborone: Government Printer, Government Paper, No. 1.

Republic of Botswana (2006), Annual Economic Report, Gaborone: Government Printer.

Republic of Botswana (2004), Household Income and Expenditure Survey 2002/3, Gaborone: Government Printer.

Rempel, H. (et al, 1983), *'The Employment Role of Micro-Enterprises in Botswana. A Study of Selected Urban and Semi-Urban Areas'*, a Preliminary Report. Gaborone: Department of Economics. University of Botswana.

Salamon, M. (2000), *'Industrial Relations: Theory and Practice'*, London: Prentice Hall.

Siphambe, K. H. (2007), Growth and Employment Dynamics in Botswana: A Case Study of Policy Coherence, Working Paper, International Labour Office.

Stiglitz, J. (2002), *Globalisation And Its Discontents*, London: Penguin Books.

UNDP (2005), United Nations Human Development Report.

United Nations Development Report (2007), *'Fighting Climatic Change: Human Solidarity in a Divided World'*, New York: UNDP.

Vroom, V. H. (1964), *'Work and Motivation'*, New York: Wiley.

Weeks, J. (2001), cited by Callinicos, A. (2003), *'An Anti-Capitalist Manifesto'*. Cambridge: Polity.

World Economic Forum (2004), *Global Competitiveness Report.*

http://www.sco.gov.bw/html/household/hies3.html

http://www.ilo.org/public/english/protection/trav/aids/publ/codeprinciples.htm

www.gov.bw.

http://www.bonela.org

http://www.weforum.org/site/homepublic.nsf/Content/Growth+Competitiveness+Index+rankings+2005+and+2004+comparisons

4

DETERMINANTS OF NON-FARM AND FARM WAGE DIFFERENTIALS IN PUNJAB–AN INTER DISTRICT ANALYSIS

Kuldip Kaur & Maneet Gill

INTRODUCTION

Generation of adequate and sustained wages and employment opportunities has become the focus of attention of the development paradigm since the inception of the planning era in India. Efforts are being made through different development plans to ensure fuller opportunities for work and better living to all sections of rural communities and in particular to assist agricultural labourers and other weaker classes to come up to basic minimum standard. (Kumar, Yadav and Hussain, 2000). Development in the agricultural sector plays an important role in removing rural poverty, as an overwhelming majority of labour force derives its livelihood from agriculture. Also, rural non- farm employment has in recent times assumed importance in economic development. The non-farm sector plays a positive role in the removal of poverty, generation of employment and decentralization of urbanization. It is a significant source of economic well being to small and landless farmers during the slack seasons.

However, the economic well being of a population including goods, consumption of food, health care and other market based goods and services is determined not only by how much each worker earns but also how equally they earn. Discrimination against segments of population on the basis of race, gender, ethnicity, religion or occupation influences a country's larger social climate and reduces development prospects, good governance and effectiveness of society's institutions. To cure the disease of discrimination in wages, a proper diagnosis is must. The diagnosis lies in pointing out the factors responsible for this discrimination. It is against this background that present study intends to analyze the factors responsible for wage differentials in non-farm and farm sectors, with following specific objectives:

1. To compute the extent of non-farm and farm wage differentials in major districts of Punjab over the study period.
2. To find out various demographic factors that determines non-farm farm wage differentials in major districts of Punjab.
3. To find out various economic factors that determine these wage differentials in major districts of Punjab over the study period.
4. To draw some conclusions and policy implications of the study.

Present study has been divided into three main sections including the present one. Section-II discusses the database and methodology used in the study. It also presents various hypotheses to be tested. Section-III presents the results derived from the analysis while Section-IV concludes the study and draws some policy implications.

DATABASE AND METHODOLOGY

For the desired analysis, the required data has been derived from various issues of Statistical Abstracts of Punjab, which is a

Government of Punjab's publications for three points of time i.e. 1980-81, 1990-91 and 2000-01, for twelve major district of Punjab. Various possible demographic determinants of non-farm and farm wage differentials considered in the study are population density, rate of urbanization, number of health institutions per thousand of population and literacy rate in these districts of Punjab. The Economic indicators considered are per capita income and female agricultural labour in these districts of Punjab. Hypotheses listed below have been tested with the help of step wise regression analysis. The regression analysis has been preceded by the computation of correlation matrix that helped establishing some negative and positive relationships between non-farm and farm wage differentials and listed variables.

Hypotheses to be Tested

1. Higher proportion of female in total work force may increase these wage differentials as women after considering the wage as supplementary income of the family may accept even lower wages than prevailing wage rates.
2. Wage differentials in non-farm and farm sector are likely to reduce with higher literacy rates, as literate workers are less likely to be exploited in farm sector. Moreover with higher literacy rates the supply of labour in farm activities may decrease, creating an imbalance between demand and supply of labour in agriculture sector. Thereby wages in farm sector may increase, reducing the non-farm and farm wage differentials.
3. Higher population density and consequently higher labour supply is likely to increase the wage differentials.
4. Urbanization may reduce the wage differentials as migration of more people to cities will decrease the supply of labour for farm sector, hence more wages in the farm sector may be offered.
5. Increasing per capita income may reduce the wage differentials as labourers are less likely to offer them till the discrimination in wages exists.

6. Wage differentials in non-farm and farm sector are likely to reduce with better health facilities, as healthy workers in both non-farm farm sectors may contribute equally.

Hence it was hypothesized that:

$$\frac{\partial D}{\partial X_1}>0, \quad \frac{\partial D}{\partial X_2}<0, \quad \frac{\partial D}{\partial X_3}>0, \quad \frac{\partial D}{\partial X_4}<0, \quad \frac{\partial D}{\partial X_5}>0, \quad \frac{\partial D}{\partial X_6}<0,$$

RESULTS AND DISCUSSION

Table 1 below shows the extent of non-farm and farm wage differentials in major districts of Punjab over the years 1981, 1991 and 2001. It can be observed from the table that throughout the study period non-farm wages are higher than the farm wages in all the districts of Punjab. The extent of these wage differentials went on increasing over the years.

Table 1
Extent of Non-Farm and Farm Wage Differentials in Major Districts of Punjab over the Years 1981, 1991 and 2001 (Rs.)

District	*1981*	*1991*	*2001*
Gurdaspur	10.67 (.52)	32.09 (.62)	85.56 (.53)
Amritsar	5.43 (.75)	37.86 (.58)	86.99 (.52)
Kapurthala	13.55 (.52)	38.09 (.56)	61.04 (.62)
Jalandhar	14.76 (.48)	38.17 (.53)	94.95 (.47)
Hoshiarpur	18.56 (.38)	29.67 (.61)	90.24 (.48)
Rupnagar	16.41 (.40)	42.62 (.52)	79.92 (.53)
Ludhiana	22.72 (.36)	48.7 (.53)	90.66 (.52)
Ferozpur	15.94 (.52)	54.08 (.49)	88.04 (.53)
Faridkot	14.03 (.54)	50.69 (.52)	81.3 (.55)
Bəthinda	18.82 (.45)	45.28 (.54)	84.95 (.52)
Sangrur	19.19 (.43)	63.47 (.42)	103.99(.47)
Patiala	15.79 (.46)	67.34 (.43)	50.77 (.67)

Note: Figures in the brackets are ratio of farm to non-farm wages.

The wages in Sangrur district of Punjab in non-farm sector were 103.99 Rs. higher than the wages in farm sector in 2001. The same difference in 1981 was only of 19.19 Rs. The lowest differences in wages of non-farm and farm sector was in case of

Patiala district in the year 2001. This difference ranged between Rs. 50.77 to Rs. 103.99 in all the districts in the year 2001. In 1991, however, this difference ranged between Rs. 29.67 to Rs. 67.34 in all the selected major districts of Punjab. The ratio of non-farm to farm wages varied between .36 to .75 in 1981, .42 to .62 in 1991 and .47 to .67 in 2001. This means non farm sector that includes organized sector of labour market offers regulated wages to the workers whereas in the farm sector nothing of this sort exists. Hence, the wage differentials in both the sectors exist.

Table 2 and Table 3 show the results of the step-wise regression equations fitted for the year 1980-81. Selected demographic and economic factors were unable to explain the phenomenon of non-farm and farm wage differentials.

Table 2
Correlation between Non-Farm and Farm Wage Differentials and Explanatory Variables

Name of the Variable	*Wage Differentials in 1981*	*Wage Differentials in 1991*	*Wage Differentials in 2001*
Female Agricultural Labour	-.45	.09	-.07
Literacy Rate	-.03	-.59	-.08
Population Density	-.22	-.31	.12
Urbanization	-.02	.19	.05
Per Capita Income	.29	.63	-.04
Average Health Institutions	.21	.07	.04

Per capita income of the state was the first variable to enter in the model. This variable explained 8 per cent of the total variation in the non-farm and farm sector wage differentials in different districts of Punjab. The regression coefficient however was positive and non-significant indicating weak positive association between wage differentials and per-capita income. Increased population density turned out to be negatively associated with these wage differentials. It explained only 3 per cent of the total variations in non-farm and farm wage differentials. The negative association between the two indicates that increased density of population resulting in higher supply of labour as compared to demand for non-farm sector might have pushed the wages downwards in the non-farm sector too.

Table 3
Results of Step Wise Regression of Non-Farm and Farm Wage Differentials in 1981

$Y = 2.35 + .005x_5$	$R^2 = .08$
(.172) (.961)	
$Y = 6.81 + .01x_5 - .01x_3$	$R^2 = .11$
(.405) (.774) (.51)	
$Y = 12.13 + .01x_5 - .02x_3 - 1.42\,x_6$	$R^2 = .12$
(.308) (.746) (.331) (.152)	
$Y = 12.22 + .01x_5 - .02x_3 - 1.33\,x_6 - .14\,x_1$	$R^2 = .12$
(.29) (.702) (.296) (.133) (.103)	
$Y = -33.02 + .01x_5 - .01x_3 + 9.81X_6 - .81X_1 + .51x_2$	$R^2 = .24$
(.545) (.513) (.087) (.668) (.541) (1.03)	
$Y = -42.12 + .005x_5 + .0008x_3 + 10.71X_6 - .861X_1 + .49x_2 - .122X_4$	$R^2 = .24$
(.427) (.283) (.079) (.608) (.501) (.901) (.125)	

The next variable to explain the wage differentials was average number of health institutions per thousand of population in the districts indicating the health status of the workers. This variable however only explained one per cent of the variations in these wage differentials. However as hypothesized, earlier it was negatively associated with the wage differentials.

Table 4 shows the results of step-wise regression equations fitted for the year 1991. The variable per capita income explained 39 per cent of the variations in non-farm wage differentials in major districts of Punjab. However the regression coefficient (.008) was weak and positive indicating the weak positive association with the dependent variable. Literacy rate as an independent variable alone explained 22 per cent of the changes in the dependent variable. As per the hypothesis this literacy rate was negatively associated with the wage differentials indicating that higher literacy rate in the districts led to the decrease in the non-farm farm wage differentials.

Increased population density also explained 1 per cent variations in these wage differentials. Positive regression coefficient indicates that as population density increases due to more supply of labour these wage differentials also increase. Urbanization seemed to solve this problem of wage differentials to some an extent as its regression coefficient is negatively associated with the wage differentials.

Table 4
Results of Step Wise Regression of Non-Farm and Farm Wage Differentials in 1991

$Y = -22.57 + .008x_5$	$R^2 = .39$
(.843) (2.56)	
$Y = 18.51 + .096\ x_5\ -.57\ x_2$	$R^2 = .61$
(.624) (2.41) (2.173)	
$Y = 23.25 + .006\ x_5\ -.77x_2 + .02\ x_3$	$R^2 = .62$
(.732) (2.136) (1.785) (.602)	
$Y = 5.37 + .009x_5\ -1.06x_2\ +.07x_3\ -.69x_4$	$R^2 = .64$
(.126) (1.625) (1.69) (.826) (.655)	
$Y = 7.35 + .009x_5 - 1.05\ x_2 + .07x_3\ -.68x_4 -.21x_1$	$R^2 = .64$
(.151) (1.5) (1.56) (.73) (.59) (.13)	
$Y = 150.22 + .0009\ x_5\ -.87x_2\ -.102x_3 + 1.04x_4 -1.03x_1 -18.17x_6$	$R^2 = .85$
(2.38) (.167) (1.82) (1.04) (1.01) (.88) (2.68)	

Overall this variable explained only 2 per cent variations in the dependent variable. Average number of health institutions per thousand of population explained 21 per cent of the total variations in dependent variable. As per the hypothesis this variable was negatively associated with non-farm and farm wage differentials.

Table 5 also shows the results of the regression equations fitted for the year 2001. The explanatory power of the model is 22 per cent. The variable population density was found to be positively associated with the wage differentials explaining one per cent of the total variations in the dependent variable. Literacy rate as per the hypothesis was found to be negatively associated with the wage differentials, explaining 6 per cent of the total variations in the dependent variable. Rate of urbanization was found to be negatively associated with the wage differentials, explaining about 8 per cent of the total variations in the wage differentials. Per capita income here is negatively but non-significantly associated with the non-farm and farm wage differentials.

Table 5
Results of Step-Wise Regression of Non-Farm and Farm Wage Differentials in 2001

$Y = 77.54 + .011\ X_3$	$R^2 = .013$
(4.904) (.372)	
$Y = 101.47 + .032\ X_3 - .54\ X_2$	$R^2 = .069$
(2.78) (.771) (.734)	
$Y = 101.17 + .032\ X_3 - .54\ X_2 + .008\ X_1$	$R^2 = .069$
(1.914) (.627) (.692) (.008)	
$Y = 128.88 + .086\ X_3 - .988\ X_2 + .059\ X_1 - .755 X_4$	$R^2 = .139$
(1.949) (.955) (.978) (.05) (.738)	
$Y = 9.24 + 144 X_3 - .526 X_2 + .076\ X_1 - 1.09 X_4 + 26.98 X_5$	$R^2 = .208$
(.052) (1.18) (.432) (.069) (.946) (.737)	
$Y = 37.83 + .131 X_3 - .567 X_2 - .149\ X_1 - 686 X_4 + 28.91 X_5 - .001 X_6$	$R^2 = .223$
(.179) (.942) (.428) (.122) (.384) (.719) (.315)	

CONCLUSION

Thus, from the analysis, it can be concluded that except literacy rate other chosen variables at one point of time are positively related and at the other point of time are negatively related to non-farm and farm wage differentials. Education and literacy help in increasing the productivity and skill of workers, which in turn stimulate the growth of modern informal rural non-farm and farm sector with new technology. Therefore higher wages are offered in both the sectors. This helps reducing the non-farm and farm wage differentials and raising the level of development. Considering the higher literacy rate as a solution to the problem of discrimination in wages, it is thereby suggested that literacy particularly technical education in rural areas should be the prime priority in the development process.

As economic development advances there is a continuous shift in the spatial distribution of the growth of non-farm employment in developing countries like India. In the early stages of development rural areas and towns provide more non-farm employment opportunities than in urban areas. Since most of the districts in Punjab are in the developing phase, hence shift of workers with in the rural areas from farm to non-farm activities might have caused shortage of farm labour supply. This short supply as compared to demand might have increased the wages in farm sector. This explains the phenomenon of reduced non-farm farm wage differentials with increased per capita income or level of development. The positive association between wage differentials and increased per capita income in the year 2001, might be due to the fact that with shifting of labour from farm to non-farm sector, marginal productivity of workers at non-farm sector might have increased and the workers might have been offered higher wages as compared to farm sector.

The other two variables indicating solution to this problem found to be are rate of urbanization and increased number of health institutions per thousand of population as these variables have been found to be negatively associated with non-farm and farm wage differentials. Hence the study suggests that development process should continue along with development of social infrastructure, such that healthy, literate and technically sound workers may be offered equal wages in either of the sector as per their specialization and interest.

References

Ghuman, R. S., S. Singh, B. Singh (2002), "Non-farm Employment in Rural Punjab," *The Indian Journal of Labour Economics*, Vol. 45, No. 4, pp. 853-870

Jahan, F., M. H. Rahman, M. A. Kteruzzaman (2002), "An Economic Analysis of Women Working in Non-Farm Sector in a Selected Area of Kushtia District", *The Bangladesh Journal of Agriculture Economics*, Vol. XXV, No. 1, June, pp. 77-88.

Kaur. K., (Ed. P.D. Hajela and M.P. Goswami) (2000), *Economic Reforms and Employment*, Deep and Deep Publications Pvt. Ltd.

Kumar, P., M. H. Rahman (2002), "Pattern and Level of on Farm and Off-Farm Employment of Farm Householders: Evidence From an Area of Garbandha District", *The Bangladesh Journal of Agricultural Economics*, Vol. XXV, No. 1, June, pp. 89-99.

Mishra, V. N., (2001), "Role of Female Labour Force Participation in Rural Poverty and Non-Farm Employment: Indian Experience", *The Indian Journal of Labour Economics*, Vol. 43, No. 2, pp. 221-239.

Mohanty, B., T. Tripathy (2005), "Socio-Economic Implications of Gender Earnings Differentials: Education Sector in Orissa," *Economic and Political Weekly*, Vol. XL, No. 21, May 21-27, pp. 2190-2195.

Punjab Statistical Abstract, Various Issues.

Rao, M. K., (2000), *Rural Employment: The Non-Farm Sector*, Deep and Deep Publications Pvt. Ltd., New Delhi.

Sarmah, S., (2002), 'Agricultural Wages in India: A Study of States and Regions", *The Indian Journal of Labour Economics*, Vol. 45, No. 1, pp. 89-116.

Sharma, H. R., (2001), "Employment and Wage Earnings of Agricultural Labourers: A State-Wise Analysis,' *The Indian Journal of Labour Economics*, Vol. 44, No. 1, pp. 27-38.

Sidhu, H. S., J. S. Toor, (2002), "Nature and Determinants of Rural Non-Farm Activities in Punjab," *The Indian Journal of Labour Economics*, Vol. 45, No. 4, pp. 871-881.

5

LABOUR RELATIONS SCENARIO IN INDIA: A PARADIGM SHIFT

Mahesh Chandra Prasad

INTRODUCTION

Industrialisation strategies affect society and labour, and influence human resource and industrial relations policies at both the macro and micro levels. These strategies and policies should thus contend with the contextual elements of the labour market to ensure that economic and industrial development is in harmony with social and human progress. From this perspective it is necessary to take stock of some key factors of the labour market in India.

In the period following the Second World War, most of humanity has broken free from the clutches of colonialism and won political freedom. Since the end of the cold war in the late 1980s almost all the countries in the world, which pursued the path of centrally planned socialist or communist regimes, have shifted to a market economy, albeit on a negative vote. Military dictatorships have propped up intermittently in some countries, but these have usually come to be shunned. At the dawn of the new millennium, however, over a third of the world's population still suffers from illiteracy, poverty and unemployment and India is home to the largest proportion of this third.

India has everything–abundant resources and a growing market and yet its economic growth has been more or less nullified by the population growth. Over-activity in regulation and controls and underactivity in economic and social development has also deprived India from realizing its true potential. There are many explanations about what ails the Indian economy. From the perspective of labour-management relations, the arguments so far have lacked a balanced perspective. The pro-labour proponents look at labour markets and harp on poverty, unemployment and falling real wages and the share of labour in the GDP. The pro-industry proponents wax eloquent on the need to cut costs and improve competitiveness. The need of the hour is to harmonize the concerns of both labour and product markets and look at the issue not in terms of equity vs efficiency, but in terms of the promotion of equity and efficiency.

The manifest trends in the Indian economy have begun to ring alarm bells over jobless growth. The organized labour with relatively decent working and living conditions, when even some leftist trade living conditions, which even some leftist trade unions have termed the labour aristocracy, has become thinner. Economic growth is accompanied by growing imbalances among individuals and states and regions. There is growing concern about the society being the servant of the market and the perverse impact of competition on social relations. Elsewhere in the world doubts have been raised by Roderick about whether social disintegration is the price we have to pay for economic integration. Even economists in the World Bank and the International Monetary Fund have begun to pay attention to the social and labour impact of economic liberalization and stress support for providing credible systems of compensation and social safety nets for those affected. Five years since the Copenhagen Social Summit of 1995, the goal of full, productive and freely chosen employment continues to be a mirage. The Asian Crises has made many ponder on whether capital has become too productive and wonder whether globalization has gone too far.

Indian industrial units are greatly affected by disinvestments, privatization, restructuring and takeovers which, in turn, affect the labour relations scenario of the country. The process makes management and labour realize the need of each other and develop cooperative relationship between them. An attempt has been made here to describe the emerging labour management relations scenario, based on the analysis of the responses of workers and management personnel.

Globalization and competitive market economy have changed the scenario of labour relations in India. Downsizing the use of contract labour, outsourcing and employment externalization are some of the phenomena that have crept in due to these changes. Consequently, the role of major actors – the trade unions and the government have changed significantly. When the management and workers come close to establish direct relationship, trade unions lose their significance. The thrust of labour management relations lies in the changing work structure and direct employment relationship, which reduce the importance of third party intervention. Liberalization has been instrumental in bringing about significant changes in traditional practices of industrial relations. New models favour open dialogue, cooperation and joint solutions as the alternatives to the more adversarial relations of the past. Due to the changed scenario, greater direct interaction between workers and management has increased whereas the interfering role of the government and the trade unions has declined. It can be said that the system of labour management relations has been changed from the age of conflicting relations to an era of close employer-employee relations.

The following factors can be considered as significant to influence the trend in labour relations scenario in India over the past decade:

- Industrialisation strategies have changed.
- Majority of the labour force is found outside the purview of a formal industrial relations system.
- Government has less interest in promoting collective bargaining, an important tool of IR.

- Conversion of permanent jobs into contractual jobs is seen in service sectors like canteen, transport, cleaning, security, loading/unloading etc.
- Downsizing/right sizing is the most common practice now-a-days instead of retraining and redeployment of workers.
- The union membership in organized sector is decreasing day by day which reduces the union power.
- Weakening of union power results in the emergence of an unbalanced power structure between union and management.
- The weak union requires the management's patronage for its existence and the management manipulates union activities.

HISTORICAL EVOLUTION

Colonial Period (Pre-1950)

During the colonial period the government's industrial relations policy was one of laissez-faire and selective intervention at the most' (NCL, 1969). The Trade Disputes Act, 1929 provided for state intervention in the settlement of disputes. The Act was subsequently amended in 1938, following the recommendations of the Whitley Commission (also referred to as the Royal Commission on Labour) (1931) and the experience of the only provincial legislation at that time in the industrially important Bombay province, called the Bombay Trade Disputes (Conciliation) Act, 1934. The Bombay Trade Disputes Act provided for (a) compulsory recognition of unions by employers; (b) right of workers to get their case represented by a union representative or a government officer; (c) certification of standing orders detailing terms and conditions of service; (d) setting up of an industrial court; and (e) prohibition of strike or lockout under certain conditions.

During this period, besides some departmental establishments like the railways and communications, much of the industrial activity was agro-based (jute and cotton textiles, tea, etc.). In the wake of the report of the Whitley Commission and special investigations by government-appointed committees into major industries like textiles, the government began to consider some special measures aimed at securing a modicum of welfare and security for employees. Though the Whitley Commission recommended tripartite consultation, the colonial government did not accept this immediately. When the Government of India Act, 1935 placed labour in the 'concurrent' list, thereby empowering provincial governments to enact their own legislation, employer and worker representatives became concerned about the lack of uniformity in labour legislation and began to press for tripartite consultation. It was only during the Second World War that the tripartite consultation on labour was initiated, particularly to meet the exigencies of war and accelerate production. In 1942, the government invited representatives of employer and worker organizations to participate in the tripartite Indian Labour Conference (ILC). Simultaneously, the Standing Labour Committee (SLC) was set up as a subcommittee of the tripartite conference. The basic objectives of the government in instituting the ILC and SLC were to (a) promote uniformity in labour legislation; (b) lay down a pro-cedure for the settlement of industrial disputes; and (c) discuss mat-ters of all-India importance to employers and employees.

The Post-colonial Period (1947-1990)

Legal Framework: Labour is a concurrent subject. Both the central and state governments have the jurisdiction to legislate. Over 100 legislations govern the various aspects of human resources and in-dustrial relations at the enterprise level. Several of these are amended. Additionally, there is a considerable amount of free interpretation of these laws, creating a body of what is known as 'judge-made law'. While there is a plethora of legislation, the implementation is weak. The institutional framework for industrial relations includes consultative machinery and conciliation and arbitration machinery. The consultative machinery is present at all three levels of the strategic choice framework indicated by Kochan *et al.* (1987). At the top tier, tripartite consultation is provided through ILC and SLC, as discussed earlier, at the enterprise level, there are joint management councils councils and work committees. Some committees like the canteen and safety committees are statutory. Although there is a lot of effort to promote worker participation, in more than half the government enterprises, where some machinery for worker participation was established in response to governmental directives, worker participation became nebulous due to a general lack of genuine commitment and involvement in the concept.

Several voluntary arrangements gained currency during the late 1950s in the wake of the Indo-China war due to the mesmeric influence of the union minister in charge of both Planning and Labour, G.L. Nanda: the Code of Discipline (1958), Model Grievance Procedure (1958), Code of Conduct (1958), Verification of Trade Union Membership (1958), Voluntary Arbitration (1959), Code of Efficiency and Welfare (1959) and Industrial Truce Resolution (1962). When these voluntary arrangements were discussed in tripartite fora the actors could not disagree openly with such lofty ideals. The moral appeal, though outstanding, soon waned. In retrospect, it appears the actors agreed to these because they were merely voluntary and non-adhere-nce did not entail any sanctions (Mathur and Seth, 1969; Ratnam, 1992). The dispute resolution machinery consisted of four levels: bipartite negotiations, conciliation, arbitration and adjudication. Soon after Independence, some trade unions favoured adjudication more than collective bargaining because they felt that they were relatively weak in relation to employers and adjudication would help restore the balance of power. In addition, there are certain draconian legislations aimed at maintaining essential services (the Essential Services Maintenance Act, for instance). By invoking these, strikes/lockouts can be banned and industrial relations rights curbed for specified periods.

The Industrial Disputes Act, 1947 emphasized dispute resolution but there is little by way of creating an enabling environment. Other legislations like the Bonus Act, 1965, which intended to reduce strife on account of bonus disputes, actually led to increased strife. The more people a firm employs the more the laws that apply to it. As shall be discussed later, to circumvent the limitations of such legislative 'harassment' employers often tend to substitute labour with capital, under report numbers employed or resort to subcontracting, employment of casuals, etc. Legal restrictions on introducing new work practices, the introduction of new technology and modernization, the adjustment of the workforce in line with changing business requirement through layoffs, retrenchments or closure of business, etc. are some of the most current and contentions issues in the wake of the ongoing economic reforms.

Period of Structural Adjustment (1991-2007)

Liberalization and Deregulation

In the wake of the New Industrial Policy (June 1991), industrial licensing was abolished in all but 18 industries related to the security and the social and environmental concerns of the country. Private sector competition was introduced, though selectively, in areas hitherto reserved for the public sector. The government has also declared that it has no plans for further nationalization. Majority foreign holding is now allowed in almost all industries except those which are of strategic importance. The system of capital issues control was abolished, the import-export regime drastically simplified and the rupee convertibility introduced on trade account. Budgetary support to public sector firms was withdrawn. Even reservations to the small scale sector were withdrawn in most cases.

IMPACT OF LIBERALIZATION ON LABOUR RELATIONS

There are doubts as to whether liberalization really leads to competition. The spate of mergers and acquisitions and the domination by a few brands or major players once again points out that in the era of globalization economies of scale do matter. Though the number of players first increased due to the easing of entry barriers, eventually few have remained. Actually, in sectors like oil, air transport, telecom, banking, etc., there are doubts whether the number of players who will ultimately remain in the field will be fewer than the number before liberalization. Domestic enterprises find it hard to compete even in home territory because they are not used to competition and have, so far, mostly operated in a seller's market. Both captains of industry and academics are asking the government to liberalize the domestic economy first before exposing it to globalization. The private sector is asking for its privatization first. The Eleventh Finance Commission (2000) observed that economic liberalization has not resulted in the liberalization of PSEs from government controls. The dismantling of public monopolies has been accompanied by the creation of regulatory authorities which are subordinate to political and bureaucratic control. When ineffective regulatory authorities replace inefficient public utilities, the result is a transition from a bad to a worse situation. A chamber executive remarked, 'The evil of licensing is replaced by the devil of tendering.' Technology is redefining competition. After nationalization, nationalized banks expanded their branch network into remote and rural areas and into virtually every street corner in urban areas. Eventually, many of them have remained unviable. The new, foreign banks with the latest technology are now open 24 hours a day, seven days a week through automatic teller machines. Not just that, E-banking has metamorphosed the banking industry. The CEO of a foreign bank said that, 'we cannot have a bank in every street corner, but we can place one in every home, every phone, every personal computer'.

The government has drafted the competition policy. What is important is that politicians, bureaucrats and captains of industry walk the talk and talk the walk. Thus far, they have only walked the walk and talked the talk. The basic ingredients of a competitive environment are still missing in India: it is marked by a demand-supply mismatch, information imperfections and a skewed distribution of resources, including purchasing power, etc. More importantly the much-needed reforms have eluded the public sector in the real sense. With most of the input and infrastructure—social and physical—still being in the hands of the government, the rest of the economy can-not gear up unless the public sector does. Still critical are reforms in the three pivotal areas of the legislature, judiciary and executive.

How different countries respond to the requirements of competitiveness may be a function of the particular stage of development it is in and the state of health of its economy. While different countries have different critical moments in history and pursue divergent industrialization strategies, it is usually observed that 'a less developed country begins the process of industrialization by creating some initial conditions conducive to investment. In industrial relations terms, it may translate to low wages and low unionization. This situation may attract initial investments by firms, which can take advantage of such labour market conditions. However, with increased investment, the initial labour market conditions inevitably change and there are pressures for higher wages and possibly unionization .... This reduces the initial advantage which attracted the new investment in the first place so other inducements are needed in order to retain attraction to external investors. This creates a critical juncture in the development process and places pressure on the existing industrial relations systems' (Sharma, 1995). The state at this stage may introduce measures such as wage controls and union repression or, alternatively, take recourse to upgrading skills and linking wages to productivity, and shift to a high wage, high value industrialization where workers get higher wages but wage costs become competitive. Wage controls cannot be prolonged and union suppression by itself cannot guarantee economic success. Therefore, these are not necessarily the answer. Yet it sometimes becomes necessary to create conditions necessary for inducing investment. Putting jobs before growth is like putting the cart before the horse. There can be growth without jobs, but there cannot be any new jobs without growth.

The policies of the international financial institutions (IFIs) have generally been criticized by most trade unions as being responsible for exacerbating the existing economic and social problems and worsening the industrial relations climate. Their policies would not have mattered much if the country had learnt to live within its means. IFI policies have affected urban India directly. Rural India has had an indirect and secondary impact. Some sectors have been affected badly and others not. Overall, India's performance in the post-reform period has been below its economic potential and negative on the social dimension. However, India has not faced an economic crisis because: (a) it has retained control on capital outflows, (b) it has not supported full convertibility, (c) of the foreign exchange remittances by migrant workers of Indian origin and investments by NRIs, which has contrib-uted to the accumulation of a sizeable exchange reserve base, and, (d) it has moved cautiously, and on a case by case basis, so far, in matters concerning disinvestment, etc.

Multinational Corporations (MNCs)

India needs foreign capital and technology resources to make optimal use of its vast natural and human resources and growing market for a variety of products and services. In the past, the policies of self-reliance and import-substitution restricted the scope for foreign capital and technology in India. The deregulation of foreign investment in India in 1991 can be considered a watershed. The extent of its liberalization and of the foreign investment climate is such that as a chief executive of one MNC put it, 'India has opened up its economy with far less discrimination than most other countries, including the Far East and South-East Asian economies at their commensurate state of development.'

The role of foreign direct investment (FDI) was recognized in India in its Industrial Policy Resolutions of 1948 and 1956 but not in the key industries, which were reserved for exclusive growth in the public sector till recently. The Foreign Exchange Regulation Act (FERA), 1973 put, barring certain exceptions, a ceiling of 40 per cent on foreign equity participation in India. Multinational Corporations (MNCs), which did not want to dilute their stake, were asked to leave the country. FERA has been a major deterrent to FDI in India till the New Industrial Policy (NIP).

The Monopolies and Restrictive Trade Practices Act was amended to remove the threshold limits with respect to assets in monopolies and dominant undertakings. In high priority industries, automatic permission is given for foreign equity of up to 51 per cent as against 40 per cent in the past. In several areas foreign equity of up to 100 per cent is permitted. The prior approval of the government is not required for investment in deregulated industries. This provides MNCs with greater flexibility in the planning and diversification of their operations. Specific high technology and priority industries are now given automatic approval to conclude foreign technology agreements within certain set guidelines. Permission is no longer necessary for the hiring of foreign technicians and the testing of locally developed technologies outside of India. The Foreign Investment Promotion Board (FIPB) negotiates with a number of large international firms to promote substantial investment and gain improved access to advanced technology and world markets. The bulk of investments in the post-1991 liberalization era has come through the FIPB route. The main attraction for MNCs in India is the size of its market, which is not only large but also growing phenomenally. A vibrant credible judicial system, a strong bureaucracy, competitive human and natural resources, and the continued popularity of English as a business language add to the attraction.

The Indian industry is concerned about the role of MNCs in India. In the early 1990s, many Indian companies engaged in foreign tie-ups and many foreign companies increased their stake in Indian operations. A spate of mergers and acquisitions, too, followed, with many alliances souring for one reason or the other. Established Indian brand names began to be replaced by foreign brand names and a new practice of charging royalty for the use of brand names, both by Indian and foreign companies, created a flutter.

Both Indian employers and Indian trade unions broadly share similar perceptions and concerns about MNCs which are along the following lines:

1. MNCs are interested in capturing the Indian market but not in building a manufacturing base in India. Continued import of components is cited as proof of this allegation. Very few Indian companies are being developed to source parts from India for the overseas operations of MNCs. Few exceptions include the case of Sundaram Fasteners which won a global tender to supply radiator caps for General Motors, worldwide. Recently, the Korean auto giant, Daewoo also acquired control over its Indian operations, increased its stake and set its eyes on developing the Indian unit to source auto components for its worldwide operations.
2. MNCs focus on the short-term rather than the long-term. MNCs are keen to generate and repatriate profits quickly.
3. MNCs are using India as a dumping ground to bring in technology and products which are being phased out in their home countries.
4. MNCs use Indian partners to establish a foothold in India on a 50/50 or 40/40 basis and to get speedy sanctions and approval. Once established, however, they seek to edge out, as in the story of the camel and the Arab the Indian partner.
5. MNCs set up joint ventures with Indian partners and simultaneously, also set up 100 per cent subsidiaries in competitive areas without Indian partnership. They thus use the insights obtained through partnership with Indian companies in joint ventures to secure an unfair advantage,

allowing the 100 per cent subsidiary to compete with the joint venture firm.

6. A significant proportion of MNC investment is geared towards either increasing their stake in existing businesses or, mainly, supplying second-hand machinery to relocate obsolete plants in their home/a third country to India. Such MNC investment does not generate many new jobs, and even if it does, obsolete plants become the breeding grounds for sickness and, therefore, job losses.
7. MNCs come to India like 'cowboys'. They choose a partner hastily, make mistakes and then want to break off the relationship. Alternatively, they get into alliances with different Indian companies for different product lines. In the telecom sector, all the joint venture partners who bid for cellular tenders have already parted company. Alliances in the deregulated airlines industry have also soured.
8. MNCs cause de-industrialization. The ghost of the East India Company still haunts the average Indian psyche. The East India Company came on business and colonized the country for over two centuries, contributing to the deindustrialization of the country. Now even established Indian brand names in several industries are not able to face or withhold foreign competition due to the financial muscle and brand image of foreign competitors in the auto (two, three and four wheeler), electronics (television sets), white goods (refrigerators, for instance) and soft drinks industries.
9. An impression is gaining ground, in the wake of the renegotiation of certain power projects, that MNCs have a tendency to pitch their investment costs and prices to a level which is higher than necessary, pushing up the prices that consumers have to pay. Confessions about huge development costs breed suspicion about corruption.

10. Since the mid-1990s, revelations about foreign exchange irregularities involving ITC-BAT and the controversy concerning the control of ITC by its UK partner, BAT has not augured well for the image of MNCs in India.
11. MNCs are capitalizing on the weaknesses of traditional and small-scale Indian businesses in rural areas by quickly patenting herbal products and indigenous snacks (Bikaner bhujia, for instance). The entry of some multinationals into businesses like salt (the salt satyagraha launched by Mahatma Gandhi in Gujarat was an emotive movement during the freedom struggle) in the border areas of Gujarat, agriculture (Cargill) in Karnataka, ecologically unfriendly chemicals projects in Goa (Dupont's pact with the Thapars), and the use of India as a dumping ground for the disposal of dangerous chemicals wastes have rendered MNCs rather unwelcome in the minds of several Indians.

RECENT ECONOMIC CHANGES AND LABOUR MARKET

A remarkable feature of the economic reforms in India has been that the adverse impact on the growth rate of the economy was short lived and the recovery was quick. The decline in the growth rate was quite sharp in 1991-92 but the recovery started immediately thereafter. GDP increased by 6.3 per cent in 1994-95 and grew at over 7.5 per cent per annum for three successive years, 1994-95, 1995-96 and 1996-97. Inflation was under control and there was a large inflow of foreign capital (Parikh, 1999). However, growth of GDP decelerated to 5-5.5 per cent after 1996-97 and industrial growth declined to less than 6 per cent. Industrial investment–both private corporate and public-has slowed down and rate of inflation rose during 1998. Fiscal deficits continued to be around 8 per cent of GDP while the rate of growth of exports declined. This downward trend has been attributed to several factors–overvalued exchange rate, East Asian crisis, infrastructure bottlenecks, lack of demand for industrial goods because of reduction in rural incomes due to relatively poor performance of agricultural sector, large deficit of the government leading to high interest payments, controversy about the sustainability of economic reforms, etc. However, the performance of the economy as measured by the Gross Domestic Product (GDP), has been marginally better in the post-reform period compared to the pre-reform period-the growth of GDP during the period 1980-81 to 1990-91 to 1999-00 (Parikh and Radhakrishna, 2002, p. 6). Thus, the economy after the reform period is on a higher growth path of above 6 per cent. Though still below the long-term growth rates of East Asian countries, the performance of the 1990s translates to a respectable growth rate of 4 per cent in per capita terms. The recent economic changes have their implications for employment and labour market as well, which are discussed in subsequent sections.

The latest and seventh quinquennial NSSO survey (61st Round) throws new light on the employment and unemployment scenario in the country. It shows a reversal of the declining trend in employment growth rate which was witnessed earlier. Employment growth increased from an annual rate of 0.98 per cent in the period 1993-94 to 1999-00 to 2.89 per cent in the period 1999-2000 to 2004-05. Interestingly, there was also an unprecedented acceleration in the labour force growth rate from 1.03 per cent to 2.93 per cent which was above the population growth rate. This could have had serious implications for the unemployment scenario, had it not been for the sharp increase in the workforce, that is employment.

A closer look at the employment elasticities reveals that the elasticity for agriculture and allied sectors is very high at 1.52 as compared to the earlier trend. This does not appear to be sustainable. Hence for Scenario 2, the elasticity of employment of agriculture and allied activities has been moderated to a lower figure of 0.7 for the purpose of projections while other sectoral elasticities are kept unchanged. Keeping the labour force growth rate at 2.93 per cent and GDP growth rate at 9.1 per cent, these projection shows that it will take up to 2009 to reach the point where the labour force will equal the workforce.

Table 1
Employment and Unemployment UPSS

	1993-94	*1999-00*	*2004-0*	*5 1993-04 to 1999-00*	*1999-00 to 2004-05*
	In million			CAGR	
Labour force	381.94	406.05	469.06	1.03	2.93
Workforce (Employment)	374.45	397.00	457.82	0.98	2.89
Number of Unemployment	7.49	9.05	11.24	-	-
As a proportion of labour force in per cent					
Unemployment Rate	1.96	2.23	2.39	-	-

Source: Yojana, January 2008

Table 2
Employment Projection

Sector	*Employment in 2004-05 (million)*	*Projected Elasticity*	*GDP growth rate (%)*	*Employment growth rate (%)*	*Projected Employment 2009*
Agriculture, Forestry & Fishing	267.57	0.70	3.73	2.61	296.62
Mining & Quarrying	2.74	0.82	4.73	3.88	3.19
Manufacturing	53.51	0.34	10.90	3.71	61.9
Electricity Gas & Water Supply	1.37	0.33	6.90	2.28	1.5
Construction	25.61	0.88	12.07	10.62	38.35
Trade, Hotels & Restaurants, Transport, Storage & Communication	64.49	0.45	11.97	5.39	79.56
Financing, Insurance, Real Estate & Business Services	6.86	0.94	10.33	9.71	9.94
Community, Social & Personal Services	35.67	0.28	7.60	2.13	38.81
Total	457.82	0.36	9.13	3.29	529.87
Labour Force	469.06	-	-	-	526.50
Unemployment rate	2.39%	-	-	-	-
Labour Force growth rate	2.93%	-	-	-	-
Employment growth rate	2.89%	-	-	-	-

Source: Yojana January 2008.

CONCLUSION

At the time India became an independent nation in 1947, it was one of the few major industrial powers in the whole of Asia. But in the 1990s, it is at the bottom of the newly industrializing countries.

India has allowed itself to get marginalized in a world that has become increasingly interdependent. India's share in world exports declined from 1.4 per cent in 1955 to 0.5 per cent in 1990; its share in world imports also declined from 1.3 per cent to 0.7 per cent during the corresponding period. Significantly, however, in the wake of the first phase of reforms during 1984-85, India's exports and imports picked up substantially. Certain international developments like the Gulf War, however, precipitated the balance of payments crisis.

India's competitiveness in terms of its human resources is considered to be the least. The World Competitiveness Report (IMD and WEF, 1990) puts India at the bottom of the 10 newly industrializing countries in terms of the competitiveness of its human resources. The World Competitiveness Report examines the competitive advantage of human resources on the basis of skills, motivation, flexibility, age structure and health of the people. The criteria included in this factor are: population, employment, unemployment, educational attainment, vocational training, public expenditure on education, management quality, income levels and health factors. During the 1990s, the UNDP Report on Human Development ranked India in the bottom 35 of 160 countries in terms of the Human Development Index that takes into account three parameters, i.e., longevity (life expectancy), knowledge (adult literacy) and decent standard of living (per capita income). In terms of the Human Freedoms Index, covering 40 indicators of freedoms to exercise choices in cultural, social, economic and political affairs, India scored 14 points to obtain a medium freedom ranking (11-30 points) (UNDP, 1999). One lesson that India has learnt is that 'inward looking country strategies (have) failed, outward looking country strategies (have) succeeded.' Hence, the shift from import-substitution to export-orientation and the concomitant thrust on productivity and quality.

Globalisation finally forces the Indian industrial units for disinvestments, privatization, restructuring, merger and acquisition, which ultimately affect the labour management relations. The emerging processes before deregulation, denationalization and disinvestments caused the state to gradually withdraw itself from some social and economic sectors. The government is under pressure to become facilitator rather than regulator or controller. Employers have become more powerful whereas trade unions have lost their influence and the movement has reached a turning point where rights are being curtailed, organizations are under attack and permanent employment is converted into contractual jobs. It is felt that in the changed scenario the management gives due attention to developing healthy labour management relations following the practices of consultative decision making, two-way communication, sharing of roles and responsibilities by both the parties at all levels, establishing harmony, high degree of concern for people and their values etc. Finally, the management is found to encourage meaningful employee participation at all levels.

The study confirms the realization and practice of the above practices by all concerned as it is most important for growth and development of individuals as well as the organization. However, such role realization helps not only in developing better labour relations but also in improving the status of organization in a competitive market. In the Indian scenario, when poverty dominates and unemployment increases, the role of government should not be laissez faire but proactive in case of employees availing VRS, suffering due to lay-off, retrenchment, closure and outsourcing. Creation of alternative employment opportunities, extending social Safetynet and providing rehabilitational measures will be more helpful in removing the insecurity and anxiety from among the working class and developing better labour relations system in the country. Care for growth and development, joint effort of labour and management, role realization and mutual trust are important factors in promoting better labour-management relations in the country.

References

Ahluwalia, I. J. (1992), *Redefining the Role of the State: India At Crossroads.* Pape, presented at the Korea Development Institute, Senior Policy Forum on Private Sector led Development Strategy and the Role of Government in Developing Countries al. Seoul, Korea, October 15-17. New Delhi: Centre for Policy Research, Mimeo.

All India Trade Union Congress (AITUC) (1990), *34th Session of AITUC: Report, Resolutions and All Documents,* Madras: AITUC.

Asian Productivity Organisation (APO) (1991), *Labour-Management Consultation in Asia.* Tokyo: Asian Productivity Organization.

Broke, Ronald J., Copper, & Carry L. (2000), *The organization in Crisis Downsizing, Restructuring and Privatisation*, Blackwell, Oxford (UK).

Davala (ed.) (1992), *Employmentand Unionism in Indian Industry.* New Delhi: Frederick Ebert Foundation.

Davala, S. (1996), *Multinationals and Labour Policies,* New Delhi: Frederick Ebert Foundation.

Gupta, S. P. (1989), *Planning and Development in India: A Critique.* New Delhi. Allied.

Gupta, S. P. (1999), 'Trickle Down Theory Revisited: The Role of Employment and Poverty,' V. B. Singh Memorial Lecture, *41st Annual Conference of the Indian Society of Labour Economies*, IGIDR, Mumbai, November 18-20.

International Labour Organization (1992), *World Employment Report,* Delhi: ILO.

International Labour Organization (1999), *National Renewal Fund,* Delhi: ILO.

International Labour Organization-Asian Pacific Project on Tripartism (1993), *Tripartism in India.* Bangkok. Mimeo.

Kannappan, S. (1993), Industrial Relations and Employment Policy in India, *The Indian Journal of Labour Economics,* April-June, pp. 133-142.

Kumar, N. (1986), 'Foreign Participation, Market Structure and Employee Compensation in Indian Manufacturing', *India Journal of Industrial Relations,* 31(3): 297-309.

Mathur, K. and N. R. Sheth (1969), *Tripartism in Labour Policy: The Indian Experience.* New Delhi, Shri Rain Centre for Industrial Relations.

National Commission on Labour (Government of India) (1969), *Report of the National Commission on Labour,* New Delhi, Government of India.

Rangarajan, C. (2008), Employment and Growth, *Yojana,* January.

Ratnam, Venkata, C. S. (2000), *Improving Workplace Relations in India,* International Management Institute, New Delhi.

Reddy, Y. R. K. (1992), Industrial Relations in the Strategic Environment, *Indian Journal of Industrial Relations,* Vol. 1. 28, No. I.

Reutner, Friedrich (1993), *Turn Around Strategy for Successful Restructuring,* Blackwell, Oxford (IJK).

Sahoo, C. K. and Tripathy, S. K. (2006), *Labour Relation Scenario, JIMS8M,* October-December.

Sen, Ratna (2003), *Industrial Relations in India Shilling Paradignis,* McMillan India Limited, New Delhi.

Sharma, B. (1995), *Aspects of Industrial Relations in ASEAN,* Singapore: Institute of South-east Asian Studies.

Sheth, N. R. (1993), Labour Relations in the New -Economic Environment, *Vikalpa.*

Singh, N. K. (1987), *Human Resource Development in Indian Public Sector,* New Delhi, Standing Conference of Public Enterprises.

Srivastava, K. B. L. (2001), *Changing Power Dynamics in the Emerging Industrial Relations Scenario, Manage Merit and Latour Studies,* October, Vol. 26, No. 4.

Tulpule, B. (1993), *New Industrial Policy, Employment and Structural Adjustment in India,* Indian Worker, August.

Venkata Ratnam (2001), *Globalization and Labour-Management Relations,* Response Book, Sage Publication, New Delhi.

Venkata Ratnam, C. S. (1989), *Employers' Dilemma,* Bombay: Employers Federation of India and SOLAR Foundation.

Venkata Ratnam, C. S. (1992), *Managing People,* New Delhi: Global Business Press.

Venkata Ratnam, C. S. (1999), The Role of the State in Industrial Relations, Globalisation and Labour Manage went Relations in South Asia, Indian, *Industrial Relations Association,* New Delhi.

Walker, K. F. (1975), *Workers Participation in Management: An International Perspective.* Geneva: IILS Bulletin.

6

LEVEL OF LIVING OF RURAL LABOUR– A CASE STUDY

M. S. Gupta

INTRODUCTION

Rural labour comprises persons living or working in rural areas. It constitutes the most marginalized section of our society. More than five decades of development has benefited this section the least. Rural labour in household enterprises, especially female labour has been one of the major victims of modernization as the new industrial products displaced their traditional activities. The problems of rural labour are multi-dimensional and concerned with economic, social and political. These problems have given birth to many challenges before the society. They are very much different in nature as compared to those, which existed in earlier days. Most rural households are below the poverty line and are still deprived of education. They are facing various problems like unemployment, under- employment, low wage rate, low income, etc. resulting in chronic poverty. They also face problems like poor working conditions, malnutrition, under-consumption and exploitation. These problems are closely interwoven and have taken a shape of serious challenge before the economy as well as the society, which should be tackled in a cautions manner so that no imbalance could take place.

Though the government has initiated several measures since independence to ameliorate their conditions, the level of their living has somewhat improved particularly during eighties and nineties. Undoubtedly, this is a position trend. But at the same time, the labour class has also become conscious of the fast deteriorating situation, which has turned them into militant organizations. They have been forced to join militant organizations or private senas to snatch wealth and power from others to grab land, to take home crops from the fields and to satisfy their revenge by bloodshed. Rural areas are burning of hatred and revenge turning peaceful villages into full of tension and killings. Today, the confrontation is not only between people belonging to the lower castes and those belonging to upper castes but also within the people of same caste. The time has come now to think over this crucial problem, which may be considered as one of the major problems of India in present era.

OBJECTIVES

The present case study primarily aims at examining the socio-economic and political conditions of rural labour. The study highlights the present economic condition of rural labours in respect of wealth, internal as well as external sources of income and wage structure of rural labour. It also examines the working and living condition of rural labour and the impact of agrarian reforms.

HYPOTHESIS

Rural labour is basically a socio-economic problem and these problems are increasing day by day despite adequate safeguards and numerous legislations. The working condition of the rural labour in various organizations relating to households, construction, transportation, trade and commerce, brick manufacturing, basket making, bidi making, hotels and restaurants, etc., are far from satisfaction and against the spirit of rural labour welfare legislations.

METHODOLOGY

The present study is an empirical study by applying sociological methods to test the impact of socio-economic and political condition of rural labours. As the study has been applied to examine the different variables of the problems of rural labour and correlation among them, sampling is based on random sampling. It has been collected from each area on interview basis. Utmost care has bee taken and respondents from all castes, categories, income groups and religions have been included in our sample. A sample survey has been conducted of different localities of Patna District. The survey has covered the rural workers both male and female. It has covered the child labour including boys and girls. The survey has covered three hundred rural labours without any discrimination of age, occupation, caste, religion and sex. Hence, the source of information is based on primary data.

PROFILE OF PATNA DISTRICT

Patna is the capital of Bihar and is situated at the bank of river Ganga. It is surrounded by 8 districts namely; Bhojpur, Jahanabad, Nalanda, Vaishali, Saran, Begusarai, Samastipur and Lakhisarai. According to 2001 Census, it has the highest population rank with 4709851 persons (5.68 per cent to the total population) in 37 Districts of Bihar. The sex ratio of Patna District is 873, which is the lowest in the state. It is the most densely populated District among the Districts of Bihar with 1471 number of persons per sq. km. The literacy rate of persons of Patna District is 63.82 per cent while the literacy rates in males and females are recorded at 73.81 per cent and 52.17 per cent respectively.

Profile of Patna Town

Patna, the headquarter of the district as well as the capital of the state, is the largest city in Bihar, having a population of million plus (more than ten lakhs) as per the provisional population figures of 2001 Census. The position of Patna among the cities of India, so far as population is concerned, is quite low. The city has a glorious past and can boast of a very rich cultural heritage. In the early nineteenth century Buchanan Hamilton (1807-14) estimated its population at 312,000. At the Census of 1872, however, the population actually returned was 158,900 only. it seems that there were large omissions at this Census and the actual number was perhaps more. At the next Census (1881) also, the population returned was 170, 654 only. Between 1881 and 1921 the population of Patna was almost continuously on the decline mainly due to decrease in the river-brone trade and perhaps, due to repeated epidemics of plague. The population recorded during the Census of 1911 was 136,153which marked a slight increase over the 1901 population of 134,785, but the 1901 figure was admittedly low because of the virulent plague, which was raging at the time of Census. A recount made six months later disclosed the population of this town as 153,739. In 1921, the population of Patna was at its lowest (119,976). It had continued to fall in the decade 1911-21 in spite of the fact that the New Capital area had been set up consequent upon designation of the city as the capital of the newly created Bihar Province. Perhaps the Non-Cooperation Movement to some extent affected the figures of 1921 also.

LOCATION AND STUDY DESIGN

The study was carried out in four Blocks of Patna District, three villages each from Bakhtiyarpur Block and Sampatchak Block and two villages each from Danapur Block and Phulwarisharif Block with rural labours consisting of male and female (Table A). It was expected that the problems and the attitudes of rural labour might differ in nature as the exposure of rural labours from these villages and Blocks might have different movements in the society. Thus, the study not only shows how much rural labours have helped in highlighting their problems but it also provides its impact on various types of rural labour population who differ in their socio-economic criteria.

A questionnaire was developed to assess the present level of problems of rural labour on various aspects mentioned above and was self administered to the rural labours of ten villages in four Blocks of Patna District.

Sample Size

It was proposed that from each of the 10 villages selected from 4 Blocks of Patna District, 30 respondents would be selected at random for the study aggregating 300 hundred rural labours as random samples. All the selected rural labours were taken aside and questionnaire was self-administered. The rural labours selected from 10 villages of 4 Blocks were of right age for highlighting their socio-economic and political problems.

Table A
Coverage of Rural Labour by Type of Blocks/Villages and Sex of the Rural Population

Blocks/ Villages	*Rural Population*		
	Male	*Female*	*Total*
Sampatchak (Sona Gopalpur, Sohgi, Chainpur)	322	264	586
Bakhtiyarpur (Narauli, Lakhipur, Bidhipur)	293	245	538
Phulwarisharif (Makinpur,Chihut)	160	133	293
Danapur (Shivala, Dariyapur)	149	138	287
Grand Total	924	780	1704

*Villages selected are shown in brackets

Obstacles During Field Work Of Research Study

During the fieldwork of research study, we have faced a variety of obstacles from rural labour, which has taken additional time in completing the fieldwork. The major obstacle we faced was that majority of the respondents were either illiterate or less educated and incapable to understand the questions asked by the investigators while few of them were not giving much importance because there was no advantage from such surveys. Few of the respondents were annoyed with us as they were assuming us Government agents and they were annoyed and dissatisfied with Government policies. We also found lack of awareness among rural labours and this was mainly due to poor economic condition, illiteracy and also threat from upper class of society. Some respondents also tried to furnish wrong information, which was detected through supplementary and counter questions during filling up of questionnaire. In case of female respondents, they either did not want to turn up or hesitated in giving answers of the questions.

FINDINGS OF THE STUDY

Rural labour, which constitutes a large section of the workforce in India, is probably the most deprived and disadvantaged group in the country. The Government has initiated several measures since independence to ameliorate their conditions. Although their levels of living have somewhat improved particularly during the 1980s, the rural labourers have been largely bypassed by the general socio-economic development witnessed after independence. Various public works programmes and social security measures sponsored by the state have played an important role in India towards mitigating the plight of rural labour.

Bihar, one of the most populous states of India (comprising a little more than 10 per cent of the country's population), is economically the most backward. Along with a very high proportion of population below poverty line, Bihar has the lowest per capita income among the major states of India and also fares very badly with respect to most of the other socio-economic indicators of development. With about 87 per cent of the population in rural areas (as against 74.3 per cent of India as a whole), Bihar is the most rural state in the country, next only to Assam. The state has the lowest per capita rural income in the country. It has a very high density of population. The average per capita operational holding in the state was 0.87 hectares in

1985-86 as against 1.7 hectares for India as a whole and about 2.8 hectares for Punjab. About three- fourths of the operational holdings are marginal (less than one hectare) in which the average size is merely 0.31 hectare. Further, the fragmentation of land holdings is much more pronounced compared to other states. Although the state has a very low amount of land per capita, in some parts of the state there are still significant numbers of landholders having large amount of land in their possession, in violation of the ceiling law. Most of such landholders are absentees and consequently the state reports one of the largest landed areas under tenancy in the country, although a significant amount of land leased out is also by small and petty landholders engaged in a variety of occupations outside the village.

Block-wise Family Size Distribution

Table 1 is concerned with family size distribution of four Blocks taken under study. The table clearly reveals that Sampatchak has the largest family size, which is followed by Bakhtiyarpur whereas Danapur is such a Block, which has the smallest family size.

Table 1
Family Size Distribution (Block wise)

Name of Block	*Average Population Per Household*
Sampatchak	6.51
Phulwarisarif	4.81
Bakhtiyarpur	5.98
Danapur	4.78
Mean Population per Household	5.68

NFHS: Bihar 5.6 and India 5.5 (National Family Health Survey).

However, Phulwarisharif Block has larger family size in comparison to Danapur Block. The mean population per household of these four Blocks was 5.68, which was higher than the figure of 5.6 and 5.5 of Bihar and India respectively recorded by National Family Health Survey.

Literacy

Literacy among people is shown in Table 2. Out of 1702 persons of different family size, actual number of responses ever attended school and can read and write are 540 and 501 respectively in which children upto 5 years of age have not been included.

Table 2
Literacy (in per cent)

Family Size (persons)	*No. of persons*	*Ever attended@ school*		*Read and write#*	
Upto 2	37	8	1.48	6	1.20
3 to 5	607	168	31.11	155	30.9
6 to 8	717	260	48.14	240	47.9
9 to 11	317	101	18.70	98	19.6
12 and above	24	3	0.5	2	0.4
Total			100		100

In both groups, the highest actual response belongs to family size of 6 to 8 persons with 48.14 per cent and 47.9 per cent respectively while the lowest response is with family size of 12 persons and above.

Educational Level

The percentage distribution of respondents by their education level is shown in Chart 1.

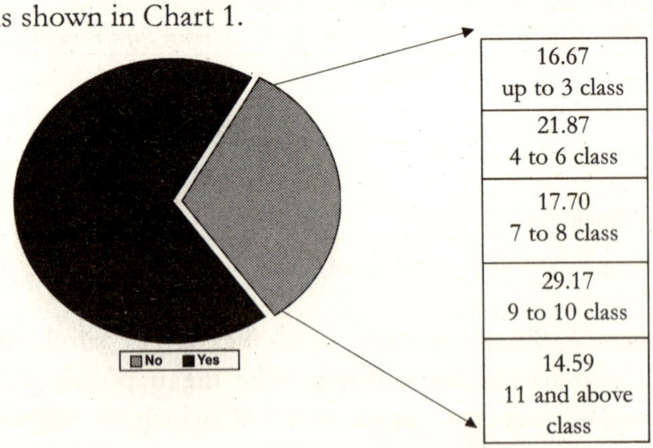

Chart 1 : Education Level of Respondents (in per cent)

The chart reveals that only 32 per cent of the respondents can read and write only. Among these respondents, highest numbers of the respondents are having 9 to 10 class level of education followed by number of respondents of 4 to 6 class level. The study further reveals that the percentage of respondents of 11-class level and above is the lowest.

House Structure

Bar-Diagram 1 shows the house structure of the respondents of the four Blocks taken under study.

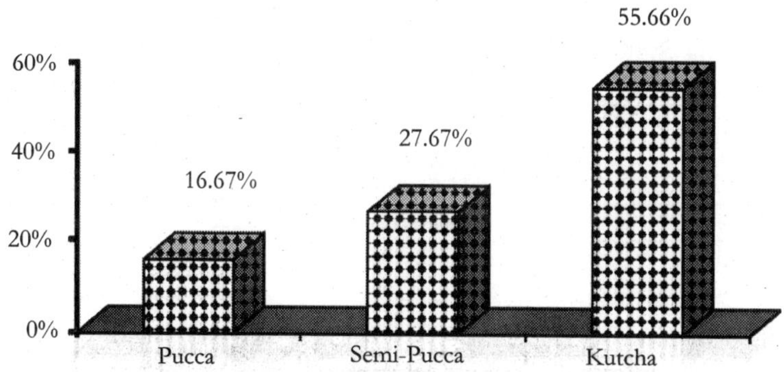

Diagram 1 : House Structure (in per cent)

It can be deduced from the diagram that majority of the respondents (55.66 per cent) have kutcha house structure while only 10.67 per cent of the respondents have pucca house structure. The house structure of the rest respondents belongs to semi-pucca structure (26.67 per cent).

Drinking Water Facility

Table 3 depicts the picture of per centage distribution of drinking water facility available to respondents. The study reveals that 48.67 per cent of the respondents use well located outside their houses for drinking water followed by hand pump/deep bore with 44.67 per cent.

Table 3
Drinking Water Facility (in per cent)

Name of items	*Per cent*
Hand Pump/ Deep Bore	44.67
Well (in residence)	6.00
Well (outside)	48.67
Piped water	00.66
Total	100

Only 6 per cent of the respondent labourers have well inside their houses while the share of piped water for drinking contributes only 0.66 per cent.

Lighting System

Table 4 is concerned with lighting system used by respondents.

Table 4
Lighting System (in per cent)

Lighting System	*Per cent*
Electricity	15.33
Kerosene	84.33
Gas	0.34
Total	100

So far as the lighting system is concerned, majority of the labourers (84.33 per cent) use kerosene oil followed by electricity about 15.33 per cent. Users of gas are very negligible with 0.34 per cent.

Land Ownership

The pie-diagram (Chart 2) shows the land ownership of rural labour.

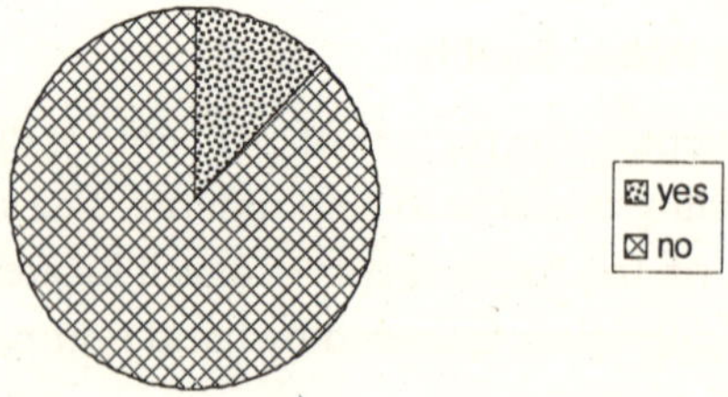

Chart 2 : Land Ownership

The diagram indicates that only 12.33 per cent of rural labourers have their own land while the rest all are landless labourers.

Cattle

Chart 3 reveals the position of cattle held by rural labourers in percentage. It is clear from the chart that 43 per cent of the rural labourers have cattle. Among these respondents, buffalo claims the highest share with 37.41 per cent followed by goat with 33.3 per cent. However, cow claims her share with 18.36 per cent followed by pig (5.44 per cent) and ox (4.76 per cent). The share of hen is negligible.

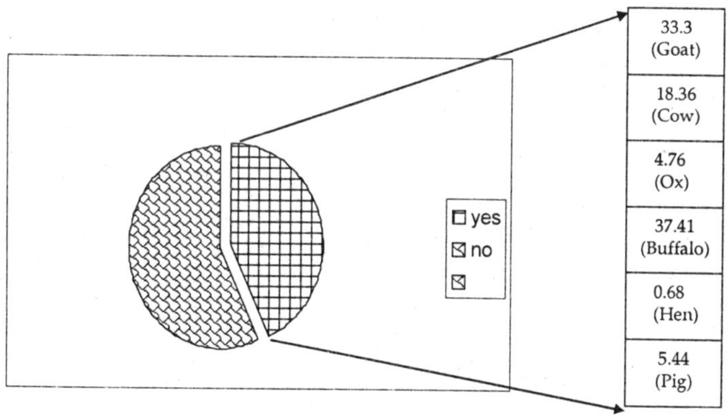

Chart 3 : Cattle (in Per cent)

Ownership Over Assets

Table 5 analyses the percentage distribution of ownership of rural labourers over assets. The table indicates that majority of rural labourers have bed/cot and mattress in all the four Blocks taken under study. Sampatchak Block is leading in availing electric and electronic goods like electric fan, radio, television and watch while use of bicycle by rural labourers is highest in Bakhtiyarpur Block in comparison to Sampatchak Block. Rural labourers of Phulwarisharif and Danapur Blocks have lower percentage of having such assets.

Table 11
Ownership of Assets (in per cent)

Name of Block	*Sample*	*Bed/Cot*	*Chair*	*Mattress*	*Table*	*Watch*	*Electric Fan*	*Bicycle*	*Radio*	*Tele-vision*	*Water Pump*
Sampatchak	90	70.00	4.44	78.88	4.44	27.77	14.44	17.77	7.77	12.22	2.22
Phulwarisarif	60	50.00	3.33	86.67	—	11.67	1.67	3.33	1.67	5.00	—
Bakhtiyarpur	90	81.11	5.55	96.67	6.67	22.22	14.44	21.11	6.67	7.78	2.22
Danapur	60	60.00	10.00	93.33	11.67	15.00	3.33	8.33	5.00	5.00	3.33
Mean		67.33	5.67	88.66	5.67	20.33	9.67	13.33	5.67	8.67	2.00

Cooked Food Items

Table 6 gives description of food items cooked by rural labourers. The food items cooked daily by labourers are mainly concerned with rice, bread, pulse and vegetables.

Table 6
Cooked Food Items Daily (in per cent)

Items	*Per cent@*
Rice	91.66
Bread	65.67
Pulses	29.33
Vegetable	68.67
Green Vegetable	10.00
Milk	4.67
Meat/Fish	3.67
Sattu (Others)	4.00

@ Due to multiple response

According to the table, rice is used by majority of the labourers (91.66 per cent) followed by vegetables (68.67 per cent), bread (65.67 per cent) and pulse (29.33 per cent). Green vegetables are consumed only by 10 per cent of the respondents while very few respondents about 3 to 4 per cent take milk and meat/fish.

Use of Leisure Time

Use of leisure time by rural labourers is shown in Diagram 2. The diagram shows that about 50.67 per cent of rural labourers chat with their friends and about 49 per cent prefer to sleep in leisure time.

The study further reveals that 27.67 per cent rural labourers get them engage in sitting alone or some household work. Only 5.67 per cent of them go for outdoor games while the percentage of movie-goers restricts to 1.67 per cent. This is mainly due to scarcity of outdoor game facilities and poverty among them.

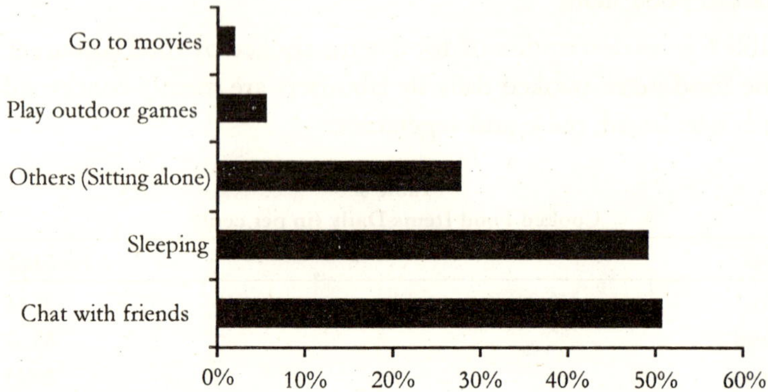

*Due to multiple responses

Diagram 2: Use of Leisure Time (in per cent)

Working Area

Diagram 3 shows the working area of rural labourers. It reveals that 72 per cent of rural labourers work in villages while 18.33 per cent of labourers work in town. Only 9.67 per cent are such labourers who work in town and village both.

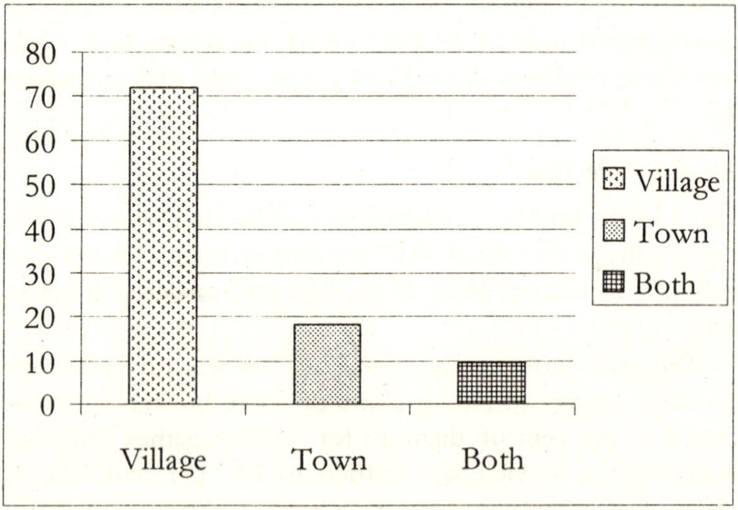

Diagram 3 : Working Area (in per cent)

Nature of Work

The pie-diagram (Chart 4) reflects the picture of nature of work done by rural labourers.

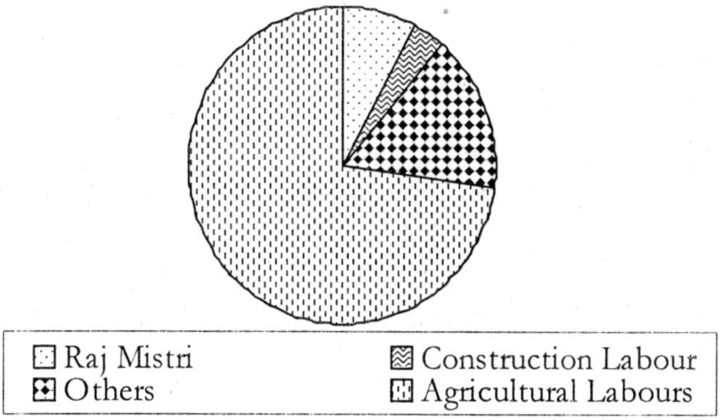

Chart 4

The diagram reveals that 72.67 per cent of rural labourers are engage in agriculture followed by 16.33 per cent in others like thela or ricksaw pulling, etc. It is also clear from the diagram that 7.67 per cent of rural labourers work as rajmistri while only 3.33 per cent are engaged in construction work.

Working Hours

The study also reveals the working hours of rural labourers which shown in Table 7.

Table 7
Working Hours (in per cent)

Working Hours	*Per cent*
Upto 5	1.67
6 to 7	11.33
8 to 9	72.00
10 to 11	9.33
12 and above	5.67
Mean Working Hours 8.62 Hours	

It is apparent from the table that majority of the rural labourers about 72 per cent work 8 to 9 hours followed by 11.33 per cent and 9.33 per cent work for 6 to 7 hours and 10 to 11 hours respectively per day. Only 1.67 per cent rural labourers work upto 5 hours per day while the mean working hours for rural labour is 8.62 hours peer day.

Working Days (Weekly)

Table 8 gives information about working days of rural labours in a week. The table reveals that only 6.67 per cent of labour gets work for all days while 30 per cent and 24 per cent get work only for four days and five days respectively in a week.

Table 8
Working Days Weekly (in per cent)

No. of Days	*Per cent*
1	1.33
2	12.01
3	20.00
4	30.00
5	24.00
6	5.67
7	6.67
Mean Working Days 4.07	100

About 32 per cent labourers are engaged only for two to three days while only 1.33 per cent gets work for one day in a week. The mean working days of rural labour is recorded 4.07 days in a week.

Working Days (Yearly)

Table 9 shows the number of working days of labourers in a year. The table reveals that 49 per cent of the labourers work from 121 to 180 days followed by 29.67 per cent working for 61 to 120 days. The lowest percentage i.e. 1 per cent of labourers works for 301 to 360 days while 3 per cent of them work for 361 days and above. The mean working days of rural labour is 143.29 days in a year.

Table 9
Working Days Yearly (in per cent)

Days	*Per cent*
Upto 60	6.67
61 to 120	29.67
121 to 180	49
181 to 240	10
241 to 300	2
301 to 360	1
361 and above	3
Total	100
Mean Days in a Year	143.29

PROBLEMS FACED

There are various problems which rural labours face during the work as is shown in Diagram 4.

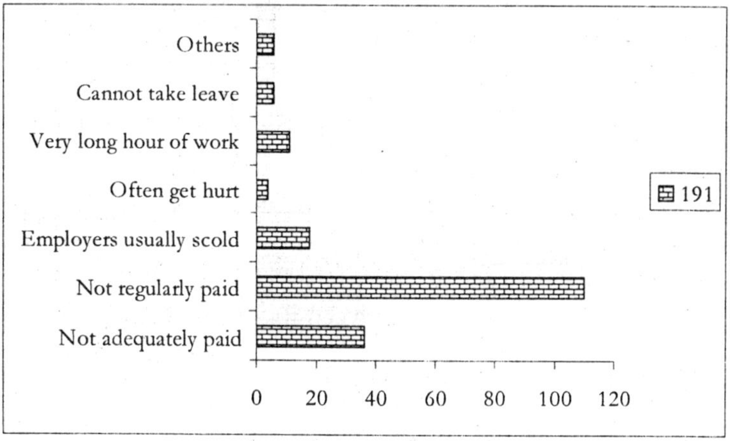

Diagram 4

The bar-diagram shows that majority of labourers face the problem of irregular payment followed by the problem of inadequate wage. The study further reveals that 18 out of 191 respondents reported that their employers scold them. Only 11 and 6 of them reported about the long hours of work and problem of leave respectively.

Mode of Wage Payment

Diagram 5 reveals the position of mode of wage payment of rural labours. It shows that 66.33 per cent of labourers get their wage in cash, 17.67 per cent in kinds and rest 16 per cent get their wage in cash as well as kinds.

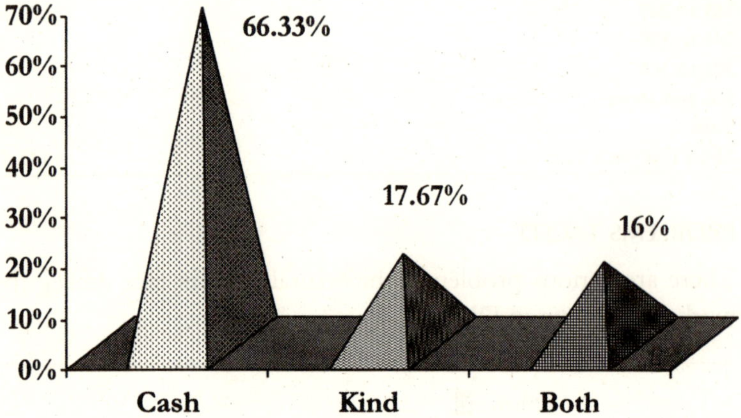

Diagram 5 : Mode of Wage Payment

Sex-wise Earning

Sex-wise per day earning of rural labour is shown in Table 10. The table reveals that highest 29.38 per cent of male respondents earn between Rs. 46 and Rs. 60 while 65.09 per cent the highest of women respondents earn between Rs. 16 and Rs. 30 per day.

Table 10
Sex-wise Per Day Earning (in per cent)

Amount in Rupees	*Male*	*Female*	*Total*
Upto 15	9.79	19.81	13.33
16 to 30	14.43	65.09	32.33
31 to 45	27.83	8.49	21.00
46 to 60	29.38	6.61	21.33
61 to 75	5.15	—	3.34
76 to 90	5.15	—	3.34
91 to 105	8.24	—	5.33
Mean Wages	46.11	23.28	38.05

The lowest percentage of male respondents 5.15 per cent belongs to two earning groups i.e. Rs. 61 to Rs. 75 and Rs. 76 to Rs. 90. Among the female respondents, 6.61 per cent is the lowest, which belongs to earning group between Rs. 46 and Rs. 60 while the mean wages for male and female are Rs. 46.11 and Rs. 23.28 respectively.

Monthly Earning

A comparative study has also been made regarding monthly earnings of rural labour, which is shown in Table 11.

Table 11
Monthly Earning (in per cent)

Amount in Rupees	*Per cent*
Upto 200	20.33
201 to 400	22.67
401 to 600	22.67
601 to 800	10.67
801 to 1000	9.67
1001 to 1200	4.33
1201 to 1600	4.33
1601 and above	5.33
n=300	
Mean Monthly Earning Rs. 566.67	

The table reveals that monthly earnings of about 65.67 per cent of rural labour is less than Rs. 600 while monthly income of 20.33 per cent of rural labour varies between Rs. 601 and Rs. 1000. Only 5.33 per cent of the labourers have monthly earning of Rs. 1601 and above while mean monthly earning is about Rs. 567.

Wage Variation

Table 12 shows wage variation among labours in rupee value. The table reveals that about 51.73 per cent of labours have wage variation between Rs. 11 and Rs. 20 while 32.75 per cent have variation upto Rs. 10.

Table 12
Wage Variation (in per cent)

Amount in Rupees	*Per cent*
Upto 10	32.75
11 to 20	51.73
21 to 30	6.90
31 to 40	1.72
41 to 50	6.90
Total	100.00
Mean Wage Variation	Rs. 14.82

The table further reveals that about 6.90 per cent each of rural labours have wage variation in two variation ranges from Rs. 21 to Rs. 30 and Rs. 41 to Rs. 50 while only 1.72 per cent of them have wage variation between Rs. 31 and Rs. 40. The mean wage variation is recorded at Rs. 14.82

Reasons for Unequal Wage

After studying wage variation among rural labours, the question arises about the reasons for unequal wage. Diagram 6 reflects the reasons unequal wage.

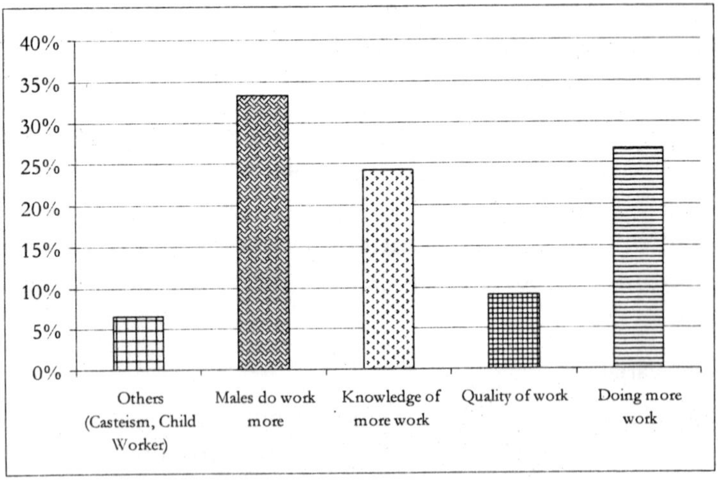

Diagram 6 : Reasons For Unequal Wage Payment

It reveals that male generally do work more in comparison to others. About 33.34 per cent of the respondents favour this reason. The second reason of wage variation is doing more work. This reason "more work more wage" is supported by 26.73 per cent of the respondents. The third prime reason of wage variation is more knowledge of work. Labour having more knowledge of work gets more wages. While wage is affected due to quality of work and others like casteism and child labour by 9.09 per cent and 6.6 per cent respectively.

Knowledge of Land Reform Programmes

It is also necessary to know how much labours are acquainted with land reform programmes. Chart 5 reveals that only 37 per cent of the respondents have knowledge of land reform programmes. Majority of them have no knowledge about this.

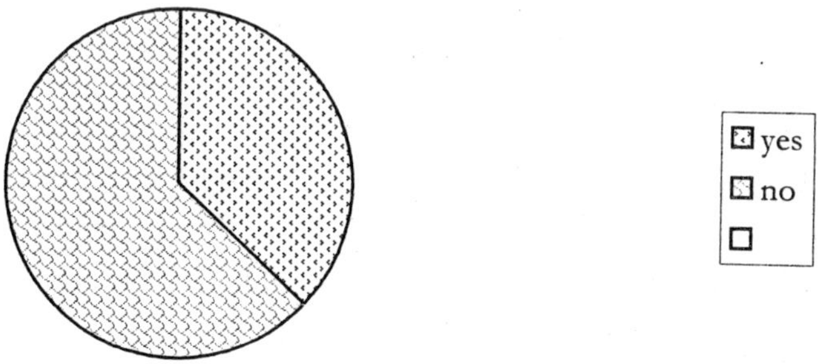

Chart 5 : Knowledge of Land Reform Programmes

Impact of Rural labour Development Schemes on Rural Labours

Chart 6 gives information about the knowledge of rural developmental schemes. It reveals that 76 per cent of the respondents have heard or some knowledge of rural developmental schemes.

In the light of Chart 6 of the study, it has become essential to know how much respondents have availed such schemes. Chart 7 reveals that about 62 per cent of the respondents are the beneficiaries of rural developmental schemes.

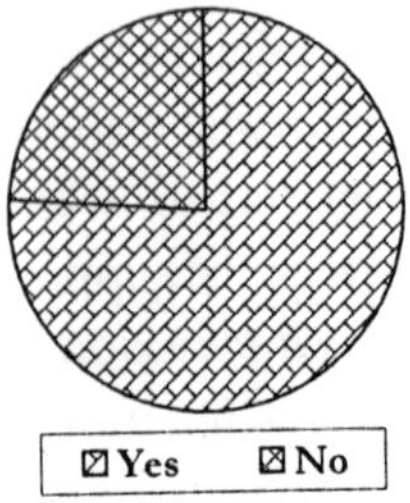

Chart 5 : Knowledge of Land Reform Programmes

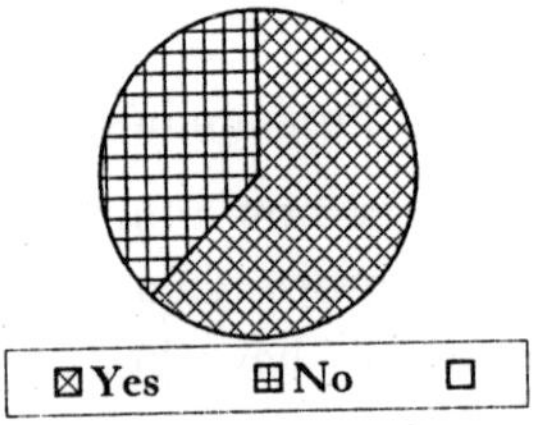

Chart 6 : Knowledge About Rural Labor Development Schemes

It is also important to study about the reasons due to which the rural labours are not being benefited of rural labour developmental schemes. Table 13 shows the various reasons due to which they are not being benefited. The highest 32 respondents out of 125 respondents are of opinion that they have no link with higher officer and this is the prime reason they are not getting the benefit of such schemes.

Table 13
Reasons for No Benefit of Rural Labour Development Schemes

Reasons	*Distribution*
No Knowledge about Scheme	12
Officer Demand Bribery	28
Fear of Seizing Property (in case of non return)	3
No Faith on Officer	5
Never Tried for Opting Loan	29
Benefit only to Literate Persons	6
No Link with Higher Officer	32
Name Allotted but Benefit Taken Over Another Person	5
Allotted Full Amount but Received Less Amount	5
n = 125	

The table further reveals that approximately the same number of respondents have neither opted for loan nor paid bribe demanded by officer concerned. 5 respondents are such whose names were in the list of beneficiaries but the benefit was taken over by another persons. It is the situation with allotted full amount but received lesser amount. 6 respondents are of opinion that these schemes are only for literate persons while 3 respondents think that their properties will be seized if they do not return the money.

An attempt has also been made to receive some effective suggestions from rural labours for better functioning of rural labour developmental schemes through Table 14.

Table 14
Suggestion For Better Functioning of Rural Labour Development Schemes

Suggestions	*Distribution*
Brokerage should be banned	41
Camp should be started for distribution	23
Distribution system should be right	13
Bribery should be prohibited	22
Employment programme should be started	55
Distribution should be started through Panchayat Samiti	7
Creating awareness programmes	7
Facility and money should be increased	2
n = 125	
Due to multiple response	

The table reveals that the highest 55 respondents are of opinion that effective employment programmes should be launched while 41 respondents are in favour of ban on brokerage for better functioning of rural labour developmental schemes. There are 23 and 22 respondents who favour distribution of schemes through camps and prohibition of bribery respectively. The table further reveals that equal number of the respondents (7) suggest distribution of schemes through Panchayat Samiti and creating awareness programmes while only 2 respondents want increase in schemes as well as money.

CONCLUSION OF THE STUDY

The main conclusion that arises from the foregoing analysis is that the rural labours play a vital and crucial role in the rural economy of Patna District. It constitutes the most marginalized section of our society. The fifty years of development has benefited this section the least. The share of agricultural labourers in the gains from the development has been the lowest while they have contributed immensely to the development of agriculture. Rural labour in household enterprises especially female labour has been one of the major victims of modernization as the new industrial products displaced traditional activities. Being unorganized and engaged in low productivity occupations, the increase in their wages and levels of consumption has been insignificant. Despite all these, the number of rural labourers in general has increased during nineties at the higher rate than the growth of population in rural areas.

Today, the rural class constitutes the largest sequent in the rural society. In fact, the present situation of rural labour is serious and critical. The labour class has also become conscious of the fast deteriorating situation, which has turned them into militants. They have been forced to join militant organisations or private senas to snatch wealth and powers from others to grab land, to take home crops from fields and to satisfy their revenge by bloodshed. Rural areas are burning of hatred and revenge turning peaceful rural areas into full of tension and killings. This class is facing socio-economic and political problems. The rural labour of Patna District is not an exception. The rural labours of this District are also facing certain challenges and are mostly illiterate. The educational schemes have also failed to reach the rural areas of this District. They are still living in a society of inequality, which has long range impact on the lives of rural labourers.

The investigator has made an extensive use of primary data, which has been drawn from a comprehensive survey of 300 rural labourers in four Blocks namely; Sampatchak, Phulwarisharif, Bakhtiyarpur and Danapur of Patna District with the help of a questionnaire. This attempt has enabled the investigator to examine the socio-economic and political problems of rural labours of Patna District, which is a burning problem of the state and hinders the development of the economy of Bihar.

The following general conclusion may be drawn from the study:

(i) Among the four Blocks of Patna District taken under study, Sampatchak Block has the highest average population per household while Danapur Block has the lowest average population per household while (Table 1).

(ii) So far as the education level of the rural labour is concerned, only 32 per cent of the rural labourers can read and write. Among these literate respondents, about 56 per cent of them have education up to 7th or 8th class while about 44 per cent of them have education above 9th class (Chart 1).

(iii) In case of land owned by rural labours, only 12.33 per cent of the respondents are in affirmative (Chart 2). The study further reveals that 43 per cent of the rural labourers have cattle mainly buffalo followed by goat and cow (Chart 3).

(iv) The ownership over assets by rural labours in the sample Blocks taken under study divided into bed/cot, chair, mattress, table, watch, electric fan, bicycle, radio, television and water pump. The position of having bed/cot and mattress is not low to such extent in comparison to water pump, chair, table and radio. However, the position of having television, electric fan, bicycle and watch is little higher to these items (Table 5).

(v) Regarding food items cooked by rural labourers, it was found that the majority of respondents favoured rice followed by vegetables, bread and pulse. Only 10 per cent of them used green vegetables while the users of milk or items made from milk, meat or fish and sattu were only of 5 per cent (Table 6).

(vi) It is very important to find out how the rural labours pass their leisure time. It was found that about 50 per cent of the respondents wanted to pass their leisure time either by chatting with friends or sleeping while about 28 per cent preferred to sit or to do some household work. The percentage of respondents either for outdoor games or movies was very low. This is mainly due to lack of facilities for outdoor games and poverty among them. Lack of infrastructure is also one of the major causes (Diagram 2).

(vii) The working area of the rural labours in the four Blocks was also examined and we have found that 72 per cent of the respondents work in village followed by 18.33 per cent in town while 9.67 per cent of the respondents are such who work in both areas (Diagram 3). It has further been observed that about 73 per cent of the respondents are engage in agriculture (Chart 4).

(viii) Regarding working hours of rural labours, it has been found that 72 per cent of the respondents work between 8 to 9 hours per day while 9.33 per cent of them work for 10 to 11 hours. Only 1.67 per cent of the respondents work upto 5 hours (Table 7). The study further reveals that the respondents having 4 working days in a week has the highest percentage (30 per cent) followed by respondents having 5 working days in a week. Only 6.67 per cent of them have work all the days in a week. The percentage of labourers having only 1 working day in a week is very low which marked at 1.33 per cent (Table 8).

(ix) The study further reveals the position of working days of rural labour of these Blocks in a year. We have found that 49 per cent of the respondents have working days between 121 to 180 days followed by 29.67 per cent between 61 to 120 days in a year (Table 9). Only 3 per cent of them have working days for 361 and above days while the percentage of respondents having working days upto 60 days in year marked at 6.67 per cent.

(x) There are various problems the rural labour face during the work. It has been observed from the study that the main problem is that they are not regularly paid followed by not adequately paid, employers usually scold them very long duration of work. The problem of often get hurt was reported the least (Diagram 4).

(xi) As far as the mode of payment is concerned, it is apparent from the study (Diagram 5) that 66.33 per cent of the respondents are paid in cash while 17.67 per cent take their payment in kind and only 16 per cent are paid in both.

(xii) Being the largest sequent of rural society, per day earning of rural labour is not satisfactory. Near about 72 per cent of the male respondents earn in between Rs.16 and Rs.60 while about 85 per cent of the female respondents are having per day earning below Rs.30. In total of male and female labours, majority of them (88 per cent) have per day earning below Rs. 60 (Table 10).

(xiii) While studying monthly earning of rural labour, we have found that 65.67 per cent of the respondents have monthly income below Rs.600 while 20.34 per cent of them earn monthly between Rs.601 and Rs.1000. Only 8.66 per cent of the respondents earn monthly between Rs.1001 to Rs. 1600 and 5.33 per cent have their monthly earning of Rs. 1601 and above (Table 11).

(xiv) During the case study, we have also found wage variation among rural labours. 51.73 per cent of the respondents have variation in their wage between Rs.11 and Rs. 20 while 32.75 per cent of them have wage variation upto Rs.10. The study further reveals that very few of them (1.72 per cent) have wage variation between Rs. 31 and Rs. 40 while 6.9 per cent of rural labour have wage variation in two wage groups i.e. Rs. 21 to Rs. 30 and Rs. 41 to Rs. 50 (Table 12).

(xv) We have further tried our level best to find out the reasons for unequal wage. It reveals that 33.34 per cent of the respondents have supported the concept that generally male labours do more work so they are paid more wages. The other main reasons for unequal wage were 'doing more work' and 'more knowledge of work'. The reasons like quality of work and others including casteism and child worker have very less importance for unequal wage (Diagram 6).

(xvi) At the age of reforms, it is important to know how much rural labours have knowledge of land reform programmes. It is a matter of fact that only 37 per cent of the respondents have knowledge about land reform programmes (Chart 5).

(xvii) Before moving to the next, an explanation is also necessary about the knowledge of rural labour development schemes. It is found that 76 per cent of the respondents have either heard or some knowledge of these schemes (Chart 6) and 62 per cent of them has been benefited (Chart 7). Those who have not benefited have various reasons. Out of 125 respondents, 32 claimed that they have no link with higher officials while 29 of them had never tried for the benefit. 20 respondents reported that they were demanded bribe while 12 respondents had no knowledge about the scheme. 5 respondents were such who were either allotted but the benefit was taken over by other or allotted full amount but received less amount or had no faith on officers (Table 13).

(xviii) In course of study, we sought for suggestions from rural labours for better functioning of rural labour developmental schemes. We found that out of 125 rural labourers, 55 rural labourers were of opinion that employment programmes should be started for better functioning of these schemes while 41 respondents favoured ban on brokerage. Almost equal number of respondents favoured distribution of these schemes through camps and prohibition on bribery while equal number of respondents supported launching of various awareness programmes and distribution of schemes through Panchayat Samiti (Table 14).

SUGGESTIONS OF THE STUDY

From the outgoing analysis, it is clear that the rural labour community suffer a lot of social and economic problems viz., increase in population, illiteracy, poor wage structure, low earnings, unhealthy working conditions, lack of infrastructure, lack of protection, etc. Though rural labourers have played a significant role in the rural economy of Patna District, rural living in Bihar is still like flying on mono engine plane. If the single engine shuts off due to malfunctioning, the high flier hurdles down to crash into a dead heap. Hence, a multiform attack should be organized on problems of rural labour. Some remedial measures may be suggested as follows:

(1) There must be a check on increasing population through different control methods because it is not possible to provide employment to the increasing population in rural areas. It is also not possible to increase infrastructure at once in accordance with the needs of the rural society due dearth of funds. Hence, the control over population will be one of the remedial measures for rural labour in Bihar and Patna District.

(2) Illiteracy is also one of the major hindrances of rural labour in Bihar and Patna District. As educational facilities are not in proper way and due to this reason, the illiterate rural labour are not aware of their rights. So, literacy must increase among rural labourers and this is also the responsibility of the state government to caste to their educational needs by encouraging them to send their children to educational institutions.

(3) For making the education system on India level and commercial, it is essential to interpret the necessities of electricity, communication, irrigation, roads, railways, public sector and whole industries as well as modernization of agriculture so that the inhabitants of Bihar and Patna District might know where Bihar exists on the map of India. Only except the certain essential subjects, the complete transparency should be showed and the people should have "the right to know".

(4) There must be thrust on increasing the rural employment potential in rural and allied sectors. It must be brought about by various ways of agricultural development activities of the rural tertiary sectors with a large reduction in indebtedness and increase in productivity of rural labourers.

(5) Much stress should be made to facilitate employment to the surplus and seasonal rural labour force in their rural areas only. The rural work programme has a vital contribution towards relief of unemployment and underemployment and assuring of minimum earnings and acceleration of the pace of rural development.

(6) In Bihar, employers are openly violating the provisions of the Minimum Wages Act, 1948 especially in rural sector and make payment of wages well below the minimum wage. The state government should strict over this issue

and should also restructure the wage format in accordance with the need of the rural sector and state.

(7) It is also suggested that the allocation of manpower in rural sector should be based on capital extensive and labour intensive technology. The rural labourers have to be provided financial support and technical assistance at subsidized rates to operate dairy, poultry, piggery, etc.

(8) There must be improvement in working conditions of rural labourers. Rural skills and tools must be upgraded. Women labourers also must be trained in male type assignments and operations.

(9) Better infrastructure facilities need to be provided for encouraging self-employment among female rural labourers. Special entrepreneurship courses should be run for such women. Educated woman should be encouraged to form co-operative societies to be controlled and run exclusively by women themselves.

(10) In order to tackle the problem of inequality of assets, administration should have to play an active role for the implementation of land reform measures. In order to improve their asset position, other means of production and services should be distributed to them at lower prices. At this juncture, it is suggested that only government programmes cannot enrich the government records, the vigilance department should also make report on the nature of benefit and also detect exploitation made by the institutional agents so that deterrent action may be taken against guilty officials.

(11) Like industrial workers, there must be adequate extension of labour and social security measures for rural labour because these measures add to the purchasing power of the rural labours and improve their status.

(12) There is always a debate on self versus wage employment programmes. There is need of self-employment

programmes. The role of government is also required in this connection. The government should launch more attractive and effective self-employment programmes according to the need of rural population so that majority of this section could be benefited.

(13) Rural labour is a serious problem, which our state faces. Government legislations are only on paper. This problem can be solved through proper technical and non-technical education, awareness programmes, government legislations, etc.

(14) Regarding public expenditure, it is suggested that it should be increased in a poor state like Bihar.

(15) Although states spend most of the resources on social sector, role of centre is equally important.

(16) Though allocation of funds to the programmes is necessary condition, management or administration aspects are equally important for efficient and effective utilization of funds making the programmes successful by reaching to the poor. Hence, we should also give more weightage to the organizational aspects as compared to the allocation of funds.

(17) Macro policies are, of course, equally important in helping the poor. Inflation must be under control. Economic growth also important if the government wants to allocate more resources to have productive employment.

(18) Decentralisation of administration and giving enough power to local bodies for administering the schemes are also important for helping the poor. But this alone will not solve the problem. A system of accountability is also needed from local bodies. Involvement of NGOs will improve the delivery system.

(19) It is also suggested that the state government should reformulate its agricultural policy to boost up the

productivity of the crops on sustained basis to increase employment opportunities for rural labourers.

(20) New agricultural technology should be spread over through the information technology to the rural masses.

(21) The state should provide the basic infrastructure like electricity, road and transport, water, irrigation, hybrid seeds and facilities to make an investment platform for agriculture.

(22) To boost agricultural activities in the state, one aspect that the Government of Bihar has to address to is to ask the banks and financial institutions to invest more in agriculture of Bihar.

(23) The government should also promote cottage industries and village handicrafts, which were destroyed by the Britishers. A major section of rural labourers who are efficient in cottage industries and village handicrafts can be reverted to this section again.

(24) Productivity of agriculture should be increased. For it, the development of agriculture is essential in which various items viz., food grain, oil seeds, vegetables, fruits, milk, fish, eggs, meat, etc. may be observed. Money supply may also be increased for rapid increase in the productivity of agriculture.

(25) It is also essential to increase productivity in industrial sector for reducing economic slump. For reducing cost of production, we have to control and keep vigilance over expenditure of goods, electricity and other sources of energy, expenditure of interests, loans, price of coal and electricity, etc. We have to review on the incidence of tax also in the new light.

(26) We have to observe over to increase our domestic saving rate. Tax evasion and black money are also the great problems of the state.

(27) Lastly, the state government should improve the law and order situation in the state where there is carnages or mass killings of labourers, looting of crops, kidnapping, etc. Militant activities are prevailing in all over the state, which is hampering the overall growth of the state.

Notes

This paper was presented in International Conference orgranised by Indira Gandhi National Open University, New Delhi on March 26 to 28, 2008.

References

Agrawal, A. N. (1982), Indian Agriculture and its Problems, Ranjit Printers & Publishers.

Bhagoliwal, T. N. (2001), Economics of Labour and Industrial Relations, Shahitya Bhawan Publications, Agra.

Bhagoliwal, T. N., Labour Problems in India, Kitabghar, Kanpur.

Das, D. K. (Ed.), *Dynamics of Rural Development*, Vol. I & II, Deep & Deep Publications, New Delhi

George, T. M. (2001), Rural Labour Market, B. R. Publishing Corporation, New Delhi.

Jha, S. (1990), Agricultural Labour, Deep & Deep Publications (P) Ltd, New Delhi.

Joshi, M. V. (1999), Labour Economics and Labour Problems, Atlantic Publishers and Distributors, New Delhi.

Mamoria, C. B. and Mamoria, Satish (1983), Labour Welfare, Social Security and Industrial Peace in Labour Welfare, India, Kitab Mahal, Allahabad.

Marla, S. (1961), Bonded Labour in India, Biblia Implex Pvt. Ltd., New Delhi.

Mehrotra, S. N. (1981), Labour Problems in India, S. Chand & Co., New Delhi,

Pawar, R. (1995), Landless Agricultural Labourers and the Law, Deep & Deep Publications, New Delhi.

Pratap, K. (1992), Rural Labour in India-Problems and Welfare Schemes, Deep & Deep Publications, New Delhi.

Radhakrishna, R. and Sharma, Alakh N. (1998), Empowering Rural Labour in India: Market, State and Mobilisation, Institute for Human Development,

New Delhi.

Ram Avtar, Lectures on Rural Problems and Social Welfare in India, New Academic.

Rao, V. M. and Aziz, Poverty Alleviation in India: Programmes and Actions, Ashish Publishing House, New Delhi

Rudra, D. and Sunderam, K.P.M. (2001), Indian Economy, S.Chand & Co., Delhi.

Sajjad, Haroon (1998), Employment of Landless Labourers, B. R. Publishing Corporation, Delhi.

Srivastava, M. K. (1993), Agricultural Labour and the Law, Deep & Deep Publications, New Delhi.

Government of India, Economic Survey (Various Issues), New Delhi.

Government of India, Report of the National Commission on Labour, 1969.

Government of India, Report on the National Commission on Rural Labour, 1991.

Government of India, Five Year Plans, New Delhi .

Yojana (Various Issues).

Kurukshetra (Various Issues).

7

LABOUR MARKET IN KENYA: STRUCTURE, REFORMS AND ROLE OF THE GOVERNMENT

Jane Kabubo-Mariara

INTRODUCTION

Statistics on the characteristics of the labour force are some of the indicators required for measuring the extent of available human resources and for the purpose of human resource planning, formulating and monitoring employment policies and programmes, income-generating activities, vocational training and other similar programmes. Such statistics also facilitate the measurement of the relationship between employment, income and other social and economic characteristics (CBS, 2002). In addition, the operations and nature of the labour market determine the rate of growth, income distribution, extent of labour force participation and the poverty status of households. To understand the nature and functioning of the labour market in Kenya, this section discusses the age, gender and sectoral diversity of the Kenyan labour market. The section also briefly discusses the quality and productivity of labour.

Diversity in Labour Supply

Age: The diversity of Kenyan labour is evidenced by regional and sectoral differentials in demand and supply of labour, as well as age and gender differentials. The sectoral categories of the labour market can further be differentiated into occupational categories. Further, the Kenyan population can be classified into the active population (or the labour force) and the inactive population. The economically active population consists of the employed and unemployed persons and most of these are youthful aged between 24-34 years (Table 1). In addition to the active population, we have categories of people classified as economically inactive either by reason of inactivity or of the usual inactivity status. Population census estimates show that in 1999, 3.6 million persons were economically inactive representing 22.6% of the population aged 15-64 years with the majority being full time students[1]. The economically active population aged 15-64 years expanded by 58.2% between 1989 and 1999. The growth was higher in urban areas (75%) than in the rural areas (53.9%) (CBS, 2002). The

Table 1
Age Distribution of Economically Active/Inactive Population, 1989-1999

	*1989**	*1999**		*1999***	
Age Group	*Active (%)*	*Active (%)*	*Inactive (%)*	*Active (%)*	*Inactive (%)*
15-19	11.3	13.4	48.35	9.04	65.27
20-24	15.2	14.9	17.59	15.97	13.48
25-29	14.9	13.0	10.00	15.22	4.61
30-34	10.9	9.6	6.17	14.02	2.63
35-39	8.8	8.2	4.97	13.58	2.55
40-44	7	5.9	3.52	10.07	1.92
45-49	5.4	4.9	2.71	8.77	1.87
50-54	4.6	4.0	2.33	6.24	2.30
55-59	3.4	2.6	2.07	3.87	2.42
60-64	2.9	2.2	2.29	3.23	2.96
Total number	9.3m	15.8m	2.6m	12.3m	3.6m

Source: *Central Bureau of Statistics (2002); **Central Bureau of Statistics (2003).

economically inactive population aged 5 years and above in the 1999 census was estimated at 8.1 million people comprising 33.9% of the population.

A quick overview of the supply and demand for labour in the economy can be gleaned from labour force participation rates. Population census estimates show that the overall participation rates increased from 75.7% in 1989 to 82.6% in 1999 (Table 2). The table further shows that the rates were lowest for the 15-19 age group in the two periods but increased along the age spectrum to peak at the age group 45-49 years. Labour force participation rates for females were generally lower than those for males and the pattern was almost common in all age cohorts. The 1998/9 labour force survey estimated the overall urban and rural participation rates at 86.4% and 73.8% respectively. Available estimates also show that participation rates rose with formal education from 83.7% for those with no education to over 98.8% for those with post-graduate education.

An analysis of the age distribution showed a high concentration of the labour force within the youthful population

Table 2
Labour Force Participation Rates by Gender: 1989-1999

	*1989**			*1999**			*1999***		
Age Group	*Male*	*Female*	*All*	*Male*	*Female*	*All*	*Male*	*Female*	*All*
15-19	44.6	44.7	44.6	62.3	62.9	62.6	28.1	30.5	29.3
20-24	79.7	70.9	75.0	89.0	79.1	83.7	66.6	69.8	68.3
25-29	94.6	77.9	85.9	96.5	81.6	88.7	91.5	87.7	89.4
30-34	96.5	80.3	88.4	97.7	83.3	90.4	96.6	91.6	94.1
35-39	97.0	82.1	89.5	97.7	84.3	90.9	97.4	92.3	94.8
40-44	96.8	82.2	89.5	97.7	84.5	91.1	97.5	92.9	95.2
45-49	96.8	83.1	89.7	97.7	85.5	91.6	95.6	90.7	93.4
50-54	95.8	81.8	88.7	97.4	84.8	91.1	94.0	86.9	90.3
55-59	92.9	82.3	87.6	93.0	84.0	88.3	87.8	82.5	85.1
60-64	92.3	79.6	85.6	90.4	81.0	85.4	85.0	77.4	80.9
Total	81.1	70.7	75.7	87.5	78.0	82.6	74.7	72.6	73.6

Source: *Central Bureau of Statistics (2002); **Central Bureau of Statistics (2003).

aged 15-29 years in 1999. 14.9% of the active population was aged between 20-24 years and was the highest concentration, followed by age group 15-19 years (13.4%) and the 25-29 years cohort (13.0%). Only 2.2% of the labour force was aged 60-64 years. The same concentration in age groups was reported in the 1989 census, but with a gradual decline along the spectrum.

Child Labour: Child labour is an emerging and disturbing phenomenon in Kenya with adverse implications on the quality of future labour force. At the national level, the use of child labour in great numbers slows down economic growth and social development. Moreover, child labour prevents them from attending school and is exploitative, hazardous and inappropriate (CBS, 2003). The government policy statement (2000) addressing children's issues emphasize the need to address the root cause of child labour problem, observe and operationalize the convention of right of the child, empower the families where child labour comes from, support NGO and development parties involved in children issues (Manda *et al.*, 2003).

The labour force survey 1998/99 (CBS 2003) estimates that there were more than 1.9 million children aged 5-17 years working for pay or family gain representing 17.4% of the children population and 14.4% of the estimated workforce. Most of the working children were in the age group 10-14 years, though child labour increased with age. There were more boys than girls engaged in child labour in all age groups though there was near gender parity. However, the proportion of working girls is higher than that of working boys in urban areas. Majority of working children (95.1%) were residing in rural areas, while more rural children (40.6%) reported to have worked compared to their urban counterparts (12.8%) (CBS, 2002). Majority of the children were reported to be unpaid family workers, followed by paid employment (Table 3). CBS (2003) further reports that the majority of working children came from either large households or poor households. The main reasons given for child labour were to help in family business/farm and to augment family income. The labour force survey report recommends that the government together with key stakeholders ensure that the Children's Act (2001) provisions are enforced. Yamano and Jayne (2003) support findings by CBS (2003). In an analysis of the impact of adult mortality rates due to AIDS on primary school enrollment, the authors argue that children in relatively poor households are less likely to be in school in the AIDS pre-mortality period compared with the period after mortality. They explain that this could be because poor households are forced to take more extreme measures to adjust to major shocks to their livelihoods, even at the expense of long-run human capital development than the non-poor. For this reason, they are more likely to reallocate their children's time from schooling to take care of sick adults, or to provide labour to compensate for lost adult labour resulting from sickness.

Table 3
Child Labour (5-17 Years) by Employment Status

Employment Status	*Schooling*	*Not Schooling*	*Total*
Paid Employee	1.2	30.3	18.5
Self Employed	0.6	2.3	1.6
Unpaid Family Worker	97.9	65.7	78.7
Apprentice	0.2	0.5	0.7
Other	0.2	1.1	0.8

Source: Central Bureau of Statistics (2002).

Majority of the working children (about 63.9%) earned less than Kshs. 900 per month in 1998/99, slightly below the statutory minimum wage of Kshs. 998 per month set for unskilled employees below 18 years who work in the agricultural sector. There were more girls than boys in the low wage groups, implying gender differentials in wages (CBS 2003). Urban children were found to earn less than those in rural areas. The study gave some non-wage facilities that employers offered to the working children as: meals, which were given to 31% of respondents, accommodation (24.2%), medical, protective clothing, transport and training as given to 22.3%, 7.8%, 7.0% and 2.6% of respondent respectively.

Gender: The labour market in Kenya is also substantially differentiated by gender. For instance, there is asymmetrical division of labour with women devoting more hours than men to domestic and other unpaid work and having little access to paid employment. UNDP (1999) notes that most women in rural areas are involved in agricultural activities (80% of food crop production and 50% of cash crop production). Available evidence shows that the proportion of women in wage employment at the national level is very low (estimated at 29.2% in 1999) and this is also reflected in both rural and urban areas (CBS, 2002). Men are generally concentrated in manufacturing and women are concentrated in agriculture, forestry, community, social and personal services (Kabubo-Mariara, 2003a; Manda, 2002).

A sex-ratio analysis also reveals gender differentials in labour force participation and employment across the age cohorts. A comparison of the 1989 and 1999 population census show that there was a notable increase in the female participation in the labour force. Females outnumbered males in labour force at ages 15-24 years in both 1989 and 1999. In 1999, there were 14.5 million people who were working, out of whom 52.4% were males. Generally, employment opportunities are lower for women than men in both rural and urban areas and also across more formal and skilled job categories. Major factors contributing to this phenomenon include: household characteristics, assets ownership, imbalances in training and access, retrogressive cultural practices and lack of supportive legal framework (Manda, 2004; Kabubo-Mariara, 2002, 2003b; Wambugu, 2002; Ministry of Labour, 2004b; Odhiambo and Manda, 2003). Other factors affecting women's labour force participation include costs of child care, presence/absence of older daughters, wages and other economic incentives (Lokshin *et al.*, 2000).

Sectoral Diversity: This is exemplified by diversity in formal and informal sectors on one hand and public vs. private sectors on the other.

Formal and Informal Sectors: Labour market diversity is also evidenced by sectoral differentials in employment and earnings. The Kenyan labour market can broadly be divided into the formal and informal sectors. Schindler (2003) argues that the labour market appears to be marked by rigidities including minimum wages and other wage setting institutions, which raise wages, thus production costs for the formal sector relative to the informal sector. Other factors include taxation, regulatory and administrative procedures, which also increase the operating costs in the formal sector, but reduce informal sector costs because of weak enforcement (Schindler, 2003). The implications of these developments include an inefficient production structure, lost fiscal revenues, lower growth prospects, reduced external competitiveness and deepening poverty.

The formal sector is small and capital intensive, while the informal sector is large and labour intensive, with highly heterogeneous activities ranging from street vendors to small kiosks, hotels, open-air motor garages, dress making, tailoring units and small scale transport operations (PRSP, 2001). During the eighth National Development plan period (1997-2001) formal sector employment expanded by only 1.8% per annum while the labour force grew by 3.5%. The informal sector employment grew by 10% per annum. Most employed workers in the formal sector were skilled agricultural and fishery workers (37.3%) whereas professionals were mainly in paid employment. Professionals accounted for only 1.2% of employed persons (Republic of Kenya, 9th National Development Plan- 2002-2008).

CBS (2003) however shows that in 1999, the level of employment stood at 85.4%. The overall employment-sex ratio was 1.08 but females dominated the rural based small–scale farming and pastoralists activities. Rural areas absorbed 70.1% of employed persons. The working population was largely made up of unpaid family workers and paid employees concentrated in rural and urban areas respectively. The formal sector engaged 26.3% while the informal sector had 31.6% and the pastoralist and small–scale farming engaging 42.1% of the total work force. Females employed in traditionally male-dominated sectors were notably low. Overall, employment creation in 1999 slowed down significantly partly due to the economic recession and a steady decline in wage employment in the public sector.

Available evidence also shows that there is significant industrial segmentation of the labour market in Kenya. For instance, for the informal sector, the predominant industries in rural areas are wholesale and retail trades (65.8%), followed by manufacturing (26.4%). In urban areas, other community services, private households, transport, health and construction are dominant industries (CBS, 2003).

CBS (2003) also shows that Kenyan workers' average earnings amounted to Kshs. 7,766 per month with basic (earnings less benefits) salary as the main source in 1998/99. Average earnings in urban areas were almost twice the rural average earnings whereas male earnings were higher than females in both rural and urban areas. The overall gazetted monthly basic minimum wages in urban areas were raised from Kshs. 3347 to Kshs. 6,142 between 1998 and 2003, while the basic monthly wages for rural agricultural workers in the private sector were raised from Kshs. 1567 to Kshs. 2,529 in 2003 (Republic of Kenya, Economic Surveys, various issues).

The Kenyan informal sector is defined to cover all semi-organized and unregulated small-scale activities largely undertaken by self-employed or those employing only a few workers in the open market, in market stalls, in both developed and underdeveloped premises. The main legal feature of informal sector activities is that they are not registered (or legally bound to register) with the registrar of companies, but may have or not have operating licenses. The activities in the sector are carried out by artisans, traders and other operators but excludes all farming and pastoral activities (CBS, 2003). For statistical purposes, the informal sector is defined as a group of production units which form a part of the household sector as unincorporated enterprises owned by households. The main feature of the informal sector include ease of entry; small scale of the activity; self employment with a high proportion of family workers and apprentices; little capital and equipment; labour intensive technology; little access to organized markets, formal credit and education and training; low productivity and incomes (CBS, K-PREP, ICEG 1999).

There has been significant structural changes in the Kenyan labour market, with the informal sector becoming increasingly important as a source of employment and income, but a declining contribution of the formal sector, more so because labour supply exceeds labour demand in the modern sector. During the last decade, the sector's growth rate in employment has remained above that of the formal sector employment. As the formal sector employment has decreased, informal sector employment has continued to record sustained increase. This has seen the sector's share in total employment rise from 16% in 1980, to 63.6% in 1997 and 70% in 2000. Between 1999 and 2000, employment in the sector rose by 11%. Its share in GDP has also recorded increases, rising from 13% in 1993 to 18% in 1999. However, overall employment creation slowed down significantly in 1999, partly due to economic recession and partly due to a steady decline in wage employment in the public sector (Republic of Kenya, 2001). Sectorally, the informal sector is the second largest source of employment after small-scale agriculture (Republic of Kenya, 2000).

Public and Private Sectors: There is also considerable labour market diversity between private and public sectors. For instance, total wage employment in the private sector employment rose by 15.7% between 1995 and 2000, compared to 2.3% decline in public sector employment. The share of the private sector out of total modern sector employment rose from 57.6% in 1998 to 61.9% in 2003. Growth in the private sector employment went up from

1.6% in 2001 to 2.7% in 2003 (Republic of Kenya, Economic Survey, 2004). In the recent past, most of the growth in the private sector employment has been in manufacturing sector activities. For instance, in 2002, employment growth in the sector expanded at 7.3% compared to 0.1% in 2001. This rate was driven by the double growth of employment in the EPZs and also from the successful exploitation of the African Growth and Opportunity Act (AGOA) opportunities.

Over the same period, there has been consistent decline in public sector wage employment, mostly due to privatization of non-strategic public enterprises as part of the public sector reforms. Employment in the Central government has continued to decline due to restrictive government employment policy and natural attrition, while Local government has increased employment. Employment in parastatals has however dropped. Overall, there was only a marginal increase in total public sector employment in 2002 since 1996, due to recruitment of teachers by the Teachers Service Commission (Table 4). The public sector wage bill has also remained modest (about 36% of modern sector

Table 4
Public Sector Employment ('000s): 1995-2006

Year	*Central Government*	*Teachers Service Commission*	*Parastatals*	*Majority control by public sector*	*Local Government*	*Total*
1995	251.7	231.7	107.3	48.5	50.8	690.0
1996	242.4	239.9	107.5	47.9	52.1	698.8
1997	219.1	241.3	112.8	52.5	74.9	700.6
1998	227.6	247.7	108.9	49.9	77.1	711.2
1999	224.0	242.3	105.2	48.5	78.8	698.8
2000	222.9	236.8	104.1	48.0	80.7	692.5
2001	195.7	231.3	101.6	47.5	82.3	658.4
2002	194.9	234.3	99.0	46.7	83.9	658.8
2003	195.0	234.8	97.3	46.4	85.6	659.1
2004	194.2	234.5	96.0	46.1	87.4	658.2
2005	189.5	232.8	87.6	46.9	87.5	654.3
2006	187.7	233.3	97.2	46.8	85.0	649.9

Source: Economic Survey, Various Issues.

total wage bill) due to government's policy of slowing down wage employment except in essential services (Republic of Kenya, Economic Surveys).

The share of informal sector employment to total employment rose from 63.6% in 1997 to 70.4% in 2000. The sector's employment increased by 18.0% in 1996 and then grew by 39.0% during the four-year period between 1997 to 2000 from about 2.99 million persons in 1997 to about 4.15 million persons in 2000. Further expansion was recorded from 4.6 million to 5.1 million persons in 2001 and 2002 respectively.

Differences in earnings across the informal and formal sector are also pronounced. Total average earnings in the formal sector rose by 115.9% during the same period. Private sector earning expanded by 114.5% and the public sector earnings rose by 116.3% between 1995 and 2000. Average earnings per employee in the formal sector increased by 14.9% in 2002 and then by 13.0% in 2003. Private sector earnings rose by 14.5% and 15.2% in 2002 and 2003 respectively. The highest average earning in the private sector are those of financial sector employees while primary activities of agriculture have the least average earnings. (Republic of Kenya, Economic Surveys, various issues).

While the rural areas employ most of the Kenyan population, urban employment grow faster than rural employment. For instance, the growth of the economically active population expanded faster in urban areas at 75.0% in 1999, than in rural areas at 53.9%. The proportion of the economically active in rural areas declined from79.4% in 1989 to 77.3% in 1999. This implies that there has been a gradual shift of the economically active population from rural to urban areas. For instance, sex ratios for urban areas declined from 195 in 1989 to 146.8 in1999. Gender gaps in urban employment seem to have narrowed between the two census periods. For instance, the sex ratio for the urban working population aged 10 years and above declined from 206.4 in 1989 to 162.4 in 1999 (CBS, 2002). There is however near gender equality in rural employment.

Quality and Productivity of Labour

Understanding the skills of the labour force is important so as to facilitate matching of demand and supply of labour. The quality of labour is a function of formal education, occupational and vocational training. Available labour force survey (1998/9) and population census (1999) data however only provide details on formal schooling and this is used as the only indicator of the skills level. However, the labour force survey (1998/99) also collected information on the professional training attainment. The data generally indicates low skill level of the population but suggest modest skill improvements between 1989 and 1999 as evidenced by the decline of the economically active population without formal education from 33.6% in 1989 to 16.9% in 1999 (Table 5).

Table 5
Distribution of the Labour Force by Education Attainment: 1989-1999

Highest Level Attained	*1989 Census (10+ yrs) (% Share)*	*1999 Census (15-64 yrs) (% Share)*	*1999 Labour Force Survey (% share)*
None	33.6	16.9	16.9
Pre-Primary	-	0.2	3.5
Primary	47.1	55.6	59.5
Form 1-4	16.8	25.0	19.7
Form 5-6	1.3	1.2	
University	0.7	1.3	1.1
Not Stated	0.5	-	0.5

Source: Central Bureau of Statistics (2002); Central Bureau of Statistics (2003).

Estimates further show that 89.5% of the employed persons reported having no vocation and professional training at all. Those reporting any training had training mainly in Trade Tests (6.3%) and Ordinary Diploma (2.8%). There are marked gender differentials in education attainment of the labour force. For instance, in 1999, it was estimated that 22.9% of women had no formal schooling compared to only 9.7% of their male counterparts. Furthermore, almost all women lacked vocational and professional training (94.3%) compared to 85% of their counterparts. The same scenario is uncovered by the LFS which argues that females are disadvantaged in educational attainment with 20.2% of all females having no formal education compared to 12.5% of their male counterparts. Women were also found to constitute 62.1% of the population with no formal education (CBS, 2003).

Quality of labour has important implications for factor productivity, which in turn has implications on incomes and poverty. Studies have shown that declining labour productivity and rising labour costs in the Kenyan manufacturing sector have contributed to declining exports, especially in labour-intensive exports (Glenday and Ndii, 2000). Nielsen and Rosholm (2000) also show that investment in training and vocational education activities is expected to increase the productivity of workers, and that firms invest in training with the expectation that the returns to acquired skills will be shared between the employer through higher output and the employee through higher incomes. Their analysis shows that even after controlling for training costs, employer-sponsored training in Kenya has an average wage effect in the range of 20-80%. This supports views by Appleton *et al.*, 1999; Manda *et al.*, 2002 and Odhiambo and Manda, 2003.

Kenya experienced growth in labour productivity[2] within the first ten years of independence. This was attributed to growth in number of workers engaged in productive employment, growth in capital that each worker worked with and increase in efficiency of both workers and capital. Thereafter, productivity has recorded a negative trend attributable to macroeconomic constraints which inhibit work incentives for the Kenyan worker, rising levels of poverty and prevalence of diseases such as malaria and HIV/AIDS. Currently, labour productivity is low in virtually all sectors of the economy. Firms have increasingly become more uncompetitive, have low labour absorption rates and the existing labour is under-utilized. This has aggravated the unemployment problem by increasing labour cost thus discouraging investment in labour-intensive ventures and limits firm expansion (Ministry of Labour, 2004a). Labour productivity in manufacturing has almost stagnated (Table 6).

To enhance labour productivity in the economy, the government has set out to promote policies that will ensure that production costs of firms are minimized through productivity promotion and enhancement. To ensure this, the government will promote and build capacity of the tripartite-based Productivity Centre of Kenya (PCK) to continue mainstreaming productivity in all sectors of the economy (Ministry of Labour, 2004b). The key responsibilities of the Centre will include raising competitiveness and productivity in all sectors, improving employee work life and enhancing industrial relations, fostering co-operation and collaboration between National Productivity organizations and other related bodies; and facilitating the establishment and development of regional productivity centers within the country (Republic of Kenya, National Development Plan, 2002-2008).

MACROECONOMICS AND LABOUR DEMAND

Macroeconomic Adjustments and Stabilization

Kenya's major economic challenges are poverty alleviation and creation of productive employment. Despite efforts to promote rapid economic growth and employment, Kenya's economy faces serious balance of payment problems and increased debt burden. As a result, since the mid 1970s, unemployment has increased against the backdrop of rising population. This led the government to implement economic reforms starting in the early 1980s emphasizing stable macroeconomic environment to lay foundation for growth.

In the 1960s and 1970s, the Kenyan labour market was highly regulated by the government and was characterized by regulated wage guidelines, approved mechanism for redundancies by the Ministry of Labour and government involvement in the election of trade unions to control them. Thus, wage levels were kept low with an aim of attracting investors and encouraging labour-intensive technologies. The labour market has undergone

Table 6

Indicators of Labour Productivity in Manufacturing (1995-2006)

Year	*1995*	*1996*	*1997*	*1998*	*1999*	*2000*	*2001*	*2002*	*2003*	*2004*	*2005*	*2006*
Change in quantum index of manufacturing	3.9	3.7	1.9	1.3	1.0	-1.4	0.8	1.2	1.4	2.7	5.5	7.0
Change in numbers employed in manufacturing	3.7	2.8	1.9	1.1	0.9	-0.6	-0.8	6.1	5.2	0.9	2.3	2.5
Implicit change in labour productivity	0.2	0.9	0.0	0.2	0.1	-0.8	1.6	-4.9	-3.7	1.8	3.2	4.5
Wage costs as percentage of gross output	3.3	3.3	3.3	4.0	4.4	5.6	6.1	6.6	7.6	10.5	10.1	10.3
Wage costs as percentage of value added	35.4	37.5	40.5	39.1	38.4	38.2	38.9	38.0	37.9	36.7	34.1	29.7

Source: Republic of Kenya, Economic Survey, Various Issues

considerable liberalization since then, including: the empowerment of industrial courts to litigate labour disputes, relaxation of redundancy clause to allow employers to declare worker redundancy, removal of wage guidelines to accord more weight to labour productivity and to allow employers appeal for higher wage awards by the industrial courts from 1994. The civil service reform incentives have included-wage increase to boost their morale, adoption of modern management techniques, performance based job description and evaluation, provision of adequate space, supplies and equipment and improved efficiency in government operations. Though the government stated intentions for civil service reform in 1986, the reforms were only instituted in 1992 (Manda 2003; Ikiara and Ndung'u 1996).

The creation of productive employment and reduction of poverty can only be achieved through a steady and sustained economic growth. Not only is the pace of growth important, but also the processes and patterns of growth that would ensure jobs and income redistribution. Growth patterns and the necessary incentive structure must therefore be designed to ensure adequate job generation and to reflect the comparative advantage of domestic production. A necessary condition for sustainable economic growth, under the current drift towards market liberalization and globalization, is a sound macroeconomic policy framework, which encourages investment and competition. Significant unemployment and poverty reduction depends on how effectively policies are designed and implemented to ensure stabilization and investment led growth (ILO/EAMAT 1999).

Kenya has however had a patchy record of policy reform for stabilization and structural adjustment (especially during the 1980s). The country faced various institutional and structural constraints that undermined stabilization efforts. These constraints relate to macroeconomic policies and management and sectoral growth. The macroeconomic structure would require not only a clear focus on stabilization but also strategic policy intervention to support savings-investment drive and infrastructural development in order to encourage greater private sector participation (especially small and medium enterprises) and therefore create more employment (ILO/EAMAT 1999).

Labour market indicators show that job creation in the economy is intricately linked to economic growth and the macro economic situation. Inflation and other macroeconomic constraints have had adverse effects on employment, earnings and productivity, especially because wage compensation is based on changes in the cost of living. High interest rates and government demand for credit has also crowded out the private sector, thus directly affecting employment and growth. After 1980, private sector employment stagnated largely due to poor economic performance while public sector employment declined due to reforms and privatization (CBS 2003).

For Kenya to obtain the ethos of a working nation, the government has set broad goals. These include creation of half a million jobs a year and reducing poverty level by at least 5% within the next five years beside others (Republic of Kenya, 2003). Since it is unlikely that the formal sector can create 500,000 jobs annually, even in the medium term, the bulk of jobs will have to be created in small enterprises. To realize these goals, the country must maintain a stable macroeconomic environment. In addition, a stable macroeconomic environment is a priority if labour productivity is to be enhanced and sustained. To generate and sustain employment, it is important to continue pursuing policy reforms aimed at macroeconomic stability for economic growth ILO/EAMAT (1999).

Trade Openings and Labour Demand

The labour market is one of the main channels through which globalization can affect the developing countries because all trade reform policies have a direct bearing on employment and incomes. To become competitive, countries may need to dismantle their trade barriers, abolish legal monopolies, privatize their public enterprises and reduce overstaffing. These reform measures may lead to massive loss of jobs leading to increased unemployment. Macroeconomic instability arising from short-term capital movement may also have adverse effects on employment (Manda, 2004). ILO/ IPAR (1996) argue that the institutional oriented policy reforms had serious direct negative effects on employment, while the competition enhancing policies had mixed effects on employment, with some causing contraction, others having expansionary effects or insignificant effects on employment. Furthermore, the adjustment process failed to induce significant movement of labour across sectors and increase employment in the expanding sectors as would have otherwise been expected. In addition, job security and real wages have declined considerably during the adjustment period (ILO/ IPAR, 1996). We review the impact of trade openings on the manufacturing (local manufacturing and export processing zones) and agricultural sectors below:

Manufacturing Sector: Since the 1980s, Kenya, like other developing countries initiated economic reforms among them reforms to liberate trade and reduce control on prices and the labour market. These reforms led to improved prices and market incentives and increased export promotion. During the Fourth National Developments Plan, a number of trade reforms were implemented to make industrial sector more efficient. These included: reduction of tariffs, export incentives and removal of quantitative restrictions. By 1995, the government had virtually removed all price and foreign exchange controls; liberalized domestic trade as well as imports and the exchange rate market, reviewed the foreign exchange act and legalized the foreign exchange bureaus. In addition, export incentives had been put in place, which centered on the creation of an enabling environment for export growth through institutional reforms, reduction and restructuring of tariffs and on raw materials and capital goods, abolition of export duties, improvement of capital allowances, introduction of export earning retention schemes, stationing of commercial attaches in trading partner countries and organizing trade missions to emerging markets. However, these reforms only resulted to dismal export performance calling for more trade reforms to make the economy more competitive with regard to international trade (Manda, 2004). The later measures had significant effect on employment in Kenya. Import liberalization led to increased competition between local producers and relatively cheap import with adverse effect on employment.

Export promotion schemes included a bonded warehouse or manufacturing under bond scheme (MUB), Export Processing Zones (EPZs), both targeting new investments, a duty and VAT exemption scheme (Export Promotion Programmes Office-EPPO), targeting existing manufacturers (Republic of Kenya, Economic Survey, various issues). Among other incentives, MUB provided for bonded factories that were allowed duty free import of plant, equipment, spares and raw materials to manufacture goods for export, an additional investment incentive in the form of favorable income tax treatment of capital expenditures, and their domestic input purchases were zero rated. EPZs are gazetted as special purpose corporations that can only do business in a designated EPZ location, which may be a single factory or a unit in an EPZ industrial park, supervised by the EPZ Authority, which also licenses them. Although targeted primarily at new foreign direct investment, Kenyan companies are allowed to establish EPZ subsidiaries, but cannot do part of its business inside an EPZ and part outside (Glenday and Ndii, 2000).

The duty and VAT exemption scheme offers exemptions to imported inputs physically incorporated in the exported product or consumed in the production of the export. It excludes exemptions for plant, equipment and machinery. The program is administered by the Export Promotion Programmes Office (EPPO) in the Ministry of Finance (Glenday and Ndii, 2000). However, lack of seriousness in implementation of the export promotion schemes, lack of fiscal discipline and administrative constraints have to some extent hampered achievement of the stated objectives of these schemes. EPZs and MUB have been less attractive than the EPPs as the later support regional trade in the same goods that are produced for the domestic market. The EPPs have been extensively used by the major local manufacturing and processing companies (Manda, 2004).

Since 1997, the Kenya government has also signed several trade agreements aimed at revitalizing the manufacturing sector. These include the African Growth Opportunity Act (AGOA), African Caribbean and Pacific-European Union (ACP/EU), Common Market for Eastern and Southern Africa (COMESA) and the East African Community (EAC). The preferential regional market, led by Uganda and Tanzania, follow COMESA accounts for the dominant share of changes in Kenya's exports. Not surprisingly then, the impact of MUB and EPZ platforms, designed to target dedicated export processors for overseas markets, has been, insignificant among exports compared to the more flexible EPPO duty/VAT. However, utilization of the EPPO programme has been declining due to exchange rate and real wage appreciation as well as the tax value of the programme declining with lower duty rates. However the MUB platform has shown considerable potential, more so for contract garment manufacturing for the US market (Glenday and Ndii, 2000).

Trade openings have had mixed impacts on employment and earnings in the manufacturing sector in Kenya. One effect would be an increase in employment in the informal sector but these jobs will be insecure and with lower wages than jobs in this formal sector (Manda 2004). There could also be a general shift towards employing highly skilled manpower especially in the manufacturing sector, a decline in permanent full-time workers and an increase in part-time and full-time casual workers. Manda and Sen (2004), have shown that the overall effect of international trade on manufacturing employment was negative in the 1990s while inequality in earnings increased during the period.

Export Processing Zones: An EPZ Act was promulgated in 1990 to facilitate the development of exclusive export processing zones and to spearhead manufacturing for exports. A range of incentives were spelt out in this Act with the expectation to contribute to growth in employment and incomes for EPZ employees while also providing revenue and foreign exchange earning to the government (Chacha *et al.*, 2004; Kibua and Nzioki, 2004; Glenday and Ndii, 2000). The EPZs have been useful in employment generation in Kenya since their inception, though trade union movements have been critical of their role in creation of employment opportunities. Employment of Kenyans in the EPZs increased from 2,824 persons in 1997 to 3,645 persons and 4,684 persons in 1998 and 1999 respectively. The EPZ employees rose further by more than two-fold from 6,620 persons in 2000 to 13,758 in 2001 and then to 26,447 and 35,000 in 2002 and 2003 respectively. This increase was mainly due to opening of new factories that were exploiting the American garment market under AGOA agreement (Republic of Kenya, Economic Survey, various issues). New forms and higher levels of capacity utilization further raised the vibrancy of the EPZs sector in the global economy (Ministry of Labour, 2004b).

EPZs have also come under substantial criticism world-wide. Labour activists claim that the incentives offered to attract companies to these zones create an environment where virtually any corner can be cut in pursuit of profit. Human rights experts blame what they describe as the abuse of workers rights in the EPZs on inadequate laws, corruption in the judiciary and weak trade unions. It has also been argued that jobs in the EPZ are not as good as the 'privileged' jobs in protected activities or the public sector. For instance, the law does not impose the minimum wage on EPZs. In the past, there have been concerns that government has avoided interference with EPZ companies for fear of alienating potential investors (Mulama 2004).

Agricultural Sector: The agricultural sector plays an important role in Kenya's economic development as reflected in employment creation in the sector and contribution to the GDP. Growth in the sector has direct impact on employment generation and poverty reduction and provides raw materials to the industrial sector. The sector accounts for 25% of GDP and employs about 75% of the labour force. However, the sector's growth and employment creation is hampered by farm size, inadequate technology, unreliable rainfall, poor marketing infrastructure and information, limited access to credit, high cost of inputs and lack of land use policy. The importance of the agricultural sector in influencing the overall growth of the economy through employment and incomes has made the government continue to prioritize the sector's policies with employment and poverty reduction objectives as the major policy thrusts, pursued in the context of the objectives of ensuring food security, foreign exchange growth, employment and income generation and production of raw materials for the manufacturing sector. Farmer organizations and parastatals aid the Ministry of Agriculture in the implementation of the policies and strategies as laid out in government policy documents.

ROLE OF GOVERNMENT IN THE KENYAN LABOUR MARKET

Though a series of labour market reforms have been adopted by the government as part of economic reforms for liberalization, the government still plays an important role in overseeing the smooth functioning of the labour market in Kenya. Among other roles, the government is charged with formulating the country's employment policy, whose objectives include: promotion of productive and freely chosen employment as a priority and fundamental base for national, economic and social policy, improvement in labour productivity, provision of skills and knowledge to the labour force, stimulation of economic growth and poverty reduction, respect of basic rights of all to work irrespective of their gender or location and ensuring full participation of employers and workers organization in policy formulation. To achieve these objectives, the government employs a range of labour market institutions to regulate and oversee smooth functioning of the market. The institutions include the

National Labour Board, the National Labour court and subordinate labour courts. A wide range of interventions are then employed to ensure appropriate implementation of labour laws and regulations.

Regulatory Mechanism

Regulation of the labour market is largely guided by the government's desire to guide private sector led-growth, enhance harmonious industrial relations, ensure health and safety in workplaces and maintain reasonable wages capable of attracting investments and labour intensive techniques of production. The key components of the regulatory framework include health and safety surveillance in workplaces; decentralized collective bargaining system that provide for flexible life of collective bargaining agreements; moderation of wage awards through wage guidelines; minimum wage setting based on wage boards and councils; and a conflict resolution and dispute settlement mechanism through tripartite arrangements and the Industrial Court of Kenya (Omolo and Apiyo, 2003).

The legal and institutional framework for labour market regulation in Kenya is found within the context of: (i) the regulations of wages and conditions of Employment Act (cap 229), which provides the laws and regulations governing wages in various sub-industries and therefore the regulations of remuneration and conditions of employment for different industries. (ii) Trade Union Act (cap 233), which lays down the regulations governing the functioning of trade unions. (iii) Trade Disputes Act (*cap 234 of 1965, revised in 1980 and 1991*), which provides for the settlement of trade disputes and establishment of boards of inquiry and a standing industrial court, to control and regulate strikes and lock-outs, make provisions for collection of union dues and related matters. (iv) The Employment Bill Act (2004), which provides for rights and conditions of workers and includes clauses for pre-mature dismissals and harassment of employees and also for basic minimum conditions for employment.

Wage Guidelines and Collective Agreements

Wage guidelines were introduced in 1973 to guide the industrial court in adjudicating trade disputes and registration of collective bargaining agreements. The objectives of these guidelines have remained employment creation, the promotion of equitable earnings distribution between sectors, industries and rural urban areas and the control of inflation. Wage guidelines affect wage determination for the private sector by setting the minimum and maximum limits for negotiated wage settlements with productivity as the major factor in determining earnings. The wage guidelines do not affect the public sector wages where determination is based on recommendations made through schemes of service and periodic salary reviews by commissions/committees and task forces established under presidential directives. This leads to public sector wages lagging behind private sector wages by large proportions (ILO/EAMAT 1999).

Termination and Dismissals

Kenyan labour laws distinguish among three types of termination from employment (1) normal termination of service (2) summary dismissal and (3) termination on account of redundancy. The Trade Disputes Act (cap 234) and the Employment Act (cap 226, 1984) of the laws of Kenya contains the legal provisions for regulating these issues. The Employment Act provides the conditions for termination on account of redundancy. These include notification of the employees and adequate compensation including terminal benefits and severance pay. The Act also provides that no employer has the right to terminate a contract of service without notice or with less notice than provided for by statutory provision or contractual term. Summary dismissal may however be meted on an employee who engages in gross misconduct such as absenteeism, neglects duty, drunkard-ness, use of abusive language, disobeys commands within ones scope of duty, engages or/ and commits criminal offences. The Act also provides for compensation incase of wrongful dismissal. The compensation ranges from payment of withheld salaries to reinstatement or re-engagement of the victim.

Labour Market Interventions

The government employment policies are contained in various documents and acts of parliament. Principally the Constitution of Kenya provides protection of fundamental rights and freedom of the individual and there is a whole range of statues that govern the labour market. The Ministry of Labour in collaboration with the relevant government ministries and departments, the tripartite partners (COTU and FKE), private sector stakeholders and development partners are responsible for the formulation and implementation of labour policies necessary for creation of productive and durable employment opportunities. The Ministry of Labour has the overall responsibility of co-coordinating and overseeing all activities concerning the labour force. These include industrial relations, social security, factory inspection and employment policy.

The Labour Regulation Act provides for establishment of employees and employers association and aims to promote sound labour relations including freedom of association, effective collective bargaining, dispute settlement, social justice and economic development and other related matters (Republic of Kenya 2004a, 2004b, 2004c). In 2003, the government adopted a national wage policy whose objectives were among others to assure wage earners a reasonable share of the national product, to create a harmonious and just relationship between employers and workers in different sector of the economy with due consideration to the demands of the national economy (Republic of Kenya, Economic Survey, 2004). The wage policy is based on payment of controlled minimum wages, where a wage guideline is issued to the industrial court to be applied in wage award determination, considering productivity and changes in the cost of living. Almost every year during Labour-Day celebrations, the government announces some increases in the minimum wages, usually set for agricultural workers (in the agricultural wages order) and the urban and other workers (in the general wages order).

Labour market regulation is argued to be inappropriate for the smooth functioning of the market. Available evidence indicates that the existing minimum wage policies in Kenya may have had a significant adverse impact on the labour market. Both minimum wage and tax growth are highly positively correlated with informal sector employment (Schindler, 2003). Schindler (2003) further argues that removal of labour market rigidities such as minimum wages would help in improving the overall efficiency of labour allocation. He argues that minimum wages in an economy of weak growth contribute to a large flow of mostly unskilled and low-income worker groups into the informal sector or unemployment. Relaxing minimum wages is likely not only to improve overall productivity, but also to alleviate poverty through productive employment creation in the formal sector. Although Schindler advocates for improvements in the formal sector in order to minimize effects of an inefficient informal sector, other studies argue for boosting the informal sector given its increasingly important role in employment and incomes generation (Wambugu, 2002).

NEED FOR LABOUR MARKET REFORM IN KENYA

Economic Reforms

Kenya's civil service expanded rapidly after independence to become by far the largest in East Africa but was characterized by wastefulness and ineffectiveness. By the late 1980's, it was clear that Kenya could no longer sustain such high level of civil service (Manda, 2003). The public sector reforms were therefore deemed necessary to reduce the number of public employees to a manageable level. The reforms were also found necessary to make the labour market more efficient and investor-friendly in order to promote private sector-led growth and poverty alleviation. The government needed a management and incentive system to create a more results–oriented public sector. Economic reforms have had a great impact on structure of the Kenyan labour force (Oiro et al., 2004). Civil service and parastatal reforms have resulted in considerable personnel reduction. The private sector on the other hand, has been changing to cope with increased competition and advances in information technology resulting in labour lay-off. The economic reforms have led to changes in employment situation with respect to labour force participation by women and increased unemployment. However, women's employment is still characterized by low productivity, low pay and long hours of work (Republic of Kenya, 8th National Development Plan).

The formal sector of the economy has largely failed to meet the challenges of employment creation and income generation due to slow economic growth and declining level of investment resulting from high cost of production, increased competition from cheap imports and the public sector reforms. On the other hand, low productivity, inadequate technological skills, limited credit facilities and lack of institutional support characterize the expanding informal sector (Republic of Kenya, 9th National Development Plan). Deregulation towards a more flexible wage determination scheme, and also towards an easing of income and other taxes, would help revert the inefficiencies of the informal sector and also encourage growth of the more efficient formal sector (Schindler, 2003).

The wage guidelines introduced in 1973 to guide the industrial court in adjudicating trade disputes and registration of bargaining agreement did not distinguish between skilled, non-skilled and less-skilled workers (Republic of Kenya, 8th National Development Plan). The plan further stipulates the need to do away with wage guidelines and allow market forces to prevail in wage determination.

The inability of the country to create enough productive and sustainable employment opportunities has led to growth of unemployment to huge proportions in Kenya. Critical challenges to job creation in Kenya include; slow economic growth rate, neglect of the labour market, job selectivity, high population growth rate and gender disparity. Others include, neglect of the cultural and entertainment sector, wage rigidity, low labour productivity, poor technology, low quality and unproductive jobs in the informal sector, inefficient labour administration systems, inadequate health and safety at workplace, insecurity, HIV/AIDS, lack of foreign employment policies and weak implementation, monitoring and evaluation systems among others. Though attempts have been made to address these challenges, unfocussed policy prescription, weak implementation and lack of monitoring and evaluation systems are major setbacks (Ministry of Labour, 2004a).

Kenya lacks a consistent and comprehensive implementation framework for its employment policy and strategies, which leads to high levels of unemployment and under-employment. There is need for a framework aimed at harmonizing government's interventions and programmes on employment, otherwise the government should leave market forces drive labour market functions.

Labour Law Reform and the African Growth and Opportunity Act (AGOA)

The need to review labour laws in Kenya has been influenced by several legal and socio-economic factors among them the fact that the country has gone through protracted socio-economic change imposed on it by forces beyond its control. They include, structural adjustment and economic liberalization programs which have laid emphasize on privatization thereby triggering labour relation crises.

New labour laws are expected to meet the conditions set by the United States of America under that country's African Growth and Opportunity Act (AGOA). Through AGOA, the US Government seeks to have better access to US market as a means of encouraging the developing countries to stay on reform course and to better their economic well being. The conditions which are to be observed by beneficiary states range from adopting new trade policies to enacting legislations which uphold the rule of law.

Kenya as a beneficiary of AGOA is expected to demonstrate that it affords its workers: protection of internationally recognized workers rights; prohibition of the use of any form of forced/ compulsory labour; legislation on minimum age for employment of children and acceptable conditions of work with respect to minimum wages, hours of work and occupational safety and health. The new legislation is supposed to prohibit forced labour to control the employment of persons below 18 years and create acceptable conditions of work with respect to minimum wages, hours of work and occupational health and safety.

Another requirement of AGOA is that the collaborating states should uphold the rule of law, practice, political pluralism and observe the right to due process, to fair trial, and offer equal protection under the law.

CONCLUSION

This section presents a situational analysis of the labour market in Kenya, documenting the structure, reforms and regulatory mechanisms that drive the Kenyan labour market. The key issues and policy priorities identified in this chapter include: First, there is diversity of the Kenyan labour market manifested in gender, age, regional and sectoral differentials in labour demand and supply. Further, although Kenya experienced growth in labour productivity within the first ten years of independence, labour productivity recorded a negative trend and was quite low at the turn of the 21st Century in all sectors of the economy. Firms have increasingly become more uncompetitive, have low labour absorption rates and the existing labour is under-utilized. Second, macroeconomic stability is important for labour market development: primarily employment growth, enhanced efficiency and productivity in all sectors of the economy. However, inflation and other macroeconomic constraints arising from poor implementation of policy reforms and other macroeconomic shocks have had adverse effects on employment, earnings and productivity. Kenya therefore has to make concerted effort to maintain a stable macroeconomic environment in order to generate and sustain employment growth and labour productivity. Third, inspite of the adoption of economic reforms and liberalization, the government still plays an important role in regulating the labour market functions, aimed at employment generation, stimulation of economic growth and enhancing industrial relations, while ensuring adequate compensation for workers. Labour market regulation is however argued to introduce rigidities in the labour market, removal of which would help in improving overall efficiency of labour allocation. Finally, the analysis suggests a number of labour market policies that need review so as to improve the functioning of the labour market. These include: a more flexible wage determination scheme in order to help revert the inefficiencies of the informal sector and harmonizing government's interventions and programmes on employment.

Notes

1. Its important to note that CBS, 2003 focuses on overall labour force as persons aged between 15-64, while CBS, 2002 considers the population over 5 years old. This difference, together with differences in coverage and methodology may explain some of the differences in estimates from the two data sets.
2. Labour productivity is defined as the average output per worker. Labour productivity at the national level can be computed by taking the entire economically active population as the labour input and the total value of goods and services produced as the output (ILO/EAMAT, 1999).

References

Appleton, S., A. Bigsten and D. K Manda (1999), 'Educational Expansion and Economic Decline: Returns to Education in Kenya, 1978–1995', Working Paper No. 99-6. Oxford: Centre for the Study of African Economies.

Central Bureau of Statistics (2002), Kenya 1999 Population and Housing Census Analytical Report on labour Force, Vol. IX. Central Bureau of Statistics, Nairobi.

Central Bureau of Statistics (2003), The 1998/99 Labour Force Survey Report, Central Bureau of Statistics, Nairobi.

Chacha, R. N. J. Kabubo-Mariara, T. Kiriti and M. Mwangi (2004), Technological Capability Acquisition in Kenya's Export Processing Zones, African Technology Policy Studies Network, Mimeo, Nairobi.

Glenday G. and D. Ndii (2000), Export Platforms in Kenya, HIID Development Discussion Paper No. 752.

ILO/EAMAT, (1999), Kenya: Meeting the Employment Challenges of the 21st Century, International Labour Organization, Addis Ababa.

ILO/IPAR (1996), "Adjustment Policy, Employment and Labour Market Institutions in Kenya", Mimeo, Nairobi

Ikiara G. K. and N. S. Ndung'u (1996). Employment and Labour Market during Adjustments in East and Southern Africa: The Case of Kenya, Employment Department, International Labour Organization, Geneva.

Kabubo-Mariara J. (2003a), Wage Determination and Gender Wage Gap in Kenya; Any Evidence of Gender Discrimination? AERC Research Paper No. 132, African Economic Research Consortium, Nairobi.

Kabubo-Mariara J. (2003b). Labour Market Outcomes, Poverty and the Role of Gender: The Case of Kenya. Chapter 10 in "*Trade Unions and Poverty Alleviation in Africa*", Mohammed Mwamadzingo and Ditiro Saleshando (2003) eds. ILO, Harare and Geneva; ISBN No. 92-2-114143-8.

Kabubo-Mariara J. (2002), Labour Force Participation in Kenya, *African Journal of Economic Policy*, Vol. 9, 2:103-115.

Kibua T. N. and B. K. Nzioki (2004), Are Export Processing Zones Relevant in a Liberalised Environment? The Kenyan Case. IPAR Discussion Paper No. 45, IPAR, Nairobi.

Lokshin M., E. Glinskaya and M. Garcia (2000), The Effect of Early Childhood Development Programs on Women's Labour Force Participation and Older Children's Schooling and Kenya, World Bank, Gender and Development WP Series No. 15.

Manda D. K. (2004), "Globalization and the Labour Market in Kenya", KIPPRA Discussion Paper No. 31. Nairobi, Kenya Institute for Policy Research and Analysis.

Manda D. K. (2003), "*Incentive Structure and Efficiency in the Kenyan Civil Service*", In (ed.) Kayizzi–Mugerwa, Reforming Africa's Institutions: Ownership, Incentives and Capabilities, United Nations, New York.

Manda D. K. (2002). Wage Determination in Kenyan Manufacturing in A. Bigsten and P. Kimuyu eds. Structure and Performance of Manufacturing Sector in Kenya, McMillan, Britain.

Manda D. K., P. Kimalu, N. Nafula, D. Kimani, R. Nyaga, J. Mutua, G. Mwabu and M. Kimenyi, (2003), Costs and Benefits of Eliminating Child Labour in Kenya, KIPPRA Working Paper No. 10. Nairobi, Kenya Institute for Public Policy Research and Analysis.

Manda D. K., G. Mwabu and M. S. Kimenyi (2002), Human Capital Externalities and Returns to Education in Kenya, *KIPPRA Discussion Paper* No. 13.

Ministry of Labour and Human Resource Development (2004a), Draft Employment Policy and Strategy for Kenya, Nairobi.

Ministry of Labour and Human Resource Development (2004b), Draft Sessional Paper on Employment Policy and Strategies for Kenya. Mimeo, Nairobi.

Mulama J. (2004), Economy-Kenya: EPZ's Failing to Deliver on Workers' Rights, Inter Press Service, Mimeo, Nairobi.

Nielsen H. S. and M. Rosholm (2002), Evaluation of Training in African Enterprises, World Bank, Mimeo.

Odhiambo W. and D. K. Manda (2003), Urban Poverty and Labour Force Participation in Kenya, Mimeo, Kenya Institute for Public Policy Research and Analysis (KIPPRA), Nairobi.

Oiro M., G. Mwabu and D. K. Manda (2004), Poverty and Employment in Kenya. KIPPRA Discussion Paper No. 33, Nairobi. Kenya Institute for Public Policy Research and Analysis.

Omolo J. O. and Apiyo, H. A. (2003), Employment and Labour Market Policies in Kenya, Studies on the Harmonisation of Employment Policies and Labour Legislation in East Africa, Mimeo, Nairobi.

Republic of Kenya (2004a), A Report of the Labour Law Review, Mimeo, Nairobi.

Republic of Kenya (2004b), The Draft Employment Bill, Government Printers, Nairobi.

Republic of Kenya (2004c), The Labour Institutions Act, Government Printers, Nairobi.

Republic of Kenya, Economic Survey-Various Issues. Government Printers, Nairobi.

Republic of Kenya, National Development Plans, Various Issues, Government Printers, Nairobi.

Schindler M. (2003), Labor Market Duality and Possible Reforms, IMF, Mimeo.

Wambugu A. (2002), Education, Employment and Earnings in Kenya, Mimeo. Göteborg University.,

Yamano T. and T. S. Jayne (2003), Working-Age Adult Mortality and Primary School Enrollment in Rural Kenya, World Bank, Mimeo.

SECTION-II

GENDER AND SUSTAINABLE DEVELOPMENT

8

GENDERED EMPLOYMENT AND SUSTAINABLE DEVELOPMENT

Angela Dziedzom Akorsu & Patrick Kwashie Akorsu

INTRODUCTION

This chapter seeks to complement the others in this book by presenting insights on gendered employment and sustainable development, with particular reference to Ghana. The central theme is that gendered employment, which is a reflection of gender or social division of labour rather than a reflection of a person's competencies and capabilities, is a development problem. The interest is in women's work and not men's work due to outcomes that give men advantages over women. Women face peculiar and persistent labour market barriers as well as new challenges in the wake of the current economic globalization. It is argued that ignoring the problems of women's work has serious socio-economic implications for women and their families as well as for attaining sustainable development. Also, assuming that economic growth is bound to solve employment problems of women as the Neo-liberal economists seem to suggest is misleading. After all, the causes of gendered employment are rooted in gender relations that are far more complex than the market forces of demand and supply. Therefore, there is the need for targeted interventions not only in the creation of employment opportunities for women, but more especially in ensuring sustainable empowerment for women in the labour market. To this end, a radical employment policy that seeks to transform perceptions is of paramount importance.

The chapter is organized into six sections. Section two presents conceptual explanations on gender and gendered employment, section three deals with explanations for gendered employment while the fourth section focuses on gendered employment in relation to sustainable development. In section five, the policy implications of gendered employment is examined. The last section outlines the conclusions. References to Ghana are made throughout the chapter to illustrate, and to buttress the discussions.

CONCEPTUALIZING GENDER AND GENDERED EMPLOYMENT

Gender as a concept refers to the social interpretations of the sexes. Thus, unlike the biological differences between the sexes which are universal, gender differences vary from place to place and changes over time. These differences are learnt through a socialization process that is often referred to as gender construction or 'gendering'. Through gendering, each individual, male or female acquires his or her gender identify, with its accompanying roles prescribed by society. In almost all societies, women and men perform different roles – *gender roles*. These roles are not based on natural talents and capabilities but on what society considers appropriate for each sex. Traditionally, women have been responsible for chores such as nursing, cooking, cleaning, washing, baby sitting etc. and these activities are not considered productive work and are therefore not paid for. Men's work on the other hand is considered productive work and is paid for. By definition then, the men do the important things. The gender roles are reinforced by *patriarchy* – male dominance over female or women's subordination to men. Patriarchal controls take many forms. Economic resources such as land are often owned and controlled by men (Bashin, 1994).

Gendered employment therefore brings to mind differences in the kinds and nature of work that women and men engage in. The term 'gendered' refers to "the activities that cultures have attached to one or the other sex" (Reskin & Padavic, 1994:6). Assigning different tasks to men and women not on the basis of their capabilities but on the basis of their sex can therefore be conveniently termed gendered employment. Though gender involves the interaction between males and females, the interest here is in women's work and not men's work. This is because women are disadvantaged in the interactions and face peculiar and persistent labour market problems. Gendered employment takes various forms and is multidimensional.

The first dimension is the categorization of women's work as paid/unpaid. Traditionally, women's labours are not considered as economic activities, since women engage in unpaid household labour such as cooking, washing and childcare. Novarra, (1980) states that "six key tasks are performed by women in nearly all societies: provision of food, home making, child care, nursing the sick, teaching and manufacture of clothing". Unfortunately as the name suggests, such activities do not generate income for the women and so are not considered as economic activities. This means that women involved in such activities are not regarded as part of the labour force since the labour force is defined as "comprising of all those who furnish the supply of labour for the production of economic goods and services" (ILO, 1995). Also, unpaid labour means there is nothing like sick leave, annual leave, and a specific number of working hours. Indications however, are that, there has been some progress especially in terms of increases in female labour force participation rates in recent times. More and more women are engaging in economic activities, thus improving their financial and social well-being. Bradley (1989:10) confirms that, "more women in the world are currently in paid employment than anytime this century" and in Ghana, women constitute about 54% of working adults (GPHC Report, 2000). This however does not mean that all is well with women's work.

Increases in the labour force participation if satisfactory at all, satisfies only the quantitative aspects of women's work. Qualitative analysis leaves much to be desired.

The second dimension of gendered employment is *occupational sex segregation.* Occupational sex segregation takes two main forms, namely, horizontal and vertical segregation.

Horizontal segregation refers to the existence of separate labour markets within the labour market rather than a single labour market, within which there is limited or no mobility. This segregation may be based on race, caste or sex. More often than not, the segregation of the labour market is on the basis of sex with certain jobs labeled "female" and others "male". According to Bradley (1989), a job is often labeled "female" when at least eighty per cent (80%) of the workers are of the female sex and vice versa and he posits that there are seven times as many "male" occupations than "female" occupations world-wide. This means that women are crowded in a limited number of low productivity and low paying jobs. Women are often found either in the survival activities of the informal sector or in restricted segments of the formal sector. This is confirmed by Lim (1996:11) that, "In Latin America and the Caribbean, 71% of the economically active women are concentrated in the service sector. In developed countries, the figure is about 60%. The concentration of female labour force in the agricultural sector is more than 80% in sub-Saharan Africa and at least 50% in Asia". The situation presented by Lim above is not different from what pertains in Ghana. The Ghana Living Standards Survey indicates that about 50.3% of employed women work in agriculture and its related works. According to Amu (2005), "a much higher concentration of them are found at the lower echelons of economic activity and are therefore less likely to influence policy decisions in their favour". In the informal economy, working conditions are often founded on scrounging, on under-payments, on overworking, on de-humanizing labouring and on absolute poverty. Informal economy workers are neither organized by trade unions nor protected by state legislation. According to Britwum et al. (2006: 108), "the structure and character of the informal sector operations present problems to effective membership organization and interest representation for the sector". They therefore often lack the social security that dignifies life and yet, as high as 85.1% of the economically active women in Ghana work in the informal sector (Table 1).

Table 1
Distribution of Economically Active Population by Sector and Sex

			Males		*Females*	
Employment Sector	*Total Number*	*Percentage of Economically Active*	*Number*	*%*	*Number*	*%*
Public	533,811	5.9	343,021	7.5	190,790	4.3
Private Formal	705,569	7.8	445,252	9.8	260,317	5.8
Semi-Public/Parastatal	258,928	2.9	167,733	3.7	91,195	2.0
NGOs	76,519	0.8	46,739	1.0	29,780	0.7
Private Informal	7,263,081	80.3	3,446,446	75.6	3,816,635	85.1
Others	201,410	2.2	107,106	2.4	94,304	2.1
Total	9,039,318	100%	4,556,297	100	4,483,021	100

Source: Ghana Population and Housing Census Report (2000).

Vertical segregation is the segregation of labour markets into higher level jobs that are usually associated with males and lower level jobs that are associated with females, with an invisible "glass ceiling" that women cannot easily break through in order to get to the top positions. Vertical segregation is nearly as pronounced as horizontal segregation. As Hakim, (1979) puts it, "it is merely a situation of women work, men give orders". In Ghana, it is obvious that in all industries and occupations, men occupy the top management positions (Table 2). The seriousness of this problem is clearly seen in a situation where, even in the so-called "female" dominated occupations such as nursing, men are in the majority in the top management positions.

Table 2
Distribution of Workforce by Sex and Occupation

Occupation	*Male %*	*Female %*	*All*
Professional/Technical	5.7	2.7	4.1
Administrative/Managerial	0.4	0.1	0.2
Clerical	3.7	1.2	2.3
Sales/commercial	7.8	27.3	18.5
Service workers	5.5	4.0	4.7
Agriculture	59.0	50.3	54.3
Production	17.9	14.4	16.0
All	100	100	100

Source: Ghana Living Standards Survey (2000).

A third dimension of gendered employment is *wage discrimination.* This is a situation where women earn lower wages compared to men. According to the Human Development Report (1997), women around the world earn an average of seventy-five per cent (75%) of men's wages. In Ghana, while there was a reduction in all earnings between 1992 and 1999, there was a sharper decline in women's earnings. The worse form of wage discrimination however is when women are paid less even for work of equal value as men.

A fourth dimension of gendered employment consists of all *the peculiar problems women have had to deal with in the world of work.* Wherever women find themselves in the labour market, they have peculiar problems to contend with. The fact that more and more women in Ghana are moving away from unpaid household labour and engaging in all sorts of economic activities does not mean that they are no more engaging in unpaid labour. Rather, empirical observations indicate that in addition to the unpaid labour, they also engage in economic activities. This combination of unpaid and paid work often breeds conflict between gender roles and the roles of career women. In Ghana, great importance is attached the domestic roles of a woman more than to her career roles. A good woman or an "obaa sima" is one who keeps her home efficiently, not one who is succeeding in the corporate world. This unspoken pressure from society as against the women's own ambitions is a challenge for working women. Sexual harassment is among the numerous problems that women have to contend with and which make their working life close to unbearable. Empirically, Some women have left work situations by resigning as a result of an unwanted harassment from a superior, some women have been victimized and discriminated against because they have rejected sexual advances from a superior at work, and others as a result of a low self esteem and a feeling of vulnerability; have resorted to unhealthy sexual bribery (Britwum, 2000:37). In all of these cases, the woman is the looser and the assertion that sexual harassment retards the capabilities of females to perform to their fullest potential at the workplace is confirmed.

EXPLANATIONS FOR GENDERED EMPLOYMENT

The patriarchal control which men exert over women is manifested in their control of women's labour. According to Britwum (2000), "men can force women to sell their labour or can prevent them from working productively outside the home". This explains women's unpaid family work. In view of this, Britwum concedes that patriarchy is rooted in economic gains and that women's compliance to offer their labour free is the result of ideological control and even outright violence. As a result of women's unpaid gender roles in the event that they have had to participate in the labour market, they tend to engage in works that are similar to their traditional caring and nurturing chores such as nursing and this is often the result of sex stereotyping.

Also, the importance attached to the domestic roles of women present a subtle pressure on them and unfortunately, this is often used against women in the form of a "glass ceiling" that prevents them from getting promoted to top positions. Thus, "the slow career progression of women in public life for example derives from the tendency on their part to be dominated by a domestic culture" (Britwum, 2000).

Patriarchy which is male dominance over women and within which, male control over women sexuality is situated, provides an explanation for the reason why women are usually the victims of sexual harassment at the workplace and as Britwum and Anokye (2006: 19) contend, "sexual harassment is an issue of power, not [simply] sex".

As a result of the above ideological positioning of male and female, a person's life is greatly determined by society. It may determine access to education, to work, to resources for work and so on. Thus, *our gender is perhaps the single most important factor in shaping who we become* (Mosse, 1993:4). By extension therefore, gender is perhaps an important factor in determining the kind and nature of work women do. These ideological perceptions are often transferred into the labour market.

Some have also explained gendered employment in purely economic terms. The Human Capital Theory for instance, which is rooted in the neoclassical ideology, is used to explain the earning differentials between males and females. Essentially, Human Capital Theory is based on the idea that the acquisition of skills is an investment decision and claims that people are rewarded with good jobs to the degree that they possess human capital - knowledge and skills achieved trough formal education. What this means is that, a person's qualification is the basis of job screening. Thus, by extension, a woman's low earning is the result of her low investment in her human capital. Of course, it is a hard fact that women usually invest less in education and training and therefore lack certain necessary skills required by employers. In Ghana, there are more educated males than females. Table 3 illustrates this situation.

However, a major criticism against this economic approach to gender discrimination in the labour markets is that, a lot more things influence income than simply the level of one's human capital. These include, market shortages/excesses, capitalist dynamics, occupational monopolies and group memberships and social positioning such as gender, class affiliation and race. Granted, formal education is not the only way to invest in human capital (Becker, 2006). Women have always formed valuable human capital through the performance of their domestic roles. Therefore, to say that because women invest less in higher education, they lack competences needed for any actual work is misleading. Also, such a position glosses over the deeper issues of disadvantage – the very reasons why women are less likely to invest in education and accumulate the same work experience as men (Elson, 1999:619). After all, the main reason for women's low investment in formal education is the result of their position in gender relations. This assertion is confirmed by Psacharopoulos and Tzannatos (1992) who conclude that there is no evidence that the significant gap between the wages of men and women can be explained by differences in education and work experience. Similar findings have been found in Korea, Indonesia, Bangladesh, Malaysia, Japan, Philippines and Thailand (Elson, 1999).

Table 3
Distribution of Educational Attainment by Sex (6 Years and above)

Educational Attainment	*Male %*	*Female %*	*All %*
None/Pre-school	36.8	48.2	42.6
Primary	20.3	19.7	20.0
Middle/JSS	25.6	21.2	23.4
Secondary/SSS	8.2	5.3	6.7
Vocational/Technical	2.9	2.0	2.5
Post Secondary	2.0	1.4	1.7
Tertiary	4.2	2.2	3.1

Source: Ghana Population and Housing Census Report (2000).

With regard to wage discrimination, another economic reason is intrinsically linked to horizontal and vertical segregations in the sense that women are over crowded in restricted occupations as well as restricted levels hence, a case of a surplus supply as against scarce demand which tend to lower the price. While the social explanation is that women's work requires dexterity rather than skill and are considered light, clean, safe, physically undemanding, and therefore less valued than men's work.

Employers have also argued for the need to make financial allowances for losses incurred from women who leave the job for maternity leave and other parenting duties. This may seem a genuine concern but the question posed on this issue is: "who pays for the kids?" (Folbre, 1994). The fact that labour market institutions are suggesting that women pay for the kids, as it were, is an indication of women's social positioning as bearers of the 'burdens' of reproduction, when in fact the society at large benefits from reproduction. Elson (1999: 612) reacts strongly to this position when she says: "Labour market institutions cannot escape the fact that 'someone' has to pay for the kids. Just as there is no such thing as a free lunch, there is also no such thing as a free replenishment of the pool of labour". This however does not suggest that the concerns of employers are unfounded, but rather that women alone should not be made to bear the cost.

Also, assuming that economic growth is bound to solve employment problems of women as the Neo-liberal economists posit is misleading. The markets, with their demand and supply forces have failed to address the problems of women's work. For instance in Ghana, though the economy has been growing at an average of five per cent per annum since the 1990s, income inequality as measured by the Gini Coefficient increased from 0.48 to 0.60. Of interest to the discussion in this paper is that, not only is the gap between the rich and the poor widening, but as it does, the gap between men and women also widens. To illustrate, whiles there was a reduction in all earnings between 1992 and 1999, there was a sharper decline in women's earnings. According to calculations by Baah (2004:50), "men's earnings fell by 4%, but women's earnings fell by 23%". It is clear that women are still disadvantaged even in the midst of economic growth. This need not be surprising since the causes of gendered employment go beyond economic forces but are rooted in gender relations that are far more complex than the market forces of demand and supply. According to Elson (1999:619), "male employers are not just economic men, interested only in maximizing profits, but are likely to be interested in perpetuating their advantage in the social and political spheres of life too". Otherwise, there is no economic reason for discriminating against women in the labour market since such discriminations have been found to be inefficient and inefficiency hinders the attainment of sustainable development.

WOMEN'S WORK AND SUSTAINABLE DEVELOPMENT

The loss of confidence in orthodox development theory and practice has been the result of the over emphasis on economic gains and the glosses over issues of social equity. Meanwhile, economic growth is not an end in itself but only a means to an end. This fact has been succinctly stated as, 'man himself is the chief means of the production of that wealth of which he is the ultimate aim' (Uthoff & Pernia, 1986:1). It has been proven that ignoring the social dimensions of development is the best only for the production of enclaves in an economy in favour of a privileged few. Current development paradigms therefore seek to measure development in terms of economic growth along with human development and focus on social equity, with particular focus on the well being of the poor and the vulnerable, most of whom are women.

Equity can be achieved when the only asset for the poor–labour–is adequately protected and rewarded along the lines of ILO Decent Work framework which emphasizes among other things, equal opportunities for men and women to secure decent employment and income (Akorsu, 2007). There is also an extended interest in women's work and not men's work because, assigning different tasks to men and women not on the basis of their capabilities but on the basis of their sex as is the case of gendered employment, signifies outcomes that give men advantages over women (Reskin & Padavic, 1994:6) and according to Elliott, (1994:19), 'inequalities…threaten the prospects for sustainable development in many ways".

Thus, the quest for sustainable development, a concept that has been explained at length in this volume, accentuates the need for social equity especially in the world of work. Wismer, (1989) defines sustainable development as:

> an integrated approach-including social, environmental, cultural and spiritual well being as well as economic progress in its field of endeavour. It places particular emphasis on...social equity in development planning, promoting, for example, decentralization and democracy in the workplace and the broader community".

From the above definition, it can be deduced that ignoring issues of discrimination against women in the labour market is equivalent to ignoring sustainable development. For instance, women's work has socio-economic implications for women and their families and in the long run, for the entire society. The low earnings of a woman very likely will translate into malnourished children and high child mortality even if she is not a single parent, for it has long been realised that the concept of the man as a *benevolent breadwinner* is only a myth in many societies. Thus, if sustainable development is as Allen (1980) puts it, the satisfaction of human needs and improvement in the quality of human life (including the life of women and children), then wage discrimination against women in the labour market is detrimental to the attainment of sustainable development.

Also, though it has been shown earlier that the concentration of female labour force in the agricultural sector is more than 80% in sub-Saharan Africa and at least 50% in Asia, they are often restricted to subsistence production. Men often take over more of the farming land to produce cash crops for urban markets. This restricts the land available to women to meet the nutritional needs of their families and this has two implications. First, women may have to use lands further away from where they live and this will increase the burden and time for farming. Meanwhile, according to Bryson,(1981), the time lost could have been invested in other economic activities as was the case among the Luo women of Kenya, who used the extra time gained as a result of improved farming technology in trading activities. Secondly, women may be forced to degrade the land on which future livelihoods will depend, for maximum current benefit. This possibility is confirmed by

Elliott (1994:19) that, "inequalities in access to resources threaten the prospects for sustainable development in many ways".

According to (Repetto, 1988), sustainable development is:

> "a strategy that manages all assets, natural resources, and human resources as well as financial and physical assets for increasing long term wealth and well-being. Sustainable development as a goal rejects policies and practices that ...leave future generations with poorer prospects and greater risks than our own"

If indeed, sustainable development is as described above, then working conditions in the informal economy will hinder the attainment of sustainable development because the informal economy is characterized by scrounging, under-payments, overworking, de-humanizing labouring and absolute poverty (Breman, 2003). Informal economy workers are neither organized by trade unions nor protected by state legislation. Yet, the majority of working women in Africa, and Ghana in particular, work in the informal economy where working conditions leave even current generations with poorer prospects and greater risks.

The implications of women's work even for the much cherished economic growth is that it is a waste of human resources and as Elson (1999:619) posits, *it violates the condition for productive efficiency*. It is a fact that some women have talents and capabilities perhaps even more valuable than those of some men and these can be tapped efficiently for development purposes, and so to underestimate the productive potential of women is inefficient. Meanwhile, sustainable development is about efficient utilization of such valuable resources or assets. This assertion is confirmed by Mosse (1993: 208) who states that leaving out women and by extension, issues of gender relations in any development agenda means *half a chance of succeeding*.

POLICY IMPLICATIONS

The problems of women's work cannot be solved by accident or by market forces of demand and supply since they did not occur by accident. Interventionist measures are necessary.

Existing Legislation and Initiatives in Ghana

For Ghana, the legal framework for ensuring gender equality at work is in place. Article 24 of the Ghanaian Constitution does not support discrimination of any kind in terms of employment opportunities. It says:

"Every person has the right to work under satisfactory, safe and healthy conditions, and shall receive equal pay for equal work without distinction of any kind. Every worker shall be assured of rest, leisure and reasonable limitation of working hours and periods of holidays with pay. Every worker has the right to form or join a trade union of his/her choice for the promotion and protection of his/her economic and social interest".

These clauses of the constitution are informed by the global framework. For instance, the first clause is based on ILO convention 100 on equal remuneration (1951) as well as convention 111 on discrimination (1958). The Constitution also provided legal grounds for inputs into the current Labour Act, (Act 651 of 2003), which also emphasizes equal pay for work of equal value. These clauses are however not exhaustive in protecting women and the constitution is silent on the enforcement of these laws. Most Ghanaian women are not even aware of them.

Regarding education and training, Article 25 of the Constitution also touches on educational opportunities for all-basic education shall be free, compulsory and available for all; higher education shall be made equally accessible to all; functional literacy shall be encouraged and intensified as far as possible. In addition to these laws, there are attempts to increase the number of female enrolment at tertiary and especially technical institutions. The quota system is used for this purpose. The aim is to improve the skill level among females, so as to make them employable and to diversify their work. There is also an award system for girls who excel in technical courses. Training is offered to women in small business as well as functional adult literacy programmes. These notwithstanding, female levels of education are still lower than males.

Institutional supports for women also exist in Ghana. A number of institutions have been given the mandate to promote women's needs and are involved in issues relating to women. The National Council on Women and Development (NCWD) for instance was established in 1975 and had the mandate to advise government on policy issues relating to the enhancement of the status of women. NCWD promoted income generation activities and training for women and was active in promoting law reform that resulted in the passage of the Intestate Succession Law in 1985 and the laws criminalizing harsh widowhood rites and female genital mutilation. According to the Women's manifesto, in spite of these successes, there has been dissatisfaction with the NCWD's inability to "provide policy leadership to build a strong foundation for gender equity in Ghana". (Abantu, 2004).

Thus, the Ministry for Women and Children's Affairs (MOWAC) was created in 2001 and is responsible for gender mainstreaming and all gender and children related issues. After about six years in existence, the ministry has become an implementing body, while these initiatives are important, the narrow focus of the ministry has resulted in a vital gap in its work. It has neither taken up the important role of formulating and analyzing policy, nor is it representing women and gender equality concerns in policy making. (Abantu, 2004).

A number of women's NGOs have also been working to address women's gender needs in Ghana. Examples are the Federation of Female Lawyers, Abantu for Development, The Ark Foundation and Netright. The work of these women cannot be overemphasized. The following extract sums up nicely, why women who work in the interest of women are assets:

"Social change needs a catalyst. The women's movement in the South is just such catalyst; …The resurgence of women as actors on the world stage is one of the most potent dynamics in the struggle against an unjust social order, both within and between nations" (Mosse, 1993:202).

However, the women's manifesto again states that the relationship between women's NGOs on one hand and the national machinery for women on the other hand has been difficult. The support from MOWAC to such NGOs has been minimal (ibid, 2004).

Improving Women's Work: A Move Towards Sustainable Development

In spite of these initiatives, gendered employment is persistent. It is beyond the scope of this paper to provide detailed explanations for this. However, one reason seems to be clear. The very basis of the imbalances i.e. women's subordination in relation to men is not being questioned and treated. Thus, to address women's work problems, it is necessary to question the status quo through legislation to empower women through education and to change perceptions through civic education campaigns.

Macro level interventions are also crucial since the employment problems even of disadvantaged groups such as women cannot be effectively tackled in isolation from the wider problems facing the economy. Stressing the danger of early targeting, UNESCO's second medium-term plan states, "the crippling restrictions that weigh on women are hardly likely to disappear so long as they are regarded as women's problems and not as a global problem of concern to society as a whole" (UNESCO,1985). Thus, a pre-occupation with target groups is bound to detract attention from balanced policies of employment growth. In view of this, the state need to provide macro-economic stability by controlling the financial sector, attracting foreign capital in-flaw, and heavily investing in education.

Once a macro-economic stability is achieved, targeted strategies can be developed to support women in the world of work. One very important thing is labour legislation and labour standard enforcement. A radical employment policy that seeks to transform perceptions is of paramount importance. Countries that have paid attention to labour standards like those in the Scandinavia have improved the lives of working people and bridged inequality gaps. It has been found that wage inequality among unionized workers is significantly lower than the non-unionized workers. This suggests that labour standards and regulation that encourage unionization and collective bargaining can improve the living standards of workers, including women. Since the majority of working women are found in the informal economy, it is vital to enforce standards for the whole economy. The informal economy cannot continue to be treated as outside the realm of standards, otherwise, the very essence of standard will be destroyed.

Thus, special attention must also be paid to increase representation of females in the trade unions through awareness campaigns and possibly by means of a quota system in electing the leadership of trade unions to encourage other women. This will afford them the opportunity to project their special needs such as maternity leaves with pay and with job security, childcare facilities and sexual harassment protection.

As regards the higher cost of employing women, it is increasingly becoming popular among the social partners in industrial relations that maternity leave costs need to be financed from general taxation rather than from individual employers, who also push it onto individual women. All that is required is a policy to this effect and a political will to push such a policy.

CONCLUSION

The importance of women's work cannot be glossed over in the discourse of sustainable development. Women have always been and will always be valuable resources for any development agenda. Yet, there are enormous odds against women's work, along with enormous odds against the attainment of a development that is sustainable. The indication therefore is that, women's work is key to sustainable development. Although there has been a number of initiatives and efforts to support women, women's work situations are still affected by gender considerations and attaining sustainable development continues to be illusive. What this means is that, until the very root causes are touched, until the status quo is questioned and until women's energies and expertise are valued, any attempt to attain sustainable development will have only *half a chance of succeeding* and may even be futile. There is therefore, the need for interventionist measures that question and address female subordination to males. In order to achieve this, there is need for a radical employment policy, a policy that emphasizes the need for observing labour standards for the benefit all–employers/employees, formal/informal economy workers and most importantly, males and females alike.

References

Abantu for Development (2004), Women's Manifesto for Ghana, The Coalition on the Women's Manifesto for Ghana Publication, Accra.

Akorsu, A. D. (2007), Economic Growth, Labour Standards and Social Equity: The Case of Ghana during Half a Century of Independence, A Paper Presented at Global Labour University Conference, Johannesburg.

Allen, R. (1980), How to Save the World, Kogan Page, London.

Amu, N. J. (2005), The Role of Women in Ghana's Economy, Friedrich Ebert Stiftung Research Project.

Baah, A.Y. (2004), Gender and Labour Market Liberalization in Ghana, in Gender and Labour Market Liberalization in Africa, ALRN/NALEDI Publication, Johannesburg.

Bradley, H. (1989), Men's Work, Women's Work, Polity Press, London.

Breman, J. and Das, A. N. (2000), Down and Out: Labouring Under Global Capitalism, Oxford University Press, New Delhi.

Britwum, A. O. (2000), Gender and Labour Relations, CDS/GTUC Teaching Manual.

Britwum, A. O. & Anokye, N. A. (2006), Confronting Sexual Harassment in Ghanaian Universities, Ghana Universities Press, Accra.

Britwum, A. O., Ghartey, N. K. & Abgesinyale, P. (2006), Organizing Labour in the Informal Sector–The Conditions of Rural Agriculture in Ghana, Ghana Universities Press, Accra.

Bryson, J. C. (1981), Women and Agriculture in Sub-Saharan Africa: Impliccations for Development in African Women in the Developmnet Process Nelson, N. (ed), Frank Cass and Company Limited, London.

Date-Bah, E. (1997), Promoting Gender Equality at Work-turning Vision into Reality, ILO Publication, Geneva.

Elliott, J. A. (1994), An Introduction to Sustainable Development–The Developing World, Routeledge, London.

Elson, D. (1999), Labour Markets as Gendered Institutions: Equality, Efficiency and Empowerment Issues, *World Development,* Vol. 27, No. 3, pp. 611-627.

Folbre, N. (1994), Who Pays for the Kids? Gender and the Structures of Constraint, Routledge, London.

Ghana Statistical Service (2000), Population and Housing Census, GSS Publications, Accra.

Ghana Statistical Service (2000), Ghana Living Standards Survey, GSS Publicatons, Accra.

Ghana Statistical Service (2000), Core Welfare Indicators Questionnaire–CWIQ, GSS Publications, Accra.

Hakim, C. (1981), Occupational Segregation by Sex, Department of Employment Research Paper No. 9.

International Labour Organization (1985), Equal Opportunities and Equal Treatment for Men and Women in Employment, ILO Publication, Geneva.

Lim, L. L. (1996), More and Better Jobs for Women: An Action Guide, ILO Publication, Geneva.

Sarkodie, K. A. *et al.* (2002), A Handbook on Occupational Health, Ghana Health Service/Ministry of Health Publication, Accra.

Mosse, J. C. (1993), Half the World, Half a Chance: An Introduction to Gender and Development, Oxfarm Publications, London.

Novarra, V. (1980), Women's Work, Men's Work, Marion Boyars Press, London.

Psacharapoulos, G. and Tzannatos, Z. (Eds.) (1992), Case Studies on Women's Employment and Pay in Latin America, World Bank, Washington DC.

Repetto, R. (1988b), The Concept of Susutainable Development, Discussion Paper, Green Cross International, Geneva, Green Cross Publications.

Republic of Ghana (1992), "Constitution of the Republic of Ghana", Ghana Publishing Corporation, Tama.

Reskin, B. & Padavic, I. (1994), Women and Men at Work, Pine Forge Press, California.

UNESCO (1985), Jobs for Women, UN Publication, Paris.

Uthoff, A. and Pernia, E. M. (1986), An Introduction to Human Resource Planning in Developing Countries, Background Papers For Training in Population, Human Resources and Development Planning. Paper No. 1 ILO, Geneva.

Wismer, S. (1989), Sustainable Development and Urban Life: Definitions of Sustainable Development, A Compilation of the CHS Research Bulletin, UBC Centre for Human Settlement, Vancouver.

9

MAKING WOMEN'S INFORMAL WORK VISIBLE: A CASE STUDY ON BANGLADESH

Nilufar Jahan

INTRODUCTION

In recent times, an increasing number of countries in Asia are attempting to produce information and estimates on their respective informal sectors particularly in relation to understanding how households and the economy as a whole–cope with and succeed in maintaining their standard of living in a state of crisis and poverty. With Bangladesh being a developing country and having a large informal sector, it is important to provide analysis on the role of the informal sector, especially the relationship between the role of women in the informal sector to poverty reduction and mainstreaming them into the growth process.

Bangladesh data for the informal sector remains scarce. Moreover despite recent efforts and greater concern and sensibility for gender issues, disaggregation of informal sector data by sex is also not adequately captured in official statistics. Due to the lack of statistics, those who work in the informal sector, especially women, therefore are not receiving the benefits of economic policies designed to assist disadvantaged groups. To promote better public policy and better understanding of the structure of the economy and policy responses to the informal sector, improved statistics on the size, contribution and characteristics of the informal sector are much needed.

The paper aims to explore the available statistics relating to the size, contribution and characteristics of the informal sector by gender in Bangladesh. The paper also discusses available concepts and techniques in estimating women's contribution to the informal sector in Gross Development Product (GDP).

NATURE AND EXTENT OF INFORMAL SECTOR

The informal sector focuses on the nature of employment as well as the characteristics of the enterprise. The informal sector includes all jobs or employment without any contract. It is a major provider of employment and is sometimes linked with the formal economy. In general, the informal economy is a part of the economy that is producing goods and services for sale or for some other form of remuneration.

The Fifteenth International Conference of Labour Statisticians defines the informal sector as "a group of production units which, according to the definitions and classifications provided in the United Nations System of National Accounts (Rev.4) form part of the household sector as household enterprises or, unincorporated enterprises owned by households" (ILO para.6).

The informal sector continues to grow since the 1980s. The International Labour Organization's (ILO) publication on key indication on labour market (ILO 2001) provided information on informal sector employment by gender, although for a limited number of countries in Asia (Table 1).

The informal economy despite its heterogeneity nature and given that the economy is by its very nature unidentified by the national accounts of Bangladesh estimating its size, composition and contribution of the informal economy is an extremely difficult exercise. The most serious limitation is that in Bangladesh, no survey has ever been undertaken on the informal sector. The available data, those collected by the Bangladesh Bureau of Statistics only provide

Table 1
Employment in the Informal Sector by Gender

Region/ Country	*Informal sector employment as percentage of total employment*				
	Year	*Men & Women*	*Men*	*Women*	*Sources and definition used for informal sector*
South Asia					
Bangladesh	1993	10**	10	16	Annual establishment and institution survey 1992-93:household based economic activities.
India	1993	44.2			Estimatesbased on surveys of the unorganised sectors 1992-93: enterprise engaged in the production and/or distribution of goods or services not for the sole purpose of own household use.
Pakistan	1992	67.1	65.9	80.6	Labour Force Survey, pilot study 1992: persons working in unincorporated enterprises owned by own account workers irrespective of the size of the enterprise, or by employers with less than 10 persons engaged.
Southeast Asia					
Indonesia	1995	20.6	19.1	22.7	Survey of small scaleand cottage household industries 1995: small scale industries employed 1 to 4 persons while cottage household industries engaged 5 to 9 persons.
Myanmar	1996	54.2	52.6	56.9	Survey on establishments and employment 1996: self employment activities undertaken on own account and production of goods or services for sale.
Philippines	1998	25.6			Survey of household-operated activities 1988.
Thailand	1994	47.6	46.1	49.4	Labour Force Survey, 1988 to 1994: enterprises engaged less than 10 persons, excluding employees of government organizations.

Notes: Data seems to be understated the size of the informal sector in Bangladesh, however this is the first data released for the informal sector by gender.

Source: ILO (2001).

very little sectoral idea for the measurement of the informal employment outside informal enterprises. Furthermore data, which are available, are not comprehensive. Only a few sectoral analyses have been undertaken mostly by excluding agriculture from their measurement of the informal sector and have considered only the urban informal sector (Amin 1989, 2002, Hussain 1995).

Hussain (1995) from a field survey of the slum and squatter settlements of Dhaka found that female were mainly employed as domestic maids, day labourers and readymade garment industry workers. The proportion of home based informal workers was around 60 per cent and for ready made garment industry workers 84 per cent. Amin (1989) found that women in the informal sector are engaged in relatively low status occupations. A survey undertaken on Dhaka by Amin (2002) revealed that around 68.0 per cent of women surveyed were engaged in domestic work as maids with brick-breaking accounting for the second largest group.

Amin (2002) revealed that the sector grew 40 to 50 per cent in the 1980s to around 60 to 65 per cent in the 1990s in the Asian countries. The findings also suggested that in the South Asian Countries the informal sector would continue to grow in the following decades, especially by greater participation of women in the service sector.

Classification in the Informal Sector

It has been widely believed that the marginalised population is concentrated in the informal economy. Informal employment consists of both self-employment in informal enterprises (i.e., small and/or unregistered) and wage employment in informal jobs (i.e., without secure contracts, worker benefits, or social protection). In all developing regions, self-employment comprises a greater share (60-70%) of informal employment (outside of agriculture) than wage employment (Chen 2003).

Following 1990 UN publication "Methods for Measuring Women's Participation and Production in the Informal Sector', the sector can be classified into four categories:

First category is the visible sector:

- they are micro business people, self employed individuals, house workers (suppliers to the stores, handicrafts, quilt sewing, packet suppliers, etc). They are legal workers but work outside the preview of formal economic activity.

Second category includes:

- self employed street workers, both legal and illegal. Street vendors selling cake, fruits, sari (dress) clothes and prostitution. The sex workers contribute significantly to the economy. The ILO noted recently that the illegal sex trade produces up to 10-15 per cent of the GDP in some Asian countries (Alex 2003).

Third category includes the invisible informal sector:

- unpaid work within the household, e.g. -wives who milk family cows, rear chickens for eggs for marketing the by-product, and

Fourth category has been characterised by

- domestic service, resident and non- resident individuals perform these activities within a household and receive compensation (gardeners, housekeepers).

Who Operates in the Informal Sector?

In 2000, the total labour force in Bangladesh was 58.07 million persons, of which women accounted for only 38 per cent (BBS 2004). Of these 78 per cent of females are engaged in the agricultural sector (ILO 2002). A very insignificant percentage of women working in the informal sector might be counted in this official statistics. However it is expected that the largest part of the women working in the informal sectors were not considered in the statistics published by the Bangladesh Bureau of Statistics (BBS).

According to the ILO and World Bank, around 90 per cent of the female workers particularly from South Asia are working in the informal sectors. Most of the women are in wage employment and over represented in the lower status occupations. Further, they are particularly vulnerable and kept mostly invisible in the national economy (Table 2). The strongest area of women's economic activity is in small firms, micro-enterprises and agriculture enterprises. In most cases, they are unregistered and have increasingly been brought into trade through the practice of contracting out production. Women working in the informal sector as in small businesses, home work, sex workers or in domestic services are outside the scope of labour legislation.

Home based workers were a small number in the 1980's but in recent years the number of home based workers has increased sharply. Recently, commercial home work accounts for a large share of the informal sectors employment while the sector is multifaceted and rather hidden. However if someone visits their home (Dhaka and its surrounding areas, such as Mirpur, other district town; Jamalpur, Rajshahi, Dinajpur, Jessore and many other districts in Bangladesh) it is very easy to locate these home-based workers usually undertaking craft business, sewing or working on contract for supplying dresses or craft work. Own account workers are the most common labour group in the informal sectors.

Estimation undertaken by Amin (1989, 2002) and Mahmud (2001) for available urban and national level (the informal sector as a percentage of total non-agricultural employment) employment in Bangladesh shows that the size of the informal sector is rising over the years (46.6 per cent in 1974, 52.4 per cent in 1984 and 59.0 per cent in 1995-96). As a proportion of urban employment, the informal sector accounted for about 60 per cent, although in the authors view the estimation appeared as an under-estimation of the real numbers.

In a recent study Hossain (2004) found that the very poor group of females worked for 161 days a year compared to 122 days for the poor and 115 days for those who considered

Table 2
Women's Employment by Enterprise Type (*Broad Category*)

Nature of work	*Own account worker/ self employed*	*Hired/ Family labour*	*Comments*
Mobile hawker	mostly own account worker		
Street vendor	Own account worker	hired or family labour	Sometime work as a family unit
Construction worker	own account worker or piece rate worker for brick breaking	Hired	
Waste picker			
Home worker	Usually wage worker/own account worker		More wage workers but flexibility in working hours gives some own accoutn charateristics
shop keepers	self employed/ wage labour	hired/family	wage labour but offered lower wages than men
Sex worker	self employed/ wage labour/ own account worker		Some time works as a daily wage worker or maybe own account worker
Domestic servants/maids	wage labour	hired	page worker paid in terms of money and in kind
Gardener	wage labour	hired	paid worker

themselves as self sufficient but vulnerable to economic shock. From these numbers, it has been found that it is the more economically depressed/distressed women who participate more in economic activities. The study also found that the wage rate is the most important factor influencing women's economic participation

Women in Bangladesh employed in different types of activities such as Bidi rolling, fishery, street vendor, agro processing, sewing, construction work, prostitution (Halim 2004, Amin 2002) and in all those stages of employment men earn more than women. Formal sector jobs have offered the best level of earnings and benefit within the economy, such as women employed in the labour intensive export earning companies, in garments and textiles earned specific wages rather than women working at home based work or an illegal work. Recent comparative surveys in Bangladesh and in Tanzania provide some information into the gender gaps in earnings in the informal sector. In both countries, earnings are highest among employers, followed by own account workers and then wage workers, who earn the least. With one exception, women earn less in each of these employment categories than men (the exception is that female employers in Tanzania earn more than male employers). The earning gap between women and men is considerably less in Tanzania than in Bangladesh. In Bangladesh, men own account workers (non agriculture sector) earn more than three times the earnings of women own account workers, while male employers earn about four times more than female ones (Table 3).

Table 3
Monthly Mean Earnings by Employment Stauts in Bangladesh and Tanzania (Take/day)

	Own Account Work		*Wage Worker*		*Employer*	
	Women	*Men*	*Women*	*Men*	*Women*	*Men*
Bangladesh	18.81	61.35	61.69	71.44	27.29	114.84
(Number)	('355)	('925)	('211)	('939)	('292)	('1294)
Tanzania	30.59	('1265)	('195)	('320)	('88)	('148)

Source: Dasgupta and Barbattini, (2003).

As a result of this large earning gap in Bangladesh, a far higher proportion (64%) of female own account workers than male own account workers (4%) are concentrated in the lowest income group (Dasgupta and Barbattini, 2003). This study also found that men in Bangladesh were far more likely than women to belong to the top income group, representing 93 per cent of this group. In Tanzania, where the gender gap is not so stark, men represented a far lower majority (55%) of the top income group.

The shares of men and women in the informal sector show that women tend to be over-represented as unpaid family workers. The figure also depicts that men being the employers have the highest earnings; and the home workers, the poor women have the lowest; resulting in a significant gender gap in earnings, women earning less on average than men. With more representation in the lower segmentation, it ascertains that the average earnings associated with the different sorts of employment also tends to decline as more and more poor women add to the informal economy.

SIGNIFICANCE OF THE SECTOR- THE KEY ISSUES

The informal economy has been growing and becoming a permanent part of the employment sector. This sector has developed as a consequence of global economic growth and mostly associated with the increasing demand of cheap labour. Within the framework of the informal economy, the non- agricultural workforce has increased over several years and the sector has been considered as an essential means of employment generation and economic growth of the country.

Poverty Reduction

People in the informal sector work hard, but they are still vulnerable, marginalised and poor. Often, there is a significant overlap between working in the informal economy and being poor. Reducing poverty need a comprehensive and innovative policy response to the informal economy. As more than half the

Box 1
A Conceptual Framework of the Informal Economy

The top segment of figure 1 explains the visibility of the employers/ micro-entrepreneurs in a developing economy setting. At the base, the people working are the least visible group and the home workers. From official data and available field survey, two basic global facts emerge about the segmented informal economy. The first one is that men tend to be over represented in the top segment while women tend to be over represented in the bottom segment. The shares of men and women tend to vary across sectors and countries for the intermediate segments, however women are described to be over represented as unpaid family workers.

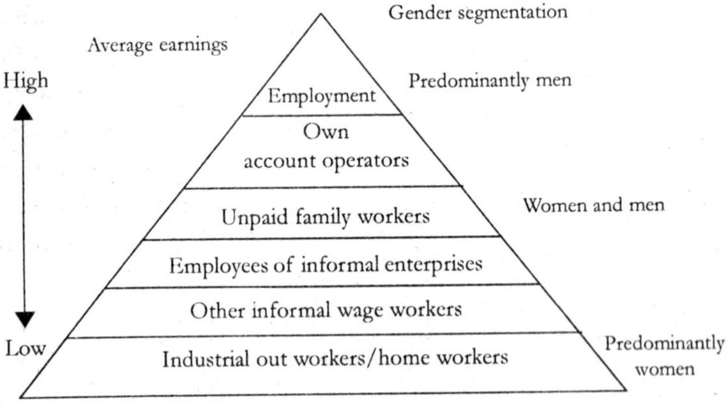

Figure 1: Segmentation of the Informal Economy
Source: adopted from Chen et al (2004).

The informal economy consists of a range of different informal enterprises and informal jobs. However on the right side of figure 1, self-employment and wage employment, the two broad components of the informal economy indicates the nature of the informal economy and the earnings at the various sub-components of each stage in the informal economy. The group on the right hand side- employees of informal enterprises, other informal wage workers and industrial workers/home-workers are under the wage employment group while employers, own account operators and unpaid family workers are under the self-employment groups. To the left, the figure explains earning differentials or average earnings associated with the informal sector. Average earnings tend to decline as one moves down the figure.

workforce and a sizeable share of economic units operate outside the scope of existing legislation, regulations and policies and therefore, do not receive any incentives, benefits or protection thereof. A comprehensive policy would be expected to improve income, productivity, and efficiency, which would subsequently improve the economic condition of the majority of the population, particularly the poorest and the most vulnerable groups of people, women-working in the informal sectors.

Social Related Issues

Informal sectors are not entitled to either legal or social protection under the current labour legislation in Bangladesh. This implies that women in the informal sector are not protected in terms of their access to labour and other labour related social protection. The working or employment condition of the informal economy is worse than any other sector of the economy.

A project of Independent University of Bangladesh (IUB) in 2001 surveyed some 300 garment workers, sex workers, domestic servants and housewives and asked the women about their families, education and income; their work histories and preferences, child rearing, birth control and health care; and their exposure to violence in the home or workplace (Akhter *et al.* 2005).

The survey found that garment workers and some groups of sex workers—those based in hotels or houses rather than in brothels or on the streets—have more control over the circumstances of their lives than other Bangladeshi women do. They usually have more education. They have more income: garment workers earn about twice the income of maids; sex workers earn five or six times that of garment workers. Both the garment workers and sex workers have better access to health care and education for their children. They are more independent and more mobile, able to go out by themselves in society. Garment workers (though not sex workers) are less likely to be abused by husbands or in-laws and they take a more equal part in household decisions. On the other hand, servants and "floating" sex workers, those who work on the streets with little or no education, were likely to have been trafficked into their jobs and are at high risk of violence.

Ward (2005) while working with the IUB project observed that micro-credit that has helped poor women to start their own small businesses; such as tea stalls, tailoring shops, or rickshaw rentals—has been widely accepted as a solution to the problem of women's poverty in Bangladesh. However Ward (2005) thought that micro-credit would not bring many women out of poverty. Rather she found that the women didn't want to be indebted, rather they preferred a job in any sector.

Employment in the informal sectors remains outside the legal framework and faces extortion and harassment by authorities. This is frequently found in the daily lives of street vendors, garment workers, domestic household workers, sex workers, craft workers and agricultural and non- agricultural workers. The absence of regulations and adequate security or protection leaves room for abuse in the labour sector and to solicit bribes.

INFORMAL SECTOR IN BANGLADESH

Distribution of the economically active population by industry and gender indicates that expansion in the service sector has created opportunities for women to participate in the work force. The Asian Development Bank (ADB) reported that more than three quarters of employed women of 15 years and above are unpaid family labourers of whom less than a tenth are self-employed and six per cent are contract workers (ADB 2001). Most of the unpaid family labourers, who are mainly women, are employed in agriculture. Rural women are mostly involved in income-generating activities such as post harvest activities, cow fattening and milking, goat farming, backyard poultry rearing, pisciculture, agriculture, fishery, horticulture, food processing, cane and bamboo works, silk reeling, handloom, garment making, fishnet making, coir production and handicrafts. A large number of rural women are also involved in certain male dominated rural construction work such as earthwork, construction and agricultural field work.

The Bangladesh Labour Force Survey (1999-2000) reported that the participation of women in paid employment is increasing. However the sectors, especially in the service sector where women's participation are rising, are not providing a stable employment condition with good income.

Segmentation of Informal Employment and Women's Participation

The informal economy shows that women account for a major share of national employment. It has also been seen that when the informal jobs were measured by principal activities, it is mainly, female, wage worker and rural. The number of females employed in agriculture is higher than the number of men working in agriculture (Figure 2). The survey undertaken by BIDS-IRRI also has similar findings. (Hossain 2004). Following Hossains (2004) findings, it can be said that women are mostly poverty stricken with agriculture being their primary job while non agricultural work is the secondary.

(in percentage)

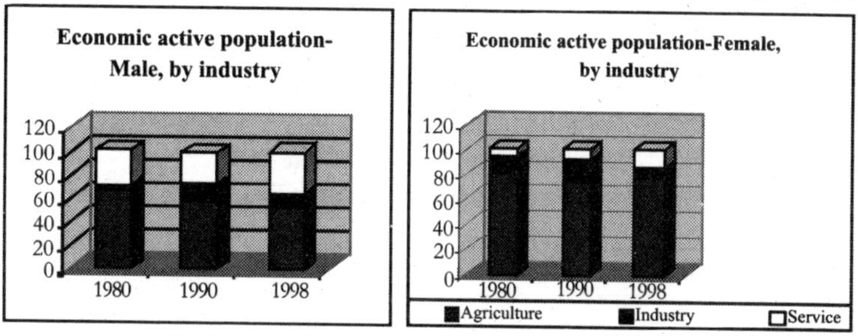

Figure 2: Distribution of Economically Active Population in Bangladesh.
Source: BBS.

Bangladesh Labour Force Survey (LFS 1999-2000) provides information on employment in 99 sectors by gender and detailed occupation. Among others, some of the sectors/industries were well matched with the characteristics of the informal sectors in general. Out of 99 sub sectors of employment, 56 groups have been identified with having possible informal sector employment. These sectors were again sub grouped, such as: sectors dominated by wage workers, or self employed or street workers, domestic or household workers (a detail listing in appendix A) to provide a rough estimation of the women's participation in the informal employment (Table 4).

While the estimated informal sectors that are included in LFS (1999-2000) grouped under house worker, wage worker, street workers and self employed categories, the LFS does not represent the entire community of the informal economy, There are others groups: such as, invisible workers, home based workers and sex workers, who are mostly women and were not included in the sectors reported in the LFS. Furthermore LFS have not accounted for multiple jobs that the most Bangladesh agricultural family workers performed. Therefore, the estimated number that have been reported as a sketch of women working in the Bangladesh informal sector is not a true reflection of the informal numbers and an underestimation of the actual number of females working in the informal sector (Table 4). However, it is presented to give an approximation in the size of female workers in the informal sector.

Table 4
Share of Employment in the Informal Sector to Total Employment by Gender

in '000

	Female	*Male*	*All*
National (informal + formal)	38	62	100
National Informal (estimated)	87.7	69	76
Male dominated (prof) supporting job	1.2	9.9	6.6
Women dominated (ag) informal job	69.4	41.2	51.9
Women dominated small scale job	5.3	1.5	2.9
Sales/Street vendors	1.6	4.3	3.3
Women dominated spinning, woven and textile	1.4	0.9	1.1
Man dominated small scale industry job	3.	10.7	7.8
Women dominated domestic work	5.8	0.5	2.5

Note: *prof:* professional, *ag:* agriculture.
Source: Own calculation based on LFS 1995-1996 and 1999-2000.

Following the table, it has been found that in total female employment, 66 per cent women are employed as wage workers (Figure 3). Wage workers, household and domestic workers belongs to the lowest segment of the working categories. They are the least visible group and tend to be over represented in the bottom income segment of the economy.

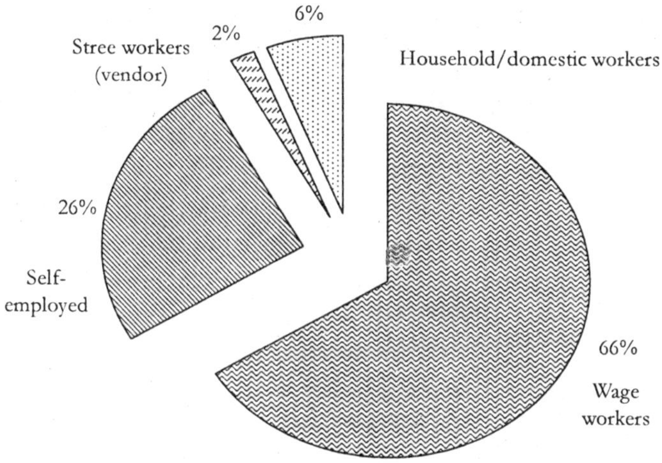

Figure 3: Women's Share in the Informal Employment to Total Female Employment

GAPS IN THE MEASUREMENT–THE UNDERESTIMATION OF WOMEN'S PARTICIPATION IN ECONOMIC ACTIVITY

Given the invisibility of the informal economy in official statistics, there are not many analyses or policy research in favour of women workers in the informal economy. In Bangladesh, official statistics do not include data on the incomes or value added activities performed by women workers in the informal economy.

Being a large contributing sector in the Bangladesh economy, the informal workforce needs to be visible to policy makers and have a voice in the policy process. The informal workers especially the women are under enumerated in official statistics. In Bangladesh national account, informal sector activities have been traditionally underestimated or absent since it has been published.

For example: women servants earn a salary, considered to be economically active are not included in the Gross National Product (GNP). Midwives earn part time and intermittently, without being considered economically active, are paid but not included in GNP. There are many examples around of our daily socio economic activities, where women are actively contributing in the economic activities of the society but those contributions are not counted in the estimation of national income.

Until the informal workers are totally counted in national accounts or statistics, policy makers will continue to ignore or underestimate the size and the contribution of the informal sectors. A major reason for this has been the lack of data and insufficient knowledge about the working ability and productivity of women in the informal sector. In many developing countries, surveys have been carried out and their results made available for national accounts (Charmes 1999, 2000). However, no attempt has been noticed yet in Bangladesh. Among other reasons, it could be that at the Bangladesh government policy level, the informal sectors have not been recognised as an important contributor in the economy. In the Bangladesh economic perspective, women are better described as a component in poverty problem-but their contribution has not been recognised as related to policy guidelines.

A recent survey undertaken jointly by the Bangladesh Institute of Development Studies (BIDS) and International Rice Research Institute (IRRI) (Hossain 2004) shed some light on the informal economy in Bangladesh. The survey acknowledged women's contribution to employment and has attempted to measure the contribution also. The IRRI-BIDS household survey reports that rural non-farm employment has been increased and nearly 43 per cent income is generated from rural non-farm income. A large proportion of rural non-farm workers are mentioned as wage labourers, however, very little is known about their earnings or income or their contribution to national production.

Measuring the Informal Sector

In the Bangladesh Labour Force Survey and National Household survey, data at the disaggregated level are available. However no data have been collected on self employment or own account workers in the informal sector. Most surveys collect information on the number of people employed and their salaries by qualification level, and age, which make the table quite hard to complete for large enterprises. Now when analysing modern sector employment, it is important to remodel the questionnaires with information especially related to the distribution by sex.

The Sample Household Survey, available for a long series of years, includes several questions on economic status, characteristics of employment, size of income from work as well as questions on demographic and social characteristics. However the results are not available by location, enterprises and sex. The current Household Survey does not furnish information on the value of output and intermediate consumption of the informal units for estimating the contribution of women in the informal sector.

Data on size and the contribution of informal sectors, especially home based workers, street vendors are very weak in Bangladesh, although a larger segment of women workers are concentrated in these two sectors. Without the efforts of highlighting the activities and measuring home based work the size of the sectors would remain unknown.

Labour Force Surveys as a Source of Data on Informal Sector Employment/Informal Employment

Labour force surveys have already been used as a source of data on employment in the informal sector (ILO 2002). In the labour force survey a few additional questions related to the informal sector or informal employment definitions and to the characteristics of informal sector employment or informal employment could explain the size of the informal sector. The additional questions could be asked of all persons employed during the reference period of the survey, irrespective of their status in employment.

The total population of the survey could be classified into employed, unemployed and economically inactive person. The employed group in the next phase would then be sub-classified by the nature of employment, such as formal and the informal, their type of production units (formal sector enterprises, informal sector enterprises, or households). The labour force survey therefore could be used as the first phase of a mixed household and enterprise survey on the informal sector. It is sometimes very difficult to provide information on informal jobs, however, an estimated total number of persons employed in an enterprise could initially be considered to provide a rough estimate of the sector.

Collection of data

The International Labour Organisation (ILO) resolution made some recommendations on data collection programmes and methods (Ferran 1998): Such as:

(a) The collection of data on the informal sector should be integrated into the regular national statistical system and should contemplate current monitoring (once a year) and in-depth inquiries (every five years), covering not only employment (numbers and characteristics of those employed), but also data on production and income. Concerning procedures for estimating the contribution of women working in the informal sector, what is needed is a cross-classification of data on production and income by gender.

(b) Data collection should be based on household surveys, using households as reporting units and household members as observation units, while for in-depth studies, establishment surveys or mixed household and enterprise surveys are preferred. In these latter cases it is the informal sector unit that is used for observation and reporting.

(c) Data might be collected either on the value of outputs and material inputs or on the transactions related to producing goods and services (gross value added as the value of output less the value of intermediate consumption. In SNA terms, intermediate consumption refers to all goods and services used during the production process).

(d) For unpaid family worker, the income of enterprise could be used to estimate the approximate contribution of women. On the other hand, an approximate estimation could be made by using time worked and wages paid in the market.

The Resolution states that "other measurement methods can also be considered, such as methods of indirect macroeconomic estimation or the comparative analysis of data from different sources".

Survey Questions

The questionnaire should include other socio-demographic and economic characteristics: such as sex, age, marital status, relationship to the reference person of the household, level of education, place of usual residence, urban vs. rural area, household/family characteristics: number of household/family members, household/family, type, hours of work and earnings; branch of economic activity (industry), occupation and status in employment; other characteristics of the job: full-time vs. part-time work, job permanency.

The current labour force survey of Bangladesh obtains some of the information mentioned here. However this information are not clearly defined and not provided by sex. Further the information that is published by the Bangladesh Bureau of Statistics is not relevant to the informal sector. If the information had been obtained from the survey question(s) on branch of economic activity, persons working in the informal sector could easily be identified those engaged in agriculture, garments, forestry, fisheries and in sex industry.

DIFFICULTIES IN MEASURING WOMEN'S CONTRIBUTION TO THE INFORMAL SECTOR

The informal sector is mainly urban and seems to be dominated by men (Box 1). However when measured by main activities, becomes rural and female dominated (Table 2). Active women not only contribute to a particular job, they are involved also in secondary activities, multiple jobs, and more broadly in pluri-activity (Charmes 1998). This statement is also true for the women in Bangladesh who are involved with the informal sector. It is a major difficulty in the measurement of women's contribution while women are involved with more than one activity.

It is also hard to obtain information on the characteristics of enterprises from employees. An estimate of employment in the informal sector by sex and status in employment can be obtained only on the basis of the surveyed answers provided by informal own-account workers and employers. It is also needed for application of the harmonized definition of informal sector recommended by the Delhi Group, which specifies the size criterion in terms of less than five paid employees (Central Statistical Organisation/India 1999).

While women are involved with this type of multi jobs, often labour force surveys while collecting information on the characteristics of the respondent's main job, can not provide the actual number of persons working in the informal work. In many countries, however, a large number of informal sector activities or informal jobs are undertaken as secondary jobs. For identification of the informal sector or informal employment, questions can be asked not only in respect of the respondents' main jobs, but also in respect of their secondary jobs. Otherwise, the size of the informal sector or informal employment is likely to be underestimated.

Informal sector employment or informal employment is usually offered in relation to a short reference period such as one week or two months. So data collected on informal sector employment obtained for a short reference period may not be representative for the whole year. Improved representation of the time dimension can be achieved by repeating the measurement several times during the year in the case of quarterly, monthly or continuous surveys, or by using a longer reference period such as one year in the case of annual or less frequent surveys.

The possibilities for disaggregating the data by branch of economic activity (industry) and other characteristics depend upon the sample size and design. Sometimes, the number of informal workers included in the survey sample is too small to make any detailed sub classifications. In Bangladesh, the difficulties are more acute as:

- informal activities of home-based work, sex-workers, or street vendors, are very difficult to capture and measure.
- the non-response rate in the surveys is generally higher for women than for men, especially regarding incomes.
- their production activities are not only hidden behind their status of so-called inactive housewives,
- but also behind the less "valuable" status of family worker in agriculture or the difficult-to-capture status of independent street or road vendor or sex worker.

CONCLUDING COMMENTS

Given the magnitude and the significance of the informal economy in regard to both poverty and growth, it would be difficult to implement and execute the country's development strategy and associated transformations without understanding the informal economy. It is very important to increase the visibility and voice of those who work in the informal economy and to promote supportive policies for the informal workforce. It could does so by promoting improved research, statistics and policy analysis on the informal economy, and by requesting other development partners, especially request may be made to ILO and other international agency such as United Nation Development Program (UNDP) to help in pursuing inventory projects concerning to the size (in terms of employment) and the contribution (in terms of GDP) of the informal sector.

Research needs to be undertaken, by using available existing data and making the efforts of providing data and estimates, disaggregated by gender, and by specific groups (home-based workers, street vendors, maids, sex worker in particular), by regional locations (mainly urban/rural) to analyse the contribution of a large uncounted labour force, who contribute significantly to the economy and support the rural economy to grow. Ignoring women's labour in the informal sector would generate policies that would harm not just women but households and families.

Notes

The views expressed in this article are of author and do not necessarily reflect those of Australian Bureau of Agricultural and Resource Economics (ABARE), Canberra, Australia.

References

ADB (2001), *Country Report 2001 Bangladesh*, Asian Development Bank: Manila. *(www.adb.org/Documents/Reports/Annual_Report/2001/ban)*

Akhter, R., Islam, A. K. M. S., Ward, K. B. Mizan, A. N. and Islam, M. (2005), "*Assessment of Knowledge, Attitudes and Practices of Domestic Violence Against Women in Dhaka, Bangladesh* "ALO/USAID grant, "Removing barriers of domestic violence from Women's full participation in civic society and democracy in Bangladesh" December 2002-July 2005, Kathyryn Ward and Ainon N. Mizan (Co-Pls, SIUC).

Amin, N. A. T. M. (2002), "*The Informal Sector in Asia from the Decent Work Perspective*", working paper on the Informal Economy, Employment Sector, International Labour Office: Geneva.

Amin, N. A. T. M. (1989), *Macro Perspectives on the Growth of the Informal Sector in Selected Asian Countries*, paper presented for the Asian Employment Programme held in New Delhi, ILO/ARTEP, 1989.

BBS (2004), Bangladesh Statistical Bulletin, Bangladesh Bureau of Statistics: Dhaka.

BBS, (2002), Report of the Labour Force Survey, Bangladesh, 1999-2000. Bangladesh Bureau of Statistics: Dhaka.

BBS, Labour Force Survey, Bangladesh Bureau of Statistics: Dhaka (various issues).

Charmes (2000), 'Measurement of the Contribution of Informal Sector and Informal Employment to GDP in Developing Countries: Some Conceptual and Methodological Issues; Paper prepared for the 9th Meeting of the Delhi Group on Informal sector Statistics.

Charmes (1999), 'The Quality of Women's Employment: A Review of Statistical and Empirical Evidence Towards an Improvement of their Situation at Work', Paper Prepared for the International Labour Office, Department of Development Policies (POLDEV), Programme "Improving the Quality of Women's Employment", February.

Chen, Martha, and Marilyn Carr (2004), "Globalisation, Social Exclusion and Work: With Special Reference to Informal Employment and Gender", *International Labour Review*, 143.1-2.

Chen, Martha (2003), "Rethinking the Informal Economy: In An Era of Global Integration and Labour Market Flexibility", New Delhi Seminar No. 531, November 2003.

CSO (1999), *Report of the Sixth Meeting of the Expert Group on Informal Sector Statistics,: Expert Group on Informal Sector*, New Delhi, 17-19 May 1999; New Delhi, Central Statistical Organisation/India.

Daily Star (2006) The recent violence in the garment sector, *The Daily Star Web Edition Vol. 5 Num 705, 710, 719 and 736 (http://www.thedailystar.net).*

Dasgupta, S. and Barbattini, S. (2003). *'Own Account Work as Work Status: Learning from the PSS in Bangladesh and Tanzania'.* In Martha Chen, Renana Jhabvala and Guy Standing (eds). *Rethinking Informality and Work.*

Ferran, L (1998) *"Note on Concepts and Techniques for Estimating the Contribution of Women Working in the Informal Sector"* New York: United Nations Statistics Division. Presented at the Delhi Group Meeting on Informal Sector Statistics, Ankara, April 28-30, 1998.

GSS (2000), *'Ghana Living Standards Survey: Report of the Fourth Round* (GLSS4)', Ghana Statistical Service, Table 4.4, p. 30.

Halim S. (2004), *Marginalisation or Empowerment? Women's Involvement in Shrimp Cultivation and Shrimp Processing Plants in Bangladesh*", in Hossain, T., Imam. M. H. and Habib. S. E. (eds.) Women, Gender and Discrimination, Rajshahi University, Rajshahi.

Hossain, M. (2004), "*Rural Non-farm Economy in Bangladesh: A View from Household Surveys*", Centre for Policy Dialogue (CPD) Occasional Paper Series, Paper 40: Dhaka.

Hossain, M. Paris. T. R., Bose. M. L. and Chowdhury A. (2004), *Nature and Impact of Women's Participation in Economic Activities in Rural Bangladesh, Policy Brief,* Centre for Policy Dialogue-International Rice Research Institute (CPD-IRRI): Dhaka.

Hussain, H. S. (1995), "Fighting Poverty: The Economic Adjustment of Female Migrants in Dhaka, *Environment and Urbanization*, Sage Publications *(http:/ / eau.sagepub.com/ cgi/ content/ abstract/ 7/ 2/ 51)*

IDRC (2004), Gender Mainstreaming, *(http:/ / www.idrc.ca/ en/ ev-83646-201-1-)*.

ILO (2002), International Labour Conference, 90 th Session, 2002 Women and Men in the Informal Economy: A Statistical Picture, International Labour Office, Geneva: 2002.

ILO (2001), '*Key Indicators of the Labour (KILM) Market*', International Labour Office, Geneva: 2001.

ILO (1993), '*Report of the 15th International Conference of Labour Statisticians*', International Labour Office: Geneva.

Jahan, N. (2007), "Can the Informal Economy Take the Lead? A Challenge to Governance", in *Readings in World Development, Vol. III: Governance and Development in Poor Countries,* (eds) by Roy, K. C. and Prasad, B., Nova Science, New York, USA; 2007.

Jahan, N. (1996), "Have Women Lost Out in the Development Process? Some Evidence from Rural Bangladesh",(with M. Alauddin.) *International Journal of Social Economics*, 23(4/5/6).

Mahmud, W. (2001), *Informal Sector in Bangladesh: A Macroeconomic Perspective,* Report prepared for the ILO as an input to a National Plan for Employment Generation in the Informal Sector, International Labour Organization: Geneva.

Noury, A. J. (2003), *Exploring the Economy's "Informal Sector", The Progress Report, (www.progress.org/ 2003/ noury03.htm)*.

UN (1990), *Methods of Measuring Women's Participation and Production in the Informal Sector*, United Nations Sales No: E.90.XVII.16, New York.

Ward, K (2005), Made in Bangladesh: An Expert on Work, Gender, and the Global Economy Tries to Improve Women's Lives and Livelihoods in a Desperately Poor Nation. Perspectives, *Southern Illinois University Carbondale (http:/ / www.siu.edu/ ~perspect/ 05_fall/ bangladesh.html)*

WIEGO (2005), Women in the Informal Sector, *http:/ / www.wiego.org/ main/ fact1.shtml*

WIEGO (2006), Programme Areas: Urban Policies Women in Informal Employment Globalizing and Organizing: Cambridge *(http:/ / www.wiego.org/ main/ areas1.shtml)*

World Bank (2004), *World Development Report 2005: A Better Investment Climate for Everyone*. Washington DC: World Bank.

Appendix-A
Employed Persons 10 Years and Over by Detailed Occupation and Sex, and Residence 1999-2000

Sectors (identifed as having informal job)	Bangladesh			Urban			Rural		
	Total	Male	Female	Total	Male	Female	Total	Male	Female
Arch. Eng. And related technician	75	61	14	59	53	6	16	8	8
Medical, dental,veterinary &work	231	174	57	76	55	21	155	119	36
Workers in religion	65	65	0	12	12	0	53	53	0
Book keepers, cashierss and related work	143	132	11	82	74	8	61	58	3
Transport and conductors	116	107	9	62	58	4	54	49	5
Clerical and related works	358	305	53	154	133	21	204	172	32
Managers whole and retail trade	58	52	6	37	36	1	21	16	5
Working proprietors (wholesale and retail)	3755	3683	72	1244	1204	40	2511	2479	32
Insurance, real estate, sec. business, serv &auc	66	62	4	25	25	0	41	37	4
Salesman, strret vendors and related workers	2318	1936	382	897	809	88	1421	1127	294
Salesman not elsewhere classified	45	44	1	17	16	1	28	28	0
Managers, catering and loging services	11	11	0	11	11	0	0	0	0
Working proprietors (catering and lodging)	202	198	4	71	67	4	131	131	0
supervisors (catering and lodging)	9	8	1	5	4	1	4	4	0
Cooks, waiters& related workers	354	308	46	125	96	29	229	212	17
Maids, related housekeeping, serv. Wokers	1105	132	973	518	62	456	587	70	517
Building caretakers, cleaners & related workers	89	59	30	85	55	30	4	4	0
Launderers, dry cleaners & pressers	122	64	58	65	28	37	57	36	21
Hairdressers, barbers, beaticians&related workers	88	87	1	23	22	1	65	65	0
Fire fighters, policeman and decoratives workers	344	332	12	146	144	2	198	188	10
Guards	345	40	305	38	7	31	307	33	274
Farm managers and supervisors	20	19	1	4	2	2	16	17	-1
Farmers	26993	11943	15050	1654	612	1042	25339	11331	14008
Farm, livestock, dairy, paultry & nursery	8702	6929	1773	331	245	86	8371	6684	1687
Forestry workers	70	53	17	8	8	0	62	45	17
Fisherman, haunters & related workers	728	651	77	71	67	4	657	584	73
Production supervisors & general foreman	73	64	9	48	40	8	25	24	1
miners, quarrymen, well & related workers	130	36	94	7	7	0	123	29	94
Metal processors	36	36	0	24	24	0	12	12	0
Wood preparers, paper makers	69	42	27	32	10	22	37	32	5
Chemical processors & related workers	9	8	1	5	4	1	4	4	0
Spinner weaver knitter dyer & textile workers	1002	666	336	239	172	67	763	494	269
Food & beverage processors	454	366	88	148	113	35	306	253	53
Tobacco preparers, cigarette makers	46	14	32	30	10	20	16	4	12
Tailors, dressmakers, sewers and related works	1793	526	1267	997	269	728	796	257	539
Shoemakers and leather goods makers	66	59	7	37	30	7	29	29	0
Cabinet makers and wood workers	470	459	11	90	88	2	380	371	9
Stone cutters, finishers	0	0	0			0	0	0	0
Forging workers, tool makers & metal workers	78	78	0	49	49	0	29	29	0
Plumbers, welders & sheet metal workers	137	133	4	96	92	4	41	41	0
Jewellery and precious metal workers	113	111	2	23	22	1	90	89	1
Glass former, potters and related workers	122	72	50	20	11	9	102	61	41
Rubber and plastic product workers	44	38	6	24	18	6	20	20	0
Paper and paper board roduct makers	45	23	22	17	11	6	28	12	16
Printers and related workers	35	31	4	14	14	0	21	17	4
Painters	65	61	4	32	29	3	33	32	1
Production and related workers	304	111	193	47	25	22	257	86	171
Bricklayers, carpenters and other workers	563	557	6	265	259	6	298	298	0
Stationary engine & equipment operators	40	35	5	16	14	2	24	21	3
Material handling	84	84	0	47	47	0	37	37	0
Transport equipment and drivers, related workers	2029	1986	43	881	872	9	1148	1114	34
Labourers. not elsewhere classified	799	663	136	276	231	45	523	432	91

Source: BBS 2002

10

GENDER AND DECISION-MAKING PROCESS IN INDIA–A CASE STUDY

C. Muthuraja

INTRODUCTION

Democratic and secular India endeavors to provide the necessary conditions for greater participation of women in all spheres of life. Equality of opportunity is guaranteed and discrimination on grounds of sex, language, religion, class or creed is prohibited. Let in reality women's participation in decision-making at all levels national to local is low. The challenges in seeking to redress this inequality in a diverse and complex country like India are enormous. They are related to over among attitudinal, institutional, cultural and socio-economic restrictions that gave grown over centuries. There is now, however, an acceptance that women's participation in decision-making in large enough numbers at every level is needed. Women's unique experiences and perspectives would enhance and alter definitions of problems and solutions and would also empower them. Obstacles, which do not let women participation fully, need to be identified and removed. Often structures and social norms are barriers; and stem from social conditioning, which inhibits women from aspirations to decision-making positions. Governmental and non-governmental interventions should facilitate and promote women's participation in decision-making.

In the privacy of a home, men and women seem to be keeping decision-making gender based. Micro level studies show that when women determine issues it is generally in the traditional spheres and at a later stage in their lives. Women will assume leadership positions and be successful if they are enabling to develop that capability within the domestic sphere and the public sphere.

Agricultural women workers play a significant role in domestic and socio-economic life of the society. Development of the country is not possible without developing the important and substantial segment i.e., agricultural women of our society. Today, more than ever before, there is an emphasis on planned and desirable change, especially in agricultural societies of developing nations, in the form of agricultural development. But the success of national programmes mainly depends on the rational decision-making process of agricultural women.

There is much debate with regard to the measurement of the status of women workers and determinates thereof, therefore no clear indicators are available. Some researchers however argue that, in the case of women workers in agriculture, their participation in decision-making is a fairly good indicator of their status. In general, males take an active role in decision-making in different areas of home operations, because the influence of women in home has not been recognised. Therefore, it is necessary to bring forth the decision-making process of women in home operations.

WOMEN AND DECISION MAKING PROCESS IN INDIA

Rani and Bhave (1981)[1] has revealed that the decision making pattern among rural women of Ranga Reddy district of Andra Pradesh indicates that with regard to decision making patterns pertaining to purchase of land, amount to be spent on seed, purchase of fertilizers, purchase of farm power and farm implementshusband was the leading person to take decisions.

Husband and wife both are involved in decisions about place of education, amount to be spent on children's education and marriage of children. Wife holds a responsible position in deciding about the quantity of food material to be purchased and the type of material for clothing.

Fatima (1984)[2] in 'Rural Development and Women's Liberation, Caste, Class and Gender in a grass-root organisation in Tamil Nadu, South India' has highlighted the real position of rural women in Tamil Nadu and has observed that women do all the domestic work. Every day she has to get firewood and buy cooking oil and other requirements. Men spend their wages, as they like. Women are criticised if they ever spend money on themselves, and are considered to be fully responsible for their family's welfare. Education, is given only to sons, not to daughters who will one day marry and leave the parents. As a result of this, many women are illiterate. Their economic contribution is not recognized. Harijans and other landless women suffer as women and also because of their caste and class. Harijan women are paid particularly low wages, although they work very hard and in some areas they are experiencing increasing difficulty in finding paid agricultural work. Due to mechanization, unemployed men are replacing them. Landlords often sexually exploit Harijans and other women agricultural labourers.

Devi (1988)[3] has made a study on management in farm and home of rural women in eight randomly selected villages of Gannavaram taluk of Krishna District of Andhra Pradesh State. She reveals that significant differences are observed between the role expectation of rural women by themselves and experts and their actual role performance in farm and home management. No significant difference was noticed between the role expectation of rural women by their husbands and their actual role performance in farm and home management and all the three economic categories of rural women, viz., the low, medium and high, differed significantly between their role perceptions and their actual role performances.

Sharma (1995),[4] in 'The Impact of Women Workforce in the Unorganised Sector on Household Management: A study of Agra City' has observed that with the exception of decisions relating to food, which are made solely or dominantly by wives, decisions on rest of the areas tend to be made jointly with equal participation by wives and husbands. In decisions pertaining to the acquisition of household durables, for example, the greater proportion of wives (42.7 per cent) claim to have decided on the matter jointly and equally with their husbands. The remaining 57.3 per cent, however shows that the decisions have been made more prominently by the wives.

Vencatesan (1996)[5], Devi (1996)[6] and Dhruvarajan (1996)[7] have revealed that the view of women as housewives engaged exclusively in domestic chores has led to erroneous definitions of productivity on the one hand, and a skewed view of women's work and child care roles on the other. The reasons for low work participation are withdrawal from the workforce due to marriage, pregnancy or other social reasons as well as repeated pregnancies leading to prolonged interruptions in work status. Limited skill and low literacy lead to limited occupational mobility.

Tuteja (2000)[8] made a study on contribution of female agricultural workers in family income and their status in Haryana state and observed that female agricultural workers contribute significantly in household income on all farm sizes and their earnings are found most crucial for the landless and small farm households. The proportionate contribution of females declined with increasing farm size while vice versa is true for absolute income. The assessment of the level of control of female workers over their earnings revealed that women belonging to land owning classes enjoyed the financial power of their earned money to some extent but female workers from small and landless households usually surrendered their earned income to the family pool and they had no freedom to spend their earned money. Female agricultural workers contributed significantly to household income, but they lacked education, health and other support services and frequently do not have access to economic resources.

Sabarwal (2003)[9] in "Gender Bias within Household: Evidences from India" has revealed out of the all the factors studied female labour free participation rates seem to be most unambiguously related to lowering female mortality at all age levels. Labour force participation of women increases their economic worth and thereby their survival chances as more resources are allocated to them within the household. Female labour force participation rates indicate opportunities available to women to earn an independent income through paid employment. This opportunity tends to enhance the social standing of a woman in the household and the society.

EMPIRICAL STUDY: RESULTS AND DISCUSSION

Participation of women agricultural workers in decision-making is a fairly good indicator of their status. Sivagangai district, Tamil Nadu is purposively chosen as the study area for reasons such as (i) it is one of the backward districts of Tamil Nadu; (ii) it is one of the drought vulnerable districts of Tamil Nadu; (iii) it is one of the districts having lower level of human development; (iv) it is also one of the two districts (Sivagangai and Ramanathapuram) where cropping intensity is unity indicating the absence of more than once crop being raised; (v) it is the district where irrigation intensity is high as compared to that of Ramanathapuram reflecting the severity of the dry land agriculture therein; and (vi) it has low work participation rate (11th rank in Tamil Nadu) with relatively higher female work participation rate (4th rank in Tamil Nadu).

The geographical advantage of the district under study provided an opportunity to compare and contrast the living conditions of agricultural labourers in unirrigated area with those of irrigated area. For this, the sample was drawn from both irrigated and unirrigated regions. The classification of the district under study into irrigated and unirrigated regions was made on the basis of the irrigation intensity at taluk level. A taluk with the highest irrigation intensity was taken to represent irrigated area while the taluk with the lowest irrigation intensity was chosen to characterize the unirrigated area. The analysis of irrigation intensity revealed that Manamadurai taluk had the highest irrigation intensity while Illayankudi taluk had the lowest irrigation intensity. Accordingly, Manamadurai taluk was considered as irrigated region whereas Illayankudi taluk was termed as unirrigated region.

Decision-making process of agricultural women workers in home operations of the study area are classified into two groups i.e., irrigated area (Manamadurai Taluk) and unirrigated area (Ilayangudi Taluk). To know the extent of participation and pattern of decision-making process of women in home operations, few areas are selected keeping in mind their importance for development. The extent of participation of women in different areas of decisions related to home activities are (1) Construction of a house (2) Deciding education of children (3) Marriage of children (4) Consumption of household articles (5) Collection and preparation of food (6) Borrowing and giving loans (7) Attending functions (8) Attending social gatherings and (9) Deciding family planning

Data regarding extent and pattern of participation of agricultural women workers in different areas of decisions related to home activities are presented in Tables 1 to 9.

Construction of a House

Decision on construction of a house is gaining importance as housing is spreading to rural areas and its utility is being realised. It has been observed from the study that in majority of the cases, women has nil or no participation in construction of a house. In the case of irrigated area, the participation of women in construction of a house are higher than the unirrigated area. The pattern of decision-making of women in home activities data shows that irrigated area has 30.67 per cent on construction of a house, whereas the unirrigated area has only 18.67 per cent. The overall pattern of participation of women is 24.67 per cent, which

Table 1
Extent of Participation of Women in Decision-making—Manamadurai Taluk

Decision-making Areas	*Extent of Participation*				
	Nil	*Only consulted*	*Opinion considered*	*Final Dec...n*	*Total*
Construction of a house	92	28	16	14	150
	(61.33)	(18.67)	(10.67)	(9.33)	(100.00)
Deciding education of children	52	39	26	33	150
	(34.67)	(26.00)	(17.33)	(22.00)	(100.00)
Setting marriage of children	34	56	31	29	150
	(22.67)	(37.33)	(20.67)	(19.33)	(100.00)
Purchasing household articles	80	37	18	15	150
	(53.33)	(24.67)	(12.00)	(10.00)	(100.00)
Collection & Preparation of food	'54	17	33	46	150
	(36.00)	(11.33)	(22.00)	(30.67)	(100.00)
Borrowing & giving loans	101	13	17	19	150
	(67.33)	(8.67)	(11.33)	(12.67)	(100.00)
Attending functions	96	23	18	13	150
	(64.00)	(15.33)	(12.00)	(8.67)	(100.00)
Attending social gatherings	75	26	23	26	150
	(50.00)	(17.33)	(15.33)	(17.33)	(100.00)
Deciding family planning	09	12	23	28	72
	(12.50)	(16.67)	(31.94)	(38.89)	(100.00)

Note: The figures in parentheses indicate the percentage of their respective categories.

Table 2
Extent of Participation of Women in Decision-making–Ilanyangodi Taluk

Decision-making Areas	*Extent of Participation*				
	Nil	*Only consulted*	*Opinion considered*	*Final Decision*	*Total*
Construction of a New house	113	14	12	11	150
	(75.33)	(9.33)	(8.00)	(7.33)	(100.00)
Deciding education of children	86	21	21	22	150
	(57.33)	(14.00)	(14.00)	(14.67)	(100.00)
Setting marriage of children	99	19	17	15	150
	(66.00)	(12.67)	(11.33)	(10.00)	(100.00)
Purchasing household articles	108	15	13	14	150
	(72.00)	(10.00)	(8.67)	(9.33)	(100.00)
Collection & Preparation of food	95	23	17	15	150
	(63.33)	(15.33)	(11.33)	(10.00)	(100.00)
Borrowing & giving loans	80	26	25	19	150
	(53.33)	(17.33)	(16.67)	(12.67)	(100.00)
Attending functions	74	26	23	27	150
	(49.33)	(17.33)	(15.33)	(18.00)	(100.00)
Attending social gatherings	69	33	24	24	150
	(46.00)	(22.00)	(16.00)	(16.00)	(100.00)
Deciding family planning	15	05	19	30	69
	(21.74)	(7.25)	(27.54)	(43.47)	(100.00)

Note: The figures in parentheses indicate the percentage of their respective categories

Table 3

Extent of Participation of Women in Decision-making–Total

Decision-making Areas	*Extent of Participation*				
	Nil	*Only Consulted*	*Opinion Considered*	*Final Decision*	*Total*
Construction of a New house	205 (68.33)	42 (14.00)	28 (9.33)	25 (8.33)	300 (100.00)
Deciding education of children	138 (46.00)	60 (20.00)	47 (15.67)	55 (18.33)	300 (100.00)
Setting marriage of children	133 (44.33)	75 (25.00)	58 (19.33)	34 (11.33)	300 (100.00)
Purchasing household articles	188 (62.67)	52 (17.33)	31 (10.33)	29 (9.67)	300 (100.00)
Collection & Preparation of food	149 (49.67)	40 (13.33)	50 (16.67)	61 (20.33)	300 (100.00)
Borrowing & giving loans	181 (60.33)	39 (13.00)	42 (14.00)	38 (12.67)	300 (100.00)
Attending functions	170 (56.67)	49 (16.33)	41 (13.67)	40 (13.33)	300 (100.00)
Attending social gatherings	144 (48.00)	59 (19.67)	47 (15.67)	50 (16.67)	300 (100.00)
Deciding family planning	24 (17.02)	17 (12.06)	42 (29.79)	58 (41.13)	141 (100.00)

Note: The figures in parentheses indicate the percentage of their respective categories.

Table 4
Pattern of Decision-making–Manamadurai Taluk

	Who Made Decision								
Decision-making Areas	*W*	*WH*	*WHO*	*WO*	*H*	*HO*	*0*	*Total*	*WP*
Construction of a New house	09	20	10	07	64	23	17	150	46
	(6.00)	(13.33)	(6.67)	(4.67)	(42.67)	(15.33)	(11.33)	(100.00)	(30.67)
Deciding education of children	28	34	08	06	44	20	10	150	76
	(18.67)	(22.67)	(5.33)	(4.00)	(29.33)	(13.33)	(6.67)	(100.00)	(50.67)
Setting marriage of children	24	68	11	06	25	10	06	150	109
	(16.00)	(45.33)	(7.33)	(4.00)	(16.67)	(6.67)	(4.00)	(100.00)	(72.67)
Purchasing household articles	10	34	08	06	68	16	08	150	58
	(6.67)	(22.67)	(5.33)	(4.00)	(45.33)	(10.67)	(5.33)	(100.00)	(38.67)
Collection & Preparation of food	41	31	06	05	47	15	05	150	83
	(27.33)	(20.67)	(4.00)	(3.33)	(31.33)	(10.00)	(3.33)	(100.00)	(55.33)
Borrowing & giving loans	14	07	04	04	94	20	07	150	29
	(9.33)	(4.67)	(2.67)	(2.67)	(62.67)	(13.33)	(4.67)	(100.00)	(19.33)
Attending functions	08	18	06	05	85	22	06	150	37
	(5.33)	(12.00)	(4.00)	(3.33)	(56.67)	(14.67)	(4.00)	(100.00)	(24.67)
Attending social gatherings	21	28	10	06	64	17	04	150	65
	(14.00)	(18.67)	(6.67)	(4.00)	(42.67)	(11.33)	(2.67)	(100.00)	(43.33)
Deciding family planning	31	11	04	04	12	08	02	72	50
	(43.06)	15.28)	(5.55)	(5.55)	(16.67)	(11.11)	(2.78)	(100.00)	(69.44)

W = Women alone, WH = Women and her husband, WHO = Women, her husband and other family members, WO = Women and other family members, H = Husband alone, HO = Husband and other family members, 0 = other family members.

Note: The figures in parentheses indicate the percentage of their respective categories.

Table 5

Pattern of Decision-making–Ilayangudi Taluk

Decision-making Areas	*Who Made Decision*								
	W	*WH*	*WHO*	*WO*	*H*	*HO*	*0*	*Total*	*WP*
	W	WH	WHO	WO	H	HO	0	Total	WP
Construction of a New house	06	11	06	05	95	19	08	150	28
	(4.00)	(7.33)	(4.00)	(3.33)	(63.33)	(12.67)	(5.33)	(100.00)	(18.67)
Deciding education of children	17	26	12	06	79	06	04	150	61
	(11.33)	(17.33)	(8.00)	(4.00)	(52.67)	(4.00)	(2.67)	(100.00)	(40.67)
Setting marriage of children	10	19	12	06	88	09	06	ISO	47
	(6.67)	(12.67)	(8.00)	(4.00)	(58.67)	(6.00)	(4.00)	(100.00)	(31.33)
Purchasing household articles	09	14	07	04	99	11	06	150	34
	(6.00)	(9.33)	(4.67)	(2.67)	(66.00)	(7.33)	(4.00)	(100.00)	(22.67)
Collection & Preparation of food	10	26	11	06	82	11	04	150	53
	(6.67)	(17.33)	(7.33)	(4.00)	(54.67)	(7.33)	(2.67)	(100.00)	(35.33)
Borrowing & giving loans	14	22	09	05	74	20	06	150	50
	(9.33)	(14.67)	(6.00)	(3.33)	(49.33)	(13.33)	(4.00)	(100.00)	(33.33)
Attending functions	22	28	12	07	66	10	05	150	69
	(14.67)	(18.67)	(8.00)	(4.67)	(44.00)	(6.67)	(3.33)	(100.00)	(46.00)
Attending social gatherings	19	24	16	07	65	13	06	150	66
	(12.67)	(16.00)	(10.67)	(4.67)	(43.33)	(8.67)	(4.00)	(100.00)	(44.00)
Deciding family planning	34	09	09	08	05	02	02	69	60
	(49.28)	(13.04)	(13.04)	(11.59)	(7.25)	(2.90)	(2.90)	(100.00)	(86.96)

W = Women alone, WH = Women and her husband, WHO = Women, her husband and other family members, Wo = Women and other family members, H = Husband alone, HO = Husband and other family members, 0= other family members.

Note: The figures in parentheses indicate the percentage oftheir respective categories

Table 6
Pattern of Decision-making–Total

Decision-making Areas	*Who Made Decision*								
	W	*WH*	*WHO*	*WO*	*H*	*HO*	*0*	*Total*	*WP*
Construction of a New house	15	31	16	12	159	42	25	300	74
	(5.00)	(10.33)	(5.33)	(4.00)	(53.00)	(14.00)	(83.33)	(100.00)	(24.67)
Deciding education of children	45	60	20	12	123	26	14	300	137
	(15.00)	(20.00)	(6.67)	(4.00)	(41.00)	(8.67)	(4.67)	(100.00)	(45.67)
Setting marriage of children	34	87	23	12	113	19	12	300	156
	(11.33)	(29.00)	(7.76)	(4.00)	(37.67)	(6.33)	(4.00)	(100.00)	(52.00)
Purchasing household articles	19	48	15	10	167	29	14	300	92
	(6.33)	(16.00)	(5.00)	(3.33)	(55.67)	(9.67)	(4.67)	(100.00)	(30.67)
Collection & Preparation of food	51	57	17	11	129	26	9	300	136
	(17.00)	(19.00)	(5.67)	(3.67)	(43.00)	(8.67)	(3.00)	(100.00)	(45.33)
Borrowing & giving loans	28	29	13	09	168	40	13	300	79
	(9.33)	(9.67)	(4.33)	(3.00)	(56.00)	(13.33)	(4.33)	(100.00)	(26.33)
Attending functions	30	46	18	12	151	32	11	300	106
	(10.00)	(15.33)	(6.00)	(4.00)	(50.33)	(10.67)	(3.67)	(100.00)	(35.33)
Attending social gatherings	40	52	26	13	129	30	10	300	131
	(13.33)	(17.33)	(8.67)	(4.33)	(43.00)	(10.00)	(3.33)	(100.00)	(43.67)
Deciding family planning	65	20	13	12	17	10	04	141	110
	(46.10)	(14.18)	(9.22)	(8.51)	(12.06)	(7.09)	(2.84)	(100.00)	(78.01)

W = Women alone, WH = Women and her husband, WHO = Women, her husband and other family members, WO = Women and other family members, H = Husband alone, HO = Husband and other family members, 0 = other family members.

Note: The figures in parentheses indicate the percentage of their respective categories

Table 7
Factors Affecting Participation of Women in Decision-making Process–Manamadurai Taluk

Particulars	*Level of Participation*			
	Low	*Medium*	*High*	*Total*
Age (Years)				
14-30	32 (40.51)	39 (49.37)	8 (10.13)	79 (52.67)
31-45	12 (40.00)	15 (50.00)	3 (10.00)	30 (20.00)
46-60	15 (46.88)	14 (43.75)	3 (9.38)	32 (21.33)
61& above	3 (33.33)	5 (55.56)	1 (11.11)	09 (6.00)
Level of Education				
Illiterate	16 (37.21)	23 (53.49)	4 (9.30)	43 (28.67)
Primary	34 (38.20)	46 (51.69)	9 (10.11)	89 (59.33)
Secondary	4 (28.57)	7 (50.00)	3 (21.43)	14 (9.33)
Higher & above	1 (25.00)	2 (50.00)	1 (25.00)	04 (2.67)
Type of Family				
Nuclear	36 (40.00)	41 (45.56)	13 (14.44)	90 (60.00)
Joint	22 (36.67)	36 (60.00)	2 (3.33)	60 (40.00)
Caste				
Backward Class	26 (37.14)	39 (55.71)	5 (7.14)	70 (46.67)
SC/ST	26 (32.50)	43 (53.75)	11 (13.75)	80 (53.33)
Land Ownership				
Landless	40 (35.71)	54 (48.21)	18 (16.07)	112 (74.67)
Below I Ha	12 (40.00)	15 (50.00)	3 (10.00)	30 (20.00)
Between 1-2 Ha	2 (28.57)	3 (42.86)	2 (28.57)	07 (4.67)
Between 2-3 Ha	0 (0)	1 (100.00)	0 (0)	01 (0.67)
Economic Status				
Lower	37(52.86)	29(41.43)	4(5.71)	70(46.67)
Medium	24(36.92)	30(46.15)	11(16.92)	65(43.33)
Higher	5(33.33)	8(53.33)	2(13.33)	15(10.00)

Note: The figures in parentheses indicate the percentage of their respective categories

Table 8
Factors Affecting Participation of Women in Decision-making Process–Ilayangudi Taluk

Particulars	*Level of Participation*			
	Low	*Medium*	*High*	*Total*
Age (Years)				
14-30	33 (42.31)	35 (44.87)	10 (12.82)	78 (52.00)
31-45	7 (33.33)	12 (57.14)	2 (9.52)	21 (14.00)
46-60	11 (31.43)	17 (48.57)	4 (11.43)	35 (23.33)
61 & above	6 (37.50)	8 (50.00)	2 (12.50)	16 (10.67)
Level of Education				
Illiterate	26 (44.07)	27 (45.76)	6 (10.17)	59 (39.33)
Primary	38 (46.91)	36 (44.44)	7 (8.64)	81 (54.00)
Secondary	3 (37.50)	4 (50.00)	1 (12.50)	08 (5.33)
Higher & above	0 (0)	2 (100.00)	0 (0)	02 (1.33)
Type of Family				
Nuclear	39 (45.88)	34 (40.00)	12 (14.12)	85 (56.67)
Joint	26 (40.00)	33 (50.77)	6 (9.23)	65 (43.33)
Caste				
Backward Class	29 (44.62)	30 (46.15)	6 (9.23)	65 (43.33)
SC/ST	36 (42.35)	39 (45.88)	10 (11.76)	35 (56.67)
Land Ownership				
Landless	44 (35.77)	69 (56.10)	10 (8.13)	123 (82.00)
Below I Ha	11 (47.83)	9 (39.13)	3 (13.04)	23 (15.33)
Between 1-2 Ha	1 (25.00)	2 (50.00)	1 (25.00)	04 (2.67)
Between 2-3 Ha	0(0)	0(0)	0 (0)	0 (0)
Economic Status				
Lower	39 (45.88)	38 (44.71)	8 (9.41)	85 (56.67)
Medium	23 (38.33)	31 (51.67)	6 (10.00)	60 (40.00)
Higher	1 (20.00)	3 (60.00)	1 (20.00)	5 (3.33)

Note: The figures in parentheses indicate the percentage of their respective categories.

Table 9
Factors Affecting Participation of Women in Decision-making Process– Total

Particulars	*Level of Participation*			
	Low	*Medium*	*High*	*Total*
Age (Years)				
14-30	65 (41.40)	74 (47.13)	18 (11.47)	157 (52.33)
31-45	19 (37.25)	27 (52.94)	5 (9.80)	51 (17.00)
46-60	26 (38.81)	31 (46.27)	7 (10.45)	67 (22.33)
61 & above	9 (36.00)	13 (52.00)	3 (12.00)	25 (8.33)
Level of Education				
Illiterate	42 (41.18)	50 (49.02)	10 (9.80)	102 (34.00)
Primary	72 (42.35)	82 (48.24)	16 (9.41)	107 (56.67)
Secondary	7 (31.82)	11 (50.00)	4 (18.18)	22 (7.33)
Higher & above	1 (16.67)	4 (66.67)	1 (16.67)	06 (2.00)
Type of Family				
Nuclear	75 (42.86)	75 (42.86)	25 (14.28)	175 (58.33)
Joint	48 (38.40)	69 (55.20)	8 (6.40)	125(41.67)
Caste				
Backward Class	55 (40.74)	69 (51.11)	11 (8.15)	135(45.00)
SC/ST	62 (37.58)	82 (49.70)	21 (12.72)	165 (55.00)
Land Ownership				
Landless	84 (35.74)	123 (52.34)	28 (11.91)	235 (78.33)
Below I Ha	23 (43.40)	24 (45.28)	6 (11.32)	53 (17.67)
Between 1-2 Ha	3 (27.27)	5 (45.46)	3 (27.27)	11 (3.67)
Between 2-3 Ha	0 (0)	1 (100.00)	0 (0)	01 (0.33)
Economic Status				
Lower	76 (49.03)	67 (43.23)	12 (7.74)	155 (51.67)
Medium	47 (37.60)	61 (48.80)	17 (13.60)	125 (41.67)
Higher	6 (30.00)	11 (55.00)	3 (15.00)	20 (6.67)

Note: The figures in parentheses indicate the percentage of their respective categories

shows that women are not able to have any influence on decision-making on construction of a house. In irrigated area, husband of the respondents is only deciding factor i.e. the pattern of decision-making on construction of a house is 42.67 per cent. In the case of unirrigated area, the percentage of pattern of decision-making on construction of a house by husband of the respondents is 63.33, which is higher than irrigated area. The overall pattern of husband deciding the decisions on construction of house is 53 per cent. This explains how agricultural women workers have been marginalised, neglected in decisions related to home activities.

Education of Children

Decision regarding education of children is gaining importance as education is spreading to rural areas and its utility is being realised. It includes such areas as age of sending children to school, in which school to send, subjects to be taken and level of education. Out of these, women's participation is assessed only in decisions regarding level of education as, for age and type of school; there is hardly any choice because there are generally schools run by Government having fixed minimum age for admission. As majority of the women workers are ignorant and illiterate, they have no clear knowledge about subjects. As regards extent of participation of respondents in decision about the level of education, it is found that majority of the respondents (46 per cent) are having no participation at all in decision-making followed by 20.00 per cent, who are only consulted and 18.33 per cent of women who made final decision for action. As regards decision-making pattern in the family, it is observed that in majority of the households (41 per cent), it is decided by husband only. Respondents are involved in participation on decision-making in level of education is found to be 45.67 per cent. In terms of comparisons on the basis of level of education between irrigated and unirrigated area, irrigated area has higher percentage (50.67) of women's participation than unirrigated area, which has only 40.67 per cent. This difference mainly because, the respondents of irrigated area has more saying in the family than the respondents of unirrigated area, relatively higher level of education, knowledge, etc. over respondents of unirrigated area.

Marriage of Children

Marriage is a social and economic compulsion in the society, practiced from the early days of human history. Even though it is a compulsion but it is cumbersome for rural societies. It is very difficult to set the marriage of their children in the agriculture societies because agricultural societies are having more number of children in their family. Therefore, it is a Himalayan task for the respondents for setting marriage for their children. In the present study it is 116 respondents in irrigated area, 51 respondents in unirraged area and 167 respondents of the total sample as a whole were participated in decision on setting marriage of children. In the case of irriaged area, it is evident that the more number of respondents has a participation in decision than unirrigated area; this is because of backward nature of domestic and social status prevalence in the unirriaged area. As regards to the pattern of decision-making on setting marriage of children, it is found that in more than half of the households, husband (32.00 per cent) and wife and husband jointly (28.67 per cent) decide about setting marriage of children in irrigated area. In the case of unirrigated area, it is found that in more than half of the household, husband alone takes the decisions. It is also evidence that, when area is irriageted or developed, then there is a more chance for more women participation. The overall district position in pattern of decision-making of women in setting marriage of children is 52.00 per cent, which shows a relatively better status than decision on other household activities.

Consumption of Household Articles

The socio-economic status can be measured by many factors including the consumption. Consumption level plays a vital role in deciding the status of the families in the rural society. Purchasing of any articles by household depend on their income, taste, etc. In the case of rural family system, the purchasing of household articles mostly decided and done by men folk. When development takes place in the special area or in a specific family, then there may be a chance for women to have more participation in decision-making on purchasing of household articles. Extent of participation of respondents in deciding about purchasing household articles in irrigated area reveals that majority of the respondents (53.33 per cent) are having no participation at all in decision-making followed by 24.67 per cent who are only consulted, 12.00 per cent of women whose opinion is considered for action, and only 10 per cent of the respondents are involved in final decision-making. As regards in the unirrigated area, it is found that majority of the respondents (72.00 per cent) are having no participation at all in decision-making followed by 10 per cent of the respondents are only consulted and 9.33 per cent of the respondents is involved in final decision. It is observed that in the unirrigated area more number of women having no participation than irrigated area on decision on purchasing household articles. As regards decision-making pattern in the family, it is observed that in majority of the households (45.33 per cent- irrigated area; 66.00 per cent- unirrigated area and 55.67 per cent district as a whole) it is husband alone decide about the purchasing of household articles followed by women and her husband jointly (22.67 per cent in irrigated area; 9.33 per cent in unirrigated area and 16 per cent in the district) i.e., it is jointly decided by respondent and her husband. Thus, decision on purchasing of household articles also has higher participation of women in irrigated area than unirrigated area.

Collection and Preparation of Food

Primarily women are engaged in collection and preparation of food in all the communities. In the case of rural and agricultural communities, women has complete or more participation in collection and preparation of food. This process requires a special skill, which most of the women naturally have. As it has been observed from the data, about 74 per cent of respondent in irrigated area and 36.67 per cent of respondents in unirrigated area are participating in decisions on collection and preparation of food. In irrigated area most of the women are able to decide what they want to prepare the food for the family, whereas in unirrigated area their role in decisions on collection and preparation of food is negligible. As regards to extent of participation of women in decisions on collection and preparation of food indicates that around 45.33 per cent of respondents are participated in the decisions. Within the district the irrigated area has 53.33 per cent and the unirrigated area has only 35.33 per cent of participation on decision on collection and preparation of food. In irrigated areas, the participation in pattern of decisions are shared by husband alone (31.33 per cent) women alone (27.33 per cent) and women and her husband jointly (20.67 per cent). Whereas in the case of unirrigated area, the decisions are mostly done by husband alone (54.67 per cent) followed by women and her husband jointly (17.33 per cent) This fact reveals that irrigated area has more saying for women in decision on collection and preparation of food than unirrigated area, where husband alone dominate.

Borrowing and Giving Loans

Decision in this regard comprised of whether to borrow or not or to give or not, from where to borrow and how much amount to borrow and other related matters. In the present study, extent of participation of respondents indicates that about 67.33 per cent of women have no participation in the decision on borrowing and giving loans, where as it is 53.33 per cent in unirrigated area. The women respondents who made a final decision in irrigated areas are 12.67 per cent and it is also 12.67 per cent in unirrigated area. As regards decision-making pattern in the family, it is found that in more than half of the household husband alone decided about borrowing money for consumption and other and giving loans in both irrigated and unirrigated areas. But, in irrigated area the husband alone deciding the borrowing and giving loans is 62.67

per cent whereas in unirrigated area it is 49.33 per cent per cent. This data reveals that even in the irrigated area husband has more participation in decision on borrowing and giving loans. This is not favourable trend for women. This kind of situation must be changed through creating awareness and by developing educational facilities for women. The participation of women in decision-making on borrowing and giving loans is 19.33 per cent in irrigated area whereas in unirrigated area it was 33.33 per cent. The district level pattern of participation of women is 26.33 per cent, which gives bad impact upon the society. It should be changed through proper policy measures.

Attending Functions

Participation in decisions on attending functions is a concrete measure to know the social status of respondents of the family. Attending functions by women respondents indicates that how much women has a freedom to decide and attend the functions. In the present study, the decision on attending functions by the respondents in irrigated area, 64 per cent of the respondents has no participation in decision, followed by 15.33 per cent of women are only consulted and only 8.67 per cent of respondent are made final decision As regards in unirrigated area, 49.33 per cent of the respondents has no participation in decisions followed by final decision are made by 18 per cent of the respondents. With reference to pattern of decision-making by women in irrigated area, it is found that more than half of the households (56.67 per cent) husband alone decided about attending functions. In unirrigated area also husband alone (44 per cent) decide the decision on attending functions.

Attending Social Gathering

In our society, attending social gathering is routine and compulsory one because our rural society is known for many social gatherings. Participation of women in decisions on attending social gathering is a unique one in our agricultural societies. In the present study it is inferred that participation in decision-making in the family, nearly

50 per cent of the respondents has no participation in decisions in irrigated area followed by 17.33 per cent of respondents are only consulted and 17.33 per cent of respondent are made the final decision. In the case of unirriaged area, it is found that 46 per cent of respondents has no participation in decisions followed by 22 per cent of women are only consulted and 16 per cent of respondents are made the final decision. As regards the pattern of decision-making in both irrigated and unirrigated area, husband alone (42.67 per cent and 43.33 per cent) decided to attend social gatherings.

Deciding Family Planning

As it has been observed from the data, nearly half of the women respondent's had adopted family planning measures. They are the ones who are most affected by adoption or non-adoption of family planning. Thus, an attempt is made to know their participation in decision-making about family planning. It is found that in majority of the cases (38.89 per cent) respondents are found to be participating in final decision-making followed by women whose opinion are considered (31.94 per cent) and 16.67 per cent of women are only consulted in irrigated area. In the case of unirrigated area, majority of the cases (43.47 per cent) respondents are found to be participating in final decision followed by 27.54 per cent of the respondents of women opinion are considered. As regards the pattern of decision-making on deciding family planning, it is found that 69.44 per cent of women participation in irrigated area and 86.96 per cent of respondents in unirrigated area. The difference in pattern of decisions is explained by socio-economic status of the family of these villages.

FACTORS AFFECTING PARTICIPATION OF WOMEN WORKERS IN DECISION-MAKING PROCESS

Participation of women in decision-making process on home activities and its extent and pattern depends on various factors. For knowing the relationship between participation in decision-making and other variables, scores of 0, 1,2 and 3 are awarded as per extent of participation (i.e.) Nil-0, consulted-1 opinion considered-2 and final decision-3 for each of the area related to home activities. Sum of the scores is divided with the number of areas applicable to that respondent in order to get average score for getting overall level of participation of the respondent in decision related to home activities. The minimum obtainable score i.e., 3 was divided into 3 parts to get low (up to 1) medium (1.01-2.00) and high (2.01-3.00) level of participation. Data regarding relationship between level of participation in decision on home activities and different variable is presented in Table numbers 4, 5 and 6. As it reveals in Table 4 that in irrigated area, the age group of 14-30 years and 31-45 years have medium level of participation than other age groups. Respondents with higher level of participation are more in the lower age groups. Those with low level of participation are lower in the higher age groups.

Education came out to be an important variable influencing the involvement of women, as more than two - third of illiterate and primary education level respondents are having low level of participation. As many as 53.49 per cent and 51.69 per cent illiterate and primary level education respondents also having medium level participation. Whether the family is nuclear or joint also affected to a great extent the participation of women in decision-making process as these two variables are having significant association. It is observed that 45.56 per cent of the respondents from nuclear families are having medium level participation and respondents of joint families (60.00 per cent) are also having medium level of participation. At the same time, nuclear family respondents are having higher level of participation than joint family.

Caste of the respondents and level of participation in decision-making are having significant association. Respondents with high level of participation in the SC/ST groups are low compared to Backward class group. Land ownership of women is a different phenomenon in rural societies. Participation of women in decision-making and land ownership has a strong association. Most of the respondents of the study area are landless women workers and it is evident from the study that when the higher level of land ownership, the participation on decision is higher. As regards association between socio-economic status and participation level in decision-making, it is also evident from the data that the level of participation is lower for women belonging to medium socio-economic status group as compared to higher socio economic status group. In the case of unirrigated area, the association between the age of the respondents and the level of participation reveals that most of the respondents of 14-30 years of age group have medium level of participation and only 12.50 per cent of higher age group respondents have higher level of participation. As regards the association between the level of education and participation level, since in the unirrigated area most of respondents are illiterate and has only primary education, their participation is at only medium level. More than half of the respondents belong to the nuclear family group in the unirrigated area. The respondents of joint family have relatively more in medium level of participation than nuclear family group and nuclear family group has higher participation level than joint family group. The caste group of the respondents and their participation level explained that SC and ST respondents have higher level of participation than Backward class in decisions. In the unirrigated area majority of the respondents are landless women workers but with land owning respondents, it is found that higher land ownership group has of lower level of participation in decisions. The socio-economic status of the respondents are also influenced the decision of women respondents. The respondent who has lower level of economic status is participating at higher level.

On the whole, district level data shows that only the 14-30 age group of respondents has higher level of participation than higher age groups In terms of association between level of education and level of participation in decisions mostly illiterate and the respondents who has only primary education has higher level of participation. In case of family type of the respondents, the respondent of the nuclear family groups has higher level of participation than joint family and majority of respondents of joint family has of medium level of participation in decisions. The Backward class caste group has relatively low in higher participation in decisions than SC and ST group. It is unique fact that most of the respondents of the study area are landless women workers and the association between landowning respondents and level of participation in decisions reveals that higher level of land ownership has lower level of participation. The socio-economic status of the respondents is also influencing the level of participation. At the district level lower and medium economic status respondents has higher level of participation in decisions.

SUMMARY AND CONCLUSION

The present study focuses on participation of women in decision-making process of unirrigated area on home operations. As regards the extent of participation, in majority of the home decisions, the level of participation for women are nil or low and only smaller percentage of respondents are made the final decision on home activities. The pattern of decision-making in home operations also reveals that the level of participation generally are low in all the home activities except the area on deciding family planning (86.96 per cent) where the women has highest level of participation. The level of participation in decision on home activities, husband alone is decided almost all the decisions except the decision on family planning. The areas like construction of a new house, decorating the house, household repairs and purchasing household articles were highly male dominated decisions. The only one area i.e. deciding family planning is decided women alone in majority of the cases.

As regards the level of participation of women in home decisions between the irrigated and unirrigated area of the district, it is found that in majority of the home decisions the level of participation of women are low. Only few areas of decision-making process like deciding family planning has higher level of participation by women in both irrigated and unirrigated area of the district. It is to be noted that irrigated area has higher level of participation by women in majority of the home decisions than unirrigated area of the district.

As regards the level of participation in home decisions by women of unirrigated area, it is observed that in the unirrigated area also, the factors like age, level of education of respondents, the type of family, caste, land holdings and economic status are influenced more on the level of participation of women. In the study area, majority of women has lower level of participation in home decisions because most of the respondents are illiterate, landless and belonging to SC/ST group. In terms of comparison between irrigated and unirrigated area with regards to factors affecting the level of participation of women in home decisions, it is found that irrigated area has higher degree of association between the level of participation on decisions and factors like age, caste, type of family etc. than unirrigated area. Participation of women in decision-making process in home operations is affected by a number of factors. Various characteristics of the respondents are found to be influencing their participation in decision-making. Women of 14-30 years and 31-45 years age group are involved more in decision-making related to home operations as in rural societies the status of women usually increases with the increasing age. Elder women are considered more important for consultation before making the final decision due to their experience. Educated women are also found to be influencing the decision in the family due to more exposure about the world. They are able to discuss family matters with husband and other family members. In nuclear families the participation of women in decisions is found to be more as compared to joint families as in joint families there are other members to whom the wife can consult whereas in nuclear families, husband is the only consultant for the wife before embarking the final decision.

The factors affecting the participation of women in decision-making process of women in home activities of irrigated and unirrigated area reveals that there is a strong association between the level of participation on decisions and factors like age, level of education type of family caste, land holding and economic status, It is found that majority of the women respondents are illiterate, landless, lower economic status and socially backward. These reasons are influencing the decision-making process of women in home activities. Because of this environment, majority of the women has no or low level of participation in majority of the decision-making areas in home activities of irrigated and unirrigated area of the study.

SUGGESTIONS AND POLICY IMPLICATIONS

Women agricultural workers are not a matter of choice but a matter of economic compulsion to supplement the family income. Women agricultural workers are facing many problems like poor living conditions, pathetic working conditions, very long working hours, low (absolute/relative) wages, wage discrimination in terms of gender etc. The extent of participation of women agricultural workers in the decision-making process shows that all the women agricultural workers are engaging women fully or partially i.e., the participation and contribution of women is significant but they are receiving of poor response from the family. This condition leads to a situation, where women are notable to decide for their way at family activities. The husband and other members of family are influencing mere in decision-making process of family work. Women agricultural workers act as a family head in many households but in real terms, the men folk and other family members are making the decisions and ignoring the women's choice. This will create gender bias in decision-making process in family work. In order to improve the conditions of women agricultural workers and to strengthen their decision-making power, the following are the specific actions to be taken.

The educational status of women agricultural workers needs immediate attention in order to create awareness and educational training facilities.

National and International institutions are urged to adopt codes of conduct guaranteeing that neither they nor their sub-contractors will employ women workers in conditions that violate their right.

There is a problem of the absence of effective implementation of labour laws. The government should form a committee under the chairmanship of retired academician (University Professor), inclusive of members from agricultural workers, government officials, non-government organizations and more importantly members of women agricultural workers. This committee will act as 'suggestive body' for strengthening the conditions of women workers particularly women agricultural workers and try to make good understanding about women agricultural workers in order to strengthen the decision-making power.

The available evidence shows that the women's participation in the total labour force is very low and a vast majority of them are engaged in agricultural operations. They have to come on the front line to accept the challenge if they are displaced from their work. The farm operations in which women's participation is maximum are labour-intensive and involve drudgery. The technologies available in research institutes suggest that most of them are male oriented and there are very few technologies pertaining to farm operations exclusively preformed by women. Therefore, studies should be conducted to identify the farm operations performed by women in different agro-climatic and socio-economic situations and research efforts should be geared up to the development of appropriate techniques whose adoption will reduce the drudgery of women and improve their efficiency and physical output.

The policies of the Government must recognise the actual role of the women labour force and especially of the rural women. The main potential for the women labour absorption in India is agriculture and allied occupations such as food grains processing, dairy, poultry and fishery as well as forestry including collection and sale of forest products and the development of these occupations must get the due preference. Besides, the Public Works

Department and engineering departments, the Khadi and Village Industries Commission, the handloom, coir, silk and other such small scale industries may provide more gainful job opportunities to the women workers. The voluntary organizations may also provide more job opportunities and training facilities to the women workers. But to enable women to participate economically in an effective manner requires certain pre conditions. First, articulation of their own feelings, fears, needs and potential to the intervening groups who must share their problems and instill confidence in these to organise is very much needed. Formation of grass root organisations, co-operatives could initially provide effective answers to solutions.

The wage structure and working conditions of women workers should also be improved. They are the weaker section of the society and they must get incentives and protection. Since farm women constitute a substantial share of female workforce, they should be "Target Group" for all the welfare programs and policy proposals undertaken by the Government. Women's organisations can also play an important role in awakening the women workforce and they can act as policymaking body in order to change the attitudes towards work, earning and standard of living of women agricultural workers.

Notes and References

1. Rani, Jhansi and Bhave. A. M. (1981), 'Decision-making Pattern Among Rural Families', *Indian Journal of Adult Education,* Vol. 42, No. 9, pp. 17-20.

1. Burnad Fatima (1984), 'Rural Development and Women's Liberation-Caste, Class and Gender in a Grass-roots Organization in Tamil Nadu, South India', *IDS Bulletin,* Vol. 15, No. 1, Institute of Development Studies, Sussex, pp. 45-50.

3. Laxmi Devi (1988), *'Rural Women-Management in Farm and Home',* Northern Book Centre, New Delhi, pp. 81-122.

4. Poonam Sharma (1995), 'The Impact of Women Workforce in the Unorganised Sector on Household Management: A Study of Agra City', *Political Economy Journal of India,* Vol. A, No. 1, pp. 63-69.

5. Jayshree Vencatesan (1996), "Women's Multiple Roles and Coping Strategies: Myths and Realities", *Indian Journal of Gender Studies,* Vol. 3, No. 1, pp. 39-56.

6. Lakshmy Devi K. R. (1996), "Determinants of Labour Force Participation among Women in Kerala-Some Evidence from a Micro-Level Study", The *Asian Economic Review,* Vol. 38, No. 1, pp. 102-115.

7. Vanaja Dhruvarajan (1996), "Hinduism, Empowerment of Women and Development in India", *Labour, Capital and Society,* Vol. 29, Nos. 1 and 2, pp. 16-40.

8. Usha Tuteja (2000), "Contribution of Female Agricultural Workers in Family Income and their Status in Haryana", *Indian Journal of Agricultural Economics,* Vol. 55, No.2, April-June, pp. 136-148.

9. Shwetlena Sabarwal (2003), "Gender Bias within Household: Evidences from India", *Labour and Development,* Vol. 9, No. 1, pp. 84-95.

11

EMPLOYMENT IN PROMOTING CAPABILITY DEVELOPMENT IN INDIAN WOMEN

Krishna Kant Jha

INTRODUCTION

Lack of satisfaction at the pace of human development in the 1980s inspired the United Nations to convene a series of global conferences in the 1990s to identify the problems involved and to commit the world community to address those problems. These World Summits set a series of goals, named as the Millennium Development Goals (MDGs), which has become the anchor around which international agencies have to organize their developmental activities. The ongoing discussion on the modus operandi and the feasibility of achieving these targets has focused largely on the lack of resources. While resources are no doubt important in a developing country like India, it is equally important to adopt the right kind of policies and institutions.

This paper argues that a well-designed employment policy accommodating the women in the interest of their capability development will go a long way towards promoting some human development outcomes linked to the MDGs.

REDUCING INCOME POVERTY OF WOMEN

The importance of employment in the context of poverty stems from the fact that poor people rely mainly on the use of their labour power–whether as wage-labour or in self-employment to earn their livelihood. How much labour power they are able to use i.e. the quantity of employment–is an important determinant of their income. Also important, however, is the return to labour, which depends to a large extent on the portfolio of assets (including physical assets, human capital and social capital) with which they pursue their livelihood. If either the quantity of employment or the rate of return to labour is low, a worker is likely to live in poverty. For growth to be able to reduce poverty fast, the nature of the growth process must be such that the forces creating underemployment and low returns to labour are weakened. Whether this will happen or not, depends on three sets of underlying factors: (1) *The growth factor:* the rate at which the production potential of the economy expands, as represented by an upward shift of the production possibility frontier; (2) *The elasticity factor:* the extent to which an upward shift of the production possibility frontier enhances the employment potential–the latter being defined as the scope for improving the quality and quantity of employment; and (3) *The integrability factor:* the extent to which the women are able to integrate into economic processes so that, when growth occurs and the employment potential expands, they can take advantage of the greater scope for improving the quality and quantity of employment.

IMPACT OF EMPLOYMENT ON WOMEN'S EMPOWERMENT

Since it is women who bear children and in most societies still carry the primary responsibility for rearing them, women's employment have a strong impact on their own capabilities and the capability of their children. If women are empowered through the rout of employment capability, they would not only be better able to look after themselves but would also be able to do more for their children's health and education.

The principal mechanism through which women's employment exerts its influence is by affecting the process through which decisions are taken within the household. Maternal health, children's education and child nutrition are all outcomes of complex processes in which an important role is played by households' decisions about how to allocate the limited resources available to them to different members of the household and to different uses. An employment strategy that seeks to redress female disadvantage in the labour market may affect the decision-making process in the household in a manner that will promote children's health and education.

The important policy question then revolves around the issue how to strengthen the bargaining power of women. In a pioneering work, Boserup (1970) had speculated that creating employment opportunities for women outside the household would be an effective way of improving their bargaining power. The argument is based on the premise that society attaches more value to working for cash than to working for subsistence. The work that women do in a traditional household–cooking, caring, engaging in subsistence production, and so on–may be intrinsically no less valuable for the well-being of the household than the income that men earn working outside. But the fact remains that it is working for cash outside the household that gives men a superior status in traditional societies. If women's status and thus, their bargaining power is to be improved, they too must be given opportunities to earn income outside the household (L. Osmani 2007; Kabeer 1997).

PRIMARY EDUCATION TO WOMEN

One of the major constraints to promote education is that of the demand for education especially for women. For education to spread, parents must be willing to send their female children to schools but in many societies they are found to consider their female children liabilities to be shifted to someone else as soon as possible; and in poor family, to be keener to utilize their male children's labour for the benefit of the household economy than to educate them. Sending children to school involves costs both the direct costs of clothes, books, fees, etc. and the indirect opportunity cost of forgone income as parents lose the contribution of children to the household economy. Only if the perceived benefits of education outweigh, these costs would desire be transformed into effective demand. Employment can play a crucial role in achieving this transformation.

There are a number of pathways through which expansion in employment opportunities can stimulate the demand for education. The first is by raising the returns to education. In an economy where employment opportunities are scarce, and seasonal unemployment and chronic underemployment are rife, parents will understandably be loath to invest in children's education – in terms of incurring the direct costs of schooling as well as forgoing the children's economic contribution to the household. The cost-benefit calculation will, however, tilt in favour of schooling as the prospect for productive employment improves. This will raise the demand for education.

This pathway relates the expected rate of return to education in future to demand for education at present. One of its limitations is that when parents are credit-constrained, higher expected rate of return to education in future will not necessarily lead to higher investment in education today (Ranjan 1999). Prospects of better employment opportunities for their children will certainly make the parents want to invest more in their education, because they know that any investments made today will be more than paid for when the children grow up and get good jobs. The problem, however, is that the parents may be too poor today to bear the costs, while at the same time imperfections in the credit market do not allow them to borrow against future earnings of children.

Under such conditions, employment can still be a major determinant of the demand for education, but the relevant variable in this case is not the expected future earnings of children and the current employment prospects of the parents themselves. It is only when child labour is not considered essential for the survival of the family that parents would be able to send their children to school. Creation of productive employment opportunities for poor parents is, therefore, an important pathway through which the demand for education can be strengthened.

While a general expansion in employment opportunities will help to achieve the education goal, it is arguable that expansion in women's employment would have an especially salutary effect. There are two distinct but related pathways through which this may happen. One of them operates through improvement in women's status and the other through fertility decisions, children's health and nutrition. The nutritional status of children is the outcome of what has come to be known as the nutrition-infection nexus. Poor nutritional status can be a consequence of either low level of nutritional intake through the food consumed or frequent infections caused by the lack of hygiene and healthcare. Quite often these two factors reinforce each other's effect. The causal role of the nutrition-infection nexus suggests that there are three major proximate determinants of child nutritional status--viz. food, hygiene and care. For policy purposes, it is important to identify the underlying socio-economic variables that shape these proximate determinants.

Household income is obviously one such variable. Higher income will enable parents to provide better food consumption, a more hygienic living environment and better care for their children. Well-designed employment strategies can play an important role here by enabling households to earn higher incomes. But the potential role of employment in combating child malnutrition goes far beyond the contribution, it can make to household income.

This wider role comes into play through women's employment in particular, in so far as employment can empower women and raise their status relative to men. This is because women's status happens to be one of the most powerful underlying variables that determine children's nutritional status. Women's status affects child nutrition through a number of pathways. Better status strengthens women's bargaining power within the household and enables them to take better care of themselves in terms of greater access to food and healthcare. Another pathway consists in the link between improvement in women's status and their ability to take care of children after they are born.

The hypothesis is that women tend to spend more on children's nutrition and healthcare than men do; therefore, if women's status within the household improves they will be able to bargain harder for allocating household's resources more towards children's well-being.

INDIAN WOMEN ARE UNEMPLOYED AND POWERLESS

Legal protection of women's rights has little effect in the face of prevailing patriarchal traditions. System of patriarchy is a historic construct; it has a beginning and it will have an end. Its time seems to have nearly run its course—it no longer serves the needs of men and women and in its inextricable linkage to militarism, hierarchy, and racism. It threatens the very existence of life on earth. As long as both men and women regard the subordination of half the human race to the other as "natural," it is impossible to envision a society in which differences do not connote either dominance or subordination. In other words, the path from gender inequity to gender equity leads to a fundamental change in all human decisions. In the context of the process model we are using, it leads to a radical and pervasive change in the structure and behavior of all psychosocial feedback loops.

Since human nature is "gendered to the core", it follows that gender inequity is the most fundamental of all inequities. Just as all branches of a tree grow out of the trunk and are fed from a common root; all social inequities derive from the common root of gender inequity. Gender equity is the door that opens wide the way toward new possibilities for justice and peace at all levels.

Women are Subordinate in Most Marriages and do not Come Forward for Job

Exposure to and interactions with the outside world are instrumental in determining the possibilities available to women in their daily lives. The situation of women is affected by the degree of their autonomy or capacity to make decisions both inside and outside their own household.

The position of women in northern India is notably poor. Traditional Hindu society in northern rural areas is hierarchical and dominated by men, as evidenced by marriage customs. North Indian Hindus are expected to marry within prescribed boundaries: the bride and groom must not be related, they have no say in the matter, and the man must live outside the woman's natal village.

"Wife givers" are socially and ritually inferior to "wife takers", thus necessitating the provision of a dowry. After marriage, the bride moves in with her husband's family. Such a bride is "a stranger in a strange place." They are controlled by the older females in the household, and their behavior reflects on the honour of their husbands. Because emotional ties between spouses are considered a potential threat to the solidarity of the patrilineal group, the northern system tends to segregate the sexes and limit communication between spouses—a circumstance that has direct consequences for family planning and similar "modern" behaviours that affect health. A young Indian bride is brought up to believe that her own wishes and interests are subordinate to those of her husband and his family. The primary duty of a newly married young woman, and virtually her only means of improving her position in the hierarchy of her husband's household, is to bear sons. Sonalde Desai points out that the perception that sons are the major source of economic security in old age is so strong in the north that "many parents, while visiting their married daughters, do not accept food or other hospitality from them. However, given women's low independent incomes and lack of control over their earnings, few can provide economic support to their parents even if parents were willing to accept it."

In the south, in contrast, a daughter traditionally marries her mother's brother or her mother's brother's son (her first cousin). Such an arrangement has a dramatic impact on women. "In southern India, men are likely to marry women to whom they are related, so that the strict distinction found in the north between patrilineal and marital relatives is absent. Women are likely to be married into family households near their natal homes, and are more likely to retain close relationships with their natal kin." But this does not mean that they have freedom to seek market job.

Child Marriages keep Women Subjugated

A 1976 amendment to the Child Marriage Restraint Act rose the minimum legal age for marriage from 15 to 18 for young women and from 18 to 21 for young men. However, in many rural communities, illegal child marriages are still common. In some rural areas, nearly half the girls between 10 and 14 are married. Because there is pressure on women to prove their fertility by conceiving as soon as possible after marriage, adolescent marriage is synonymous with adolescent childbearing: roughly 10-15 per cent of all births take place to women in their teens.

A May 1998 article in the *New York Times* states:

Child marriages contribute to virtually every social malaise that keeps India behind in women's rights. The problems include soaring birth rates, grinding poverty and malnutrition, high illiteracy and infant mortality and low life expectancy, especially among rural women.

The article cites a 1993 survey of more than 5,000 women in Rajasthan, which showed that 56 per cent of them had married before they were 15. Barely 18 per cent of them were literate and only 3 per cent used any form of birth control other than sterilization. Sixty-three per cent of the children under age 4 of these women were severely undernourished.

"Each year, formal warnings are posted outside state government offices stating that child marriages are illegal, but they have little impact."

One man interviewed for the article has seven daughters. He borrowed some 60,000 rupees to pay for the dowries for six of his daughters, ranging in age from 4-14. He reported that "the weddings mean that he can now look forward to growing old without being trapped in the penury by the need to support his daughters." (NYT).

Women are Kept Subordinate, and are Even Murdered by the Practice of Dowry

In India, 6,000 dowry murders are committed each year. This reality exists even though the Dowry Prohibition Act has been in existence for 33 years and there are virtually no arrests under the Act. Since those giving as well as accepting dowry are punishable under the existing law, no one is willing to complain. It is only after a "dowry death" that the complaints become public. It is estimated that the average dowry today is equivalent to five times the family's annual income and that the high cost of weddings and dowries is a major cause of indebtedness among India's poor.

A December 1997 article in *India Today,* entitled, *Victims of Sudden Affluence* states, "A woman on fire has made dowry deaths the most vicious of social crimes; it is an evil endemic to the subcontinent but despite every attempt at justice, the numbers have continued to climb. With get-rich-quick becoming the new mantra, dowry became the perfect instrument for upward material mobility." A study done by a policy think-tank, the Institute of Development and Communication, states, "the quantum of dowry exchange may still be greater among the upper classes, but 80 per cent of dowry deaths and 80 per cent of dowry harassment occurs in the middle and lower stratas."

The article goes on to state, "So complete is the discrimination among women that the gender bias is extended even toward the guilty. In a bizarre trend, the onus of murder is often put on the women to protect the men. Sometimes it is by consent. Often, old mothers-in-law embrace all the blame to bail out their sons and husbands." Despite every stigma, dowry continues to be the signature of marriage. Proper employment opportunity is only way out to save the women.

Divorce is not a Viable Option

Divorce is rare—it is a considered a shameful admission of a woman's failure as a wife and daughter-in-law. In 1990, divorced women made up a miniscule 0.08 per cent of the total female population. Maintenance rights of women in the case of divorce are weak. Although both Hindu and Muslim law recognize the rights of women and children to maintenance but in practice, maintenance is rarely set at a sufficient amount and is frequently violated.

Both Hindu and Muslim personal laws fail to recognize matrimonial property. Upon divorce, women have no rights to their home or to other property accumulated during marriage; in effect, their contributions to the maintenance of the family and accumulation of family assets go unrecognized and unrewarded.

Women's Rights to Inheritance are Limited and Frequently Violated

In the mid-1950s the Hindu personal laws, which apply to all Hindus, Buddhists, Sikhs and Jains were overhauled, banning polygamy and giving women rights to inheritance, adoption and divorce. The Muslim personal laws differ considerably from that of the Hindus and permit polygamy. Despite various laws protecting women's rights, traditional patriarchal attitudes still prevail and are strengthened and perpetuated in the home.

Under Hindu law, sons have an independent share in the ancestral property. However, daughters' shares are based on the share received by their father. Hence, a father can effectively disinherit a daughter by renouncing his share of the ancestral property, but the son will continue to have a share in his own right. Additionally, married daughters, even those facing marital harassment, have no residential rights in the ancestral home.

Even the weak laws protecting women have not been adequately enforced. As a result, in practice, women continue to have little access to land and property, a major source of income and long-term economic security. Under the pretext of preventing fragmentation of agricultural holdings, several states have successfully excluded widows and daughters from inheriting agricultural land.

On the basis of the aforesaid facts, we can argue that employment is only panacea of which will enable them to be treated as human being in the society.

Women in Panchayat Raj Institutions

The highest national priority must be the unleashing of woman power in governance. That is the single most important source of societal energy that we have kept corked for half a century.

—Mani Shankar Aiyar, journalist, *India Today*

Through the experience of the Indian Panchayat Raj Institutions (PRIs), 1 million women have actively entered political life in India. The 73rd and 74th Constitutional Amendment Acts, which guarantee that all local elected bodies reserve one-third of their seats for women, have spearheaded an unprecedented social experiment which is playing itself out in more than 500,000 villages that are home to more than 600 million people. Since the creation of the quota system, local women–the vast majority of them illiterate and poor–have come to occupy as much as 43% of the seats, spurring the election of increasing numbers of women at the district, provincial and national levels. Since the onset of PRIs, the percentages of women in various levels of political activity have risen from 4-5% to 25-40%.

According to Indian writer and activist Devaki Jain, "the positive discrimination of PRIs has initiated a momentum of change. Women's entry into local government in such large numbers, often more than the required 33.3 %, and their success in campaigning, including the defeat of male candidates, has shattered the myth that women are not interested in politics and have no time to go to meetings or to undertake all the other work that is required in political party processes…PRI reminds us of a central truth: power is not something people give away. It has to be negotiated, and sometimes wrested from the powerful."

Contrary to fears that the elected women would be rubber stamp leaders, the success stories that have arisen from PRI are impressive. A government-financed study, based on field work in 180 villages in the states of Uttar Pradesh, Rajasthan and Madhya Pradesh and coordinated by the Centre for Women's Development Studies in New Delhi, has found that a full two-thirds of elected women leaders are actively engaged in learning the ropes and exercising power. Says Noeleen Heyzer, executive director of UNIFEM, "This is one of the best innovations in grass-roots democracy in the world."

Women leaders in the Panchayati Raj are said transforming local governance by sensitizing the State to issues of poverty, inequality and gender injustice. Through the PRI, they are tackling issues that had previously gone virtually unacknowledged including water, alcohol abuse, education, health and domestic violence. According to Sudha Murali, UNICEF Communications Officer in Andhra Pradesh, women are seeing this power as a chance for a real change for them and for their children and are using it to demand basic facilities like primary schools and health care centres.

The PRI has also brought about significant transformations in the lives of women themselves, who have become empowered, and have gained self-confidence, political awareness and affirmation of their own identity. The panchayat villages have become political training grounds to women, many of them illiterate, who are now leaders in the village panchayats. Says Sudha Pillai, joint secretary in India's Ministry for Rural Development, "It has given something to people who were absolute nobodies and had no way of making it on their own. Power has become the source of their growth."

By asserting control over resources and officials and by challenging men, women are discovering a personal and collective power that was previously unimaginable. This includes women who are not themselves panchayat leaders, but who have been inspired by the work of their sisters; "We will not bear it," says one woman. Once we acquire some position and power, we will fight it out...The fact that the Panchayats will have a minimum number of women (will be used) for mobilizing women at large." It is this critical mass of unified and empowered women which will push forward policies that enforce gender equity into the future.

An observation by Deepak Tiwari in India's No.1 Weekly News Magazine, displays the promising future made possible by the PRI. He notes, "'Learning politics' is the latest fad for young village girls, who dream of joining the growing band of women panchayat representatives, 164,060 at last count, in the state."

But when we empirically examine the economic advancement of women in terms of their capability developments the myth of PRI proves futile. In villages, the concept of 'Mukhiapati' has emerged who controls the whole affairs in a close nexus with the unemployed and corrupted youth of the village.

Let us examine the following statistical summary to observe some facts about the Indian women:

Statistical Summary

Social Indicator	*India*	*World*	*Developing World*	*Kerala*	*Sri Lanka*
Infant Mortality Rate, per 1000 live births	73	60	66	16	17
Maternal Mortality Rate, per 100,000 live births	570	430	470		140
Female Literacy, %	58	77.6	70.4	86.93	90.2
Female School Enrollment	47	62	57	63	67
Earned Income by females, %	26	58.0	53.0	49.8	35.5
Underweight Children, %	53	30	30		38
Total Fertility Rate	3.2	2.9	3.2	1.9	2.1
Women in Government, %	6	7	5		9
Contraception usage, %	44	56	54	56	66
Low birth weight babies, %	33	17	7		25

Kerala and Sri Lanka are added for comparison as they are recognized as having made exceptional efforts in the field of female education.

The above table suggests that in no way the Pnchayat Raj Institutions have improved the lot of Indian women.

As the Former UN Secretary General Kofi Annan stated, "Gender equality is more than a goal in itself. It is a precondition for meeting the challenge of reducing poverty, promoting sustainable development and building good governance."

This recognition is currently missing in India. Transforming the prevailing social discrimination against women must become the top priority and must happen concurrently with increased direct action to rapidly improve the social and economic status of women. In this way, a synergy of progress can be achieved. Capability development in women is significant in the modern society, so now let us have a concept of capability evelopment.

CAPABILITY EXPANSION THE REAL HUMAN DEVELOPMENT

Moving away from the crude identification of development with statistics on economic growth, capability approach stresses the necessity to place human beings at the centre of the meaning of development. Throughout his career, Amartya Sen has been preoccupied with questions of social justice. Inequalities between women and men have been especially important in his thinking, and the achievement of gender justice in society has been among the most central goals of his theoretical enterprise.

What Amartya Sen and others in this school (such as Martha Nussbaum, a feminist philosopher) emphasize, is the removal of barriers. Having capabilities for them is having opportunities. So, this approach stresses the broadening of opportunities—e.g, removing racism, removing sexism, removing inadequate education, removing conditions which generate poor health, removing restrictions on the opportunities due to traditional, cultural and religious blind faith. The UN Human Development Reports draw in particular upon the theoretical work of the economist Amartya Sen. In this work, the central focus is upon the development of human capabilities, and this is sometimes described as the "capabilities approach." The development of human capabilities is seen as at the core of human development and as the condition for people to be able to live lives of respect and value.

But, what exactly do people like Amartya Sen and others in this school (such as Martha Nussbaum, a feminist philosopher) mean by capabilities? That's what the UN Human Development Reports do—they record the achievements of different societies in terms of what they provide in areas such as education and health. But, they say nothing about how the struggle to end racism, sexism, inequality in education and health itself transforms people and develops their capacities. They say nothing about the role of human activity. Rather, their focus is upon creating a level playing field and removing the barriers to equality which restrict opportunities.

Essentially, this perspective is liberalism, liberal reformism. It certainly rejects the neo-liberal worship of the market with all its inhuman effects and it accepts the importance of the role of the State in supporting human welfare. However, it implicitly argues that broadening and equalizing opportunities—something that States should do—is the answer to neo-liberalism. The difference between this liberal reformism which dominates current discussions of human development and the concept of revolutionary practice that we see in the Bolivarian Constitution is most obvious when it comes to talking about education. In the capabilities approach, what matters is how much States choose to spend on education—i.e., what their priorities are. What proportion of the society is illiterate? What proportion has completed high school? What proportion has gone to university? And, it would also ask what is the gender difference in this data —in order to explore the effect of sexism and patriarchy in preventing human development. Do all castes and races have the opportunity for education or are they excluded?

But, what it doesn't ask is—what kind of education? Is it education delivered vertically from the top to the bottom? Is it education that involves the memorization by students of accepted truths? Are truths accepted by and acceptable to those at the top? Is it education that supports the maintenance of existing power structures? Or, is education as a process in which people learn through their own activity?

These are the very types of questions posed by *Paulo Freire,* who was himself profoundly influenced by Marx. Freire distinguishes very clearly between the delivery of "banked knowledge" and knowledge which develops from a critical process which examines the world and our place in the world. "In the banking concept of knowledge,"-Freire pointed out, "knowledge is a gift bestowed by those who consider themselves knowledgeable upon those whom they consider to know nothing." In other words, it is a gift from above. The state provides a gift; the teacher provides a gift.

In contrast, Freire's own concept of education (what he calls "problem-posing education") stresses revolutionary practice— this relation between our activity and the development of our capacities." Problem-posing education," he notes, "affirms men and women as being in the process of becoming—as unfinished, uncompleted beings"; it is, he stresses, a "humanist and liberating praxis"—one which "posits as fundamental that the people subjected to domination must fight for their emancipation" There is no place in the liberal concept of human development for this emphasis upon practice. Whether education comes as a gift from above to the deprived who are below or whether it emerges from our critical problem-posing and reflections appears irrelevant. Again, let me stress the relationship to Marx's point. When he first developed his concept of the coincidence of the changing of circumstances and self-change, it was in a particular context. He was criticizing the idea that we can give people a gift, that we just change their circumstances for them and they will be themselves different people. And what Marx said right before introducing his concept of revolutionary practice was . . . you are forgetting something rather important. You are forgetting that it is human beings who change circumstances. You are forgetting that "the educator must himself be educated." This idea that we can change circumstances for people and thus change them, he noted, divides society into two parts—one part of which is superior to the other. In other words, the same point that Paulo Freire was making—the idea that knowledge is a gift bestowed by those who consider themselves knowledgeable upon those whom they consider to know nothing.

The fact that the liberal concept of human development does not put human activity and practice at its core means that it is essential to develop a revolutionary concept of human development. That is especially essential here in Venezuela. Why? Because what is the Bolivarian Revolution about if it is not about development through practice? Revolutionary practice is not a concept buried in the Constitution. It lives every day in the idea of combining education and work—a concept not only at the core of Mision Vuelvan Caras but also in the new ideas of education in workplaces. And, it is obviously present in the idea of the communal councils, where people can work together in their neighborhoods to diagnose and begin to resolve their needs.

Precisely because there is little explicit consideration of this revolutionary concept of human development, it is important to develop these ideas here. Once we understand the concept of revolutionary practice, we recognise that without practice, we can not have the full development of human capacities. People don't develop all their potential if they can't make decisions in their communities. If the State is hierarchical and issues instructions from above through transmission belts, we cannot have people's complete development, both individual and collective. If people are prevented from using their minds within the workplace but instead follow directions from above, we have what Marx described as the crippling of body and mind, producers who are fragmented, degraded, alienated from "the intellectual potentialities of the labour process." The more we explore these ideas, the more we recognise that this is what socialism for the 21st century. We must be a profound democracy as practice, a process in which we simultaneously transform society and ourselves.

AMARTYA SEN'S ETHICS OF SUBSTANTIAL FREEDOM

Sen's perspective of positive or, as he calls it "substantial freedom" is concerned with enhancing the lives we lead and the freedoms we enjoy, in other words, expanding the freedoms we have reason to value, so that our lives will be richer and more unfettered and we will be able to become fuller social persons, exercising our own volitions (capacities for deliberate choice) and interacting with—and influencing—the world in which we live." In his view, positive freedom is "intrinsically important as the pre-eminent objective of development," that is, of public policy.

Public policy—the programs and rules by which government and other public agencies arrange our lives in society—is supposed to be the means by which human beings pursue what is good or ethically desirable in the public sphere. Perhaps it is not too much of a stretch to treat Sen's perspective as an ethical perspective that may also help us evaluate the interactions between people in families and other associations.

We should try to explain what Sen means by "substantial freedoms." Substantial freedoms are valuable things that can be divided up and delivered to human beings (or groups of people in a region) in varying amounts. In that respect they are like money and freedom from coercion, things which can be preconditions for substantial freedom but are not very good indicators of it. In the case of money, a person can have very little, a middle amount, or a lot. In the case of freedom from coercion, the same can be said: one can be a slave, constantly subject to the whims of an overseer, or one can have maximum available freedom from coercion by one's fellow humans in their private or governmental capacities. What society does, and to some extent what individuals do, can determine how much substantial freedom we have.

But substantial freedom has to be distinguished from other things that we "often have reason to value": from negative freedom, i.e., freedom from coercion, and happiness, on the other.

SUBSTANTIAL FREEDOM AND INCOME LEVEL

Monetary income alone cannot be used as a reliable indicator of substantial freedom. An increase in income might be converted into an increase in substantial freedom, but the conversion is not automatic or equally easy for everybody. A sick person is normally less able than a healthy one to convert a given increase in income into a wider range of real opportunities, i.e., into greater substantial freedom. The same might be said of a person who lives in a dangerous neighbourhood that makes her fearful to go outside as compared to a person who lives in a safer neighbourhood.

Thus it is often more effective, in the promotion of substantial freedom, to invest in public programs that will provide access to inexpensive health care or make neighbourhoods safer places than to divide the money that would be used on these programs among the individual people who happen to be sick or who live in the affected neighbourhoods.

SUBSTANTIAL FREEDOM: GREATER THAN NEGATIVE LIBERTY, LESS THAN HAPPINESS

Substantial freedom is somewhere between negative liberty and well-being or happiness. Sen appears to believe that the more substantial freedom one has, the happier one is likely to be. But the correspondence between negative liberty and happiness is not so close. Yet negative liberty can be a precondition for substantial freedom. Thus, perhaps we have a scale.

Negative liberty ———Substantial freedom———Happiness

What is Negative Liberty or Negative Freedom?

Negative liberty corresponds to what is sometimes called negative or non-interference rights. These rights can be summed up as freedom from coercion. Negative liberty includes the freedom from assault (murder, rape, etc.), the freedom from enslavement and kidnapping, the freedom from theft of the products one has created solely from one's own labour, the freedom not to be prevented from making deals with other willing deal-makers, etc. (The only limits normally imposed by a pure system of negative liberty is that those who have it must respect the similar liberties of others.)

Substantial freedom differs from negative freedom in this way. A women who is without resources (a plot of land of her own to farm, seeds to plant, water to irrigate, education, access to health care, ability to pay for what she needs, powerful friends, etc.) may live a life that is unpleasant and short. But if she is not attacked or robbed by others or enslaved against her will, then her negative freedom is not violated. Yet we might forgive her for thinking that neither is her negative freedom worth very much to her. Substantial freedom, by contrast, provides people with real opportunities that negative freedom by itself does not.

Happiness is at Least Partly up to us Alone

Happiness, on the opposite end, always requires the right attitude on the part of the person who is happy. Whatever else it requires, happiness implies that the happy person is not always wishing for something that he or she does not possess. We can easily imagine persons very rich or famous or physically healthy or politically powerful who are miserable because they strongly desire what they do not have and cannot easily get.

Substantial Freedom is Close to but not Identical with Happiness

The ability not to be frustrated just because one does not possess some conceivably valuable things is an attitude (something mental rather than physical). As an attitude it lies essentially in the power of the individual whose attitude it is. It is not something that other people can control. Yet positive freedom is something that people can promote for persons outside themselves. They can also sometimes create it in what they themselves are not yet, that is, in their own future lives. Pursuing education is a way of doing this. So positive or substantial freedom, though essential for happiness or true well-being according to Sen, is not equivalent to happiness.

SUBSTANTIAL FREEDOM AND "CAPABILITY"

Sen sometimes uses the term "capability" to explain what he means by positive freedom. A capability lies between a raw capacity and an excellently executed activity. Most human beings are born with the raw capacity to participate in deciding about the conditions of our collective life together, just as most human beings are born with the raw capacity to see colours. But developing the capability to distinguish turquoise from sky blue or even dogs from cats is something that has to be developed by experience and (informal or formal) education. Likewise, developing the capability to reason together with others about social problems in order to reach a decision is not something we are born with, but we have to learn partly by seeing how it is done when others do it, partly by practice ourselves.

But having a capability is not a guarantee of use. A women, who can lift weights because she has practiced doing so, still has this capability when he is asleep or reading a book and not lifting weights. What makes it a capability and not a raw capacity is that she could move to activate it relatively quickly.

Raw capacity——Capability——Activity (done with excellence)

Substantial Freedom and Well-Being

Just as capability is linked to activity but not identical to it, so substantial freedom is not identical to the achievement of well-being. Sen, sometimes defines the latter in terms of being well and doing well. To understand the distinction between substantial freedom and well-being, consider the difference between a person like Gandhi who fasts, that is, deliberately goes without food, in order to witness to an ethical position that might otherwise be ignored and a women who is starving because she lacks the opportunity to get food. Neither are "doing well" in terms of their nutritional intake, an important aspect of health, but the person who can choose to fast has considerably greater substantial freedom. They similarly lack well-being, at least in one respect, but one has an element of substantial freedom that the other lacks.

The Constitutive and Instrumental Roles of Positive Freedom

Sen makes a number of important distinctions himself in clarifying the nature of positive freedom. He distinguishes for instance, its constitutive and its instrumental role in "development" (which is the goal of public policy especially in the face of poverty, famine, etc.). To say that freedom is constitutive of development is to say that the use of freedom is part of what well-being is. Sen has in mind chiefly rights to active political participation, at the local and higher levels, in determining the shape of one's social and economic environment.

There are important freedoms that have an instrumental role in making positive freedom possible. One of Sen's chief points as an economist is that we should not act as if there is just one of them. He lists five groups of instrumental freedoms:

Political Freedoms: The opportunities that people have to determine who should govern and on what principles, and also include the possibility to scrutinize and criticize authorities, to have freedom of political expression and an uncensored press, to enjoy the freedom to choose between different political parties, and so on. They include . . . opportunities of political dialogue, dissent and critique as well as voting rights and participatory selection of legislators and executives.

Economic Facilities: The opportunities that individuals enjoy to utilize economic resources for the purpose of consumption, or production, or exchange. The quantity of income as well as how it is distributed is important. Availability and access to finance are also crucial. Not being able to get credit can be economically devastating.

Social Opportunities: Arrangements that society makes for education, health care, etc.

Transparency Guarantees: These relate to the need for openness that people can anticipate; the freedom to deal with one another with a justified expectation of disclosure and clarity. These guarantees play a clear role in preventing corruption, financial irresponsibility and violation of society's rules of conduct for government and business.

Protective Security: A social safety net that prevents sections of the population from being reduced to abject misery. Sen refers to "fixed institutional arrangements such as unemployment benefits and statutory income supplements to the indigent as well as ad hoc (temporary) arrangements such as famine relief or emergency public employment to generate income for destitute.

Interconnections: One of Sen's major accomplishments in the area of economics is that he has shown quite persuasively a number of concrete ways in which the instrumental freedoms are interrelated and enhance each other. What makes this important is that collective choices can make a significant positive difference in people's lives.

- Access to income is no guarantee of well-being, though it can help if other conditions are met.
- Famine has never occurred in democratic countries with a free press.
- Coercive population control methods are less effective in limiting population than educating and empowering women.
- Education and subsidized health care promote longevity, better than increased income.
- Education and access to income and finance (even if in modest amounts) can do a lot to promote well-being for women and their children.

Nussbaum and Sen

Sen's position on how substantial freedoms should be distributed in particular on whether there is a threshold in terms of substantial freedoms below which no human being should be allowed to fall, is less clear than one might like. But Martha C. Nussbaum has developed Sen's ideas further in this direction. Nussbaum is also influenced by John Rawls, whose work she modifies from the perspective of substantial freedoms or capabilities.

MARTHA NUSSBAUM ON CAPABILITIES

Martha Nussbaum says that the guiding thought behind her approach is "one that lies at the heart of John Rawls' project...the idea of the citizen as a free and dignified human being."

John Rawls' political conception of justice involves a commitment by citizens to recognize each other as free and equal persons within the framework of a social order conceived on the model of nation-states. Nussbaum's approach is internationalist As such it appears to start from a somewhat stronger assumption that might strike Rawls as metaphysical rather than political. Nussbaum's view of the person is somewhat more fully elaborated than Rawls, but no more than Rawls does it try to restrict conceptions of the good to one, and it generally accepts Rawls' view on the importance of distinguishing the principles of justice to be enforced by justifiable law and the diversity of comprehensive doctrines operating within the principled framework.

THE BASIC IDEA ABOUT HUMAN BEINGS

Martha Nussbaum affirms a "liberal" view that is compatible with the feminist affirmation of the value of women as persons. "At the heart of this tradition of liberal political thought is a twofold intuition about human beings: namely, that all, just by being human, are of equal dignity and worth, no matter where they are situated in society, and that the primary source of this worth is a power of moral choice within them, a power that consists in the ability to plan a life in accordance with one's own evaluation of ends." To these two ideas is linked one more, that "the moral equality of persons gives them a fair claim to certain types of treatment at the hands of society and politics. This treatment must do two things respect and promote the liberty of choice, and respect and promote the equal worth of persons as choosers."

Nussbaum's view holds that "the core of rational and moral personhood is something all human beings share, shaped though it may be in different ways by their differing social circumstances. And it does give this core a special salience in political thought, defining the public realm in terms of it, purposefully refusing the same salience to gender, rank, class and religion." Her approach to women's issues is "part of a systematic and justifiable program that addresses hierarchy across the board in the name of human dignity."

Her view is that political theory should be based on "the conception of human beings as essentially rational agents." The key type of reason to be emphasized is practical (i.e., moral and political) reason.

THE ROLE OF CAPABILITIES

At the heart of Nussbaum's liberal theory of justice and human rights is (her version of) Amartya Sen's concept of substantial freedoms or capabilities. Sen developed this notion as a way of addressing questions of justice and human development. Before we can talk intelligently about just distributions, we have to decide on a dimension whose relative value is important. If, for example, equal distribution is just, we have to know equal distribution of what? In relation to human development, specifically, poverty, the question is to know precisely what we should be striving to increase.

Workers on such issues have converged on what is now widely known as the capabilities approach. This approach holds that we should focus on what are the people of the group or country in question actually able to do and be? Importantly, the capability approach considers people one by one. For instance, it does not lump individuals into families and ignore the relations and unequal distributions of power within families.

Preference utilitarianism is an influential approach among planners today. This approach says that social planners should aim to maximize the satisfaction of preferences that individuals have before social policies are applied to them as if preferences are not affected by social arrangements. The capability approach rejects the preference standard as a proposed standard of what is socially valuable. Nussbaum points out that preferences may be distorted (A slave or an abused woman may eventually become convinced that a moderately comfortable enslavement or oppression is the best she can do and not "prefer" greater freedom.

Nor does the capability approach concern itself with the distribution of resources alone, because resources have no value in themselves disconnected from their promotion of human functioning, i.e., what humans actually do and what they are. The capability approach asks social planners to inquire into the needs individuals have for resources and their diverse abilities to convert resources into functioning.

THE BASIC CAPABILITIES

A necessary component of Nussbaum's capability approach is the list of basic capabilities. She asks an Aristotelian question, What activities characteristically performed by human beings are so central that they seem definitive of a life that is truly human? Two more precise questions are then formulated, (1) Which changes or transitions are compatible with the continued existence of a being as a member of the human kind and which are not? (2)What kinds of activity must be there if we are going to acknowledge that a given life is human? The latter is posed when she invites us to consider stories of anthropomorphic creatures that do not quite get classified as human.

Her list includes the:

1. *Life:* Being able to live to the end of a human life of normal length ; not dying prematurely.
2. *Bodily Health and Integrity:* Being able to have good health, including reproductive health; being adequately nourished; being able to have adequate shelter

3. *Bodily Integrity:* Being able to move freely from place to place; being able to be secure against violent assault including sexual assault; having opportunities for sexual satisfaction and for choice in matters of reproduction
4. *Senses, Imagination, Thought:* Being able to use the senses; being able to imagine, to think, and to reason and to do these things in a way informed and cultivated by an adequate education; being able to use imagination and thought in connection with experiencing and producing expressive works and events of one's own choice; being able to use one's mind in ways protected by guarantees of freedom of expression with respect to both political and artistic speech and freedom of religious exercise; being able to have pleasurable experiences and to avoid non beneficial pain.
5. *Emotions:* Being able to have attachments to things and persons outside ourselves; being able to love those who love and care for us; being able to grieve at their absence, to experience longing, gratitude and justified anger; not having one's emotional developing blighted by fear or anxiety.
6. *Practical Reason:* Being able to form a conception of the good, and to engage in critical reflection about the planning of one's own life are basic liberties for a human being. This entails protection for liberty of conscience.
7. *Affiliation:* Being able to live for and in relation to others, to recognize and show concern for other human beings, to engage in various forms of social interaction; being able to imagine the situation of another and to have compassion for that situation; having the capability for both justice and friendship. Being able to be treated as a dignified being whose worth is equal to that of others is also a basic librty.

8. *Other Species:* Human must be capable to live with concern for and in relation to animals, plants and the world of nature.
9. *Play:* Being able to laugh, to play, to enjoy recreational activities are also basic things to be done.
10. *Control Over One's Environment: (A) Political:* being able to participate effectively in political choices that govern one's life; having the rights of political participation, free speech and freedom of association . . . *(B) Material:* being able to hold property (both land and movable goods); having the right to seek employment on an equal basis with others.

There are two important qualifications on this list: First, they are a list of separate components. They are distinct in quality and all are of central importance. Second, they are related to one another in complex ways that can only be discovered empirically. It is to be noted that that in her formulation of the basic capabilities, the formula "being able to" is found in almost every example.

CLASSIFICATION CAPABILITIES

Nussbaum classifies capabilities into three types:

(a) *Basic capabilities* are the innate equipment of individuals that is the necessary basis for developing more advanced capabilities. She points out that most infants have the basic capabilities for practical reason and imagination, though without a good deal more development and education they cannot use it. Healthy children have basic capabilities in all ten of the areas in the above list.

(b) *Internal capabilities* are states of persons that are sufficient conditions for the exercise of the corresponding function (given suitable complement of external conditions). Internal capabilities build on pre-existing basic capabilities by processes such as exercise, education and training. Most adults have the internal capabilities of use of speech, capabilities that would not exist without the informal education that occurs along with socialization. Many internal capabilities require a more structured educational environment.

(c) *Combined capabilities* are defined as internal capabilities plus the external conditions that make the exercise of a function a live option. The aim of public policy is the promotion of combined capabilities; this requires two kinds of efforts (1) the promotion of internal capabilities (say, by education or training) and (2) the making available of the external institutional and material conditions.

THE CAPABILITIES APPROACH AND SOCIAL JUSTICE

Thus, the capability approach has been preoccupied with questions of social justice. Inequalities between women and men have been especially important in this thinking and the achievement of gender justice in society has been among the most central goals. Against the dominant emphasis on economic growth as an indicator of a nation's quality of life, emphasis has been given on the importance of capabilities, what people are actually able to do and to be. Frequently our arguments are in favour of the shift in thinking deal with issues of gender.

WOMEN'S CAPABILITY (OUTCOME OF SURVEYS)

Women and men are different biologically but all cultures interpret and elaborate these innate biological differences into a set of social expectations about what behaviours and activities are appropriate, and what rights, resources and power they possess. While these expectations vary considerably among societies, there are also some striking similarities. For example, nearly all societies give the primary responsibility for the care of infants and young children to women and girls and that for military service and national defense to men.

Like race, ethnicity and class, gender is a social category that largely establishes one's life chances, shaping one's participation in society and in the economy. Some societies do not experience racial or ethnic divides, but all societies experience gender asymmetries-differences and disparities- to varying degrees. Often these asymmetries take time to change, but they are far from static. In fact, they can at times change quite rapidly in response to policy and changing socioe-conomic conditions.

The term *gender equality* has been defined in a variety of ways in the context of development. This work defines gender equality in terms of equality under the law, equality of opportunity (including equality of rewards for work and equality in access to human capital and other productive resources that enable opportunity) and equality of voice (the ability to influence and contribute to the development process).

Rights

In no region do women and men have equal social, economic, and legal rights. In a number of countries, women still lack independent rights to own land, manage property, conduct business, or even travel without their husband's consent. In much of Sub-Saharan Africa, women obtain land rights chiefly through their husband as long as the marriage endures and they often lose those rights when they are divorced or widowed. Gender disparities in rights constrain the sets of choices available to women in many aspects of life-often profoundly limiting their ability to participate in or benefit from development.

Resources

Women continue to have systematically poorer command over a range of productive resources, including education, land, information and financial resources. In South Asia, women have only about half as many years of schooling as men on average, and girls' enrollment rates at the secondary level are still only two-thirds of boys. Many women cannot own land and those who do generally command smaller land holdings than men. And in most developing regions, female-run enterprises tend to be under capitalized, having poorer access to machinery, fertilizer, extension information and credit than male-run enterprises. Such disparities, whether in education or other productive resources, hurt women's ability to participate in development and to contribute to higher living standards for their families. Those disparities also translate into greater risk and vulnerability in the face of personal or family crises in old age and during economic shocks.

Despite recent increases in women's educational attainment, women continue to earn less than men in the labour market-even when they have the same education and years of work experience as men. Women are often limited to certain occupations in developing countries and are largely excluded from management positions in the formal sector.

Limited access to resources and weaker ability to generate income, whether in self-employed activities or in wage employment, constrain women's power to influence resource allocation and investment decisions in the home. Unequal rights and poor socioeconomic status relative to men also limit their ability to influence decisions in their communities and at the national level. Women remain vastly underrepresented in national and local assemblies, accounting for less than 10 per cent of the seats in parliament, on average (except in East Asia where the figure is 18-19 per cent). And in no developing region do women hold more than 8 per cent of ministerial positions.

Moreover, progress has been negligible in most regions since the 1970s. And in Eastern Europe, female representation has fallen from about 25 to 7 per cent since the beginning of economic and political transition there. Societal institutions social norms, customs, rights, laws as well as economic institutions, such as markets, shape roles and relationships between men and women and influence what resources women and men have access to, what activities they can or cannot undertake and in what forms they can participate in the economy and in society. They embody incentives that can encourage or discourage prejudice. Even when formal and informal institutions do not distinguish explicitly between males and females, they are generally informed (either explicitly or implicitly) by social norms relating to appropriate gender roles. These societal institutions have their own inertia and can be slow and difficult to change but they are far from static.

Like institutions, households play a fundamental role in shaping gender relations from early in life and in transmitting these from one generation to the next. People make many of life's most basic decisions within their households-about having and raising children, engaging in work and leisure, and investing in the future. How tasks and productive resources are allocated among sons and daughters, how much autonomy they are given, whether expectations differ among them- all this creates, reinforces, or mitigates gender disparities. But families do not make decisions in a vacuum. They make them in the context of communities and in ways that reflect the influence of incentives established by the larger institutional and policy environment.

Violence

The UNDP has in several reports made links between economic crisis and human insecurity at all levels. Structural inequalities brought about by globalisation generate violence at the household, community and national levels. In East Asia, while national economies show signs of recovery from the collapse of the financial markets during the Asian Financial Crisis of 1997-8, the human costs of the crisis include continued social stress and fragmentation. Increasing domestic violence, street crime and suicides have been reported in Malaysia, Thailand and Korea. In Korea, a hotline for women received an escalating number of calls from women suffering from domestic violence–seven times as many as during the previous year.

International trade and the advent of the Internet have led to an expansion of the global sex industry, including trafficking in women, prostitution and sex tourism. The opening up of borders within the former Soviet bloc together with the shrinking of opportunities for women in the formal economy in the region, have caused many women to migrate to other parts of Europe looking for work. However, restrictive immigration policies in Western Europe increase women's vulnerability to sexual exploitation by the organised criminal groups on which they often depend for movement.

In Pakistan, crises in national and religious identities have turned urban populations to fundamentalist models of law. This has been linked to the increased incidence of 'honour-killings' where the perception of what defiles honour is continually widening so that male control does not simply extend to a woman's sexual behaviour, but to all of her behaviour, including her movements, her language and her actions. In any of these areas, any form of defiance by women is perceived as undermining male honour and women may be killed by men for such trivial matters as answering them back, bringing their food late and going on forbidden visits.

During periods of social upheaval, violence against women may be tolerated to an even greater extent as social norms that control men's behaviour break down. The sanctions against violence that may be applied by family and community, or the protection that they may offer, can be disrupted by migration, displacement and economic strain on individuals. Women may also be afforded less protection by the State as crime and justice systems divert their attention to general criminal matters, deprioritising still further what continues to be seen predominantly as the 'private' crime of domestic violence. When the State is under pressure to cut social spending, provision for victims of gender and sexual violence may be withdrawn. The options available for women to challenge attacks upon them may therefore become far fewer, so that violence can be perpetrated with impunity.

For development agencies, this entails developing responses that address violence in different and changing contexts on the basis of sound analysis. The integration of examination of the incidences of violence against women and of the factors and indicators that may point to its increase into the analysis of the external context, is essential. An internal analysis of the institutional context and of the composition and culture of the development agency is equally important. Even though there is a trend within international organisations and development agencies to identify violence against women as a corporate priority for action, much work remains to be done within these organisations before we see violence against women as a development concern legitimate as the more traditional areas such as production, education, or public health. Violence against women is probably still regarded as an important, but fairly marginal concern in most international development and relief agencies. It has to be recognised, therefore, that violence against women is a systematic strategy to maintain women in a state of subordination and fear, and that systematic and strategic measures like programmes on education, training and economic independence are need to combat it.

Attitudes: Marriage and Children or Job?

Women represent an increasing share of the world's labour force –over a third in all regions except Southern and Western Asia and Northern Africa. However, women remain at a disadvantage in securing paid jobs. Wage differentials, occupational segregation, higher unemployment rates and their disproportionate representation in the informal and subsistence sectors limit women's economic advancement. Socio-cultural attitudes, employment policies and a lack of options for balancing work and family responsibilities or for controlling the timing and spacing of births contribute further to inequality in the labour market. A close study of the following tables establishes a link between the two different attitudes: (i) attitude towards compulsory marriage and children (ii) attitude towards education and market job.

The table clearly indicates that South Asia which comprises of Indian sub-continent and where society believes in compulsory marriage and children for female, the women due to this reason have the smallest share in the job market. Improvement in a period of 14 years is also meagre; it has come to 17% in 1994 from 13%

in 1990. In 2004, it is one third of the highest representation of 51% of CIS .

For women, education and training is very important for getting paid job. The following table will show the trend in effort for education by the women.

Table 1
Showing Share of Women in Non-agricultural Wage Employment

Region	*1990*	*2004*
South Asia	13%	17%
Developed Nations	41%	46%
Western Asia	17%	20%
South east Asia	37%	38%
North Africa	20%	20%
Oceania	28%	37%
Eastern Asia	38%	41%
Latin America , Caribbean	38%	43%
CIS	48%	51%
Sub Saharan Africa	32%	35%

Source: Millennium Development Goals Report, 2006.

Table 2
Showing Proportion of Children of Primary School Age Out of School by Sex

Region	*Girls*	*Boys*
South Asia	29%	22%
South Eastern Asia	10%	10%
Latin America & Caribbean	8%	7%
Eastern Asia	1%	1%
Developing Countries	22%	18%

Source: Millennium Development Goals Report, 2006.

It is evident from the table above that South Asian women are the least concerned with the school going also. The figures show that all the developing countries of the world are better placed in comparison with the South Asian countries. Moreover, most of the girls in South Asian countries leave the school at the primary level due to their marriage in childhood. Even if some of them continue, they do so in the interest having a better groom. A small faction of these school going girls in south Asia prosecute their study for getting a paid job.

WOMEN'S ATTITUDE IN THE MOST DEVELOPED COUNTRIES

USA and Japan are the two most developed countries of the world both in terms of GDP, human development and capability expansion. Behaviour of women in these two countries should be adopted by the women living in the other part of the world. Let us examine their attitude in terms of marriage and children.

Childless by Choice–women in USA

The above anaysis in section (c) shows that there is a contrast relationship between lust for marriage and children and that for education and job on the part of the women. As the former is feature in countries in South Asia, later is prevailing in the most developed countries of the world- USA. This will be evident from the following facts:

In 1997, Candace Korasick, a 32-year-old graduate student from Columbia, launched the Child Free Web site to link up with others like herself married people who do not want children. Within days of posting the site, Korasick says, she was inundated with grateful e-mails from other deliberately childless couples, and was even offered cash donations toward maintaining the site. Korasick and her husband, John, 30, are members of a small but growing demographic group in the U.S. According to the Census Bureau's 1998 Current Population Survey there, a greater percentage of women of all ages are not having children. In that year, 5.7 million (or 18.4 per cent) married women of childbearing age (defined by the Census as between 15 and 44 years old) were childless. And many of them like it that way. The National Centre of Health Statistics confirms that the per centage of women of childbearing age who define themselves as voluntarily childless is on the rise: from 2.4 per cent in 1982 to 4.3 per cent in 1990, to 6.6 per cent in 1995 (the most recent available figure). That's 4.1 million women saying no to motherhood in 1995.

It is a trend that applies to all age groups: for the 25 to 29 bracket, 28 per cent were childless in 1998, up from 16 per cent in 1976; for 30 to 34 year olds, it was 20 per cent compared with 11 per cent in 1976; for 40 to 44 year olds, 19 per cent were childless, up from 10 per cent in 1976. "Fertility of American Women," says: "From the data we have gathered so far, it looks like childlessness is continuing to go up."

The reasons for opting out of parenthood range from religion to ideology to simple lifestyle preference. Yet, whatever their motives, these couples say what they are either overlooked or looked down upon by the surrounding, child-oriented society. "When I refer to 'my family,' people seem baffled," says Candace Korasick. They say, "I thought you did not have kids. I absolutely consider my husband and myself a family, but other people do not even use family terminology for us." Yet these childless couples are bold enough to face the situation.

In recent years, a number of *websites* including Korasick's, (*web.missouri.edu/~cak307*) have popped up, such as Child-free by Choice (www.childfree.net) and Childfree Families (*http//24.89.14.183/cf.nsf/main*), as well as social networks such as No Kidding!, an organization with 68 chapters in North America, up from 47 last year. The members of this group are not only clamoring to be recognized by society but also by businesses. "Couples without children are totally ignored as a group, and businesses lose money that way," says Karen Smith, co-founder of the Leavenworth, Wash.-based organization, Childless by Choice. "We are not to be lumped with single people or empty-nesters. After all, we have different ages, we have different priorities, different expenses and we are at completely different life stages." Adds Scott Wenzel, 39, a computer consultant from Knoxville, Md., who is married and childless: "We're probably the largest and least recognized group in Western society right now."

Yet, as consumers, this diaper-free brigade wields considerable financial clout. According to analysis done for American Demographics by Third Wave Research Group, a Madison,

Wis.-based demographic marketing firm, childless couples spend more per person in almost every consumer category than their married with-children counterparts. In general, married couples without kids have more discretionary income than households with children, says Ed Wallander, a principal at Third Wave.

"Marketers may take childless couples for granted when marketing to married couples as a whole," says Wallander. "But their discretionary income and their buying patterns as well as their size and their growth show that couples without children should be recognized as a unique marketing opportunity." He points out that in some spending categories, the higher per-person outlays by childless couples are especially notable: compared with couples with kids, they spend 60 per cent more on entertainment, 79 per cent more on food and 101 per cent more on dining out. They also spend a lot on booze, clothing and surprisingly pets. "Some cliches are true," says Elinor Burkett, author of The Baby Boon: How Family-Friendly America Cheats the Childless (Free Press, 2000). "Childless couples very often have pets and they spend a lot of money on them. They also tend to be insanely generous to their nieces and nephews. Part of it may be over-compensation."

The spending behavior of childless couples rests on some attractive demographic qualities. Two-income couples without children are better educated than two-income couples with children. As of 1998 census report, 30 per cent of childless couples consisted of two college graduates, compared with 17 per cent of those with kids. The childless are more likely to have professional or managerial occupations (24 per cent versus 16 per cent of dual-employed couples with children). Although there is little difference in income (55 per cent of childless couples have incomes over $50,000 versus 54 per cent of couples with children), childless families have no child-related expenses to contend with. They don't have to save for their child's college education, let alone pay pre-school tuition. They do not need to pay for diapers or baby food or their children's health care. There are no pediatrician bills, no orthodontists and no family-size. They also do not structure their lives around the academic year and school vacations or choose their residence according to the quality of the school district.

Women in USA not only remain childless by choice but also they can live without spouse. 51% of women in America now live without spouse. In most of the developed countries including Japan, an Asian country, number of unmarried and other forms of single women is growing fast ensuring their economic independence. The report follows:

51% Women in America Living Single

In 2005, 51 per cent of women said they were living without a spouse, up from 35 per cent in 1950 and 49 per cent in 2000. Coupled with the fact that in 2005, married couples became a minority of all American households for the first time, the trend could ultimately shape social and workplace policies, including the ways government and employers distribute benefits.

Several factors are driving the statistical shift. At one end of the age spectrum, women are marrying later or living with unmarried partners more often and for longer periods. At the other end, women are living longer as widows and after a divorce, are more likely than men to delay remarriage, sometimes delighting in their newfound freedom.

In addition, marriage rates among black women remain low. Only about 30 per cent of black women are living with a spouse, compared with about 49 per cent of Hispanic women, 55 per cent of non-Hispanic white women and more than 60 per cent of Asian women.

In a relatively small number of cases, the living arrangement is temporary, because the husbands are working out of town, are in the military or are institutionalized while most women eventually marry, the larger trend is unmistakable.

"This is yet another of the inexorable signs that there is no going back to a world where we can assume that marriage is the main institution that organizes people's lives," said Prof. Stephanie

Coontz, director of public education for the Council on Contemporary Families, a non-profit research group. "Most of these women will marry or have married. But on average, Americans now spend half their adult lives outside marriage."

Professor Coontz said that this was probably unprecedented with the possible exception of major wartime mobilizations and when black couples were separated during slavery.

William H. Frey described the shift as "a clear tipping point, reflecting the culmination of post-1960 trends associated with greater independence and more flexible lifestyles for women." "For better or worse, women are less dependent on men or the institution of marriage," Dr. Frey said. "Younger women understand this better and are preparing to live longer parts of their lives alone or with unmarried partners. For many older boomer and senior women, the institution of marriage did not hold the promise they might have hoped for, growing up in an 'Ozzie and Harriet' era."

Emily Zuzik, a 32-year-old musician and model who lives in the east village of Manhattan said she was not surprised by the trend. "A lot of my friends are divorced or single or living alone," Ms. Zuzik said, "I know a lot of people in their 30s who have roommates."

Ms. Zuzik has lived with a boyfriend twice, once in California where the couple registered as domestic partners to qualify for his health insurance plan. "I do not plan to live with anyone else again until I am married," she said, "and I may opt to keep a place of my own even then."

Linda Barth, a 56-year-old magazine editor in Houston who has never married, said, "I used to divide my women friends into single friends and married friends. Now that does not seem to be an issue."

Sheila Jamison, who also lives in the East Village and works for a media company, is 45 and single. She says her family believes she would have had a better chance of finding a husband had she attended a historically black college instead of Duke.

"Considering all the weddings I attended in the '80s that have ended so very, very badly, I consider myself straight up lucky," Ms. Jamison said. "I have not sworn off marriage, but if I do wed, it will be to have a companion with whom I can travel and play parlor games in my old age." Carol Crenshaw, 57, of Roswell, Ga., was divorced in 2005 after 33 years and says she is in no hurry to marry again. "I am in a place in my life where I am comfortable," said Ms. Crenshaw, who has two grown sons. "I can do what I want, when I want, with whom I want. I was a wife and a mother. I do not feel like I need to do that again."

Present Status of Japanese Women

Population

The birthrate in Japan is declining and its population is ageing. The total fertility rate (the total live birthrate for women in all age groups for that year, in other words, it refers to the number of births per woman during her lifetime) has declined since it fell below 2.00 in 1975. Increase in the percentage of unmarried persons is thought to be one of the reasons behind the decline in Japan's total fertility rate.

The average age at first marriage has risen annually and stood at 27.0 years for women and 28.8 years for men in 2000. Approximately half of Japanese women in their late 20s, the age group that used to enjoy the highest birthrate, remained unmarried. The lifelong single rate (the percentage of people still single at 50 years old) has increased dramatically since 1960, particularly for men.

The ageing rate (the proportion of the total population aged 65 years or older) has also risen rapidly. The declining birthrate and greater life expectancy are thought to be the main factors behind the aging of society. The average life expectancy of women was 84.62 years in 2000 and that of men was 77.64 years.

The following diagrams explain the facts more clearly:

Trends in the Live Births and the Total Fertility Rate

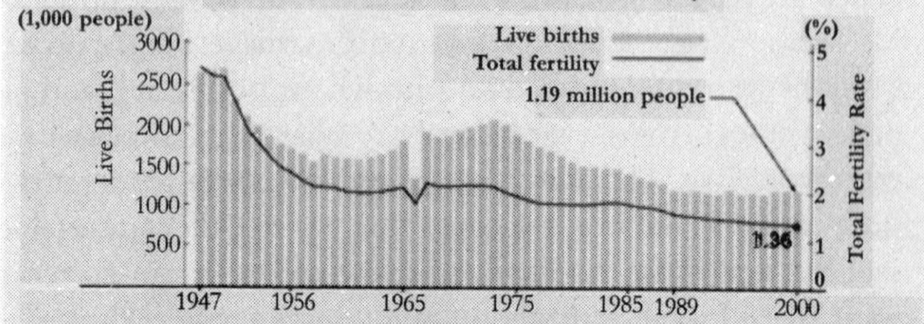

Source: "Vital Statistics of Japan", Ministry of Health Labour and Welfare

Changes in the Aging Rate and Population Aged 65 Years and Over

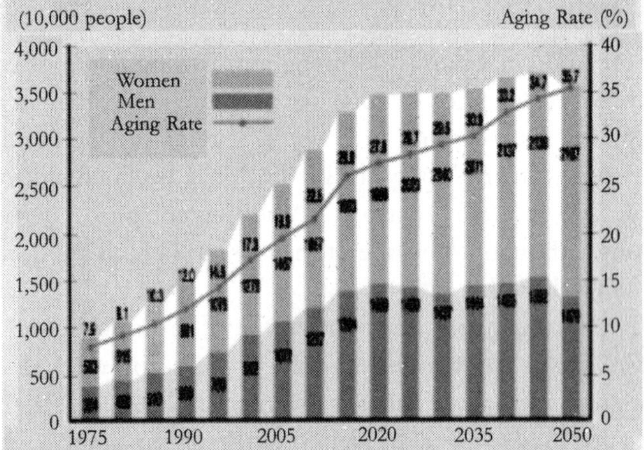

Source: Until 2000: Population Census, Ministry of Public Management, Home Affairs, Posts and Telecommunications; 2005 onwards; Population estimates for 1 October of each year (middle estimate) taken from Future Population Estimates for Japan (Jan. 2002 Estimates), Japan Institute of Social Insurance and Population Issues

Education

The percentage of students advancing into high school in Japan is extremely high with the percentage of girls exceeding that of boys.

Although the majority of boys advancing into institutions of higher education enter universities (undergraduate), girls may advance into either universities (undergraduate) or junior colleges. In recent years however, the percentage of girls advancing into universities (undergraduate) has increased and their advancement into junior colleges has declined. Their major fields of study show a tendency to diversify. The following diagram supports the fact.

Trends in Female and Male Advancement into Schools by School Category

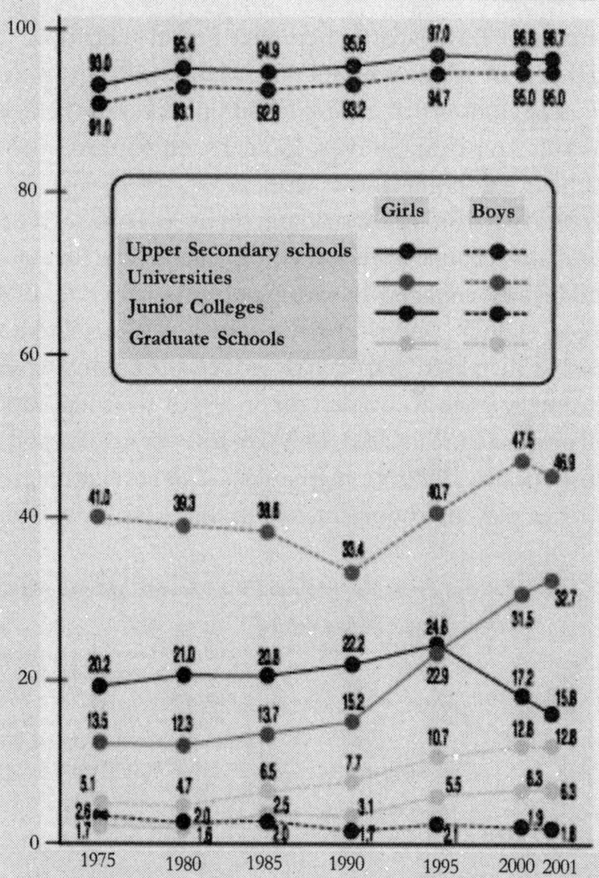

Source: "School Basic Survey", Ministry of Education, Culture, Sports, Science and Technology

Employment

The labor force participation rate of women in Japan remains a M-shaped curve with their participation declining due to marriage, childbirth and child raising. Women's aspirations to work are not realized although many women have a great desire to work throughout their childbirth/child raising years. The latent labor force participation rate, which adds the number of unemployed women who wish to work to the labor force population, approximates an upside down U-shaped curve as shown in the diagram below.

Looking at how Japanese couples spend their time, we see that regardless of whether or not their wives work, husbands spend little time on housework, raising children or care for the elderly. As a result, working wives have to shoulder both their responsibilities at home and at work.

Diversification of work patterns may be given as a distinguishable change in recent employment. The proportion of the labor force engaged in work patterns other than regular employees, including part-timers, dispatch workers and contract workers, has increased, particularly noticeable among women.

Japanese women accounted for 55.8% of the total labor force engaged in agriculture in 2000, 14.3% in forestry in 2000 and 17.0% in the fisheries in 1999. Women engaged in agriculture, forestry and fisheries play an important role in their respective industries

Women's Latent Labour Force Participation Rate Avoids AM-Shaped Curve

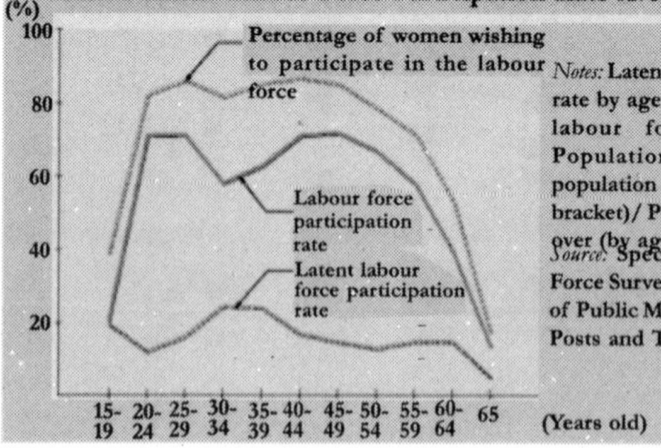

Notes: Latent Labour force participation rate by age bracket Population of the labour force (by age-bracket) Population of the non-working population that want to work (by age-bracket)/ Population aged 15 years and over (by age-bracket)

Source: Special Survey of the Labour Force Surveys (August 2001). Ministry of Public Management, Home Affairs, Posts and Telecommunications

Usage of Time by Married Couples

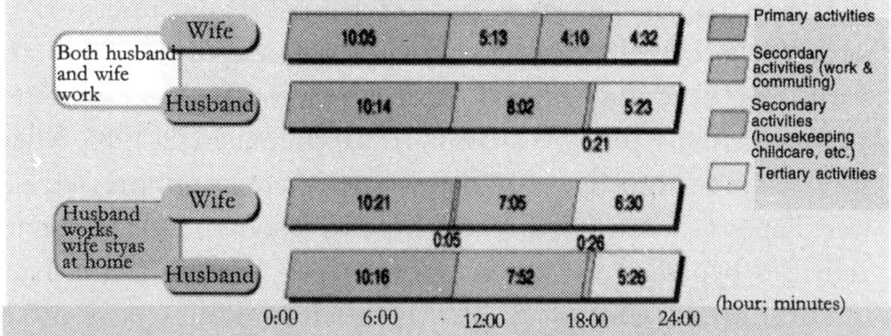

Note: Primary activities refer to activities essential to daily lie such as sleeping and eating. Secondary activities refer to activities of a highly obligatory nature undertaken as part of our social life and encompass work and housework. Tertiary activities refer to activities not included in the above the individuals participate in during their free time. "Nursing and "shopping" are included in 'housekeeping childcare, etc'. *Source:* '1996 Survey on Time Use and Leisure Activities', 1996, Ministry of Public Management, House Affairs, Posts and Telecommunications

and contribute greatly to the management of their respective lifestyles and to the maintenance and revitalization of their local communities. Looking at the status of women's participation in local policy decision-making processes reveals that the percentage of women members of agricultural committees responsible for organizing matters pertaining to the use of farmland falls far below the percentage of the total labor force accounted for by women. Notwithstanding, this percentage has increased from 0.74% in 1997 to 0.80% in 1998 and 1.64% in 1999 and the trend is to rise gradually

INDIAN WOMEN'S LIVES

India's famous female Prime Minister, Indira Gandhi, owes her entrance into power to her status as the daughter of India's founding Prime Minister and heir to the dynastic, Nehru-Gandhi political family line which eventually gave India three prime ministers. She downplayed her pioneering role as a woman in politics by saying, "I do not regard myself as a woman. I regard myself as a person with a job." The percentage of women in the parliament in India is currently 9 per cent, down from a peak of 10 per cent in 1988. By comparison, women make up 14 per cent of the representatives in the U.S. Congress.

The Western feminist movement of the 70s and the simultaneous media boom brought another wave of change to

Indian feminism. The emergence of formal feminist networks is new, but informal women's networks for sharing, learning and socializing have long existed. Radical protests in India were few and anti-feminist protests arose in India, continued till 1985, where some women argued that Indian women were not oppressed and were happy as wives and mothers. Much of modern Indian feminist activities bypassed the majority of India's women, those living in rural areas, ending up aiding mostly middle-class, urban women.

Historically, Indian women enjoyed a social status unparallel in human history according to the most widely accepted interpretation of ancient Hindu texts. The Indian dancer Mallika Sarabhai put it this way: "Hinduism is the only philosophy in the world where the woman does not come out of the man." Despite such a widely held egalitarian belief in traditional Hindu culture of today only women are forbidden to know, hear or read the Vedas, the sacred Hindu texts. Women are denied an equal share of inheritance because in most families, only the sons inherit the wealth of the parents, as married girls are no longer considered part of the family. Similarly, only a son can continue the family line or perform the funeral rites that ensure the soul of the dead's safe passage through the Hindu purgatory.

Ancient rites are still performed over pregnant women in traditional households to elicit the birth of a male and magically hope to change the sex of the unborn if it happens to be female. Although dowries were officially banned in India in 1968, they are still pervasive through private negotiations between families. While sons bring dowries to their parents, daughters are seen as a burden because they require dowries in order to be married, sometimes placing their parents, particularly in the middle and lower classes in debt. Compulsion of sending off in a compulsory marriage has made the 'liability-status' of a daughter. Even if a couple in India has only child, the daughter and after a huge investment she gets a lucrative job, able to be treated as asset economically, is liability on this account.

For these and other reasons, some feminists see the Indian family as the most oppressive institution, because women's roles are defined solely in terms of others. The traditional roles for women are the child, adolescent, wife, daughter-in-law, mother, mother-in-law and widow. At marriage, a woman often loses her identity and is referred to by her own parents as the "son-in-law's wife." In other sectors of Indian society, women change their first and last names to that of their husbands, obliterating their identity and sealing the husband's feudal-like ownership of his wife.

The rare act of divorce is seen as a reflection on the woman, who is viewed as westernized, amoral and unmindful of her duties as a good Indian woman and wife. The growth in the number of divorces in India is seen as either a sign of demoralization of Indians or as a sign of self-assertion and independence.

There is a wide disparity in the literacy rate between men and women. In 1991, the literacy rate of women aged seven and above was 39 per cent, compared to 64 per cent for men. Only five countries in the world have a larger male-female literacy gap. Encouragingly, the literacy rate among women is growing at 11 per cent a year, whereas for men it is 9 per cent. Girls are better educated in the state of Himachal Pradesh than other parts of India. As a result, the state has seen a reduced rate of poverty, mortality, illness, malnutrition and related deprivations. Here, schoolgirls wait for lunch during the mid-day meal plan, funded by the charity Maria Seva Sangha in Bangalore. A World Health Organization study showed that such mid-day meal programs greatly benefit girls and young women. In poor homes in India, girls are often fed smaller meals or no lunches. WHO research shows that providing girls with lunch motivates them to work harder to stay in school rather than getting involved in child labor or illegal activities.

Widows who make up more than 60 per cent of the women over the age of 60 rarely remarry and live out their lives in a culture that often shuns them as bad luck. Widows are supposed to remain celibate, wear white, curb any romantic impulses, not wear the Bindi on their forehead and deny themselves pleasures to honour their dead husbands while widowers can remarry freely, often to child brides.

Typical of the dichotomy in Indian women's lives is the fact that prostitutes are both scorned and sought. Poverty and domestic desertion are major factors contributing to women entering prostitution. The so-called Devadasi belt in central/southern India, is the home of organized criminal networks trafficking in young women. Devadasi means "maid or servant of god," referring to the ancient practice among communities in India of dedicating their daughters to the service of a temple deity. The girl is "married" to the God and has to earn her living by dancing and singing in praise of the God. Although the custom is now illegal, girls who are dedicated to the deity when very young are often sold into prostitution. According to research published in the Journal of the American Medical Association, the incidence of HIV infection has risen in female prostitutes from less than 10 per cent in 1990 to between 40 per cent and 50 per cent in a 1996 survey of Mumbai (formerly Bombay) and other cities. The survey found a 14 per cent HIV incidence among women who are not prostitutes, which was disturbingly high given their low-risk behaviour. These women erroneously believe themselves to be at low risk because of their presumed "monogamous" marriages.

Indian culture discourages communication between men and women regarding sexual behaviour and promotes fidelity after marriage for both sexes, particularly for the woman. Arranged marriages based on astrological signs and family traits rather than individual personalities are the norm for the majority of couples. Love marriages, where the individuals select their own spouse, are still rare and premarital sex, while a mark of distinction for men, is a badge of shame for women.

Indian women's social status improves immensely within her extended family once she is pregnant and bears children (preferably male). A mother who cannot produce boys is considered deficient or even damned. "Better to be mud than a barren woman" goes one proverb. Although biologically untrue, it is considered the mother's fault if a daughter is born and the father's triumph if it is a boy. Girls are seen as only temporarily a part of their own families because they move to the groom's family upon marriage, depriving the girl's family of income and leaving her parents with no one to look after them as they age. Also, when girls marry, dowries further cement the belief that a girl is a lifelong burden. Similar beliefs are held in emigrant communities of South Asians, most notably among Indian-Americans. A small percentage of Indians travelling to America on family visits exploit America's relaxed laws on abortion and terminate unwanted (reportedly disproportionately) female fetuses while away from home thus avoiding Indian familial, social and even legal issues.

Despite a constitutional prohibition outlawing sex determination tests in 1994, amniocentesis and more recently ultrasound are regularly used for gender determination and resulting female feticide. One in ten children in India do not live to age one. The number is worse for girls, who are innately stronger as babies—but are more likely to be deprived of food and medical care. UNICEF documents show that one fourth of the 12 million girls born in India do not survive to see their 15th birthday and one-third of these deaths occur before their first birthday. Nearly 50 million women are missing from the Indian population. The continuous decline in female/male ratio has resulted in a national ratio of 927 women for 1,000 men, the worst ratio among the ten most populous countries in the world. In the state of Punjab, the ratio is 793 women to 1,000 men, arguably the worst in India. In Rajasthan, the ratio is so skewed that some women marry one man and indirectly the man's brothers. The extended set of pseudo-husbands do much of the traditional housework while the woman is obligated to satisfy the sexual demands of her husband and his brothers.

Despite explicit legal prohibitions, child marriage is still prevalent especially in North India, where 75 per cent of rural marriages involve brides under 18. The average age of a Hindu bride is 15 to 16. Tradition holds that girls should be married soon after her first menstrual period, allegedly to guard against promiscuity. Women 15 to 29 years old have more than three-fourths of the children born in India. Illiterate women are estimated to have four children while women with at least high school education have only 2.2 children each, close to the number of 2.1, the target for stabilizing the population. Currently, India has one of the highest birth rates in the world with a nationwide average of 3.4 children per woman in her lifetime. This number is a tremendous decline from the average of 5.9 in 1960.

Since 1970, the use of modern contraceptive methods has risen from about 10 per cent to 40 per cent. The use varies widely by state, from a high of 53 per cent in Maharashtra to a low of 20 per cent in Uttar Pradesh. The most striking aspect of contraceptive use in India is the predominance of sterilization, which accounts for more than 85 per cent of total modern contraceptive use. Female sterilization, though physiologically much more difficult and risky, accounts for 90 per cent of the sterilizations. Mortality rates reach as high as 500 per 100,000 sterilization operations, a grim symbol of how medical standards have been lowered to meet the government's sterilization targets. Since the legalization of abortion in India in 1971, the reported number of legal procedures has reached an estimated 600,000 annually. However, other estimates suggest that at least twice as many illegal (and unsafe) abortions take place in unlicensed clinics.

Indian streets are largely male-dominated so unwanted touching and harassment of women in public places, known as Eve teasing, is common including groping on crowded buses, pressing up against women on streets and unwelcome touching in movie theaters. North Indian men are particularly renown for their disregard of women's rights and it is on the plains of Uttar Pradesh and Bihar that Indian women are often subject to physical (and verbal) harassment if wearing modern western garb, which is considered provocative.

Wife beating is perhaps the most prevalent form of violence against Indian women, occurring in as much as 50 per cent of families across India. Indian men who one minute worship Hindu goddesses and the next beat their wives depend on Hindu fatalism to ensure submission, because a woman's fate is supposedly set at birth and so nothing can change that destiny. Surveys reveal that not bearing a child, especially a son, were major causes of violence. Attitudes towards domestic violence, especially among women, are startling. Among literate women, 63 per cent found some justifications for wife beating while among illiterate women, it is 76 per cent.

The Indian women who suffer the most are the indigenous peoples, known as "tribals." Despite four and a half decades of constitutional protection, they remain the most backward ethnic group in India on the three most important indicators of development: health, education and income. Tribal women's lives are characterized by over-work, illiteracy, sub-human physical living conditions, high fertility and malnutrition. India's population of 68 million tribals is the largest indigenous population in the world. The literacy rate of rural tribal women is below 13 per cent, the lowest of all groups in India. The school dropout rate for tribals at the secondary level is as high as 87 per cent and for girls it is almost 90 per cent. Consequently, there is a negligible amount (0.06 per cent) of tribal women in colleges and universities.

The traditions of India, which are focused strongly on the extended family, contrast dramatically with the individualism and the nuclear family of the West. Building on this tradition of women's focus on families may be a way to make life better for India's women according to development agencies. They see women as the real agents for change because their research shows that raising a woman's income through training, education and micro-credit lending raises household income. Women spend their extra money on their families while men spend it on liquor or cigarettes.

Even today in the 21st Century, women in India are socially forced to acquire 'ardhangni' (half limbed) status by marriage. Their half limbs which would earn livelihood are made handicapped by socialization and another half, the genital organs, are made so strong that they can downpour bringing flood of children. This is the root cause of poverty in India. The following figures on work force participation of women in India support this fact.

Table 3
Total Workers in India 2001

Population/ Workers	*Persons*	*Males*	*Females*
Total			
Population	1 ,025,251,059	5 30,422,415	494,828,644
Workers	4 02,512,190	2 75,463,736	127,048,454
% of Workers	3 9.26	5 1.93	25.68
Rural			
Population	7 40,255,371	3 80,438,194	359,817,177
Workers	3 10,655,339	1 99,199,602	111,455,737
% of Workers	4 1.97	5 2.36	30.98
Urban			
Population	2 84,995,688	1 49,984,221	135,011,467
Workers	9 1,856,851	7 6,264,134	15,592,717
% of Workers	3 2.23	5 0.85	11.55

Note: Workers include both main workers and marginal workers.
Source: Census of India.

In this way, women in most of the under developed countries in a patriachal structure of the society are just slave of men to obey their male masters responsible for giving birth to children and fostering them at the cost of their own capability development. However in some advanced countries like USA and Japan, women have acquired some capability which should be followed by women in other parts of the world.

CONCLUSION

- As women receive greater education and training, they will earn more money.
- As women earn more money as has been repeatedly shown they spend it in the further education and health of their children, as opposed to men, who often spend it on drink, tobacco or other women.
- As women rise in economic status, they will gain greater social standing in the household and the village, and will have greater voice.
- As women gain influence and consciousness, they will make stronger claims to their entitlements-gaining further training, better access to credit and higher incomes and command attention of police and courts when attacked.
- As women's economic power grows, it will be easier to overcome the tradition of "son preference" and thus, put an end to the evil of dowry.
- As son preference declines and acceptance of violence declines, families will be more likely to educate their daughters and age of marriage will rise.
- For every year beyond 4th grade that girls go to school, family size shrinks 20%, child deaths drop 10% and wages ris 20%.
- As women are better nourished and marry later, they will be healthier, more productive and will give birth to healthier babies.

Only through action to remedy discrimination against women in terms their opportunities of getting market jobs can be the vision of India's independence—an India where all people have the chance to live health and productive lives—be realized.

References

Abzug, Bella, and Davis, Susan (1998), "India." Mapping Progress: Assessing Implementation of the Beijing Platform.

Bunch, Charlotte (1997), "The Intolerable Status Quo: Violence Against Women and Girls." *The Progress of Nations* 1997 New York: UNICEF.

Burns, John F. (1998), "Though Illegal, Child Marriage is Popular in Part of India." *The New York Times.* May 11.

Boserup, E. (1970), Women's Role in Economic Development. St. Martin's Press: New York.

Carr, Marilyn., and Chen, Martha and Jhabvala, Renana (1996), *Speaking Out: Women's Economic Empowerment in South Asia.* Southampton Row, London: Intermediate Technology Publications LTD.

Census Bureau of America.

Desai, Sonalde (1994), *Gender Inequalities and Demographic Behavior: India.* New York: The Population Council, Inc.

Enigma (1996), *'The Progress of Nations"*, New York: UNICEF.

Kabeer, N. (1997), "Women, Wages and Intra-Household Power Relations in Urban Bangladesh", *Development and Change*, Vol. 28, No. 2.

Martha C. Nussbaum, (1999), Sex and Social Justice, Oxford University Press, 46.

Martha C. Nussbaum (1999), Sex and Social Justice, Oxford University Press, 46.

Neft, Naomi and Levine, Ann D. (1997), *Where Women Stand: An International Report on the Status of Women in 140 Countries.* New York: Random House.

Omvedt, Gail (1990), "Violence Against Women: New Movements and New Theories in India", *Kali Primaries.*

Osmani, L. N. K. (2007), "A Breakthrough in Women's Bargaining Power: The Impact of Microcredit", *Journal of International Development*, Vol. 19, pp. 695-716.

Osmani, S. R. (2006), "Exploring the Employment Nexus: The Analytics of Pro-poor Growth", in R. Islam (ed.), Fighting Poverty: The Development-Employment Link. Lynne Rienner, Boulder.

Purushothaman, Sangeetha (1998), *The Empowerment of Women in India: Grassroots Women's Networks and the State,* New Delhi, Sage Publications.

Rajan, "Will India's Ban on Prenatal Sex Determination Slow Abortion of Girls?", Internet.

Ramalingaswami, Vulimiri., and Jonsson, Urban., and Rohde, Jon.

Reardon, Geraldine (1995), *Power and Process.* Oxford: Oxfam.

Times of India, "Protest Against Atrocities in Women", Internet, p. 3.

Sen Amartya (1999), "Development as Freedom", New York: Random House, 14, 15.

Tinker, Anne (1996*), Improving Women's Health in India,* Development in Practice Series, The World Bank.

United Nation Development Programme, (1999).

Venkateswaran, Sandhya (1995), *Environment, Development and the Gender Gap,* New Delhi: Sage Publications.

Vinayak, Ramesh (1997), "Victims of Sudden Affluence", *India Today.* December 15.

SECTION-III

Labour and Migration

12

RURAL-URBAN MIGRATION AND ITS IMPACT ON LAND, LABOUR AND CREDIT CONTRACTS IN SOURCE AREAS: AN EMPIRICAL STUDY

Mamata Swain

INTRODUCTION

Migration is often considered as a development-fostering process, which helps man to overcome 'the tyranny of space' and equilibrates the unequal factor endowments of different regions. People move from labour surplus and capital scarcity areas to labour deficit and capital abundant areas. But the question arises: why labour moves to places where capital is available and not the other way round? It is observed that labour migration takes place from backward/rural areas to advanced/urban areas mostly for employment, higher wage, larger income and better life. But there is large scale evidence that the migrants are exploited in various ways at the destination areas. As a matter of fact, movement of capital to labour surplus areas is easier if planned efforts are geared to achieve equal development throughout the entire geographical spread of the state. Thus, uneven spatial development or disparity in development causes population mobility.

Admittedly, economic development all over the world is observed to be associated with gradual transfer of labour force from the rural to urban sector. Many economists have probed into causes for rural-urban migration. While Ravenstein (1985, 1989) emphasized higher economic opportunities, W. Arthur. Lewis (1954), John Fei, and Gustav Ranis (1961) have developed dualistic models of development and stress that higher wage in the modern industrial urban sector pulls the surplus labour from the traditional agricultural sector and/provides the incentives to migrate. But Sjaastad (1962) and Todaro (1969, 1976) have applied human capital approach to migration. Sjaastad (1962) explains migration as the outcome of the investment decision of an individual to maximise income over his productive life at the possible destinations when both costs and returns are estimated in monetary and non-monetary components. Todaro extending Sjaastad's model, emphasized that the stream of potential migrant depends on the prevailing urban wages and a subjective estimate of the probability of obtaining a job in the modern sector, which depends on the urban unemployment rate. The decision to migrate depends on 'expected' rather than actual urban-rural wage differentials and the probability of successfully obtaining employment in the urban modern sector. Thus, the conventional explanations are very much simplistic as they emphasize the simple fact that the source areas are relatively labour abundant and capital scarce and labour moves to the place where it gets higher remuneration.

While these models put stress on individuals as the deciding units, Stark (1991) considers migration as a household strategy to stabilise family income and to spread risk in the face of incomplete and imperfect land, labour and capital markets and prevalence of transaction costs in rural areas. Haan (1999) questions the negative view on migration and argues that it is an essential element in the livelihood strategy of rural as well as better-off people.

Of course, the neo-classicals see the rationale of migration as a welfare promoting device or an investment decision on the part of a rational individual or the family on the basis of costs and benefits. On the other hand, Marxists emphasize the forced nature of migration. They see migration as an action of last resort for the pauperised peasant. Pauperisation and proletarianisation of peasants take place due to penetration of capitalist market forces. With development of capitalism the patron-client relationship gradually disappears. The pressure of capitalist development ruins the traditional petty producers and transforms them into proletariats. The peasants being alienated from land are forced to migrate for their survival. Amin (1974) argues that choice of the migrant is nothing but the immediate and apparent cause, the root cause lies in the overall development strategy of the state, which causes unequal allocation of factors of production. The conventional economic theory of migration is purely tautological and applies an individualistic functionalist approach, which ignores the relations of production. The transformation of the socio-economic organization in the rural areas that causes exodus of a part of its population needs to be examined carefully to provide meaningful explanations of migration.

What is interesting is that migration is not only the consequences of unequal development, it also aggravates unequal development (Mukherjee, 1981). Mukherji (1981) holds that unlike in developed economies where migration occurs in association with a quantitative change and a vertical shift in the labour force, labour migration in low income countries occurs as a spatial symptom of disease of underdevelopment and regional disarticulation in the space economy.

Also, it is argued that not only economic factors are responsible for migration but also social and cultural institutions, embedded in local customs and ideologies determine the rate and pattern of migration. Push-pull theories of migration have also been developed which emphasize both the positive and negative aspects of migration (*Lee,* 1966). The minus or the push factors include inadequate income in native place, inability to carry out cultivation, occurrence of natural-calamities, indebtedness, disturbing development in the family, etc.. Plus or pull factors comprise better employment and income earning opportunities in destination area, urge to see new places and learn new things etc.. While push factors are actually experienced and known, the pull factors like better work opportunity, higher income and improved living standard in receiving or destination areas are mere conjectures or expectations and thus uncertain. Therefore, many emphasize that push factors are real and more important in explaining migration. It is assumed that man is sedentary and risk averse by nature and unless forced by adverse circumstances, man does not want to leave his native place.

The economic factors that affect rural-urban migration can be categorised into three sets of variables. The variables relating to industrial/urban sector are: growth rate of industrial output, rural urban income differential, urban risk. Higher the growth rate of industrial output and larger the differential between urban and rural income and lesser the risk of getting the job, higher the pull force for rural-urban migration. The factors relating to the agricultural sector are: growth rate of agricultural output, income in rural areas, agricultural unemployment or underemployment, distribution of land holdings and poverty. The lower growth rate in the agricultural sector, lower income in rural areas, large scale of unemployment, skewed land distribution and poverty are the major push factors inducing rural-urban migration. Other variables affecting migration are:- distance, education and family contacts. Rural people prefer to migrate to nearer areas and to areas where other family members or relatives have previously migrated. Higher the level of education, higher is the inclination to move to high-income areas with greater opportunities.

The neo-classical explanations of migration in terms of better economic opportunities, higher wages, higher expected income are the obvious explanations put forth for migration after it has taken place. These models have less predictive value. Many believing in the sedentary nature of human beings see migration as a compulsive adjustment process under adverse circumstances. The socio-economic contexts in which migration takes place are of more academic interest and Standing (1981) following the Marxist framework has provided a materialistic interpretation of rural-urban migration. According to him the conditions for migration are as follows:

(i) The decision to migrate is considered as an acceptable response to adversity or frustrated aspiration;

(ii) The peasants deem their exploitation as .being unjust and not inevitable, which means in practice that some reciprocal relationship must have been violated to cause a sense of deprivation.

(iii) The revolt must appear to have minimal chance of success, or the class solidarity of the oppressed must have been undeveloped or have given way to disjointed anomie.

(iv) The fourth condition is that the potential migrant must have had cause to reject customary forms of oppression and exploitation because of a sense of deprivation or inability to satisfy his traditional level of subsistence.

Thus, a variety of reasons have been adduced for rural-urban migration. Many empirical studies have also been undertaken to analyze the motives for migration and the impact of rural-urban migration on destination areas (Breman; 1985,-1996). Though the causes of migration and the impact of migration on destination areas have been explored by many, the impact of migration in the areas of origin or sending areas has been sparingly dealt with. Impacts on destination areas as unfolded by several empirical studies are: subordination of labour to capital, increased control over labour, long-term labour contracts, low wage, long working hours, out-migration of local labourers, segmentation of the labour market etc. The probable effects of labour migration on source areas as propounded by many are: tightening of labour market, upward pressure on wages, adoption of labour-saving technology by employers, increase in female and child labour, etc.

In this paper an attempt is made to analyze the causes and determinants of rural-urban migration and to examine its impact on land, labour and credit contracts in the source area with primary data collected from three villages in Orissa, India.

METHODOLOGY

This study is based on primary data collected from three villages in Orissa in Eastern India. The villages were selected on the basis of rough indicators of their agricultural advancement and differing historical contexts. The agriculturally advanced village is Charapara, which receives perennial canal irrigation from the 11 Pattamundai Canal. The village is situated in the agriculturally advanced district of Cuttack in the Eastern Coastal plain of Orissa. The moderately advanced village is Harinababi, which is also canal irrigated. This village is situated adjacent to the village Charapara. Historically these two villages were under *zamindari* settlement located in the mainland of Orissa. In the case of *zamindari* settlement, the British conferred the proprietary right in land on the *zamindars*. The *zamindars* or the landlords were merely the intermediary between the Government and the cultivators having responsibility for the collection of land revenue. By conferring ownership rights to the intermediaries, the Britishers rendered the numerous actual tillers of land to virtual tenants and the *zamindars* exploited them by rack renting, debt bondage and rural usury.

The backward village is Sandhagaon, which is non-irrigated and situated in the district of Ohenkanal in the mid-central table land of Orissa. Ohenkanal is considered as an agriculturally backward district of Orissa. Historically, the village Sandhagaon was under the rule of semi-independent *Rajas* located in the *Tributary Mahals* or feudatory states of Orissa and constituted some hilly tracts and inaccessible areas and, was sparsely populated. The *Tributary Mahals* were under the rule of semi-independent kings and were permanently settled. The tributary chiefs were expected to pay annual tributes in specified instalments. The tributes were fixed in perpetuity. Exploitation of tenants in the *Tributary Mahals* or *Garhjats* was more excessive than in *Zamindari* areas where there was temporary settlement and land revenue was revised from time to time. Mainly shifting cultivation was practised in *Garhjats*.

The study covered all the households of the three study villages. A household questionnaire was prepared and canvassed among the informant households. Data were collected from heads of households by direct interview method.

Categorisation and Classification of Farmers

A careful observation of the three study villages reveals that the position of a household in the class hierarchy is determined at two levels. At the first level, it is the category of farm household like owner cultivator, part tenant, pure tenant, pure lessor and agricultural labourer that counts in determining the class position in the village. Secondly, within each category the peasants are further classified according to size class of land ownership holding.

All the households in each village have been divided mainly into five categories viz. owner cultivator (OC), part tenant (PRT), pure tenant (PT), pure lessor (PL), landless labourer (LL) depending on the behaviour of hiring labour, renting land and the surplus of production and income over consumption. The category of landless labourer includes casual labourer, attached labourer and farm servant and a residual category has been added to contain those households who do not fit into any of these categories. The categorisation of the households is based on the viewpoints of the residents i.e. how they perceive their class position and rank themselves in a class hierarchy. The farmer categories in descending order of class hierarchy are defined below.

Owner Cultivator (OC): The owner cultivator cultivates his owned land only and does not lease in land from others for cultivation. In the study villages the owner cultivators are considered to be at the top of the class hierarchy. Most of them hire in labour for agricultural operations and they have adequate surplus after consumption.

Part Tenant (PRT): The part tenant cultivates his owned land as well as leased-in land. In the study villages, a cultivator who leases in land is considered as of lower status than an owner cultivator, and most of the tenants use their own labour as well as hired labour for agricultural operations. They are just able to meet their consumption needs with hardly any surplus left after consumption.

Pure Lessor (PL): The pure lessor leases out all of his owned land and his operational holding is nearly zero. He does not have much surplus after consumption.

Pure Tenant (PT): The pure tenant is the landless tenant possessing no cultivable land of his own. He leases in land as he has some means of production like a pair of bullocks and a plough. He and some of his family members may be casual labourers and hire out labour on a regular basis. The pure tenant is usually a deficit household and his income from cultivation and wage labour hardly meets his annual consumption needs.

Landless Labourer (LL): The landless labourer does not have any owned land and he hires out labour to earn his livelihood. He is a chronically deficit household.

Others: In this category are included salaried people, pensioner and single widow family.

In rural areas land is the mainstay of livelihood and land ownership not only indicates possession of property and wealth but also is a source of power and prestige. Therefore, the farmer categories i.e. the owner cultivator, part tenant, the pure tenant and the pure lessors have been further classified into four farmer classes on the basis of size of land ownership holding. The farmers have been classified into four classes: Marginal, Small, Medium and Large Farmer. Each farmer class has been defined as follows:

Marginal Farmer (MF): Farmer with a holding size of less than one hectare of unirrigated land or 0.5 hectare of irrigated land;

Small Farmer (SF): Farmer with a holding size of 1 to 2 hectares of unirrigated land or 0.5 to 1 hectare of irrigated land;

Medium Farmer (MDF): Farmer with a holding size of 2 to 4 hectares of unirrigated land or 1 to 2 hectares of irrigated land;

Large Farmer (LF): Farmer with a holding size equal to or exceeding 4 hectares of unirrigated land or 2 hectares of irrigated land.

Data relating to migration have been analyzed with respect to farmer categories as well as farm classes.

THE CONTEXT

As the pattern of migration is context dependent, in this section-an attempt is made to study the nature of class and caste relationship existing in the study villages. The distribution of households in three villages as per farmer category and caste is presented in Table 1. It is well known that in rural areas in a hierarchical society, class and caste relationships are intertwined to a significant extent and considerably overlapping. An analysis of the caste configuration in the three study villages reveals that in Charapara out of total 43 households, 27 are *'Khandayats'* and the rest 16 belong to scheduled castes. The *khandayats* are upper castes in the caste hierarchy and are traditionally believed to belong to the warrior caste: supposedly fighting for the king during war and at other times cultivating their land. The scheduled castes are the lower castes and traditionally do sweeping and scavenging jobs and hire out their labour. The scheduled castes live in a separate cluster at the outskirts of the village. It is noted from Table 1 that all the labourer house-holds and the pure tenants in Charapara belong to scheduled castes.

In village Harinababi; out of total 22 households, 20 belong to the caste *'gudia'* and the rest 2 are *'khandayats'*. Gudias are a middle caste in caste hierarchy and are traditionally known to prepare and sell sweets and snacks. Now they are considered under Socially Economically Backward Classes (SEBC) just above the scheduled castes. The cultivators in Harinababi have less access to government facilities in comparison to cultivators of Charapara who have familial or social ties with government officials, those who invariably come from higher castes.

In the non-irrigated village Sandhagaon; out of total households of 33, 13 are *'karan'* by caste and the remaining 20 are scheduled castes. The '*karans*' are an upper caste and are traditionally held to have accounting jobs near the king. The *karans* lead an ostentatious life. In Sandhagaon, all pure tenants and casual labourers belong to scheduled castes. But there is one owner cultivator, one tenant owner and one pure lessor household belonging to scheduled castes. Whereas in Charapara, there is not a single scheduled caste household owning land, in Sandhagaon there are landowning scheduled castes. Thus, strict caste rigidity is observed in the advanced village Charapara.

Table 1
Distribution of Households Farmer Category and Caste

Village/	*Caste*					
Category	*Khandayat*	*Karan*	*Gudia*	*SC*	*Total*	*Percentage*
Charapara						
OC	13	-	-	-	13	30.2
PRT	4	-	-	-	4	9.3
PL	9	-	, -	-	9	20.9
PT	-	-	-	5	5	11.6
LL	-	-	-	11	11	25.6
Others	1	-	-	-	1	2.3
Total	27	-	-	16	43	100.0
Harinababi						
OC	2	-	12	-	14	63.6
PRT	-	-	5	-	5	22.7
PL	-	-	3	-	3	13.6
Total	2	-	20	-	22	100.0
Sandhagaon						
OC	-	4	-	1	5	15.2
PRT	-	3	-	1	4	12.1
PT	-	-	-	6	6	18.2
PL	-	5	-	1	6	18.2
LL	-	-	-	9	9	27.3
Others	-	1	-	2	3	9.1
Total	-	13	-	20	33	100.0
Grand Total	29	13	20	36	98	

Note: OC - Owner Cultivator, PRT - Part Tenant, PT - Pure Tenant, PL - Pure Lessor, LL - Landless Labourer.

The owned land area has been taken into account to determine the class status of a household. The owned landholding pattern of households according to farmer category and class is contained in Table 2. An acre of irrigated land has been calculated to be equivalent to two acres of non-irrigated land, as the cropping intensity in the case of irrigated land is almost twice the cropping intensity of non-irrigated land and likewise the price of one acre of irrigated land is about two times the price of one acre of non-irrigated land.

Table 2
Distribution of Owned Landholding According to Tenancy Status and Farmer Class

	Charapara		*Harinababi*		*Sandhagaon*	
Category	*No. of House Holds*	*Avg. Size of Holding (Acres)*	*No. of House Holds*	*Avg. Size of Holding (Acres)*	*No. of House Holds*	*Avg. Size of Holding (Acres)*
Owner Cultivator						
MF	-	-	2	1.9	1	0.2
SF	2	2.8	6	3.4	3	3.7
MDF	6	7.1	6	6.0	1	
LF	5	13.7	-	-	-	-
Total	13	9.0	14	4.3	5	3.4
Part Tenant						
MF	3	2.1	3	1.3	3	1.3
SF	1	2.7	1	4.2	-	-
MDF	-	-	1	7.0	1	5.0
LF	-	-	-	-	-	-
Total	4	2.2	5	1.8	4	2.2
Pure Lessor						
MF	5	1.1	3	1.4	3	1.6
SF	3	4.3	-	-	1	3.0
MDF	1	8.0	-	-	2	5.0
LF	-	-	-	-	-	-
Total	9	2.0	3	1.4	6	3.0
Grand Total	26	5.5	22	3.6	15	2.9

Table 2 shows that the average landholding size is the highest i.e. 5.5 acres in Charapara and then 3.6 acres in Harinababi and the lowest 2.9 acres in Sandhagaon. In the advanced village Charapara, there are 5 LFs under the owner cultivator category and there is none in Harinababi and Sandhagaon. Now we analyse the distribution of owned land among different classes (Table 3). Our purpose is to see whether there is significant inequality in ownership holding and how it varies across villages. Table 3 shows that the peasants are more differentiated in the advanced village Charapara in comparison to other two villages. In Charapara MFs constituting 31 per cent of households own only 8 per cent of owned land, whereas the LFs constituting about 19 per cent of households account for 48 per cent of owned area. In village Harinababi, the MFs are 36 per cent of the total households and they own only 15 per cent of the landholding. On the other hand, the MDFs constituting 32 per cent of the households occupy nearly 54 per cent of owned land. In the non-irrigated village Sandhagaon, about 47 per cent of households are MFs and they own 21 per

Table 3
Distribution of Owned Area According to Farmer Class

Class	*No. of Households*	*% of Total*	*% of Owned Area*
Charapara			
MF	8	30.8	8.1
SF	6	23.1	14.7
MDF	7	26.9	29.7
LF	5	19.2	47.5
Total	26	100.0	100.0
Harinababi			
MF	8	36.4	15.0
SF	7	31.8	30.9
MDF	7	31.8	54.1
LF	-	-	-
Total	22	100.0	100.0
Sandhagaon			
MF	7	46.6	20.9
SF	4	26.7	32.1
MDF	4	26.7	47.0
LF	-	-	-
Total	15	100.0	100.0

cent of owned area, whereas the MDFs constituting 27 per cent of the households possess 47 per cent of the owned land. It is clearly discernible from Table 3 that the peasantry is more differentiated in the advanced village Charapara.

Thus, our data suggest that caste rigidity, inequality in land ownership and above all, differentiation of peasantry are more pronounced in the irrigated villages than the non-irrigated village.

DETERMINANTS OF MIGRATION

Having discussed the socio-economic context of the three study villages, an attempt is made in this section to analyse the characteristics of migrants and the reasons for their migration. To start with we try to analyze how the level of agricultural development and the social structure affect the extent of rural-urban migration. Table 4 shows that in the irrigated village Charapara; out of 43 households, 20 households have at least one member emigrating to urban areas. Thus, the emigration ratio is 46.5 per cent. The emigration ratio is calculated as the ratio of number of households with members emigrating to total number of households in the village. In the irrigated village Harinababi the emigration ratio is the highest i.e. 59.1 per cent followed by Charapara (46.5%) and Sandhagaon (24.2%). Thus, the emigration ratio is quite high in the irrigated villages where inequality in land ownership and caste rigidity are more pronounced. As the non-irrigated village Sandhagaon is located amidst industrial complexes like Talcher colliery, Talcher Thermal Power Station and Fertiliser Corporation of India, many villagers get jobs in these enterprises. Residing in their own villages, they commute to their work places. Therefore, if work opportunities are available in the native place, people will have less incentive to emigrate. Lack of employment avenues in their native place compels them to migrate to urban areas.

The next logical question that follows is that 'who migrates?' How the migrants can be distinguished from non-migrants? What are the characteristics of persons who have larger propensity to

Table 4
Number of Emigrants per Household According to Farmer Category

Village\ Category	*Total No.of Households*	*No.of Households with Members Emigrating*	*%of Total*	*Total No. of Emigrants*	*No.of Emigrants per Household*	*1*	*No.of Households with Emigrants 2*	*+2*	*No.of Households Head is Emigrant*
Charapara									
OC	13	9	69.2	16	1.78	5	2	2	1
PRT	4	2	50.0	2	1.00	2	-	-	-
PL	9	8	88.9	9	1.13	7	1	-	7
PT	5	-	-	-	-	-	-	-	-
LL	11	1	9.1	1	1.00	1	-	-	-
Others	1	-	-	-	-	-	-	-	-
Total	43	20	46.5	28	1.40	1 5	3	2	8
Harinababi									
OC	14	9	64.3	17	1.89	4	3	2	1
PRT	5	1	20.0	1	1.00	1	-	-	1
PL	3	3	100.0	3	1.00	3	-	-	3
Total	22	13	59.1	21	1.62	8	3	2	5

Contd...

Village\ Category	Total No.of Households	No.of Households with Members Emigrating	%of Total	Total No. of Emigrants	No.of Emigrants per Household	No.of Households with Emigrants 1	2	+2	No.of Households Head is Emigrant
Sandhagaon									
OC	5	1	20.0	1	1.00	1	-	-	-
PRT	4	2	50.0	6	3.00	-	1	1	-
PL	6	3	50.0	4	1.33	2	1	-	3
PT	7	-	-	-	-	-	-	-	-
LL	8	1	12.5	1	1.00	1	-	-	-
Others	3	1	33.3	1	1.001	1	-	-	1
Total	33	8	24.2	13	1.63	5	2	1	4

migrate? The socio-economic attributes of migrants are more or less found to be fairly uniform across villages. Mostly young able-bodied adult men migrate to urban areas for employment. They are not necessarily the poorest men of the sending areas. In most cases, they are more educated. The migrant households are socio-economically and educationally better placed than the non-migrants. There is a positive relationship between land holding size and migration. Also, the higher castes have a larger propensity to migrate.

To find out the determinants of migration, some regression equations have been estimated and regression co-efficients have been computed. Table 5 presents the regression results with migration as the dependent variable and the land owned as the index of class position and caste as explanatory variables. In Charapara, the number of members emigrating from a household (MIGR) is positively and significantly related to total owned cultivable land (OLANDT) of the household. There is positive and significant relation between the ratio of migrating members to total family members (MIGRRAT) and owned land per family member including emigrants (OLANDRAT). Thus, land-rich and better-off families have more propensity to migrate. But there is negative and strong association between the ratio of adult members migrating (MIGRRA) and owned land per adult members including the emigrants (OLANDRA). This purports to say that due to adverse land man ratio, the disguised unemployed adult family members have a tendency to emigrate.

The caste (CASTE) coefficients are found to be negative and significant. Caste has been entered as a dummy variable with value equal to one if scheduled caste but zero if otherwise. This implies that the scheduled castes are less mobile than the higher castes. Thus the signs of all the regression coefficients in the village Charapara are as expected.

In the village Harinababi there is weak and positive relationship between MIGR and OLANDT and between MIGRRAT and OLANDRAT. MIGRRA is negatively related to OLANDRA but

Table 5
Result of Least-Squares Regression Analysis: Migration and Land Ownership (All Households)

Village	*Dependent Variable*	*Explanatory Variables*	*B*	*S.E. (B)*	*T-Value*	*Sig(T)*	*R Square*	*F-Value (k-1, n-k d.f.)*	*Sig(F)*
Charapara									
	MIGR	OLANDT	0.14	0.026	5.62	0.000	0.43	31.56	0.000
		Constant	0.19	0.148	1.26	0.214		(1.41)	
	MIGRRA	OLANDRA	-0.04	0.019	-1.94	0.060	0.44	15.17	0.000
		Caste	-0.46	0.084	-5.43	0.000		(2.38)	
		Constant	0.46	0.061	7.45	0.000			
	MIGRRAT	OLANDRA T	0.03	0.022	1.29	0.205	0.40	13.06	0.000
		Caste	-0.14	0.039	-3.54	0.001		(2.40)	
		Constant	0.14	0.029	4.79	0.000			
Harinababi									
	MIGR	OLANDT	0.13	0.102	1.25	0.228	0.07	1.55	0.228
		Constant	0.49	0.441	1.10	0.285		(1.20)	
	MIGRRA	OLANDRA	-0.03	0.099	-0.34	0.739	0.006	0.11	0.739
		Constant	0.33	0.141	2.37	0.028		(1.20)	
	MIGRRAT	OLANDRAT	0.07	0.115	0.63	0.539	0.02	0.39	0.539
		Caste	0.08	0.051	1.47	0.156		(1.20)	

Contd...

Village	*Dependent Variable*	*Explanatory Variables*	*B*	*S.E. (B)*	*T-Value*	*Sig(T)*	R *Square*	*F-Value (k-1, n-k d.f.)*	*Sig(F)*
Sandhagaon									
	MIGR	OLANDT	0.14	0.079	1.79	0.083	0.09	3.20	0.083
		Constant	0.21	0.179	1.16	0.255		(1,31)	
	MIGRRA	OLANDRA	-0.07	0.035	-2.03	0.052	0.27	5.54	0.009
		Caste	-0.25	0.074	-3.33	0.002		(2,30)	
		Constant	0.28	0.066	4.26	0.000			
	MIGRRA T	OLANDRAT	-0.11	0.139	-0.79	0.435	0.14	2.50	0.099
		Caste	-0.13	0.065	-1. 95	0.060		(2,30)	
		Constant	0.14	0.063	2.25	0.031			

is not significant. Thus, the signs of all the co-efficients are as expected.

In the non-irrigated village Sandhagaon, there is strong and positive association between MIGR and OLANDT. And there is negative strong relation between MIGRRA and OLANDRA. But OLANDRAT and MIGRRAT are negatively associated in contrast to the irrigated villages but not significant.

MOTIVATION FOR MIGRATION

As discussed in the introductory section, views of economists vary considerably in explaining rural-urban migration. Our field study unfolds that, size of land ownership holding of a family remaining constant, when there is expansion of the size of the family due to new births and with growth of small children into adults, the food requirement of the family increases. It becomes increasingly difficult to meet their consumption needs from their own-farm production. Initially they undertake temporary adjustment mechanisms like borrowing money from private moneylenders by pledging their precious assets like gold ornaments, brass utensils and land. Usually, they borrow from their lessors or employers who are the agriculturist moneylenders. These moneylenders charge exorbitant interest rates on advanced loans either in explicit or implicit manner by tying up with unpaid or under-paid labour services. If the borrower does not repay the principal amount with interest charged within the stipulated time, the collateral kept as security is confiscated by the lender. Also, the lender exploits by undervaluing the collateral (Bhaduri, 1983). Thus, gradually the land-poor but labour-surplus households lose their precious and productive assets and feel insecure. Sometimes they also sell their assets like land and bullocks at low prices to meet emergency needs. If the financial stringency recurs, the household as a whole has to think of a strategy that will provide a solution to the problem on a permanent basis. That is why some family members prefer to migrate to urban areas in quest of jobs. If they succeed in getting a job, they take up the job even if it involves unskilled labour, which they would not have taken up in their native place because of blemish to their social status. Thus the impersonalised atmosphere in the urban area widens their feasible choice set and getting employment becomes easier. However, all migration cannot be explained in this manner as some family members being educated and the so-called rural elites obviously migrate to urban areas to hold white collar jobs. Due to the extended family system, they continue to maintain link with their family members in the village and regularly send money to their parents. The remittances that a household receives help in consolidating one's class position in the village.

A category-wise comparison of the migration ratio as contained in Table 4 reveals that in village Charapara, the emigration ratio is the highest for pure lessors (89%) followed by OCs (69%) and PRTs (50%) and it is the lowest for the landless class. The same gradation is observed in Harinababi. In Sandhagaon, the emigration ratio is the same 50 per cent for the PLs and PRTs and 20 per cent for OCs and the lowest (12.5%) for the landless labourers. In irrigated villages, it is observed that the semi-absentee emigrants lease out their entire land-holdings. Therefore, in the case of PLs, the emigration ratio is the highest. PRTs are found to be less mobile than the OCs. But in Sandhagaon, there are resident pure lessors. Therefore, the emigration ratio is low in the case of PLs. In Charapara and Sandhagaon, the PTs and LLs are found to be quite immobile. Thus, the poorest or the landless class are the least mobile in all the villages. As they do not have the minimal fund required for job hunting, they are incapacitated to move elsewhere for better life. Besides, as their resource base is poor, they feel insecure to take up a new venture. They hesitate to take risk and believe in the status quo. Moreover, being uneducated they are not aware of better prospects and opportunities available outside their village economy.

An analysis of the types of jobs for which the family members have migrated (Table 6) shows that in Charapara most of the OC household emigrants i.e. 63 per cent are employed in managerial

Table 6
Percentage of Emigrants and Type of Job According to Farmer Category

Village\ Category	*Govt. or Semi-Govt. Job*				*Purely Private Sector Job*					
	Managerial	*Clerical*	*Skilled Worker*	*Un-skilled Worker*	*Managerial*	*Clerical*	*Skilled Worker*	*Un-skilled Worker*	*Self Employed*	*Total*
Charapara										
OC	18.8	25.0	6.3	-	12.5	6.3	-	31.3	-	100.0
PRT	-	-	-	50.0	-	-	-	50.0	-	100.0
PL	-	22.2	-	11.1	-	-	-	66.7	-	100.0
LL	-	-	-	-	-	-	-	100.0	-	100.0
Total	10.7	21.4	3.6	7.1	7.1	3.6	0.0	46.4	0.0	100.0
Harinababi										
OC	-	11.8	5.9	23.5	5.9	5.9	-	41.2	5.9	100.0
PRT	-	-	-	-	-	-	-	100.0	-	100.0.
PL	-	-	-	-	-	-	-	100.0	-	100.0
Total	0.0	9.5	4.8	19.0	4.8	4.8	0.0	52.4	4.8	100.0
Sandhagaon										
OC	-	100.0	-	-	-	16.7	-	-	-	100.0
PRT	16.7	-	-	16.7	-	-	16.7	16.7	16.7	100.0
PL	-	-	75.0	25.0	-	-	-	-	-	100.0
LL	-	-	-	-	-	-	-	-	100.0	100.0
Others	100.0	-	-	-	-	-	-	-	-	100.0
Total	7.7	15.4	23.1	15.4	0.0	7.7	7.7	7.7	15.4	100.0

and clerical jobs. Managerial jobs include administrative jobs and all class I and class II employees of state government like engineers, doctors, supervisors and superintendents. Clerical jobs refer to class III employees of the state government like teachers, cashiers, clerks. In the case of PRTs, all the emigrants are employed in unskilled work. For PLs, 78 per cent are engaged in unskilled manual labour. One landless labourer has sent his son to an urban area to work as a hotel boy. In Harinababi, 64 per cent of the OC emigrants are engaged in unskilled manual labour and in the case of PLs, cent per cent emigrants are engaged in unskilled manual labour. Most of them are working in informal sector. As the residents of Harinababi belong to the middle caste in comparison to higher caste residents of Charapara, they have mainly migrated for unskilled manual work.

In the non-irrigated village Sandhagaon, 75 per cent of the PLs have emigrated for skilled work like helper and operator and they are industrially trained. A casual labourer has migrated to his wife's native place, as employment is available there likewise in the irrigated village Charapara, it is observed that most of the married daughters of landless labourers prefer to come back to this village as work is available here and are settling permanently. Thus, there is considerable immigration of labourers to irrigated villages.

An inter-class comparison of migration for different jobs (Table 7) reveals that most of the MDF and LF emigrants are engaged in managerial and clerical work whereas the MF and SF emigrants are mostly unskilled workers. The landless labourers hesitate to migrate as they do not have the initial sum that is required to start job hunting. Thus, the class cleavage is gradually becoming solidified. The education level of the emigrants has been given in Table 8 and naturally the education level of emigrants tallies with the jobs in which they are engaged.

The distance traversed by the emigrants as per farmer class is given in Table 9. It is revealed that in the irrigated villages, most of the migrants have moved to places which are at a distance of more than 100 kms including Calcutta and distant states like Uttar

Table 7

Percentage of Emigrants and Type of Job According to Farmer Class

Village\ Category	*No. of Emigrants*	*Govt. or Semi-Govt. Job*				*Purely Private Sector Job*				*Self Employed*	*Total*
		Managerial	*Clerical*	*Skilled Worker*	*Un-skilled Worker*	*Managerial*	*Clerical*	*Skilled Worker*	*Un-skilled Worker*		
Charapara											
MF	7	-	-	-	28.6	-	-	-	71.4	-	100.
SF	4	-	50.0	-	-	-	-	-	50.0	-	100.
MDF	7	-	-	-	-	14.3	14.3	71.4	-	-	100.
LF	9	33.3	44.4	11.1	-	11.1	-	-	-	-	100.
LL	*1	-	-	-	-	-	-	-	100.0	-	100.
Total	28	10.7	21.4	3.6	7.1	7.1	3.6	17.9	28.6	0.0	100.
Harinababi											
MF	4	-	-	-	-	-	-	-	100.0	-	100.
SF	7	-	28.6	14.3	14.3	-	-	-	28.6	14.3	100.
MDF	10	-	-	-	30.0	10.0	10.0	-	50.0	-	100.0
Total	21	0.0	9.5	4.8	19.0	4.8	4.8	0.0	52.4	4.8	100.0
Sandhagaon											
MF	6	16.7	-	16.7	33.3	-	16.7	-	-	16.7	100.0
SF	2	-	50.0	50.0	-	-	-	-	-	-	100.0
MDF	3	-		33.3	-	-	-	33.3	33.3	-	100.0
LL	**1	-		-	-	-	-	-	-	100.0	100.0
Others	1	-	100.0	-	-	-	-	-	-	-	100.0
Total	13	7.7	15.4	23.1	15.4	0.0	7.7	7.7	7.7	15.4	100.0

Notes: * He has become a hotel boy in urban area. ** He has migrated to his wife's native place and is a casual labourer.

Table 8
Percentage of Emigrants and Level of Education According to Farmer Category

Village\Category	*Illiterate*	*Minor*	*Secondary*	*Graduate*	*ITI Training*	*AMIE/ Engineering*	*Total*
Charapara							
OC	-	-	37.5	37.5	12.5	12.5	100.0
PRT	-	50.0	50.0	-	-	-	100.0
PL	-	33.3	55.6	11.1	-	-	100.0
LL	100.0	-	-	-	-	-	100.0
Total	3.6	14.3	42.9	25.0	7.1	7.1	100.0
Harinababi							
OC	-	23.5	47.1	29.4	-	-	100.0
PRT	-	100.0	-	-	-	-	100.0
PL	-	100.0	-	-	-	-	100.0
Total	0.0	38.1	38.1	23.8	0.0	0.0	100.0
Sandhagaon							
OC	-	-	100.0	-	-	-	100.0
PRT	-	16.7	50.0	-	16.7	16.7	100.0
PL	-	-	25.0	-	75.0	-	100.0
LL	100.0	-	-	-	-	-	100.0
Others	-	-	-	100.0	-	-	100.0
Total	7.7	7.7	38.5	7.7	30.8	7.7	100.0

Note: ITI refers to Industrial Training Institute, AMIE refers to Associate Member of Institute of Engineers

Pradesh, Punjab, Delhi and Karnataka and even Nepal. But in Sandhagaon, most of the emigrants are employed within 50 kms radius of the village. Thus, the residents of Sandhagaon are less mobile than that of irrigated villages.

Table 9
Percentage of Emigrants and Distance Traversed According to Farmer Class

Category	*0-50 Kms.*	*50-100 Kms*	*Above 100 Kms*	*Neighbour State*	*Distant State*	*Total*
Charapara						
MF	-	14.3	28.6	42.9	14.3	100.0
SF	-		75.0	25.0	-	100.0
MDF	14.3	-	28.6	2.6	28.6	100.0
LF	33.3	11.1	44.4	-	11.1	100.0
LL			100.0	-	0.0	100.0
Total	14.3	7.1	42.9	21.4	14.3	100.0
Harinababi						
MF		-	-	100.0	-	100.0
SF	-	14.3	42.9		42.9	100.0
MDF	10.0 I	20.0	30.0	20.0	20.0	100.0
Total	4.8	14.3	28.6	28.6	23.8	100.0
Sandhagaon						
MF	66.7	-	33.3	-		100.0
SF		50.0	-	-	50.0	100.0
MDF	33.3		66.7	-	-	100.0
LL	100.0	-	-	-	-	100.0
Others		-	100.0	-	-	100.0
Total	46.2	7.7	38.5	0.0	7.7	100.0

A village-wise comparison of duration of migration (Table 10) unveils that in the advanced village Charapara, 36 per cent of the migrants had emigrated more than fifteen years back and 39 per cent have migrated within the last 5 years. Those who have migrated within last five years belong to the second generation and are much younger. They have migrated mostly for clerical and managerial jobs. In Harinababi and also in Sandhagaon, the largest proportion i.e. 38 per cent of the migrants have moved within the last 5 to 10 years. Thus, the households in these two villages have been mobile quite later than that of Charapara.

Table 10
Percentage of Emigrants and Duration of Emigration According to Farmer Class

Category	*0-5 Years*	*5-10 Years*	*10-15 Years*	*Above 15 Years*	*Total*
Charapara					
MF	28.6	-	14.3	57.1	100.0
SF	25.0	50.0	-	25.0	100.0
MDF	71.4	14.3	-	14.3	100.0
LF	22.2	22.2	11.1	44.4	100.0
LL	100.0	-	-	-	100.0
Total	39.3	17.9	7.1	35.7	100.0
Harinababi					
MF	-	-	50.0	50.0	100.0
SF	-	57.1	28.6	14.3	100.0
MDF	30.0	40.0	20.0	10.0	100.0
Total	14.3	38.1	28.6	19.0	100.0
Sandhagaon					
MF	33.3	16.7	16.7	33.3	100.0
SF	-	-	50.0	50.0	100.0
MDF	-	66.7	-	33.3	100.0
LL	-	100.0	-	-	100.0
Others	-	100.0	-	-	100.0
Total	15.4	38.5	15.4	30.8	100.0

But it is to be noted that in the case of irrigated villages those emigrants who have migrated more than fifteen years ago are the marginal farmers. They did not have sufficient income from cultivation to meet their consumption. That is why they had to migrate mainly to Calcutta. They had to take up unskilled manual jobs like gardener, peon, and cook in private sectors. They were low paid, working for long hours and there was no job security. Thus, the emigration of marginalised peasantry from Charapara and Harinababi to Calcutta was not due to any pull factor of growth and income but under the push factor of indebtedness, pauperisation and unemployment and as a survival strategy of the last resort. Though the emigrants stayed in urban area, their family members used to stay in the villages. It was quite impossible on their part to maintain their family in urban areas with the meagre salary that they were getting. They were paid individual wage and not the family wage. Thus, in destination areas migration culminated to subordination of labour to capital and exploitation of labour. Under such a situation, the neo-classical explanation of migration in terms of benefit (expected income) and cost does not hold good. According to Marxists, crisis occurs when relations of production not only impede the development of productive forces but entail declining living standards and economic stagnation. Thus, the out-migration observed in our study areas can be better understood in a Marxist framework in terms of exploitation and as a symptom of feudal crisis.

To explain this in detail, one needs to trace the evolution of property rights in Orissa. This study being an empirical one, the historical perspective does not come under the ambit of the paper. However, briefly the historical roots of migration can be explained. In Orissa, during the native Hindu rule, the Maratha rule and the Mughal periods, there was no absolute property rights in land. The cultivating peasantry enjoyed security of tenure on the land, they cultivated as long as they paid the required share of the produce to the authority. During the British rule in the year 1804, the *zamindars* were conferred proprietary rights on land. The *zamindars* were only the rent collectors in pre-British period. Thus, the actual tillers of land became tenants and the revenue farmers became the de facto owners of land. Thus, a marginalised peasantry was created, who in later period being pauperised had to migrate to Calcutta and Assam tea gardens for employment. Thus, predominance of marginal and small land holdings in Orissa is the root cause of out-migration. The landlessness and skewed distribution of land holdings observed in today's Orissa can legitimately be traced back to its colonial past.

INCREASE IN PURE LESSOR AND PURE TENANCY

Having discussed the causes and determinants of rural-urban migration, now we intend to delineate its impact on land, labour and credit relations in source areas. In our study villages mostly the able adult young male family members have emigrated to urban areas for employment. It is observed that after the departure of the emigrant, initially his father self-cultivates the land with remittance money. But with passage of time, when he grows old and becomes physically weak, he is no more able to cultivate or supervise field work. The emigrant's sons, even if they grow up, hesitate to take up cultivation work, as cultivation is deemed as an inferior occupation in the village society. Therefore, the semi-absentee emigrants are compelled to lease out their entire holdings. That is why in our study villages we find mainly pure lessors and not partial lessors. When asked about the reason for leasing out land, all the lessors replied that there was no male member available in the family willing to supervise the cultivation work (Swain; 1999a. 1999b). Thus, due to out-migration of landowners, there has been a shift in the land tenure system. The area under tenancy has increased. The lands are leased on share rent basis with 50:50 ratio. Interestingly, during our survey we came across a villager who had previously out-migrated to urban areas for employment. After retirement from his job, he has come back to his native village. As he has spent most of his productive life in the metropolis, he lacks experience in cultivation. Therefore on retuning to his village, he is no more able to self-cultivate his land. At old age he lacks the will power and stamina to venture into cultivation which is a quite risky and arduous job.

Moreover, we find that as the marginal and small farmers who were once sharecropping land of large farmers have migrated to urban areas, the landless labourers are now getting scope to lease in land. Therefore, there is a visible tendency of increase in number of landless tenants or pure tenants.

INMIGRATION OF LABOUR

Due to emigration of able-bodied adult young male members to urban areas, in the sending areas the emigrant households are depending on hired labourers for their agricultural work. With the remittance money, they have been able to raise two to three crops on the same plot of land during *kharif*, *rabi* and summer season. Also, they are cultivating High Yielding Varieties of seed and applying fertiliser. In the case of HYV paddy the labour requirement is higher than the local variety. Thus, demand for labour has increased which has an upward pressure on wage. Many unemployed youths from tribal areas have migrated to these areas and are engaged as farm servants to provide dependable labour services to their employers. In village Charapara, there are seven farm servants out of which three have come from tribal areas. In each of the village Harinababi and Sandhagaon, there are two farm servants who have emigrated from tribal areas, as jobs are not available in their native place. Thus, inmigration of labour to our study areas has increased. Whereas the marginal and small farmers from our study areas have emigrated to urban areas and metropolitan cities, there is an exodus of tribal people from hilly and forest areas into these villages. Thus, unequal development and regional disparity is causing movement of population from backward areas to developed region.

DECLINE IN TRADER MONEYLENDERS

Moreover, it is observed that there has been a decline in trading-cum-moneylending activities in source areas. In our study villages many years back many cultivators were borrowing money from trader moneylenders for cultivation of cash crops like jute, potato and ground nut. They were borrowing for purchase of improved varieties of seeds and fertiliser required for cultivation of these cash crops. As there were no institutional sources of credit available to the farmers, they were borrowing from private moneylenders with onerous terms and conditions. Usually, the trader cum moneylenders advance loans for the cultivation of cash crops like jute at the time of sowing or transplanting with the condition that just after harvest the cultivator will sell the crop to the lender at a predetermined low price irrespective of the market price. Conditions vary with regard to interest payment.

In our investigation, only one respondent, a small farmer owner tenant in village Harinababi reported borrowing from the trader moneylender (Swain, 1998). He had borrowed Rs. 200 from the trader for two months. And after harvest he repaid the principal loan amount in terms of jute at the prevailing market price but towards interest he paid 2 kgs. jute extra for the principal amount of Rs. 100. As the price of jute was Rs. 380 per quintal, interest for Rs. 100 was Rs. 7.60 for two months. So the interest rate per annum was 45.6 per cent. But here the borrower is compelled to sell just after harvest when the price is very low. To that extent, there is further implicit interest charged.

It is to be noted that 10 years back, there were many trader cum moneylenders in these villages advancing loans for cultivation of jute. In 1982-1983, the price of jute increased abruptly to Rs. 1000 per quintal pulled by the increased demand for jute due to loss of jute crop in West Bengal caused by flood. The farmers expecting high price started cultivating jute the next year but the price almost halved to Rs. 500 per quintal. The price of jute is volatile in nature. Gradually, there is decreasing demand for jute as the gunny bags are now being replaced by plastic and paper bags. Therefore, in Charapara jute cultivation has declined. Moreover, almost all the cultivator households have some supplementary income like remittance income or salary income and that they no longer go to the trader moneylenders to borrow for cultivation purposes. The emigrant members of the family though reside in urban areas, send money to their family members for agricultural purposes. Thus, remittance money has helped in the decline of trader moneylenders and the exploitation thereof.

SUMMARY AND IMPLICATIONS

The study based on primary data collected from three villages in Orissa in Eastern India reveals the followings on the causes of migration, determinants of migration, socio-economic characteristics of migrants and consequences of migration on source area.

An analysis of the socio-economic context of the study villages with data on distribution of owned land area among households and their caste configuration indicate that caste rigidity, inequality in land ownership and above all, differentiation of peasantry are more pronounced in the two irrigated villages than the non-irrigated village.

The emigration ratio is higher in the irrigated villages than the non-irrigated village. As the non-irrigated village Sandhagaon is located amidst industrial complexes like Talcher colliery, Talcher Thermal Power Station and Fertiliser Corporation of India, many villagers get jobs in these enterprises. Residing in their own villages, they commute to their work places. Therefore, if work opportunities are available in the native place, people will have less incentive to emigrate. Lack of income-earning avenues in their native place compels them to migrate to urban areas,

The socio-economic characteristics of migrants are more or less found to be fairly uniform across villages. Mostly young able-bodied adult men migrate to urban areas for employment. In our study, no female members are found to emigrate. The migrants are not necessarily the poorest men of the sending areas. In most cases, they are more educated. The migrant households are socio-economically and educationally better placed than the non-migrants. There is a positive relationship between land holding size and migration. Also, the higher castes have a larger propensity to migrate.

The regression exercises with migration as the dependent variable and the land owned as the index of class position and caste as explanatory variables indicate that the number of members emigrating from a household (MIGR) is positively and significantly related to total owned cultivable land (OLANDT) of the household. There is positive and significant relation between the ratio of total members migrating and owned land per family member including emigrants (OLANDRAT). Thus, land-rich and better-off families have more propensity to migrate. But there is negative and strong association between the ratio of adult members migrating (MIGRRA) and owned land per adult members including the emigrants (OLANDRA). This purports to say that due to adverse land man ratio, the disguised unemployed adult family members have a tendency to emigrate. The caste (CASTE) coefficients reveal that the scheduled castes are less mobile than the higher castes.

A category-wise comparison of the migration ratio reveals that the emigration ratio is the highest for pure lessors in all the villages and it is the lowest for the landless class. The landless labourers hesitate to emigrate as they do not have the initial sum that is required to start job hunting. Thus, the class cleavage is gradually being solidified in this manner.

Most of the OC household emigrants are employed in managerial and clerical jobs, whereas the emigrants from part-tenant and pure lessor households are mostly engaged in manual jobs in unorganised and informal sectors. An inter-class comparison of migration for different jobs also reveals that most of the MDF and LF emigrants are engaged in managerial and clerical work whereas the MF and SF emigrants are mostly unskilled workers. The education level of the emigrants tallies with the jobs in which they are engaged.

It is revealed that in the irrigated villages Charapara and Harinababi most of the migrants have moved to places which are at a distance of more than 100 kms including Calcutta and distant states like Uttar Pradesh, Punjab, Delhi and Karnataka and even Nepal. But in Sandhagaon, most of the emigrants are employed within 50 kms radius of the village. Thus, the residents of Sandhagaon are less mobile than that of irrigated villages.

A village-wise comparison of duration of migration unfolds that in the advanced village Charapara, 36 per cent of the migrants migrated more than fifteen years back and 39 per cent have migrated within the last 5 years. Those who have migrated within last five years belong to the second generation and are much younger. They have migrated mostly for clerical and managerial jobs. In Harinababi and also in Sandhagaon, the largest proportion i.e. 38 per cent of the migrants have moved within the last 5 to 10 years. Thus, the households in these two villages have been mobile quite later than that of Charapara.

Due to out-migration of landowners, there has been a shift in the land tenure system. The area under tenancy has increased. The absentee landowners have leased out their entire land holdings. Thus, in our study area we find mainly pure lessors and not part lessor. Moreover, we find that as the marginal and small farmers who were once sharecropping land of large farmers have migrated to urban areas, the landless labourers are now getting scope to lease in land. Therefore, there is a visible tendency of increase in number of landless tenants or pure tenants.

Whereas the marginal and small farmers from our study areas have emigrated to urban areas and metropolitan cities, there is an exodus of tribals from hilly and forest areas into these villages. Thus, unequal development and regional disparity is causing movement of people from backward to developed area. The resource base of the migrant households is found to be strengthened with remittance money. No more, they depend on trader moneylenders for cash advances to cultivate remunerative crops. There has been a decline in trader moneylenders in the study area and the exploitation thereof.

As regards causes of migration, the study reveals that the emigration of marginalised peasantry from rural areas to urban centres for employment in informal sectors at low wages and without job security was not due to any pull factor of growth and income but under the push factor of indebtedness, pauperisation and unemployment and as a survival strategy of the last resort. Though the emigrants stayed in urban area, their family members used to stay in the villages. It was quite impossible on their part to maintain their family in urban areas with the meagre salary that they were getting. In the destination area, the migrant was not given family wage. He was getting only individual wage, which was sufficient to maintain himself only. Thus, the neo-classical explanation of migration in terms of benefits (expected income) and costs does not hold good in this context. According to Marxists crisis occurs when relations of production not only impede the development of productive forces but entail declining living standards and economic stagnation. Thus, the out-migration from our study villages can be better understood in a Marxist framework in terms of exploitation and as a symptom of feudal crisis.

References

Amin, Samir (1974), 'Modern Migrations in Western Africa', in Samir Amin (ed.) *Modem Migrations in Western Africa.* Oxford University Press.

Basu, A. M., Kaushik Basu and Ranjan Ray (1987), 'Migrants and the Native Bond: An Analysis of Microlevel Data from Delhi', *Economic and Political Weekly,* Vol. 22, Nos. 19, 20 and 21, May, pp. AN145-54.

Beteille, Andre (1971), *Caste, Class and Power: Changing Patterns of Stratification in a Tanjore Village.* California: University Press.

Beteille, Andre (1973), *Studies in Agrarian Social Structure,* Oxford University Press.

Bhaduri, A. (1983), *Economic Structure of Backward Agriculture,* Delhi: Macmillan Press.

Breman, Jan (1974), *Patronage and Exploitation: Changing Agrarian Relations in South Gujarat, India,* California: University Press.

Breman, Jan (1985), *Of Peasants, Migrants and Paupers: Rural Labour and Capitalist Production in West India,* Delhi: Oxford University Press.

Breman, Jan (1996), *Footloose Labour: Working in India's Informal Economy.* Cambridge: University Press.

Brown Allan A. and Egon Neuberger (eds.), (1977), *Internal Migration: A Comparative Perspective,* New York: Academic Press.

Chopra, Radhika (1995), 'Maps of Experience: Narratives of Migration in an Indian Village', *Economic and Political Weekly,* Vo1. 30, No. 49, December 9, pp. 3156-62.

Dupont, Veronique (1992), 'Impact of Migration on Industrial Development: Case Study of Jetpur in Gujarat', *Economic and Political Weekly,* Vol. 27, No. 45, November 7, pp. 2423-36.

Fei, J. C. H. and G. Ranis (1961), 'A Theory of Economic Development.' *American Economic Review,* Vol. 51, No. 4.

Gill, S. S. (1998), 'Migration of Labour in India', *The Indian Journal of Labour Economics,* Vol. 41, No. 4, Oct-Dec., pp. 617-24.

Lee, E. S. (1966), 'A Theory of Migration', *Demography*, Vol. 3.

Haan Arjan De (1999), 'Livelihoods and Poverty: The Role of Migration-A Critical Review of the Migration Literature', *The Journal* of *Development Studies,* Vol. 36, No. 2, December , pp. 1-47.

Kundu, Amitabh and Shalini Gupta (1996), 'Migration, Urbanisation and Regional Inequality', *Economic and Political Weekly,* Vol. 31, No. 52, December 28, pp. 3391-98.

Lewis, Arthur (1954), 'Economic Development with Unlimited Supplies of Labour.' *Manchester School of Economic and Social Studies,* Vol. 22, No. 2, May.

Matoussi, M. S. and J. B. Nugent (1989), 'The Switch to Sharecropping in Medjez-el-bab', in M. K. Nabli and J. B. Nugent (eds.)

Mukherji Sekhar (1981), *Mechanisms* of *Underdevelopment, Labour Migration, Planning Strategies in India,* Calcutta: Prajna.

Nabli, M. K. and J. B. Nugent (eds.) (1989), *The New Institutional Economics and Development: Theory and Applications to Tunisia.* Amsterdam: Elsevier Science Publishers BV.

Nolan, Peter (1993), 'Economic Reform, Poverty and Migration in China', *Economic and Political Weekly,* Vol. 27, No. 26, June 26, pp. 1369-77.

Ravenstein, E. J. (1885), 'The Laws of Migration', *Journal of the Royal Statistical Society*, Vol. 48

Ravenstein, E. J. (1889), 'The Laws of Migration', *Journal of the Royal Statistical Society,* Vol. 52.

Sjaastad, L. A. (1962), 'The Costs and Returns of Human Migration', *Journal of Political Economy,* Vol. 70, No. 5.

Srivastava, Ravi (1998), 'Migration and the Labour Market in India', *The Indian Journal of Labour Economics,* Vol. 41, No. 4, pp. 583-616.

Standing, Guy (1981), 'Migration and Modes of Exploitation: Social Origins of Immobility and Mobility', *The Journal of Peasant Studies* 8(2): 173-211, January.

Stark, Oded (1991), *The Migration of Labour,* Oxford: Basil Blackwell.

Swain, Mamata (1998), *Peasant Agriculture and Share Tenancy in Orissa.* Commonwealth Publishers, Delhi.

Swain, Mamata (1999a), 'Tenancy Structure in Orissa: Implications for Agricultural Growth', *Artha Vijnana,* Vol. 41, No. 3, pp. 245-61, September.

Swain, Mamata (1999b), 'Agricultural Tenancy and Interlinked Transactions' in Two Parts, *Economic and Political Weekly,* Sept. 11-17, pp. 2657-66, Sept. 18-24, pp. 2752-58, Vol. 34, Nos. 37&38.

Swain, Mamata (2000), 'Agricultural Development and Interlocked Factor Markets', *Indian Journal* of *Agricultural Economics,* Conference Number, Vol. 55, No. 3, pp. 78-108, July-Sept.

Swain, Mamata (2001), 'Dynamics of Share Tenancy Institution', *Review* of *Development and Change,* Jan-June, Vo1. 6, No. 1, pp. 51-72.

Swain, Mamata (2001), 'Rural Indebtedness and Usurious Interest Rates in Eastern India: Some Micro Evidence', *Journal* of *Social and Economic Development,* Vol. 3, No. 1.

Todaro, M. P. (1969), 'A Model of Labour Migrat!pn and Urban Unemployment in Less Developed Countries', *American Economic Review,* Vol. 59, No. 1.

Todaro, M. P. (1976), *Intemal Migration in Developing Countries: A Review of Theorj, Evidence, Methodology and Research Priorities,* International Labour Office, Geneva.

Unni, Jeemol (1991), 'Regional Variations in Rural Non-Agricultural Employment: An Exploratory Analysis', *Economic and Political Weeklyl,* Vol. 26, No. 3, January 19, pp. 109-22.

13

RURAL-URBAN MIGRATION: A CASE STUDY

M. S. Gupta

INTRODUCTION

Rural-urban migration is basically labour migration. It is thought to be the consequence of unequal development wherein people from 'backward' regions move to 'developed' regions. These developed regions may either be prosperous rural areas or expanding urban areas where the people from the regions of less employment income opportunities flock. Economists and social scientists have propounded various theories about migration, which analyses the process, causes and consequences of migration. 'Pull' and 'push' factors of migration have often been talked with regard to the causes of migration. The factors like poverty and deprivation, land alienation, population pressure, lack of employment and income opportunities, social differentiation, penetration of market economy, etc. are some of the factors which are closely linked with migration.

Bihar is one of the states of India from where the out-migration from the rural areas has taken place. Apart from the out-migration from rural areas, Patna Town is a witness of heavy in-migration from the rural areas of other districts of Bihar which results in variety of problems and imbalances viz., problems of urbanization, slums, pollution, unemployment and many other institutional, social, cultural and educational problems. Hence, a multiform attack should be organized to check the rural-urban migration. In present paper, some remedial measures have also been suggested to make the migration process more systematic, organized and less cumbersome.

OBJECTIVES

The present study primarily aims at analyzing the causes of socio-economic problems and social unrest in rural areas of undivided Bihar where from large number of rural people are rushing towards Patna town. In this process, causes responsible for out-migration of people has been analyzed. More emphasis has been laid down on economic and social factors, which have forced people of different categories to leave their places of origin and move to Patna Town. Socio-economic factors which have attracted the people of the rural areas to the urban centers have also been given due consideration. An attempt has also been made to highlight the impact of out-migration of people from the rural areas and the people living in those areas. Some considerations have been made on the consequences of rural-urban migration in Patna Town.

METHODOLOGY

The present study is an empirical study by applying sociological methods to test the socio-economic crisis, social problems of rural-urban migration in Bihar. The sociological method consists a social survey through a structural questionnaire. A sample survey has been conducted in different localities of Patna Town. As the proposed project has been applied to examine the different variables of socio-economic problems of rural-urban migration and correlation among them, sampling is based on random sampling.

Samples for the study have been collected on interview basis randomly and the utmost care has been taken. A comprehensive questionnaire has been framed and the questions are related to personal information e.g. family background, age, sex structure, marital status, family organization, causes of migration, socio-economic changes and social unrest developed in the study area and increasing rural-urban migration, etc. The survey has covered 500 rural-urban migrants without any discrimination of age, occupation, caste, religion and sex. Hence, the source of information is based on primary data.

SELECTION OF STUDY AREA

As regards the geographical coverage, Patna Town in Bihar was selected for fieldwork. The choice of Patna was influenced due to many reasons. Patna, the heartland and state capital of Bihar is becoming thickly populated and facing severe threat of migration day by day. There is a gross difference between today's Patna and 25-30 year's old Patna. As an old resident of Patna, I have seen the both situations and the period in between. Today everyone is coming from other districts of Bihar and want to settle in Patna, leaving one's palatial building in village or parental area. There are many factors responsible for this situation. The villages and sub-areas are still very backward and are lacking from basic infrastructure viz. transport, road, education, employment, medical facilities, electricity, poor farming, etc. Another factor, which holds position in several factors is caste clashes, worst law and order situation outside Patna in Bihar. It may also be added here that Patna is the state capital and on the main transport route for most of the labour in-migrating from other places. However, migration in bulk from other districts or places is also creating problems for Patna in all respect including the law and order situation. This is the reason I have chosen this research project.

LOCATION AND STUDY DESIGN

The study was carried out in Patna Town. It was expected that the problems and the attitudes of respondent migrants might differ in nature as the exposure of migrants from different villages and Blocks might have different movements in the society. Thus, the study not only shows how much migrants have helped in highlighting their problems but it also provides its impact on various types of migrant population who differ in their socio-economic criteria.

In this context, a questionnaire was developed to assess the various aspects migrants mentioned above and was self administered to the migrants of Patna Town.

SAMPLE SIZE

To examine the different variables of rural-urban migration from various districts of Bihar, sampling has been the basis on random sampling. A sample survey has been conducted through questionnaire concerning socio-economic and political conditions of migrants to Patna from various districts of undivided Bihar. The survey has covered 500 respondents, selected at random basis for the study as random samples. All the selected respondent migrants were taken aside and questionnaire was self-administered. The respondent migrants selected were of right age and without any discrimination for highlighting their socio-economic and political conditions.

FINDINGS OF THE STUDY

Migration is a very important subject of study and research in a backward economy. The subject of migration has attracted the attention of increasing number of social scientists. In a backward region, migration means migration of labour from less developed areas to more developed areas. "Rural to urban migration" , the most important of the migration streams, is generally attributed to pull factors like the difference between average income opportunities in the urban and rural areas.

The present research work is an attempt to study the socio-economic and political conditions of migrants to Patna from other districts of Bihar.

Bihar, one of the most populous states of India, is economically the most backward. Although a very high proportion below poverty line, Bihar has the lowest per capita income among the major states of India and also fares very badly with respect to most of the other socio-economic indicators.

In this situation, migration only to a particular place in a backward state will further increase population pressure, affect law and order situation and create other problems. Patna is the capital of Bihar where persons are migrating heavily from other districts of Bihar, which will create its own problems.

Following are the major findings of the study:

DISTRICT-WISE BREAK UP OF MIGRANTS

Table 1 shows the position of district-wise migrants to Patna from various districts of Bihar. It shows that the highest percentage of migrants to Patna is 9.6 per cent which belongs Darbhanga followed by Hazaribagh with 8.8 per cent, Jahanabad and Ranchi both with 8.4 per cent while the lowest percentage (0.4 per cent) belongs to Muzaffarpur.

Table 1
District-wise Break up of Migrants

District	*No. of persons*	*Per cent*
Araria	4	0.8
Aurangabad	20	4.0
Bhagalpur	8	1.6
Bhojpur	30	6.0
Buxar	14	2.8
Chapra	4	0.8
Daltenganj	8	1.6
Darbhanga	48	9.6
East Champaran	14	2.8
Gaya	38	7.6
Gopalganj	4	0.8
Hazaribagh	44	8.8
Jahahabad	42	8.4
Jamsedpur	16	3.2
Jamui	14	2.8
Madhubani	16	3.2
Mirzapur	6	1.2
Motihari	4	0.8
Munger	10	2.0

Contd...

District	*No. of persons*	*Per cent*
Muzaffarpur	2	0.4
Nalanda	12	2.4
Nawada	20	4.0
Palamu	4	0.8
Patna	2	0.4
Purnia	22	4.4
Ranchi	42	8.4
Rohtas	18	3.6
Samastipur	4	0.8
Sitamarhi	24	4.8
West Champaran	6	1.2
Total	500	100.0

SOCIO-ECONOMIC CONDITIONS

Caste Distribution

Table 2 shows caste-wise distribution of migrants to Patna from other districts of Bihar. The table reveals that OBC respondents have the highest percentage i.e. 60.8 per cent among the migrants followed by Scheduled Caste with 22.4 per cent while percentage of Scheduled Tribe is only 1.2 per cent.

Table 2
Caste Distribution

Caste	*No. of persons*	*Per cent*
Upper caste	78	15.6
OBC	304	60.8
SC	112	22.4
ST	6	1.2
Total	500	100.0

RELIGION

Table 3 shows the religion of migrants. It is clear from the table that 86 per cent of the migrants are Hindu followed by Muslims with 13.2 per cent while 0.8 per cent of the migrants belong to Christian in the study.

Table 3
Religion

Religion	*No. of persons*	*Per cent*
Hindu	430	86.0
Muslim	66	13.2
Christian	4	.8
Total	500	100.0

AGE DISTRIBUTION

Table 4 shows age groups of migrants with their percentage. It reveals that 65.2 per cent of the migrants belong to age groups of 20-25 and 25-30 years while 18 per cent of the migrants belong to 15-20 years of age group.

Table 4
Age Distribution

Age Group (in years)	*No. of persons*	*Per cent*
Below 15	12	2.4
15-20	90	18.0
20-25	204	40.8
25-30	122	24.4
30-35	40	8.0
35-40	18	3.6
40-45	8	1.6
45 and above	6	1.2
Total	500	100.0

The study further reveals that migrants below 15 years of age and 40 years and above are 2.4 per cent and 2.8 per cent respectively.

SEX DISTRIBUTION

In sex-wise study of migrants, the study reveals that 98 per cent of the total migrants belong to male while only 2 per cent belong female, as it is clear from the Table 5.

MARITAL STATUS

The study reveals that the percentage of married persons migrating to Patna is very high in comparison to unmarried persons. Table-

6 shows that 86 per cent of the migrating persons are married while only 14 per cent are unmarried.

Table 5
Sex Distribution

Sex	*No. of persons*	*Per cent*
Male	490	98.0
Female	10	2.0
Total	500	100.0

Table 6
Marital Status

Status	*No. of persons*	*Per cent*
Unmarried	70	14.0
Married	430	86.0
Total	500	100.0

EDUCATIONAL LEVEL

Table 7 depicts the picture of education of migrants to Patna. It reveals that about 80 per cent of the respondents have education status upto only Middle while 11.6 per cent of the respondents are matriculate/secondary passed.

Table 7
Level of Education

Education Level	*No. of persons*	*Per cent*
Illiterate	28	5.6
Below Primary or Informal Education	100	20.0
Primary	132	26.4
Middle	166	33.2
Matric/High School/Secondary	58	11.6
Higher Secondary/Pre-university/Intermediate	12	2.4
Degree (Graduation level)	4	.8
Total	500	100.0

The study further reveals that only 2.4 per cent of the respondents are having education of Higher Secondary while 5.6 per cent of the respondents are completely illiterate.

FAMILY STRUCTURE

In course of study, the family structure of the migrants has also been taken into consideration. Table-8 reveals that 63.6 per cent of the respondents have joint family while 36.4 per cent have nuclear family.

Table 8
Family Structure

Type of Family	*No. of persons*	*Per cent*
Joint Family	318	63.6
Nuclear Family	182	36.4
Total	500	100.0

MIGRATION ON THE BASIS OF TIME PERIOD

Further the study has been made on the basis of time period of migration i.e., long term and short term migration. Out of the total 500 respondents, 234 respondents are under long-term migration while 266 respondents are under short-term migration. Hence, the study has been done first on the basis of long term migration followed by short-term migration.

Long-Term Migration

In this section, the various important items of long-term migration have been taken into consideration. They are mentioned below:

REASONS FOR MIGRATION

Under long-term migration, the study has been continued with the major reasons of migration. Table 9 reveals that among different reasons of migration, good income/wage is on the top. About 26.5 per cent of the respondents seek good income/wage followed by other factors with 23.6 per cent which includes factors like family tension, motivation from others, fear of schooling, etc.

The study further reveals that about 17.5 per cent of the respondents have migrated due to tension in villages while 12.8 per cent of the respondents are not having work/wage according to their social status.

Table 9
Reasons for Migration

Reasons	*No. of persons*	*Per cent*
For Good Income/Wage	62	26.5
Economic condition is measurable of the family	20	8.5
For good employment	26	11.1
In village do the work/wage against the own social	30	12.8
Tension in Village	41	17.5
Others*	55	23.6
Total	234	100.0

*Family tension, motivation from others, Fear of schooling, etc.

SOURCES OF MIGRATION

Besides reasons of migration, it is also important to study the various sources of migration through which people migrated to the state capital of Bihar.

Table 10
Sources of Migration

Sources	*No. of persons*	*Per cent*
Self knowledge	40	17.1
By outside contractor	4	1.7
By middlemen/agent	4	1.7
Relatives	120	51.3
With group of villagers	14	6.0
Pre-service engagement	52	22.2
Total	234	100.0

Table 10 reveals that 51.3 per cent of the respondents have been migrated through their relatives, 22.2 per cent respondents through pre-service engagements and 17.1 per cent persons through self-knowledge. Only 1.7 per cent of the migrants have been migrated each through middlemen and contractors.

PRESENT OCCUPATION

Table 11 shows the present occupation of long-term migrants. The table reveals that 32.5 per cent of the migrants are engaged in small business/trade/construction, 29.1 per cent are salaried people in private jobs and 23.1 per cent are engaged as casual labour in non-agriculture sector. The study further reveals that only 2.5 per cent of the migrants are engaged in their traditional caste occupation

Table 11
Present Occupation

Occupation	*No. of persons*	*Per cent*
Casual labour in non-agriculture	54	23.1
Salaried (private)	68	29.1
Individual/personal service (Jajmani/caste occupation)	6	2.5
Small Business/Trade/Construction	76	32.5
Others*	30	12.8
Total	234	100.0

*Casual Labour in agriculture, Attached labour, Self-business based on agriculture and allied activities, animal husbandry, poultry, aqua-culture, etc.

INCOME (MONTHLY)

Income is one of the most important aspects of migrants. Table 12 shows the monthly income of long-term migrants in Patna.

Table 12
Monthly Income

Income (Rs.)	*No of persons*	*Per cent*
Below 1500	14	6.0
1500-2000	60	25.6
2000-2500	44	18.9
2500-3000	62	26.5
3000-3500	34	14.5
3500 and above	20	8.5
Total	234	100.0

The table reveals that the highest 26.5 per cent of the respondents move in income group of Rs. 2,500 – Rs. 3,000 while 45.4 per cent of the respondents belong to income range between Rs. 2,000 – Rs. 3,000. The study further presents that only 8.5 per cent of the respondents are having their income over Rs. 3,500 and above and 6 per cent migrants have income below Rs. 1,500.

FAMILY STATUS

During the course of study, it is found that more than 90 per cent of the migrants live single and only 9.4 per cent of the respondents live with their families as is evident from Table-13. Hence, majority of them want to avoid the busy and costly city life and prefer their families to live in home districts.

Table 13
Family Status

Status	*No. of persons*	*Per cent*
Single	212	90.6
With family	22	9.4
Total	234	100.0

Short Term Migration

Under short-term migration also, the same grounds have been taken into consideration. The important items are mentioned below:

REASONS FOR MIGRATION

Under short-term migration, the study has been accelerated with the reasons of migration. Table 14 shows that among different reasons of short-term migration good income/wage holds the first position with its share of 62.4 per cent while only 3.0 per cent of the respondents have migrated due to good employment. The share of other factors is 23.3 per cent, which includes family tension, motivation from others, fear of schooling, work not suitable according to social status.

Table 14
Reasons for Migration

Reasons	*No. of persons*	*Per cent*
For Good Income/Wage	166	62.4
Economic condition is measurable of the family	20	7.5
For good employment	8	3.0
Village tension	10	3.8
Others	62	23.3
Total	266	100.0

*Family tension, motivation from others, Fear of schooling, Work not suitable according to social status, etc.

SOURCES OF MIGRATION

The study further reveals how migration has proceeded through various sources, which is clear from Table 15.

Table 15
Sources of Migration

Sources	*No. of persons*	*Per cent*
Self knowledge	84	31.6
By middlemen/agent	4	1.5
Relatives	164	61.7
With group of villagers	7	2.6
Pre-service engagement	7	2.6
Total	266	100.0

The main sources of proceeding migration are relatives 61.7 per cent followed by self-knowledge with 31.6 per cent while only 1.5 per cent of the respondents have migrated through middlemen/agent.

PRESENT OCCUPATION

Table 16 shows the present occupation of short-term migration in Patna, Bihar. The table reveals that 36.1 per cent of the migrants are engaged in casual labour in non-agriculture, 12.1 per cent are engaged in self-business based on agriculture and allied activities while only 9.0 per cent of them are engaged in personal service like jajmani and caste occupation.

Table 16
Present Occupation

Occupation	*No. of persons*	*Per cent*
Casual labour in agriculture	4	1.5
Casual labour in non-agriculture	96	36.1
Salaried (private)	20	7.5
Self-business based on agriculture and allied activities	32	12.1
Small Business/trade/construction	36	13.5
Personal service (Jajmani/caste occupation)	24	9.0
Others*	54	20.3
Total	266	100.0

* Attached labour, animal husbandry, poultry, aqua-culture, collection of fodder from nearby areas and selling, etc.

The study further reveals that the share of other occupations is 20.3 per cent which includes attached labour, animal husbandry, poultry, aqua-culture, collection of fodder from nearby areas and its selling.

WORKING DAYS (YEARLY)

Table 17 shows the number of working days (yearly) of short-term migrants in Patna. The table makes it clear that the highest 57.1 per cent of the respondents work between 200–250 days and 36.1 of the respondents work between 150–200 days in a year.

Table 17
No. of Working Days

Working Days	*No. of persons*	*Per cent*
Below 150	10	3.8
150-200	96	36.1
200-250	152	57.1
250 and above	8	3.0
Total	266	100.0

Hence, it can be deduced that 93.2 per cent of the migrants have their working days between 150–250 days in a year. The study also reveals that only 3.0 per cent of the respondents have working days below 150 days in a year.

WORKING HOURS

In course of study, the discussion about average working hours is also important with number of working days in a year.

Table 18
Average Working Hour (per day)

Hours	*No. of persons*	*Per cent*
Less than 4	8	3.0
4-8	42	15.8
8-10	152	57.1
10 and above	64	24.1
Total	266	100.0

Table 18 reveals that about 81.2 per cent of the migrants work for more than 8 hours per day. The percentage of migrants working for less than 8 hours is about 18.8 per cent in while percentage migrants working for less than 4 hours is 3.0 per cent.

WAGE DISTRIBUTION (PER DAY)

As wage is one of the most important factors, it is necessary and vital to study the wage distribution of the migrants.

Table 19
Wage per day

Wage (Rs.)	*No. of persons*	*Per cent*
Below 70	26	9.8
70-80	140	52.6
80-90	18	6.8
90-100	10	3.8
100-110	32	12.0
110 and above	40	15.0
Total	266	100.0

Table 19 shows that 52.6 per cent migrants get their wages between Rs. 70–Rs. 80 per day. The table further reveals that 62.4 per cent of the respondents have their wages below Rs. 80 per day while only 27.0 per cent of the migrants have their wages above Rs. 100 per day.

EFFECTS OF MIGRATION

A study of effects of migration on various items has also been done. Table 20 reveals that 98.4 per cent of the migrants reported increase in family income, 96.8 per cent of the migrants have reported improvement in food status, 92.8 per cent have reported improvement in living status, 64.0 per cent have reported improvement in housing and other facilities.

The table further reveals that 65.6 per cent of the migrants have reported increase in total expenditure during festivals, marriage, etc., 58 per cent of them reported increase in wage level, 66.8 per cent reported emergence of new skills, 59.2

per cent of the migrants reported to implement the skill in villages while 97.2 per cent have supported the usefulness of migration for the family.

Table 20
Effect of Migration

Variables	*Per cent*
Did the family income increase	98.4
Food status improved	96.8
Living status improved	92.8
Housing and other facilities such as toilet, hanu pump, etc. have improved	64.0
Total expenditure increased during festivals, marriages, etc?	65.6
Did wage level increase in village?	58.0
Is migration led to the emergence of new skills?	66.8
If yes, this skill can be implemented in village	59.2
In total, migration has been useful for the family	97.2

POLITICAL NETWORK

Table 21 shows the political network of respondent migrants in Patna.

Table 21
Political Network

Items related to network	*Per cent*
Do you know any union/party	47.2
Is any union/party active in your area/village	13.6
If yes, name the union/party	52.6
Are you associated with that union/party	5.4
Is there any benefit to attach with union/party	0.4

The table reveals that 47.2 of the migrant respondents have knowledge about the union or party while 13.6 per cent of the respondents have informed about active union/party in their area/village. The table further reveals that 5.4 per cent of the total respondents are associated with that party/union while only 0.4 per cent have reported benefit from such attachment.

CONCLUSION OF THE STUDY

The investigator has made an extensive use of primary data, which has been drawn from a comprehensive survey of 500 migrants in Patna with the help of a questionnaire during the year 2004–05 and 2005–06. The attempt has enabled the investigator to examine the socio-economic and political condition of migrants to Patna from other districts of Bihar. On the other hand, such type of migration in Patna itself is creating a variety of problems like over population, law and order situation, heavy out-migration of people from rural areas, etc.

The following are the general conclusion which may be drawn from the study:

1. In district-wise migrants to Patna from various districts of Bihar, the study reveals that the highest percentage of migrants to Patna is 9.6 per cent, which belongs Darbhanga followed by Hazaribagh with 8.8 per cent, Jahanabad and Ranchi both with 8.4 per cent each while the lowest percentage (0.4 per cent) belongs to Muzaffarpur (Table 1).
2. The caste-wise distribution of migrants to Patna from other districts of Bihar reveals that OBC respondents have the highest percentage i.e. 60.8 per cent among the migrants while percentage of Scheduled Tribe is the lowest i.e. only 1.2 per cent (Table 2).
3. The study further shows that 86 per cent of the migrants are Hindu, followed by Muslims with 13.2 per cent while 0.8 per cent of the migrants belong to Christian in the study (Table 3). The trend of migration in other religions has been observed very low.
4. The study of age groups of migrants with their percentage reveals that 65.2 per cent of the migrants belong to age groups of 20-25 and 25-30 years while 18 per cent of the migrants belong to 15-20 years of age group while the migrants below 15 years of age and 40 years and above are 2.4 per cent and 2.8 per cent respectively (Table 4).

5. In sex-wise study of migrants, the study reveals that 98 per cent of the total migrants belong to male while only 2 per cent belong female (Table 5).
6. Regarding marital status of migrants, it has been observed that 86 per cent of the migrating persons are married while only 14 per cent are unmarried (Table 6).
7. Regarding level of education among migrants, the study reveals that about 80 per cent of the respondents have education status upto only Middle while 11.6 per cent of the respondents are matriculate/secondary passed. The study further reveals that only 2.4 per cent of the respondents are having education above Higher Secondary while 5.6 per cent of the respondents are completely illiterate (Table 7).
8. While studying the family structure of the migrants, it has been observed that 63.6 per cent of the respondents have joint family while 36.4 per cent have nuclear family (Table 8).
9. Further the study has been made on the basis of time period of migration i.e., long term and short term migration. Out of the total 500 respondents, 234 respondents are under long-term migration while 266 respondents are under short-term migration. Hence, the study has been done first on the basis of long term migration followed by short-term migration with their major variables.
10. Under long-term migration, the study reveals that among different reasons of migration, good income/wage is on the top. About 26.5 per cent of the respondents seek good income/wage followed by other factors with 23.6 per cent which includes factors like family tension, motivation from others, fear of schooling, etc. The study further reveals that about 17.5 per cent of the respondents have migrated due to tension in villages while 12.8 per

cent of the respondents are not having work/wage according to their social status (Table 9).

11. Besides reasons of migration, an attempt has also been made to study the various sources of migration through which people migrated to the state capital of Bihar. It reveals that 51.3 per cent of the respondents have been migrated through their relatives, 22.2 per cent respondents through pre-service engagements and 17.1 per cent persons through self-knowledge. Only 1.7 per cent of the migrants have been migrated each through middlemen and contractors (Table 10).
12. Regarding the present occupation of long-term migrants, the study reveals that 32.5 per cent of the migrants are engaged in small business/trade/construction, 29.1 per cent are salaried people in private jobs and 23.1 per cent are engaged as casual labour in non-agriculture sector. The study further reveals that only 2.5 per cent of the migrants are engaged in their traditional caste occupation (Table 11).
13. So far as the income of the migrants is concerned, we found that the highest 26.5 per cent of the respondents belong to income group of Rs. 2,500–Rs. 3,000 while 45.4 per cent of the respondents move in income range between Rs. 2,000–Rs. 3,000. The study further presents that only 8.5 per cent of the respondents are having their income over Rs. 3,500 and above and 6 per cent migrants have income below Rs. 1,500 (Table 12).
14. During the course of study, it is found that more than 90 per cent of the migrants live single and only 9.4 per cent of the respondents live with their families (Table 13). Hence, majority of them want to avoid the busy and costly city life and prefer their families to live in home districts.
15. Under short-term migration also, an attempt has been made to study the reasons of migration. It has been found

that among different reasons of short-term migration, good income/wage holds the first position with its share of 62.4 per cent while only 3.0 per cent of the respondents have migrated due to good employment. The share of other factors is 23.3 per cent, which includes family tension, motivation from others, fear of schooling, work not suitable according to social status (Table 14).

16. We have further tried to find out the main sources of short-term migration like long-term migration. In course of study, it has been found that the main sources of proceeding migration are relatives 61.7 per cent, followed by self-knowledge with 31.6 per cent while only 1.5 per cent of the respondents have migrated through middlemen/agent (Table 15).

17. While studying the present occupation of short-term migration in Patna, Bihar, we have observed that 36.1 per cent of the migrants are engaged in casual labour in non-agriculture, 12.1 per cent are engaged in self-business based on agriculture and allied activities while only 9.0 per cent of them are engaged in personal service like jajmani and caste occupation (Table 16). The study further reveals that the share of other occupations is 20.3 per cent which includes attached labour, animal husbandry, poultry, aqua-culture, collection of fodder from nearby areas and its selling.

18. While studying the number of working days (yearly) of short-term migrants, it clear that the highest 57.1 per cent of the respondents work between 200–250 days and 36.1 of the respondents work between 150–200 days in a year (Table 17). Hence, it can be deduced that 93.2 per cent of the migrants have their working days between 150–250 days in a year. The study also reveals that only 3.0 per cent of the respondents have working days below 150 days in a year.

19. In course of study, the discussion about average working hours has also been taken into consideration. The study reveals that about 81.2 per cent of the migrants work for more than 8 hours per day. The percentage of migrants working for less than 8 hours is about 18.8 per cent in while percentage migrants working for less than 4 hours is 3.0 per cent (Table 18).
20. We have also tried to find out wage distribution of the migrants. The study shows that 52.6 per cent migrants get their wages between Rs. 70–Rs. 80 per day. The table further reveals that 62.4 per cent of the respondents have their wages below Rs. 80 per day while only 27.0 per cent of the migrants have their wages above Rs. 100 per day (Table 19).
21. During the study, an attempt has also been made to study of effects of migration on various items. The investigator has found that 98.4 per cent of the migrants reported increase in family income, 96.8 per cent of the migrants have reported improvement in food status, 92.8 per cent have reported improvement in living status, 64.0 per cent have reported improvement in housing and other facilities (Table 20).The study further reveals that 65.6 per cent of the migrants have reported increase in total expenditure during festivals, marriage, etc., 58 per cent of them reported increase in wage level, 66.8 per cent reported emergence of new skills, 59.2 per cent of the migrants reported to implement the skill in villages while 97.2 per cent have supported the usefulness of migration for the family.
22. Regarding the political network of the respondent migrants, the study reveals that 47.2 of the migrant respondents have knowledge about the union or party while 13.6 per cent of the respondents have informed about active union/party in their area/village. The study

further reveals that 5.4 per cent of the total respondents are associated with that party/union while only 0.4 per cent have reported benefit from such attachment (Table 21).

SUGGESTIONS OF THE STUDY

Rural-urban migration is basically labour migration. It is thought to be the consequence of unequal development wherein people from 'backward' regions move to 'developed' regions. These developed regions may either be prosperous rural areas or expanding urban areas where the people from the regions of less employment income opportunities flock. Economists and social scientists have propounded various theories about migration, which analyses the process, causes and consequences of migration. 'Pull' and 'push' factors of migration have often been talked with regard to the causes of migration. The factors like poverty and deprivation, land alienation, population pressure, lack of employment and income opportunities, social differentiation, penetration of market economy, etc. are some of the factors which are closely linked with migration.

Bihar is one of the states of India from where the out-migration from the rural areas has taken place. Apart from out-migration from rural areas, Patna town is a witness of heavy in-migration from the rural areas of other districts of Bihar which results in variety of imbalances viz., problems of urbanization, slums, pollution, unemployment and many other institutional, social, cultural and educational problems. Hence, a multiform attack should be organized to check the rural-urban migration. Some remedial measures may be suggested as follows to make the migration process more systematic, organized and less cumbersome.

1. There must be a check on increasing population through different control methods because it is not possible to provide employment to the increasing population in rural areas. It is also not possible to increase infrastructure at once in accordance

with the needs of the rural society due dearth of funds. Hence, the control over population will be one of the remedial measures for rural people of Bihar to Patna District and Patna town.

2. Satellite townships should be developed at the fringe of cities for immigrants and city dwellers.
3. The residents of central city should be encouraged to seek residential facilities in suburban areas by providing better transport facilities linking the suburban areas with city center.
4. Planned residential developments in suburban areas may minimize the central population density.
5. In order to meet the supply of convenient goods, creation of secondary commercial centers is also suggested.
6. The central functions like industry, commerce, administration and center of higher learning, etc should not be allowed to concentrate only in large cities. These functions should be kept highly decentralized.
7. Illiteracy is also one of the major hindrances of rural people in Bihar. As major population of Bihar live in rural areas where educational facilities are not in proper way. Rural literacy is a crucial variable in sending rural people to urban areas. So, to reduce the flow of rural people to urban areas, more schools and colleges of good quality need to be established in the vicinity of villages and small towns so that the flow of youths, who migrate for higher, may be checked.
8. For making the education system on India level and commercial, it is essential to interpret the necessities of electricity, communication, irrigation, roads, railways, public sector and whole industries as well as modernization of agriculture so that the rural inhabitants of Bihar might know where Bihar exists on the map of India. Only except the certain essential subjects, the complete transparency should be showed and the people should have "the right to know".

9. Another requirement for reducing the rural-urban migration is alteration of the inequality between urban and rural sector by intensifying the ongoing rural development programmes. This necessitates the launching of non-farm employment projects in the rural areas by the government with stress on major and minor irrigation projects so that employment opportunities may be created through raising farm productivity and cropping intensity.
10. Lack of development of the non-household manufacturing sector in the rural area is a major contributing factor in rural-urban migration. Hence, top priority must be given to accelerate the pace of rural industrialization. Concerted efforts are also required to integrate agriculture with agro-based and non-agro small-scale industries in the rural areas.
11. The Panchayats, which new Panchayati Raj Act have been entrusted with the responsibility to develop and promote small scale industries and village industries in rural areas at different levels, can now play important role in stepping up the pace of rural industrialization by identifying the local human and physical resources and using them in developing SSIs in rural sector. Panchayats should identify the educated unemployed manpower such as ITI and Polytechnic diploma holders and try to develop their entrepreneurial skills through requisite training to them. During the training, efforts must be made to develop group entrepreneurship among trainees so that they can jointly take up SSI projects. Moreover, there is also a need to revitalize the old Panchayat Udyogs.
12. There must be thrust on increasing the rural employment potential in rural and allied sectors. It must be brought about by various ways of agricultural development activities of the rural tertiary sectors with a large reduction in indebtedness and increase in productivity of rural people will certainly provide employment to them all the year round.

13. Much stress should be made to facilitate employment to the surplus and seasonal rural work force in their rural areas only. Its solution lies on rural work programme, which has to create employment. The rural work programme has a vital contribution towards relief of unemployment and underemployment and assuring of minimum earnings and acceleration of the pace of rural development.
14. In Bihar, employers are openly violating the provisions of the Minimum Wages Act, 1948 especially in rural sector and make payment of wages well below the minimum wage. In order to get employment, the rural labourers have no option but to move to urban area. The state government should strict over this issue and should also restructure the wage format in accordance with the need of the rural sector and state.
15. It is also suggested that the allocation of manpower in rural sector should be based on capital extensive and labour intensive technology. The rural poors have to be provided financial support and technical assistance at subsidized rates to operate dairy, poultry, piggery, fishery, etc.
16. There must be improvement in working conditions of rural labourers. Rural skills and tools must be upgraded. Women labourers also must be trained in male type assignments and operations, which will result in checking the rural-urban migration.
17. Better infrastructure facilities need to be provided for encouraging self-employment among female rural labourers. Efforts have to be made to bring the development of different skills in line with the social need and give opportunities to rural unemployed women. Special entrepreneurship courses should be run for such women. Educated woman should be encouraged to form co-operative societies to be controlled and run exclusively by women themselves. This will certainly check the migration from rural to urban area.

18. In order to check the migration, the problem of inequality of assets must be tackled very efficiently. Administration should have to play an active role for the implementation of land reform measures. It cannot be denied that the anti-land reform segment happens to be much stronger than pro-land reform segment. But if the government is determined, evasion from land reform laws will be difficult. At this juncture, it is also suggested that only government programmes cannot enrich the government records, the vigilance department should also make report on the nature of benefit and also detect exploitation made by the institutional agents so that deterrent action may be taken against guilty officials.
19. Like industrial and urban areas, there must be adequate extension of general and social security measures for people of rural areas because these measures add to the purchasing power of the rural people and improve their status. Provision of housing, roads, schools, recreational facilities, drinking water, family welfare, maternity centres and other medical facilities are essential for creating right type of attitude and motivation to the rural areas. It is the duty of the society or government to take proper care of their security. Hence, social security measures must not be restricted only to the industrial and urban areas. They must be enlarged in such a way as to cover the rural areas and for this purpose; the rural employers should be legally obliged to contribute to the social security cost of a labour in case of injury.
20. There is always a debate on self versus wage employment programmes. These programmes do not upgrade the skills of the rural persons coming to work while self-employment programmes improve the skills of rural people in order to compete in the market. So, there is need of self-employment programmes. The role of government is also required in this connection. The government should launch more attractive and effective self-employment programmes according to the need of rural population so that majority of

this section could be benefited and they have not to move somewhere else.

21. Rural-urban migration is a serious problem, which Patna town area faces. Government legislations are only on paper. This problem can be solved through proper technical and non-technical education, awareness programmes, government legislations, etc.
22. Regarding public expenditure, it is suggested that it should be increased in rural areas in comparison to urban areas where majority lives.
23. Though allocation of funds to the programmes is necessary condition, management or administration aspects are equally important for efficient and effective utilization of funds making the programmes successful by reaching to the rural areas. Hence, we should also give more weightage to the organizational aspects of rural areas in allocation of funds.
24. Macro policies are, of course, equally important in helping the rural areas. Inflation must be under control. Economic growth also important if the government wants to allocate more resources to rural areas to have productive employment.
25. Decentralisation of administration and giving enough power to local bodies for administering the schemes are also important for helping the rural areas. But this alone will not solve the problem. A system of accountability is also needed from local bodies. Involvement of NGOs will improve the delivery system. Effective implementation of programmes for poverty alleviation and social development require the active participation of beneficiaries in their designing as well as implementation. Appropriate rural institutions have also to be developed for this purpose to check the problem of rural urban migration.
26. It is also suggested that the state government should reformulate its agricultural policy to boost up the productivity of the crops on sustained basis to increase employment opportunities for rural areas.

27. New agricultural technology should be spread over through the information technology to the rural masses.
28. The state should provide the basic infrastructure like electricity, road and transport, water, irrigation, hybrid seeds and facilities to make an investment platform for agriculture in rural areas.
29. To boost agricultural activities in the state, one aspect that the Government of Bihar has to address to is to ask the banks and financial institutions to invest more in agriculture sector of rural areas of Bihar.
30. The government should also promote cottage industries and village handicrafts, which were destroyed by the Britishers. A major section of rural labourers who are efficient in cottage industries and village handicrafts can be reverted to this section again.
31. Productivity of agriculture in rural areas should be increased. For it, the development of agriculture is essential in which various items viz., food grain, oil seeds, vegetables, fruits, milk, fish, eggs, meat, etc. may be observed. Money supply may also be increased for rapid increase in the productivity of agriculture in rural areas. It will control over price rise, the purchasing power will be increased and consequently explosive unemployment will be reduced in the rural areas in short span of time.
32. It has been observed that return migration is very low. In fact, people who migrate from rural area in search of better job do not return even after their retirement because in the rural area, they do not get the same facilities as in urban areas. Hence, to increase the migration rate of people from urban area to rural areas, emphasis must be given to develop better living conditions in the rural areas.
33. Lastly, the state government should improve the law and order situation in the state where there is carnages or mass killings, looting of crops, kidnapping, etc. Militant activities are prevailing in all over the state, which is hampering the overall

growth of the state and finally, resulting in migration from rural areas to urban areas.

References

Banerjee, Biswajit (1986), Rural to Urban and Urban Labour Market (A Case Study of Delhi), Himalaya Publishing House, Bombay.

Gore, M. S. (1970), Migration and Neighbourhood, Two Aspects of Life in a Metropolitan City, Tata Institute of Social Sciences, Bombay.

Joshi, K. G. (1989), Migration and Mobility: A Sociological Study of Urban Karnataka, Himalaya Publishing House, Bombay.

Khan, N. (1983), Studies in Human Migration, Rajesh Publication, New Delhi.

Mandal, R. B. (ed.) (1981), Frontiers in Migration Analysis, Concept Publishing Company, New Delhi.

M. S. A. Rao (eds.) (1986), Studies in Migration, Manohar Publications, New Delhi.

Mehta, G. S. (1991), Socio-Economic Aspects of Migration, Deep & Deep Publications, New Delhi.

Oberoi, A. S. and H. K. M. Singh (1983), Causes and Consequences of Internal Migration: A Study of Indian Punjab, Oxford University Press, Delhi.

Premi, M. K. (1980), Urban Out-Migration, A Study of Its Nature, Causes and Consequences, Sterling Publishers Pvt. Ltd., New Delhi.

Raju, B. R. K. (1987), Development Migration, Concept Publishing Company, New Delhi.

Saxena, O. P. (1978), Rural Urban Migration in India, Causes and Consequences, Popular Prakashan, Bombay.

Sekhar, T. V. (1997), Migration and Social Change, Rawat Publications, Jaipur.

Sharma, A. N. (1997), People on the Move, Vikas Publishing House, Delhi.

———*et.al.*, (2000), Dynamics of Employment, Poverty and Human Development in Rural Bihar, Institute of Human Development, New Delhi, (mimeo).

Singh, J. P. (1986), Patterns of Rural-Urban migration in India, Inter-India Publications, New Delhi.

Singh, R. N. (1989), Impact of Out-Migration on Socio-Economic Conditions, Amar Prakashan, New Delhi.

14

TREND AND PATTERN OF OUT-MIGRATION OF RURAL LABOUR

Bipin Kumar

INTRODUCTION

Simply migration means movement of human beings in the persuit of certain cherished objectives like better employment, better wages and better quality of life. Migration takes place from one district to another, from one state to another and even within the district from one area to another. The Report of the National Commission on 'Rural Labour' defines 'a migrant labourer as "person who migrates temporarily from his place of residence to another area with a view to getting wages employment"– (National Commission on Rural Labour, p. 115). In our country or in Bihar, we are faced with the problem of migration which generally takes the form of 'rural to rural' and rural to urban' migration (The process of migration embraces essentially four crucial dimensions : space, residence, time and activity changes. (Oberai-18).

The history of migration in Bihar is very old and its migrants have not only crossed the district or state boundaries, but also have moved to other countries as well. The earliest migration stream from Bihar started around 1830, when people in large numbers migrated to some British colonies, notably Mauritius, Guyana, Trinidad and Fiji, as indentured labour. Drawn mainly from the western part of the state, sometimes kidnapped through contractors, such migrants were mostly employed in the plantation and agricultural sectors of those far-off countries. The conditions of those migrant labourers were often slave-like and they were brutally assaulted, ill-clad, ill-fed and ill-housed and their wages were low and unchanged over time. For example, there was no change in wages in Guyana during 1871-1922 and in Trinidad during 1845-1920. Even then, such migration continued from Bihar till the First World War. Within the country, since the middle of the 19th Century, the most important destinations of migrants from Bihar have been the tea-gardens of Assam and the industrial areas of West Bengal. Initially, the migration to tea gardens had started from the plain regions of the state. But later, since the close of the 19th century, the tribals from Chhotanagpur also became one of the major suppliers of plantation labour. The industrial areas of West Bengal (mainly around Calcutta and Asansol), however, had attracted migrants mainly from the North Bihar plains to work as coolies, rickshaw or "thela" pullers, night guards, workers in jute and other factories and many such low paid jobs. A large number of persons also migrated to Assam and Bengal to take up small business and petty trade. Before independence a significant proportion of the police force in Bengal consisted of Bihari migrants.

In this article our purpose is to study the problem of migration in a poor state like Bihar. There are three sections in the paper. In the *first section,* we shall deal with the theory and causes of migration. *Section second* of the article will try to capture 'the process and trend of migration in Bihar' which would be based on the available secondary information and also on the survey result conducted in some selected villages. In the *third section* of the article We have tried to analyse the impact of migration on the rural economy of Bihar which would naturally be followed the conclusion and suggestions.

SECTION-I

With the increasing pace of population rise, we also encounter the problem of imbalance between job creation and job seekers which is ultimately reflected in the process of migration which takes place from one area to another and from one state to another. There are some theories which explain the process and possible causes of migration. The 'push' theory tells us that migration from an area takes place because of area being under-developed or due to stagnation. People are pushed out of the area in search of employment and better wages. This also takes place due to backwardness and relative under-development and unavailability of jobs as it compels people to go out to other areas or state for job and better incomes. This increasing economic hardship seems to be an important factor which pushes people/workers out in search of jobs. On the other hand, 'pull' theory works and this also facilitates the process of migration when development takes place or process of industrialisation is speeded up or level of urbanisation is going up. These factors pull or attract people to urban areas and centres of development or to developed regions. As observed, even development is the most important reason giving rise to 'pull' and 'push' phenomena in migration of labourers. The process of migration is widely related to social structure. Hence, any change in the socio-economic structure will soon find its response in migration (Joshi p.1). Migration is a complex phenomena having different dimensions which is generally categorised in 'push' and 'pull' aspects. This view has been clearly recorded in the Report of National Commission of Rural Labour 1991. It is a well known fact that uneven development works both ways; when the area is under developed the labours are pushed out to areas for job and better incomes, people are pulled towards developed regions because they are attracted there expecting more job opportunities and better paid once. This is elaborated from the fact that developed regions like Punjab, Haryana, Gujarat, Maharashtra, Karnataka, Andhra Pradesh pull the agricultural labourers from relatively backward regions while the most backward regions in the state of Bihar and Orissa push their labourer to the 'developed state. 'Todaro' has propounded a theory of migration which is based on expected better income outside the place of residence of the workers. According to him, "Migration is primarily an economic phenomena". He feels that migration occurs in response to rural urban differences in 'expected' rather than 'actual earnings'. It means that migrant workers consider the possibility of available opportunities both rural and urban sectors and choose one which maximizes their expected gains. By having done so a labourer decides to migrate to an urban area when he feels that expected income is higher in urban area than the rural areas. But this view is based on unrealistic assumptions such as worker's complete information about the possibility of the job in the modern sector, that wages in traditional sector are always lower than the modern sector. But other writers have questioned Todaro's views. On the basis of a survey of unemployed in Kingston (Jamaica) Standing (1978) argued that urban unemployment rate may be an effective deterrent to migration, while a reduction in urban wage rates may increase rather than reduce migration. For the income differential models have also been termed partial, since they do not take into account non-economic factors and the structural aspects of the economy.

In order to understand better the causes of migration from rural areas, we must take into account the socio-economic factors which cause differences in rural urban incomes such as rural unemployment, stagnation, the increasing pressure on land, the lack of non-farm employment opportunity existing, unequal land distribution and also meagre investment rates in agriculture. The distress factor seems to be the most important factor in causing migration of poor from rural to urban areas. The famous study made by 'Dandekar' and 'Rath' (1971) clearly shows that 'rural poverty acts as a 'push factor'. In order to over-come the incidence of poverty, the rural poor migrate continuously to urban areas in search of livelihood. Sundaram (1996) expresses his doubt about the inadequacy of expected income differential as explaining the rural urban movement of population.

In India and more so in Bihar, agriculture still remains to be the dominant sector giving employment to majority of labour force. Majority of people including labourers are dependent on agriculture for work and income. Rapidly rising population has caused determination in the land-man ratio. Due to increased hardships, the transfer of surplus labour from rural to urban centres is taking place. Finding no job in the place of residence, people are pushed to other areas. This process is very much going on in Bihar. One aspect of this push factor is lack of work or job opportunity in rural segment, the other important aspect is the low level of wages in agriculture sector. Migration may be motivated by the various causes among which are personal, social (social tension), political, economic psychological and natural forces. Migration currents acquire significant prominence with technological change and industrial development with increasing urbanisation and economic development taking place movement of population. This is true in my case also but the push factor seems to be more prominent in case of Bihar. In Bihar it has been found that the feudal exploitation and acute poverty in villages are very much responsible for migration. Recently, there has been increase in the seasonal migration of agricultural labour to agriculturally prosperous state of Punjab and Haryana and even today, this process continues. But in last ten-fifteen years, it has been noticed that migration is taking place in industries of developed states like Gujarat and Maharashtra and construction and security work in Delhi. Distress migration seems to be dominant form and people seem to be moving out in search of work in order to survive.

Thus, the main causes leading to migration are rapid population growth, worsening land man ratio, lack of development, lack of non-agricultural work, poverty, lack of education and training, lack of support facility for government for self-employment, growing level of urbanisation, growth of infrastructure facilities etc.

SECTION-II

Bihar is predominantly agricultural state with heavy pressure of population on land. Being predominantly agricultural state with large population, it faces the problem of poverty and unemployment. The population of agricultural labour to the total agricultural worker in Bihar has increased from 28.2% in 1951 to 45.5% in 1991. Their number is estimated to have increased annually at rate of 2.5% (Ghosh and Sharma, 1990)

METHODOLOGY

For writing this paper, we have made a survey in rural areas of Bihar. We selected two districts representing two geographical regions of the state i.e. *North Bihar and Central Bihar*. We purposely selected two villages from one Block of the district keeping in mind the aim of having a comparative picture of migration. We selected *Samastipur* from North Bihar which is one of the known migration prone districts. We selected *Patna* being capital, land, one of agrarian tension prone districts of Central Bihar. While selecting these districts, blocks and villages, the access objective was to the process of migration from rural Bihar to other states. For collection of data, a questionnaire incorporating different aspects of migration such as characteristics of migration (like age, education, land, marital status etc.) work experience of migrants and their earnings was used for our survey.

An attempt has been made to analyse the survey data to know different aspects of migration from rural Bihar. We have processed the data of our survey which are being presented in the table representing different aspects of migration from some villages of rural Bihar.

From Table 1, it is evident that in Samastipur district the percentage of migration is high in Dhoboliya village of Bithan Block. The number of migrants of the village was 135 which constituted over 16% migration from the village. But in Bhikhanauliya village of the same block it was about 8.5% of the population of 1163 in the village (99 persons migrated). In Patna district which happens to be the capital district of the state as per our survey in two villages of Paliganj Block, the percentage of migration was 7.5% in Khanpura village and slightly over 4% in Mankurha village.

Table 1
Number of Out-Migrants from the Villages

District	*Block*	*Village*	*Population of the Village as per our 1997 survey*	*Number of Migrants from the villages*	*Percentage of Migrant*
Samastipur	Bithan	Dhobauliya	842	135	16.03
		Bhikhanauliya	1163	99	8.51
Patna	Paliganj	Khanpura	700	53	7.51
		Mankurha	600	25	4.16

So far as the sex ratio of out migrants from the villages is concerned, we found that the dominant features of migration of males was ranging from 84 to 100% in our survey villages. Female migration was marginal in Dhoboliya and Bhikhnauliya villages of Bithan block of Samastipur district and there was no female migration from Patna district village. This is clear from Table 2.

Table 2
Sex Ratio of Out-Migrants from the Villages

			Male Migrant		*Female Migrant*	
District	*Block*	*Village*	*No. of male migrants*	*Percentage of male migrant*	*No. of female migrants*	*Percentage of female migrant*
Samastipur	Bithan	Dhobauliya	113	83.70	22	16.29
		Bhikhanauliya	93	93.93	06	6.06
Patna	Paliganj	Khanpura	53	100.00	-	-
		Mankurha	25	100.00	-	-

When we come to the analysis of marital status of out-migrants, we found that the percentage of married persons out-migrating from the four villages of Samastipur and Patna districts was approx 90% as revealed by Table 3. It is also to be noted that the percentage of female out-migrants was 10% or less in the villages where the survey was conducted.

Table 3
Marital Status of Out-migrants from the Villages

District	*Block*	*Village*	*Married*		*Unmarried*	
			No. of Married	*Percentage of Married*	*No. of Unmarried migrants*	*Percentage of Unmarried*
Samastipur	Bithan	Dhobauliya	121	89.62	14	10.37
		Bhikhanauliya	90	90.90	09	9.09
Patna	Paliganj	Khanpura	49	92.45	04	7.54
		Mankurha	23	92.00	02	8.00

When we come to the analysis of the social status of the out-migrants from these villages, we observed that in the north Bihar villages, the percentage of SC's out-migrating from Dhoboliya was 34% and Bhikhanauliya was 90%. The dominant feature of out-migration in the two villages was mainly from backward caste (BC) people. In Dhoboliya village, the people out-migrating were from backward caste (BC) like yadavas, Mallah, business community men and a few upper caste people. In Bhikhanauliya, dominant community/caste out-migrating was yadav's and other backward castes. In villages of patna district, we found that there was mix social group out-migranting from the village. In Khanpura village, the percentage of Schedule Castes was 7.5% but the dominant group of out migrants was from upper caste (Bhumihar) and a few from BC-I Group. In adjacent village also, the trend was mixed about 40% of out-migrants mainly came from (SC) and nearly 60% from other caste in which we included BC people and a few upper caste men, which is shown in Table 4.

When we come to educational status of out-migrants. We observed that in Dhoboliya village of Samastipur district, about 44% were illiterates while in Bhikhanauliya, the percentage of illiterates was nearly 31%. In Khanpura village of Patna District, the percentage of illiterate migrants was 5.5% but in adjacent village of Mankurha, it was 52%. In Khanpura village, as the out-migrants

Table 4
Social Status of Out-Migrants from the Villages

District	*Block*	*Village*	*SC*		*ST*		*Others*	
			No. of SC's	*% of age SC's*	*No. of ST's*	*% age of ST's*	*No. of Others*	*%age of Others*
Samastipur	Bithan	Dhobauliya	46	34.07	-	-	89	65.92
		Bhikhanauliya	19	19.19	-	-	80	80.80
Patna	Paliganj	Khanpura	04	7.54	-	-	49	92.45
		Mankurha	10	40.00	-	-	15	60.00

were from upper caste so the percentage of illiterates was very low. In almost all the villages of two districts, we find that the educational status of out-migrants was mainly primary and middle school education. The percentage is high in Bhikhanauliya and Khanpura. This is linked with the social status of out-migrants. In the group of class-8 and above category, the percentage of out-migrants was near about 10% except in Khanpura village of Patna district where it was over 28%, as the people who out-migrated belong to upper Bhumihar caste. This is very much clear from Table 5.

Table 5
Educational Status of Out-Migrants from the Villages

District	*Block*	*Village*	*Illiterate*		*Class 3-7*		*Class 8 & above*	
			No.	*% age*	*No.*	*%a ge*	*No.*	*% age*
Samastipur	Bithan	Dhobauliya	59	43.70	62	45.92	14	10.37
		Bhikhanauliya	31	31.31	55	55.55	13	13.13
Patna	Paliganj	Khanpura	03	5.66	35	66.03	15	28.30
		Mankurha	13	52.00	10	40.00	02	08.00

While analysing family size of out-migrants, we observed that there was migration from small families (member having upto 3) and also from large families (number of member being 7 or above) in the family. According to our survey, medium family number ranging between 4-6 seems to be a dominant features, because in Bhikhanauliya village of Samastipur district, the percentage of out-migrant from this family size group was over 51% and in Khanpura, village of Patna district was recorded about 85%. In the nearby village of Mankurha in the same district, the size of family was large and over 64% of out-migrants, family size with 7 members and more. This is explained on the basis of social status and illiteracy of the family. This is clear from Table 6.

Table 6
Family Size of Out-Migrants from the Villages

District	*Block*	*Village*	*0-3* Family Range	*0-3* % age	*04-06* Family Range	*04-06* % age	*07-above* Family Range	*07-above* % age
Samastipur	Bithan	Dhobauliya	28	20.74	51	37.77	56	41.23
		Bhikhanauliya	25	25.25	51	51.51	23	23.23
Patna	Paliganj	Khanpura	Nil	0	45	84.90	08	15.09
		Mankurha	02	8.00	07	28.00	16	64.00

From Table 7, it is clear that migration of one member family was the dominant feature of out-migrants. In almost all these villages, percentage of out migrant from this category (i.e. one member from one family) was ranging between over 60% to over 90%. The second important category was the category of two out-migrant members from the family. Almost 20-25% migration from this group took place. The number of family was less from the category in which three members migrated which was 16% or less. Table 7 clearly demonstrates it.

When we come to the analysis of the age group of out-migrants from these villages, the dominant feature was the migration from age group of 15 to 30 years. In Dhoboliya village of Samastipur, about 66% and in Bhikhnauliya village of same district was over 74% migrated from this age group. In Patna district villages also, we found that the trend was almost the same. The percentage of migration from the villages Khanpura and Maukurha of Patna district from this age group was 67.9% and 72% respectively. The study further reveals that except one village, migration of children was also recorded in rest three villages under

Table 7
Family Size of Out-Migrants from the Villages

District	Block	Village	*No. of out-migrants from a family 1 member*		*No. of out-migrants from a family 2 member*		*No. of out-migrants from a family 2 member*	
			No. of migrant	*% age of migrant*	*No. of migrant*	*% age of migrant*	*No. of migrant*	*% age of migrant*
Samastipur	Bithan	Dhobauliya	91	67.40	26	19.25	18	13.13
		Bhikhanauliya	90	90.90	08	08.08	01	01.01
Patna	Paliganj	Khanpura	32	60.37	06	22.64	03	16.98
		Mankurha	19	76.00	06	24.00	0	0

survey. Middle age group migrants from the villages constituted 25-30% of out-migration from these villages. So, the marked feature of out-migration from these village is from the age group of 15-30 years. It means the migration of youth is dominant feature which is very much clear from Table 8.

Table 8
Age Group of Out-Migrants from the Villages

District	Block	Village	*5-15 Years*		*15-30 Years*		*30 Year & above*	
			No. of out-migrant	*% age of out-migrant*	*No. of out-migrant*	*% age of out-migrant*	*No. of out-migrant*	*% age of out-migrant*
Samastipur	Bithan	Dhobauliya	04	2.96	89	65.92	42	31.11
		Bhikhanauliya	03	3.03	74	74.74	22	22.22
Patna	Paliganj	Khanpura	02	3.77	36	67.92	15	28.30
		Mankurha	0	0	18	72.00	07	28.00

In context of further study, Table 9 explains the land ownership of out-migrants. It is deduced that except in Khanpura village of Patna district, the out-migration from the landless households was dominant over others. Over 56% to 70% migrants belong to landless class and others who migrated owned some land which negligible or inadequate for support to the family. These migrants from all social groups were mainly small and marginal farmers. Economic hardship has punished them cut in search of better paid jobs as there is lack of non-farm work, land owned is inadequate to maintain the family and meet its obligations and also there is urge for betterment of the standard of living. So even people from land owning upper caste have started migrating. In Khanpura village of Patna district over 81% of out migrants were owning land over one acre to two acres. One of the features of out-migrants were owning land over one acre to two acres. One of the features of out-migrants was that those who were landless or coming from disadvantaged social group were migrating in the agriculturally developed states. But those who belong to upper caste but own inadequate land, they are moving to cities or industrial towns. They are working there as coolies, labourers, security guards etc. in Delhi, Calcutta, Surat etc. But no body from this group was found working as an agricultural labourer outside. People from (SC's) particularly from cobbler caste are still persuing their traditional craft in the place of their out-migration.

Table 9

Land Possessed by the Migrants (In Acres)

			Landless		*0-10 Kathas*		*10-20 Kathas*		*20 Katha & above*	
District	*Block*	*Village*	*No.*	*% age*	*No.*	*% age*	*No.*	*% age*	*No.*	*% age*
Samastipur	Bithan	Dhobauliya	94	69.62	27	20.00	11	8.14	03	2.22
		Bhikhanauliya	66	66.66	10	10.10	19	19.19	04	4.04
Patna	Paliganj	Khanpura	03	05.66	04	7.54	03	5.66	43	81.13
		Mankurha	14	56.00	06	24.00	03	12.00	02	8.00

N.B. 1 Acre = 1.12 Bigha 1 Bigha = 20 Kathas.

Table 10 reveals the annual income of out-migrants of villages taken under study. The study reveals that out-migrants were getting annual income between Rs. 10,000 to Rs. 15,000. This was the dominant income range of the out-migrants. Some were getting less than Rs. 10,000 particularly those who were children. Those who earned more than Rs. 15,000 were less in number. Even percentage-wise, one fourth or less than that belonged to this category of income range except of Dhoboliya village where about 50% of out migrants belong to this category. Those who were working as supervisory staff even in agricultural sector or industrial centres, they were getting more than Rs. 15,000 per annum.

Table 10
Annual Income of Out-Migrant (In Rupees)

			Between Rupees 5000-10000		*Between Rupees 10001-15000*		*Between Rupees 15001 & above*	
District	*Block*	*Village*	*No.*	*% age*	*No.*	*% age*	*No.*	*% age*
Samastipur	Bithan	Dhobauliya	6	4.44	62	45.92	67	49.62
		Bhikhanauliya	14	14.14	66	66.66	19	19.19
Patna	Paliganj	Khanpura	2	3.77	36	67.92	15	18.30
		Mankurha	0	0	22	88.00	03	12.00

SECTION-III

CONCLUSION & SUGGESTIONS

Not all the findings and conclusions of this study are possibly very new, but in some cases we did find evidence against some of the widely believed views about internal migration. Many of the conclusions are of immense relevance to the policy planning, be they related to economy in general or its demographic dimensions in particular. To begin with, we first stress the fact that migration is an extremely heterogeneous phenomenon.

Thus, we see that migration from rural villages of Bihar is taking place and there is rising trends. People are forced to migrate in majority of cases. It is survival strategy for people migration from landless labour families. There is a new trend of migrants from upper castes and land holders from rural Bihar. Land owned was inadequate for family maintenance. Even upper caste people owning two acres of land are migrating to supplement their family earnings and betterment of their economic condition. This is a new trend which is very much obvious in the rural segment of Bihar. This is happening because land man ratio has deteriorated and economic hardship has grown. This aspect of migration needs more probing. "Surveying on large scale is needed particularly in central Bihar region to get correct picture about this new trend."

We found that in most of the cases, migrants were male and youth from the family. Most of the people who migrates are male and have got educational qualification of middle, high school or even higher secondary. We also noticed that people migrating from BC and SC's are mostly working in agriculture field in developed regions like Punjab, Haryana but in case of migrants from upper caste land owning families. We did not find any one working as agricultural labour. They were mostly engaged in work related to industries, textile mills in Surat, small scale industries in Ludhiyana, Amritsar, watchman in multi storey buildings or clerks in offices of business establishment in Surat, Delhi, Calcutta.

So far as the impact of migration is concerned, we find that there are two sides of the coin, some adverse impact is experienced particularly during the busy season in agriculture. Due to shortage of able persons in the village, agricultural wages are pushed up and raises the cost of farming. But on balance, beneficial impact is much more as economic condition of families from where migration took place has decidedly improved. Due to regular money flow from outside, they have become better off. We found a distinct trend that the families from where members migrated are using modern methods and practices of farming. They are making the needed investment in HYV seeds and fertilizers which has helped the family in getting more output from land and ultimately in improving their economic lot. We also noticed that even families who did not own land but some one has migrated from the family are using their remittances for leasing in land from others for share cropping or on fixed rent (Patta). They are making better use of resources and earning from such type of farming. We also marked that there is marked improvement in housing facility of the family from which a member migrated. There is a tendency to built brick made pakka houses.

We have a new trend of exudes of rural youth not only from landless families but also from land owning upper castes from villages of Bihar. In view of the marked tendency towards migration from rural segment of the backward state of Bihar, it seems pertinent to develop agriculture on modern lines and also encourage non-farm employment opportunity and small and cottage industries for which there is ample scope. With a view to access the process of out-migration and to stop the tendency of out-migration, our view is creation of regular employment in and around the village itself as it will help in easing the problem of population pressure and creation of slums in urban areas and also the problem of under or acute unemployment already existing in urban areas. The eleven fold suggestions made by National Commission on Rural Labour in this respect deserve attention. We must take effective measures to stop migration of children as it deprives them from schooling, robs them of their youth and proper growth and terms them into a manual labour for whole life. The ultimate solution of the problem of out-migration lies in the proper speedy and all around development of backward areas and states like Bihar. It will enable the backward state like Bihar to use its precious human resource for developing agriculture, agro-based industries and over all speedy economic development of the state and free the helpless people of Bihar from ignominy of death being caused due to terrorist attacks and accidents.

As this study has shown that push factors have been more important in the decision to migrate and at the same time, the migration has been beneficial to at least individual migrants, any policy with regard to migration should take into account this factor. A blanket anti-migration policy would be harmful for the potential poor migrants in the rural areas. A careful policy encompassing various facts of rural development and diversification of the rural economy is required. Some of the broad components of such a policy may be as follows:

(i) The state should take effective steps in reducing imbalances in the employment opportunities between the rural and urban areas. Deliberate steps may be taken to reduce the gap between the rural and urban wages.

(ii) All efforts should be made to encourage the programme of rural development. In National Rural Employment Guarantee Programme (NREGP), Swarnjayanti Gram Swarojgar Yojana (SGSY) and others similar poverty alleviation and employment generation programmes should be strengthened.

(iii) There is the need to encourage industrialisation in smaller urban centres and rural towns spread throughout the country.

(iv) There is the need to develop the social infrastructure in terms of health and education facilities in the rural areas and surrounding of small urban centres. This will naturally check the migration for the reason of attaining education.

(v) Indiscriminate expansion in higher education must be checked. It will only lead to more migration and higher unemployment. The over investment by the Government in higher education has often led to investment in idle human resources in the country.

The above policies may be effective in controlling the migration stream to the cities. However, it should be kept in mind that it would not be desirable to initiate anti-migration policies which has given the heavy population pressure in the countryside. The best way to control the rural-urban migration is to make the rural areas attractive through development programmes (Peek, 1981).

References

Dhandekar, U. M. and Rath Neelkantha (1971), "Poverty in India", the Indian School of Political Economy, Pune.

Joshi, Vidyut (1987), Ed. "Migrant Labour and Related Issues", Oxford 18th Publishing Private Ltd.

Mohan, Arbind (1998), "Pravasi Mazduron Kee Pura", Radha Krishna Prakashan, New Delhi.

Oberai, A. S. (1987), "Migration, Urbanisation and Development" International Labour Organisation, Geneva.

Oberai, A. S. & H. K. Manmohan Singh (1983), "Causes and Consequences of Internal Migration: A Study in the Indian Punjab", Oxford University Press, Delhi.

Peek, Peter (1981), "Agrarian Change and Rural Emigration", In Balan (ed).

"Report of the National Commission on Rural Labour" (1991), Government of India, Ministry of Labour.

Sharma, Alakh N. (1997), "People on the Move Nature and Implications of Migration in a Backward Economy", Vikas Publishing House, New Delhi.

Sharma, A. N. and Ghosh P. P. (1990), "Rural Labour Migrants in Bihar", A.N. Sinha Institute of Social Studies, Patna.

Standing Guy (1978), "Aspiration Wages, Migration and Urban Unemployment", *The Journal of Development Studies*, Vol. 14., No. 2.

Sensarma, Kuntal (1997), "Migrant Labour in Urban Areas; Dimensions and Determinants", *The Indian Journal of Labour Economics*, April-June.

Sundram (1886), "Agriculture Industry Inter-Relations: Issues of Migration World Congress of the International Economic Association, New Delhi.

SECTION-IV

Agricultural Labour: Some Issues

15

FEMALE AGRICULTURAL LABOUR: A SOCIO ECONOMIC PROFILE

Asha Singh

INTRODUCTION

In the emerging global restructuring, a country can improve its competitiveness by enhancing and utilizing the cognitive skills of its female labour force. Economic empowerment of women occupies an area of utmost significance for a lasting and sustainable development of the society. A rational and gender- friendly attitude towards the needs and requirements of women in the society and a holistic approach to the cause of their upliftment are the pre-requisites of such empowerment. Women form a very important segment in development at local to global level. Unfortunately in India and particularly in Bihar, the immense potential concealed within the female labour force is yet to be recognized.

Rural labour force, particularly in the unorganized sector remains as one of the most neglected, deprived and disadvantaged group in India. Sex discrimination, deprivation, unemployment, poverty and economic disparity are the main social and economic ailments of a developing country and especially of the backward regions. Bihar being one of the most underdeveloped states of India is highly inflicted with these ailments.

To describe how the female agricultural labour are socialized into the present set up of Bihar and how in particular, the lives of female agricultural labour in Jehanabad district of Bihar are economically and socially structured, is the goal of this study.

The study focuses on themes such as nature and type of rural female labour force, their working conditions, occupational hazards, literacy level and lack of awareness, policies, programmes and strategies for their welfare. Valuable suggestions have been made regarding their wage differences, skill enhancement, non-farm activities, provision of institutional credit and all such measures required to empower the rural female folk and make them realize the immense potential concealed within themselves.

OBJECTIVES

- To examine the socio economic and political conditions of women agricultural labourers in India in general and Bihar in particular.
- To assess their present economic condition in respect of wealth and their internal and external sources of income.
- To examine their working and living conditions.
- To study their wage structure, identify the causes of wage discrimination and suggest remedies to remove it.
- To evaluate the impact of agrarian reforms and other reform measures adopted by the Government of India and Bihar in particular.
- To point and niche out some positive solutions for upliftment in the socio economic status of women agricultural labourers of Bihar and particularly of Jehanabad district, which is one of the most backward and undeveloped part of Bihar.

METHODOLOGY

Present study is an empirical study based on sociological tools to test the socio economic crisis and problems of women labour folk in Bihar. A sample survey of different parts of Jehanabad district of Bihar, through a structural questionnaire was conducted by me. The sampling was based on random method. The survey has covered about 200 women agricultural labour without any discrimination of age, occupation, caste and religion. Hence, the source of information is based on primary data.

FINDINGS OF THE STUDY

Socio-Economic Profile of Female Agricultural Labourers

An attention has been made on the socio-economic status of the sample respondents, which is very helpful in analyzing the perception, orientation, opinion and participation of women in the Rural Development Programmes. The Socio-economic factors determine the attitude, and orientation of the women, and may be considered as explaining variables.

In the present study, 200 respondents were interviewed across 4 villages and details of their caste, family type, family Property, housing conditions, living status, demographic details, education, marital status, working status and occupation along with income-expenditure are analyzed to understand their socio-economic status. These aspects can be analyzed one by one as follows:

Distribution of Households by Religion and Caste Groups and Type of Family

Religion and Caste Group

In India, the caste structure shows the socio-economic status of people. Religion or caste group has a major bearing on the attitude and orientation of women. The barriers between high and low castes create obstacles in the path of economic growth by restricting social mobility of labour force and creating contract among higher castes for manual works.

An analysis of the given Table 1 reveals that about 50 per cent of respondents belong to Scheduled Caste Hindus and 43.5 per cent belong to backward caste Hindus group. The per cent of Muslims among various caste groups is very low, only 3.5 per cent.

Uttar Sarthu has highest concentration of Scheduled Caste Hindus while Kochnama has 76 per cent respondents belonging to Backward Castes. Muslims show highest concentration in Larsa, about 12 per cent, as compared to other villages. Higher concentration of Backward Caste and Scheduled Caste groups across all villages shows higher level of denied opportunities in terms of socio-economic status and development prospects.

Table 1
Religion and Caste Distribution

Religion and Caste	*Villages*				
	Uttar Sarthu (N=50)	*Ahiasa (N=50)*	*Kochnama (N=50)*	*Larsa (N=50)*	*All Villages (N=200)*
Upper Caste Hindus	0.0	8.0	0.0	0.0	2.0
Backward Caste Hindus	6.0	32.0	40.0	16.0	23.5
Most Backward Caste Hindus	24.0	0.0	36.0	22.0	20.5
Scheduled Caste Hindus	70.0	60.0	22.0	50.0	50.5
Muslims	0.0	0.0	2.0	12.0	3.5

Type of Family

The foregoing Table 2 reveals that only 39 per cent of sample respondents belong to nuclear families, while 60 per cent households have joint families, where interests of woman members is generally overruled. Joint families are very prominent in Uttar Sarthu (70%) while nuclear families are very prominent in Kochnama (56%), which is quite unlike the general trend in the sample region.

Table 2
Type of Family

Type of Family	*Villages*				
	Uttar Sarthu (N=200)	*Ahiasa (N=50)*	*Kochnama (N=50)*	*Larsa (N=50)*	*All Villages (N=50)*
Nuclear	30.0	38.0	56.0	34.0	39.0
Joint	70.0	62.0	44.0	66.0	60.5
All Households	100.00	100.00	100.00	100.00	100.00

Distribution of Households by Selected Demographic Characteristics

Sex-Group

The above Table 3 throws light on proportion of females in the overall sample population. The female group constitutes 46.6 per cent of sample population, which is much lower compared to the proportion of males, which is 53.4 per cent. The gap between male-female proportions is maximum in Kochnama and lowest in Larsa. The proportion of females is lower than male proportion across all villages, which is a remarkable hindrance in the path of development.

Table 3
Sex Distribution

Sex	*Uttar Sarthu (N=50)*	*Ahiasa (N=50)*	*Kochnama (N=50)*	*Larsa (N=50)*	*All Villages (N=200)*
Male	52.0	52.8	57.3	50.6	53.4
Female	48.0	47.2	42.7	49.4	46.6

Age-Group

Age group is a good indicator of the working force and shows clear distinction between dependent and independent population sections.

Table 4
Age Distribution

Age Group	*Uttar Sarthu (N=50)*	*Ahiasa (N=50)*	*Kochnama (N=50)*	*Larsa (N=50)*	*All Villages (N=200)*
0-6 Yrs	22.2	20.4	16.0	20.3	19.7
7-14 Yrs	22.8	21.7	18.7	23.5	21.7
15-60 Yrs	51.2	55.7	63.2	53.3	55.9
Above 60Yrs	3.8	2.2	2.1	2.9	2.7

Table 4 shows that the proportion of working population that lies in age-group 15-60 years is only 55.9 per cent while proportion of respondents above 60 years of age is about 2.7 per cent. The working age-group has highest population proportion in Kochnama (63%) and least proportion in Uttar Sarthu (51.2%), the rest of the population is dependent on this very age-group for a living. It is evident from above data that the working age group has an equally sized population dependent on it for survival.

Marital Status

Marital status shows the socio-economic attitude and orientation of people and also affects their productive capacity, as marriage involves a greater set of responsibilities.

Table 5
Marital Status

Marital Stuatus	*Uttar Sarthu (N=50)*	*Ahiasa (N=50)*	*Kochnama (N=50)*	*Larsa (N=50)*	*All Villages (N=200)*
Unmarried	50.6	49.4	46.0	51.7	49.6
Currently Married	48.4	46.2	49.8	44.5	47.2
Others	0.9	3.8	3.6	3.8	3.0

About 49.6 per cent of overall sample respondents are unmarried, the incidence being very high in Larsa (51.7%) and lowest in Kochnama (46.0 per cent). Kochnama has about 49.8 per cent respondents as currently married, which shows their higher responsibilities on family front.

Education Level

Education is a good index for human resource development. Investment on education is more powerful instrument for the socio-economic and cultural transformation of the people. Illiteracy causes ignorance, which is responsible for the narrow socio-economic attitude of the people. Narrowness of the social and economic attitude of the people hampers their productive capacity and automatically keeps them away from the formal or organized sectors.

The literacy position among the sample respondents can be studied as follows:

Table 6
Education Level

Education Level	*Uttar Sarthu (N=50)*	*Ahiasa (N=50)*	*Kochnama (N=50)*	*Larsa (N=50)*	*All Villages (N=200)*
Illiterate	61.9	60.7	48.0	51.2	55.2
Below Primary	23.8	24.5	23.1	31.7	25.9
Primary Completed	8.4	6.0	8.9	5.5	7.2
Below Matriculate	3.1	5.0	7.4	6.4	5.5
Matriculate & Above	2.8	3.8	12.6	5.2	6.2
All Household Members	100.0	100.0	100.0	100.0	100.0

All Villages.

It is found from the Table 6 that 55.2 per cent of respondents are illiterate. They were not admitted to any school at all. The proportion of illiterates is highest in Uttar Sarthu (61.9%) and lowest in Kochnama (48.0%). About 25.9 per cent of sample respondents were admitted to the school, out of which only 7.2 per cent completed primary and only 5.5 per cent were below matriculate. Only a meagre percentage (6.2%) attained matriculation and higher degrees. Only 2.8 per cent of respondents belonged to matriculate category in Uttar Sarthu, while the proportion is higher (12.6 per cent) to some extent in Kochnama.

Size of Household

The size of household has a major bearing on availability of opportunities to individual members. The average size of household shows in a better way the privileges, productive capacity and prospects of female members. The following table shows the average size of household for sample households:

Table 7
Size of Household

Size	*Uttar Sarthu (N=50)*	*Ahiasa (N=50)*	*Kochnama (N=50)*	*Larsa (N=50)*	*All Villages (N=200)*
Average size of household	6.4	6.4	6.7	6.9	6.6

Table 7 clearly shows that the average household size is 6.6 among sample households, which is quite high. The average household size is above 6 for all villages, and this indicates predominance of joint family system on one hand, and higher number of children on the other.

Age of Marriage for Women

The age of marriage for women is a good indicator of illiteracy and social backwardness. The women who are married at an age less then 18 have to undergo physical sufferings and are also denied educational opportunities. They also have greater reproductive span and may have to give birth to children at an age when their physical and psychological system is not prepared for it. Larger fertility periods also lead to higher population, which is a bigger problem.

Table 8
Age of Marriage for Women

Age of Marriage of women	*Uttar Sarthu (N=50)*	*Ahiasa (N=50)*	*Kochnama (N=50)*	*Larsa (N=50)*	*All Villages (N=200)*
Per centage of married women where age at marriage is less than 18 years	77.2	71.0	67.2	63.4	69.6

The percentage of married women whose age at marriage is less than 18 years is about 69.6 percent for all sample households, which is above 63 per cent for all villages. This situation is very alarming; especially in case of Uttar Sarthu where above 77 per cent of women have been married at less than 18 years of age.

Distribution of Households by Land and Livestock Endowment

In India, lack of income generating assets is a major cause of poverty. Due to non-possession of such assets, the unskilled poor women labours depend on physical labour only. Physical labour yields inadequate income and thereby keeps them in the vicious circle of poverty. Low and irregular income cause misery to the poverty-stricken women labour households.

The following statistics reveal percentage distribution of sample households by land and livestock endowment.

Land Owned

Table 9 clearly highlights the miserable conditions of sample respondents, as far as asset ownership is concerned. About 75 per cent of total respondents are landless, only 7.5 per cent have land up to 0.30 acres, 13 per cent have land between 0.31-1.00 acres. A meager 4 per cent have land above one acres and only 1.5 per cent have land above two acres. The proportion of landless is very alarming in Ahiasa (94%) where no respondent has land above one acre.

Table 9

Land Owned (in acres)

(In Acres)	*Uttar Sarthu* (N=50)	*Ahiasa* (N=50)	*Kochnama* (N=50)	*Larsa* (N=50)	*All Villages* (N=200)
Landless	84.0	94.0	66.0	52.0	74.0
Up to 0.30	0.0	2.0	12.0	16.0	7.5
0.31-1.00	16.0	4.0	18.0	14.0	13.0
1.01-2.00	0.0	0.0	0.0	12.0	4.0
Above 2.00	0.0	0.0	0.0	6.0	1.5
Total	100.0	100.0	100.0	100.0	100.0

Land Operated

Table 10 reveals the percentage distribution of sample households on the basis of operated land; which shows the actual usage of land, which is quite distinct from mere asset ownership.

In terms of land operated, about 68.5 per cent of respondents are landless; this proportion is very high in Ahiasa and lowest in Larsa. Only 9.5 per cent of households have more than one acre of land, which is operated. This situation shows lack of income generating assets for majority of respondents, ultimately leading to poverty and misery.

Table 10
Land Operated (in acres)

Land Operated (In Acres)	*Uttar Sarthu (N=50)*	*Ahiasa (N=50)*	*Kochnama (N=50)*	*Larsa (N=50)*	*All Villages (N=200)*
Landless	78.0	86.0	66.0	50.0	68.5
Up to 0.30	0.0	2.0	10.0	22.0	8.5
0.31-1.00	10.0	10.0	18.0	16.0	13.5
1.01-2.00	10.0	2.0	4.0	4.0	5.0
Above 2.00	2.0	0.0	8.0	8.0	4.5
All Household	100.0	100.0	100.0	100.0	100.0

Livestock Endowment

Livestock endowment also shows an important income-generating asset and has a direct bearing on economic conditions of the sample households.

Table 11
Livestock Endowment (in Rs.)

Livestock Endowment (in Rs.)	*Uttar Sarthu (N=50)*	*Ahiasa (N=50)*	*Kochnama (N=50)*	*Larsa (N=50)*	*All Villages (N=200)*
Nil	26.0	40.0	38.0	46.0	37.5
Up to Rs. 1000	6.0	2.0	4.0	8.0	5.0
Rs.1001-10, 000	44.0	50.0	38.0	36.0	42.0
Above 10,000	24.0	8.0	20.0	10.0	15.5
All Household	100.0	100.0	100.0	100.0	100.0

Table 11 depicts the picture of livestock endowment in rupees. About 37.5 per cent of respondent households have nil livestock endowment. About 5 per cent have livestock up to Rs. 1000, 42 per cent have livestock of value Rs. 1001-10, 000 and only 15.5 per cent have livestock worth more than Rs.10, 000. The livestock endowment is nil for about 46 per cent of respondents in Larsa, and is followed by Ahiasa (40%) and Kochnama (38%). In Ahiasa, only 8 per cent of respondents have livestock worth more than Rs. 10, 000. Low livestock ownership increases their dependence on physical labour only for income and survival.

Employment Status of Households

The following section reveals the working status of sample households and gives a closer view of the income prospects of female agricultural labour in the district.

Work Participation Ratio

The work participation ratio is 49% for all villages; it is highest for Kochnama (55.2) and lowest for Larsa (42.4). The percentage of workers in total respondents is only 68.2 and the rest is unemployed. The proportion of workers is highest in Larsa (73.3%) and lowest in Ahiasa (62.8%). Low work participation ratio clearly indicates lesser opportunities for employment, and low-income possibilities as revealed by Table 12.

Table 12
Work Participation Ratio

	Uttar Sarthu (N=50)	*Ahiasa (N=50)*	*Kochnama (N=50)*	*Larsa (N=50)*	*All Villages (N=200)*
Work Participation Ratio	49.7	49.1	55.2	42.4	49.1
Percentage of workers	66.0	62.8	66.1	73.3	68.2

Distribution of Workers by Employment Status

Table 13 elucidates that the population proportion of regular earners is negligible (0.3%) among respondents. Self-employed and unpaid family under member constitutes about 26 per cent of the respondents. At the same time, casual wage earners constitute a very high proportion of the total sample households. The proportion is significantly high in Ahiasa, where 80 per cent belong to casual wage-earner category, while the per centage of regular earners is nil. The proportion of self-employed is comparatively high in Larsa, about 21.9 per cent. The given data clearly shows the lack of suitable job opportunities and low payments, wages for the available work opportunities. The proportion of unpaid family under member is also remarkable across all villages.

Table 13
Distribution of Workers by Employment Status

Employment Status	*Uttar Sarthu (N=50)*	*Ahiasa (N=50)*	*Kochnama (N=50)*	*Larsa (N=50)*	*All Villages (N=200)*
Self employed	11.3	10.3	10.8	21.9	13.3
Unpaid family under member	13.2	9.6	20.0	8.2	13.1
Regular earner	0.6	0.0	0.3	0.0	0.3
Casual wage earner	74.8	80.1	68.8	69.9	73.3
Total	100.0	100.0	100.0	100.0	100.0

Workers Migrating for Work

Migration of workers for better work opportunities is caused due to lack of jobs and low wage rates at home. The workers can migrate both temporarily and for long term, depending on the job options and wage rates available at their new work places. The following table distinguishes between temporary and long term migration.

Table 14
Workers Migrating for Work

% of workers who migrate for work	*Uttar Sarthu (N=50)*	*Ahiasa (N=50)*	*Kochnama (N=50)*	*Larsa (N=50)*	*All Villages (N=200)*
Temporary	6.3	5.8	21.5	8.2	11.0
Long Term	8.8	12.2	8.1	8.9	9.4

According to Table 14, the proportion of workers who migrate temporarily (11%) is higher than long term migrating per centage (9.4%) of respondents. Temporary migration is very high in Kochnama, with about 21.5% of respondents leaving the village temporarily for work. The village Ahiasa has higher per cent of workers migrating for long terms. The main reason for high long-term migration across all villages is lack of job opportunities, low wages, lack of income generating assets and terrorism. The towns always attract unemployed youth as they offer better job options and suitable wages.

Distribution of Members of Households by Occupation

The occupation of workers has a direct bearing on the income and living conditions of households. Greater dependence on agriculture shows lack of alternative sources of employment. Agricultural labour has an uncertain source of income and generally faces low wages. Lack of industrial occupations is also an indicator of backwardness. The following table shows the main occupation and secondary occupation of sample respondents:

Main Occupation of Workers

The foregoing Table 15 clearly shows that agricultural labour is the most popular main occupation of workers in the sample households. About 45% of respondents depend on agricultural labour as their main source of income. Non-agricultural labour is the other occupation option that is very common. Business and caste occupations are not very popular. Salaried workers constitute only 10% of total workers, which is very low. There is an absolute lack of job options in the industrial sector, and agriculture seems to support majority (79%) of the population, either directly or indirectly.

Table 15
Main Occupation of Workers

Occupation	*Uttar Sarthu* (N=50)	*Ahiasa* (N=50)	*Kochnama* (N=50)	*Larsa* (N=50)	*All Villages* (N=200)
Cultivation	19.5	7.0	20.4	17.1	16.5
Agricultural Labour	46.5	55.8	34.4	43.2	45.4
Non-agricultural Labour	18.9	9.0	24.2	17.8	18.1
Caste Occupation	2.5	0.0	0.0	6.8	2.2
Business	4.4	11.5	7.0	7.5	7.7
Salaried workers	8.2	16.7	12.9	7.6	10.1
Total	100.0	100.0	100.0	100.0	100.0

Agricultural labour constitutes more than half of the working population in sample households in Ahiasa. This sector is associated with irregular income and low wages. The marginal productivity is also very low in this sector. Caste occupations are very uncommon in Ahiasa and Kochnama. Kochnama also has a higher proportion of non-agricultural labour.

Secondary Occupation of Workers

It is evident from the Table 16 that business category is the most popular secondary occupation of workers, across all villages, closely followed by agricultural labour. Salaried workers are very meager as salaried jobs are very few. Cultivation is least prevalent secondary occupation in Uttar Sarthu. About 12.5 % of respondents are involved in cultivation, as a secondary occupation. Farm and non-farm yet indirectly farm-associated activities together involved majority of the workers having secondary occupation. Lack of industrial activity is evident.

Table 16
Secondary Occupation of Workers

Occupation	*Uttar Sarthu (N=50)*	*Ahiasa (N=50)*	*Kochnama (N=50)*	*Larsa (N=50)*	*All Villages (N=200)*
Cultivation	2.9	8.2	13.8	24.3	12.5
Agricultural Labour	37.1	29.6	27.6	22.4	29.1
Non-Agricultural Labour	18.1	26.5	19.5	19.3	20.8
Caste Occupation	1.0	0.0	0.0	12.1	3.2
Business	40.9	35.7	38.8	21.5	33.9
Salaried Workers	1.0	0.0	0.3	0.4	0.5
All Workers	100.0	100.0	100.0	100.0	100.0

Information on Annual Income and Expenditure of Households

Average Annual Income per Household

The following table presents the picture of the annual income of the family on an average. This is one of the important indicators of the economic status of the family.

Table 17
Average Annual Income per Household

Average Annual Income Per Household (Rs. 000)	*Uttar Sarthu (N=50)*	*Ahiasa (N=50)*	*Kochnama (N=50)*	*Larsa (N=50)*	*All Villages (N=200)*
	20.52	21.52	26.73	29.45	24.62

The average annual income per household is very low, Rs. 24.62 thousands which shows the poor economic condition of sample respondents. The average annual income is lowest in Uttar Sarthu (about Rs. 20 thousands) and highest in Larsa (Rs. 29.45 thousands) as it is revealed from Table 17.

Distribution of Income by Sources

From Table 18, it is clear that casual wages constitute about half of the total income among sample respondents. Self-employment in agricultural sector (27%) is the second major source of income. Remittances also contribute to income of sample households to certain extent. Regular wages are very uncommon source of income, contributing only 3.8 % of total income. Uttar Sarthu had no respondent having regular wages as a source of income, while it had about 52% of respondents depending on casual wages. Larsa had about 15% respondents who were self-employed in non-agricultural field.

Table 18
Distribution of Income by Sources

Income by Sources	*Uttar Sarthu (N=50)*	*Ahiasa (N=50)*	*Kochnama (N=50)*	*Larsa (N=50)*	*All Villages (N=200)*
Self-employment (Agriculture)	30.9	19.2	29.8	27.5	27.0
Self- employment (Non-Agriculture)	5.6	13.5	7.6	14.9	10.7
Wages (casual)	52.0	39.5	40.8	44.2	43.9
Wages (Regular)	0.0	3.9	10.4	0.3	3.8
Remittances	10.8	23.5	10.0	13.1	14.0
Others	0.7	0.4	1.3	0.0	0.6
Total	100.0	100.0	100.0	100.0	100.0

Distribution of Expenditure

The percentage distribution of expenditure across different overheads is a direct indicator of consumption pattern and living standard as well as economic status of sample households.

Table 19
Distribution of Expenditure

Expenditure	*Uttar Sarthu* (N=50)	*Ahiasa* (N=50)	*Kochnama* (N=50)	*Larsa* (N=50)	*All Villages* (N=200)
Food	67.5	70.2	65.0	69.2	69.0
Clothing	7.7	8.9	8.4	8.6	8.6
Fuels	2.3	2.6	2.5	4.1	3.0
Education	1.2	1.5	1.3	2.7	1.7
Medical	2.2	3.9	3.0	4.3	3.4
Transport	1.7	2.4	2.7	1.8	2.2
Recreation	3.3	2.5	3.8	3.3	3.3
Intoxicants	2.6	3.0	2.9	2.8	2.9
Loan Repayment	0.6	0.8	5.1	0.2	1.9
Marriage/Shraddh etc.	1.3	0.5	0.7	1.1	0.9
Others	9.7	3.7	4.6	2.0	4.9
Total	100.0	100.0	100.0	100.0	100.0

Table 19 clearly shows food as the most important avenue of expenditure (69%) across all villages, closely followed by clothing. Fuels, medical and recreation are other popular categories. Intoxicants also constitute a good share of total expenditure and about 3% of respondents spend on intoxicants in Ahiasa. The expenditure on education and loan repayment is very low, which shows lesser prospects of development. Very high expenditure on food & clothing is a clear indicator of poverty conditions, which compel greater demand of basic necessities.

Information on Possession of Consumer Durables by Households

Consumer durables show the standard of living of sample households, which has a direct bearing on the socio-economic attitude, orientations, behavior, efficiency and prospects of respondents. The following table shows the possession of consumer durables by sample households:

The above table clearly shows the poor living conditions of sample respondents. Almost all households seem to have cot (about 99.5%). Cycle is other category of durables, which is possessed by about half (52.5%) of sample households. Bed, radio and chair are other categories, which are possessed by the respondents. Almost negligible households possess television, Motorcycle and Car/Jeep and other expensive items. Watches, fans and stove are owned by none of the respondents. This situation clearly shows the miserable economic conditions of sample respondents. No respondent in Uttar Sarthu and Ahiasa has an Almirah, while Ahiasa and Kochnama had no respondent with a motorcycle.

Table 20
Possession of Consumer Durables

Items	*Uttar Sarthu (N=50)*	*Ahiasa (N=50)*	*Kochnama (N=50)*	*Larsa (N=50)*	*All Villages (N=200)*
Cot	100.0	100.0	98.0	100.0	99.5
Bed	8.0	16.0	28.0	24.0	19.0
Table	6.0	4.0	16.0	6.0	8.0
Chair	12.0	10.0	26.0	18.0	16.5
Almirah	0.0	0.0	4.0	6.0	2.5
Radio	24.0	22.0	18.0	24.0	22.0
Television	0.0	0.0	0.0	6.0	1.5
Cycle	48.0	44.0	62.0	56.0	52.5
Motor Cycle	4.0	0.0	0.0	2.0	1.5
Car/Jeep	0.0	0.0	0.0	0.0	0.0
Pressure Cooker					
Watch					
Electric Fan					
Electric Stove					
Gas Stove					

Distribution of Households by Housing Conditions

Ideal housing conditions generally promote the state of health and efficiency of the workers. Lack of housing facility and inferior housing accommodation is the indicator of backwardness and poverty. Obviously, good housing facility is necessary for workers to make them efficient and committed to work.

The following sector analyses the status of homestead land, the type of house and number of rooms in sample households and gives a close view of living conditions of respondents:

Status of Homestead Land

Table 21 shows that about 96% of sample respondents live on their own land while only 3.5% depend on government land. Landlord's land constitutes only 0.5% of total land, and is absent in Uttar Sarthu, Ahiasa and Kochnama. Kochnama had 100% respondents living on their own land, while government land constituted 10% of total homestead land in Uttar Sarthu.

Table 21
Status of Homestead Land

Status of Homestead Land	*Uttar Sarthu (N=50)*	*Ahiasa (N=50)*	*Kochnama (N=50)*	*Larsa (N=50)*	*All Villages (N=200)*
Owned	90.0	98.0	100.0	96.0	96.0
Government Land	10.0	2.0	0.0	2.0	3.5
Land Lord's Land	0.0	0.0	0.0	2.0	0.5

Type of House

Table 22 further shows that about 31% of respondents live in katcha (khaprail) houses, while 8.5% live in katcha (thatched) houses. Semi-pucca houses constitute 34% of total households while pucca houses constitute only 20% of total sample households. No respondent had a fully pucca house in Uttar Sarthu. Larsa has highest proportion of respondents living in katcha (khaprail) houses, while Kochnama had highest proportion living in (fully) Semi pucca houses. Pucca houses constituted highest per cent of total households in Ahiasa compared to other villages. Bad housing conditions deter the efficiency and commitment to work of the respondents, and are a major indicator of poverty conditions.

Number of Rooms

In above continuation, Table 23 shows the accommodation (no. of rooms) available in the houses of sample respondents. About 5.5% of respondents live in single rooms, and 36.5% live in homes with two rooms. 31.5% lives in houses with more than three rooms. Ahiasa has 54% of respondents living in single or double room houses.

Table 22
Type of House

Type of House	*Uttar Sarthu (N=50)*	*Ahiasa (N=50)*	*Kochnama (N=50)*	*Larsa (N=50)*	*All Villages (N=200)*
Katcha (Thatched)	18.0	6.0	6.0	4.0	8.5
Katcha (Khaprail)	32.0	18.0	34.0	40.0	31.0
Katcha (Thatched + khaprail)	12.0	6.0	4.0	2.0	6.0
Semi-Pucca (Partially)	14.0	4.0	10.0	6.0	8.5
Semi-Pucca (Fully)	20.0	28.0	36.0	20.0	26.0
Pucca (Partially)	4.0	20.0	6.0	10.0	10.0
Pucca (Fully)	0.0	18.0	4.0	18.0	10.0
Total	100.0	100.0	100.0	100.0	100.0

Table 23
Number of Rooms

No. of Rooms	*Uttar Sarthu (N=50)*	*Ahiasa (N=50)*	*Kochnama (N=50)*	*Larsa (N=50)*	*All Villages (N=200)*
One	8.0	4.0	2.0	8.0	5.5
Two	22.0	50.0	30.0	44.0	36.5
Three	40.0	16.0	26.0	24.0	26.5
More than Three	30.0	30.0	44.0	34.0	31.5
All Households	100.0	100.0	100.0	100.0	100.0

The type of dwelling and number of rooms has a direct effect on efficiency of workers, which is very low in given villages.

Distribution of Households by Living Conditions

Drinking water source, Lighting Arrangement, type of fuel used and availability of toilet facility depict living conditions of a household. Living condition has a very significant effect on efficiency and productivity of working members and their health condition.

Drinking Water Sources

The foregoing Table 24 shows that 54.5% of sample households have own tube wells while 42.5% depend on public tube wells for water supply. 1.5% have protected dung well of their own while 1.5% depend on neighbors tube well for water supply. Larsa has about 80% of respondents having their own tube wells. Protected dung wells were absent as a drinking water source in Uttar Sarthu, Kochnama and Larsa. The dependence on public tube well is very low in Larsa (only 16%). 4% of respondents in Larsa still depended on neighbor's tube well for water supply.

Table 24
Drinking Water Sources

Drinking Water Sources	*Uttar Sarthu (N=50)*	*Ahiasa (N=50)*	*Kochnama (N=50)*	*Larsa (N=50)*	*All Villages (N=200)*
Tube well (own)	42.0	42.0	54.0	80.0	54.5
Tube well (Public)	56.0	52.0	46.0	16.0	42.5
Protected Dung Well (own)	0.0	6.0	0.0	0.0	1.5
Neighbor's Tube well	2.0	0.0	0.0	4.0	1.5
All Households	100.0	100.0	100.0	100.0	100.0

Lighting Arrangement

Lighting arrangement has a direct effect on work efficiency and productivity, and is an important indicator of economic progress and living standard.

Table 25
Lighting Arrangement

Lighting Arrangement	*Uttar Sarthu (N=50)*	*Ahiasa (N=50)*	*Kochnama (N=50)*	*Larsa (N=50)*	*All Villages (N=200)*
Dhibri*	30.0	26.0	16.0	20.0	23.0
Dhibri* + Lantern	54.0	56.0	68.0	24.0	50.0
Lantern	8.0	16.0	4.0	6.0	6.0
Electricity	0.0	14.0	10.0	50.0	18.0
All Households	100.0	100.0	100.0	100.0	100.0

(* Dhibri is a small kerosene lamp without shade used mostly in villages of Bihar).

Table 25 reveals that only 18% of respondents have access to electricity, the access being highest in Larsa (50%) and lowest in Uttar Sarthu (0%). Dhibri and lantern still offer the most prevalent source of light to majority of households across all villages. Household's dependent on dhibri is very high (23.0%) among sample respondents. This indicates backwardness and lack of basic infrastructure facilities to majority of household.

Type of Fuel Used

Table 26 shows the type of fuel used by respondents. According to the data, 61.5% of households are still dependent on cow-dung cakes for fuel. Agricultural wastes constitute the second best fuel option for sample households. Firewood constitutes a meager per cent (4.0%) and offers the only other option of fuel. Electric stoves and Gas stoves are completely absent and the sample households are still dependent on traditional sources of fuel.

Table 26
Type of Fuel Used

Type of Fuel	*Uttar Sarthu (N=50)*	*Ahiasa (N=50)*	*Kochnama (N=50)*	*Larsa (N=50)*	*All Villages (N=200)*
Firewood	0.0	12.0	2.0	2.0	4.0
Agricultural Waste	34.0	38.0	52.0	12.0	34.0
Cakes	64.0	50.0	46.0	86.0	61.5
Others	2.0	0.0	0.0	0.0	0.5
All Households	100.0	100.0	100.0	100.0	100.0

Toilet Facility

Toilet facility indicates the health and hygiene conditions of sample respondents. They indicate living standard and socio-economic status to a considerable extent.

Table 27
Toilet Facility

Type of Toilet	*Uttar Sarthu (N=50)*	*Ahiasa (N=50)*	*Kochnama (N=50)*	*Larsa (N=50)*	*All Villages (N=200)*
Pit Latrine	0.0	2.0	0.0	8.0	2.5
Water-Serled Latrine	2.0	6.0	2.0	6.0	4.0
No Latrine	98.0	92.0	98.0	84.0	93.5
All Households	100.0	100.0	100.0	100.0	100.0

Table 27 clearly indicates lack of toilet facility that is available to the houses of the respondents. About 93.5% of overall households have access to no latrines. Only 4% use Water-Serled latrine while pit latrine is used by only 2.5% of respondents. Pit latrines are absent in case of Uttar Sarthu and Kochnama. Both Uttar Sarthu and Kochnama have 98% of households having no latrine facility.

This shows the miserable living conditions of sample respondents, who do not have access to basic facilities of life.

INFORMATION ABOUT EXTENT OF INDEBTEDNESS OF HOUSEHOLDS

Lack of adequate credit facilities leads to over-dependence on moneylenders for short-term and long-term credit requirements. Low-income base of villagers increases their indebtedness, and they are unable to repay loans on time. Their dependence on agriculture and high interest charges can also be accounted for this. Ultimately, the peasants and poor villagers land in a non-ending debt-trap. Their low productivity leads to indebtedness that continues across generations.

The following table throws light on indebtedness of sample households.

Table 28
Indebtedness of Households

	Villages				
Percentage of Households Indebted	*Uttar Sarthu (N=50)*	*Ahiasa (N=50)*	*Kochnama (N=50)*	*Larsa (N=50)*	*All Villages (N=200)*
	34.0	60.0	68.0	54.0	54.0

As the data indicates, more than half (54%) of sample households are indebted, the per cent being very high in Kochnama and Ahiasa (68 % and 60% respectively). The low-income base of sample households is mainly responsible for this debt-trap situation.

Distribution of Indebted Households by Amount of Outstanding Loan

The above table clearly shows that more than half of the sample households (75%) are under a debt of Rs. 1,001-10,000. The proportion is significantly high in Ahiasa, where 60% of population has a debt of Rs. 1001-5000 and 20% have taken loans between Rs. 5001-10, 000. About 30% of respondents in Uttar Sarthu have an indebtedness of amount up to Rs. 1000. All respondents in Ahiasa and Larsa had a debt amount, which was more than Rs. 1,000, though no respondent in Uttar Sarthu and Ahiasa had a loan above Rs. 20, 000. Since half of all sample households seem to be under debt of some amount, and the loan amount is above Rs. 1,000 for majority of them, the situation is miserable. About 17.6% of households seem to be in debt-trap, with an outstanding loan above Rs. 10, 000.

Table 29
Amount of Outstanding Loan

Amount of Outstanding Loan	*Uttar Sarthu (N=50)*	*Ahiasa (N=50)*	*Kochnama (N=50)*	*Larsa (N=50)*	*All Villages (N=200)*
Up to Rs.-1000	29.4	0.0	8.8	0.0	7.4
Rs. 1001-5000	52.9	60.0	41.2	55.6	51.9
Rs.5001-10, 000	17.6	20.0	32.4	18.5	23.1
Rs.10, 001-20,000	0.0	20.08	18.5	13.0	13
Above Rs.20, 000	0.0	0.0	8.8	7.4	4.6
Total	100.0	100.0	100.0	100.0	100.0

Alternative credit facilities and government support for better income base and quick loan redemption is urgently needed in the region.

Information about Sources of Loan, Purpose of Loan and Interest Rates

Village moneylender is an important source of agro-credit in Bihar, though other sources (Commercial Banks, Rural Banks and Co-operative Banks) are also gaining popularity. Loans are taken by villagers mainly for productive works, such as seeds, fertilizers, equipments, digging of wells etc. or for unproductive works like consumption, marriage, parties etc. These unproductive loans don't add to farm productivity and are difficult to be repaid. Such loans are injurious for farmers. The following section analyses the sources of loan, purpose of loan and interest rates among the sample households.

Sources of Loan

According to the Table 30, about half (44%) of the sample respondents are still dependent on moneylenders for their loan requirements. The Land Lords/Employees happen to be the next preferred alternative source of loan, claiming about 38% of total loans. These moneylenders and landlords tend to exploit respondents by charging high interest rates and taking farm produce as repayment. Still, respondents are attracted to these non-institutional sources instead of banks or loans since these sources offer loans easily, quickly and do not demand any security. They also offer good level of secrecy.

Table 30
Sources of Loan

Sources of Loan	*Uttar Sarthu* (N=50)	*Ahiasa* (N=50)	*Kochnama* (N=50)	*Larsa* (N=50)	*All Villages* (N=200)
Commercial Bank	5.9	3.3	20.6	14.8	12.0
Rural Bank	0.0	3.0	5.9	0.0	2.8
Co-operative Bank	5.9	0.0	5.9	0.0	2.8
Money Lenders	58.8	50.0	26.5	51.9	44.4
Land Lord/Employees	29.4	43.3	41.2	33.3	38.0
Total	100.0	100.0	100.0	100.0	100.0

While commercial banks are the third preferred source (12%) of loan, Rural Banks and Co-operative Banks still have to gain recognition as a suitable loan source. Larsa has no respondent who has taken loan from Rural Banks or Co-operative Banks. Landlords/Employees are more popular source than moneylenders in Kochnama. Commercial Banks also have a good hold in Kochnama, and provide 20% of total loans in this village.

Purpose of Loan

It is also important to study the purpose of loan taken by households. As the Table 31 suggests, 24% of loans are taken for consumption purpose, 16.7% for marriage and other unproductive purposes. Only 15.7% is taken for farm and 4.6% of total loans are taken for non-farm activities. 2.8% of loans are taken for migration purpose, as well as for house-building .25% of total loans are also taken for health purpose, which has a very high proportion in Ahiasa (34.4%). On the other hand, Ahiasa has very limited per cent of loans (6.2%) taken for farm activities and no loans are taken for non-farm activities. Uttar Sarthu has half of the loans taken for consumption purpose, which is unproductive.

Table 31
Purpose of Loan

Purpose of Loan	*Uttar Sarthu (N=50)*	*Ahiasa (N=50)*	*Kochnama (N=50)*	*Larsa (N=50)*	*All Villages (N=200)*
Agriculture/Livestock	11.8	6.2	15.6	29.6	15.7
Non-farm activities	0.0	0.0	15.6	0.0	4.6
Migration	0.0	0.0	9.4	0.0	2.8
House-building	0.0	3.1	3.1	3.7	2.8
Consumption	47.1	21.8	15.6	22.2	24.9
Health	29.4	34.4	12.5	25.9	25.0
Marriage	5.9	21.9	18.8	14.8	16.7
Mixed Purposes	5.9	12.5	9.4	3.7	8.3
Total	100.0	100.0	100.0	100.0	100.0

The tendency to take loans for unproductive purposes is very high across all villages. Such loans don't add to farm or non-farm productivity, and are difficult to be repaid. They are mainly responsible for heavy indebtedness of sample households.

Average Rate of Interest

The village moneylenders charge about 55% average interest on all types of loans. The landlords/employees also charge an interest rate of about the same order (51.2%). This rate is exceptionally high as compared to banks, which charge 10.3% interest on an average. But the villagers are attracted towards moneylenders and other traditional sources as they meet their credit needs very easily without any security and provide an element of secrecy. The long and tedious process of loan sanctions by banks, which also demand securities, also add up to the popularity of moneylenders. But these lenders tend to exploit poor, illiterate farmers and villagers by charging very high interest rates, and have a tendency to seize land, farm produce as repayment. In spite of this, lending system is a necessary evil of rural economy. These village moneylenders charge 97% interest in Larsa, which is about 10 times, the interest charged by Banks in this village. The situation is equally exploitative in Uttar Sarthu and Ahiasa, facing interest rate of about 60 % in the hands of these lenders.

Table 32
Average Rate of Interest

Source of Loan	*Uttar Sarthu (N=50)*	*Ahiasa (N=50)*	*Kochnama (N=50)*	*Larsa (N=50)*	*All Villages (N=200)*
Bank	13.5	11.0	10.6	9.9	10.3
Money lenders	58.8	60.0	40.0	97.3	54.6
Landlord/Employees	57.6	53.5	40.0	33.3	51.2

This high interest rate by lenders and low popularity of bank loans is mainly responsible for high indebtedness among sample households.

Awareness of Households about Selected Development Programmes

A developmental programme can be effectively implemented or penetrated only when it is accompanied by a considerable degree of people's participation, which is the most important factor for the achievement of socio-economic goals in the society. This participation depends upon the level of awareness of the target population of the development programmes. The following table analyses the awareness of sample households about selected development programmes:

According to the Table 33, not more than 21% of respondents are aware of employment related programmes. In Ahiasa, the awareness of such programmes is extremely low, not more than 16%. This is the reality in spite of prevalence of three programmes– SGSY, SGRY AND PMGY.

Table 33
Awareness About Selected Development Programmes

Types	*Programmes*	*Uttar Sarthu (N=50)*	*Abiasa (N=50)*	*Kochnama (N=50)*	*Larsa (N=50)*	*All Villages (N=200)*
Employment Related	(a) SGSY	10.0	14.0	22.0	4.0	12.5
	(b) SGRY	22.0	16.0	26.0	22.0	21.5
	(c) PMGY	6.0	12.0	22.0	30.0	17.5
Housing Related	(a) IAY	98.0	100.0	100.0	96.0	98.5
	(b) CCSSRH	0.0	4.0	0.0	4.0	2.0
	(c) CRSP	0.0	0.0	0.0	0.0	0.0
Social Security Related	(a) NOAPS	100.0	94.0	98.0	100.0	98.0
	(b) NFBS	16.0	8.0	24.0	14.0	15.5
	(c) NMBS	36.0	64.0	60.0	66.0	56.5
PDS Related	(a) Annapurna Scheme	24.0	50.0	44.0	52.0	42.5
	(b) Antodaya Scheme	44.0	52.0	52.0	80.0	57.0
Education Related	(a) Rural Scholarship	54.0	56.0	44.0	22.0	44.0
	(b) Free Text Book	90.0	94.0	100.0	100.0	96.0
	(c) NFE Centre	96.0	98.0	100.0	96.0	97.5
	(d) Mid day Meal	10.0	10.0	22.0	32.0	18.5
	(e) SSA					
Other Schemes	(a) ARWSP	0.0	0.0	0.0	0.0	0.0
	(b) PMGSY	28.0	38.0	38.0	52.0	39.0
	(c) DPAP	2.0	16.0	30.0	20.0	17.0
	(d) NGO/SHG Mahila Mandal	10.0	10.0	20.0	24.0	16.0

As far as housing related programmes are concerned, Indira Awas Yojana (IAY) is very popular across all villages with 98.5% of sample households being aware about it. Other housing programme CCSSRH is very less popular. None of the respondents seemed to have any idea of CRSP programme.

NOAPS programme is a known name for about 98% of respondents, the awareness being perfect (100%) in Uttar Sarthu and Larsa. NMBS has more than 56% of respondents aware of it. NFBS has comparatively lesser popularity (15.5%) across all villages. Only 8% of respondents were aware of NFBS in Ahiasa.

Free Textbook and Mid-Day meal are the two most popular education related programmes, which about more than 95% of respondents are aware of. In Kochnama and Larsa, 100% respondents are aware of free textbooks scheme and in Kochnama 100% respondents are aware of Mid-day meal programmes. NFE Centre and rural scholarship are less popular programmes, though rural scholarship is known by more than half of respondents in Uttar Sarthu and Ahiasa. SSA is a programme, only 18.5% of people are aware of.

Among other schemes, the level of awareness is 40 % for PMGSY, 17.0% for DPAP and 16% for NGO/SHG Mahila Mandals. No respondent was aware of ARWSP programme in any of the sample villages.

Benefited to Households from Selected Development Programmes

Accruing benefits and evaluation of developmental programmes are supported by psychological traits like awareness, perception and motivation of the individual towards the activity. This section attempts to analyze the percentage of sample households, which have benefited from selected development programmes:

The above table clearly highlights the limited success of development programmes in providing benefits to the target population. Only 17.5% of population has benefited from PMGY programme. The proportion is significantly low in Uttar Sarthu and Ahiasa. The proportion of sample households receiving

Table 34
Benefits from Selected Development Programmes

Selected Development	*Programmes*	*Uttar Sarthu (N=50)*	*Ahiasa (N=50)*	*Kochnama (N=50)*	*Larsa (N=50)*	*All Villages (N=200)*
Employment Related	(a) SGSY	0.0	0.0	4.0	0.0	1.0
	(b) SGRY	0.0	0.0	2.0	0.0	0.5
	(c) PMGY	6.0	12.0	22.0	30.0	17.5
Housing Related	(a) IAY	28.0	60.0	14.0	14.0	29.0
	(b) CCSSRH	0.0	0.0	0.0	0.0	0.0
	(c) CRSP	0.0	0.0	0.0	0.0	0.0
Social Security Related	(a) NOAPS	6.0	4.0	8.0	12.0	7.5
	(b) NFBS	0.0	0.0	4.0	0.0	1.0
	(c) NMBS	0.0	12.0	0.0	2.0	3.5
PDS Related	(a) Annapurna Scheme	2.0	0.0	0.0	6.0	2.0
	(b) Antodaya Scheme	6.0	0.0	0.0	14.0	5.0
Education Related	(a) Rural Scholarship	6.0	10.0	2.0	00.	4.5
	(b) Free Text Book	60.0	52.0	22.0	68.0	50.5
	(c) NFE Centre	0.0	2.0	0.0	4.0	1.5
	(d) Mid day Meal	62.0	52.0	34.0	68.0	54.0
	(e) SSA	0.0	0.0	0.0	0.0	0.0
Other Scheme	(a) ARWSP	0.0	0.0	0.0	0.0	0.0
	(b) PMGSY	0.0	0.0	2.0	0.0	0.5
	(c) DPAP	0.0	0.0	0.0	0.0	0.0
	(d) NGO/SHG Mahila Mandal	0.0	0.0	0.0	0.0	0.0

benefits from SGSY and SGRY is almost negligible. Uttar Sarthu, Ahiasa and Larsa have no respondent who has benefited from SGSY and SGRY programme.

Indira Awas Yojana (IAY) has been successful to limited extent in providing houses to the needy respondents, as only 29% of total respondents have benefited from it. IAY has been more successful in Ahiasa as compared to other villages. No respondent in any village has benefited from CCSSRH, and CRSP housing programmes.

As far as Social Security Schemes are concerned, only 7.5% of total respondents have benefited from NOAPS, 3.5 % have received benefits from NFBS. Social Security Schemes seem to have attained very limited success in their aim.

PDS related schemes have benefited no respondent in Ahiasa and Kochnama. It has benefited very limited households (2% under Annapurna and 5% under Antodaya Scheme) in Uttar Sarthu and Larsa.

In the field of education, free textbook and mid-day meal schemes have been successful in benefiting only half of the sample households. They have been more successful in Larsa (68%) and Uttar Sarthu (60-62%) in comparison to Ahiasa and Kochnama. NFE centers and rural scholarship have not been able to benefit even 5% of sample households. The SSA scheme has been a thorough failure across all villages, in spite of consistent government efforts.

Among other schemes, PMGSY seems to be the only working scheme, but it has benefited only a meager percentage (2%) of households in Kochnama. Other Schemes such as ARWSP, DPAP, NGO / SHG/ Mahila Mandal have been completely unsuccessful in providing developmental benefits to sample households.

Hence, despite efforts on part of the government; none of the schemes seem to have addressed the developmental needs of sample respondents to a considerable extent. Lack of awareness and improper distribution system may be responsible for this situation. The statistics show that the existing programmes need a fresh impetus and proper supervision if all round development is desired in the sample area. A well formulated strategy and sincere execution is the need of the hour.

CONCLUSION OF THE STUDY

Women constitute half of the population and their development reflects the progress of society. The status of women in society is measured in terms of their level of income, employment, education, health as well as the role played by them in family, community and society. Women play a vital role in the social and economic transformation of a society. About 80 per cent of economically active women in India are engaged in agriculture and allied activities. There are more than 30 million women working in rural economy. Women in India have always been discriminated at all fronts against men in human resource development with utter disregard to their actual and potential contribution to the national progress in general and agricultural progress in particular. On the threshold of the twenty first century, we find that the condition of our women folk, particularly those of rural community is still very deplorable. In 2006, UNDP ranked India in the last quartile of the countries (122 out of 143 countries) in a gender–related development index (GDI).

Women in rural India, by and large, remain bogged down with domestic work, rearing cattle and other support and productive works. They are by and large not part of the decision making process and have little control over money matters and assets even though they contribute substantially in asset formation especially in rural India. Their educational backwardness and low level of awareness add to a general invisibility of their work. This trend has not changed much for the past 50 years.

Hence, the informal women labourers generally face low wages, longer working hours, denial of leaves and leisure and maltreatment. The deprivation of women is more acute in terms of health, education, nutrition, social, economic, political and demographic aspects. The plight of female agricultural labourers in Jehanabad district can be studied closely by the following findings of the field data:

(i) The district Jehanabad in Bihar has 61 per cent of population dependent on agriculture as the main occupation. There is a complete absence of industrial activity in the sample area.

(ii) About 46 per cent of population comprises of females in the sample area, while male population is much higher.

(iii) More than half of the sample population is illiterate. Only 7 per cent of members of sample households of female agricultural labourers were able to complete primary education. This is because these villages do not have adequate educational facilities.

(iv) The agricultural female labour households have 6.6 as the average household size; about 60 per cent of families are joint families.

(v) About 73 per cent of agricultural female labour households are casual wage earners. The work participation ratio is less than 50.

(vi) Average annual income of agricultural female labour households is only Rs. 24.62 thousands. About 43 per cent of this income comes in form of casual wages, and 27 per cent comes through self–employment in agriculture sector.

(vii) The expenditure pattern of agricultural female labour households is mostly focused on food and clothing expenses, which constitute about 77 per cent of total expenses. This means that more than three–fourths of the family expenditure was on basic necessities, resulting in deficit of money for other expenses and there could be no saving.

(viii) Caste plays a major role in the social stratification in Indian rural society. 43 per cent of such female households belong to backward caste Hindus whereas Scheduled caste households constitute 50 per cent. This shows that the under privileged class people of these sample villages must be guided and helped both economically and employment wise to come up in their life.

(ix) 74 per cent of sample households were landless and 38 per cent had no access to live stock of any type. Due to low asset ownership and lower earnings, these households face heavy indebtedness.

(x) About 45 per cent of female agricultural labourers lived in Katcha (Thatched or Khaprail) houses; only 20 per cent had access to Pucca houses. This clearly indicates the poor economic status of the female labourers and that the low income earned by them could not meet their daily needs. Due to this situation, it is very difficult for the female labourers to repair their houses, which are in dilapidated conditions.

(xi) Only 54 per cent of female agricultural laborer households had their own source of water supply; 79 per cent depended on Dhibri or Lantern for light; 95 per cent depended on agricultural waste and dung cakes as fuel source; about 93 per cent of such households had no latrines. The female agricultural labourers faced miserable living conditions.

(xii) Nearly 70 per cent of married women in the sample households were married at an age less than 18 years. It shows that the women are forced to share the family responsibilities at a young age. This may be the reason for their lack of awareness about their rights and privileges.

(xiii) The indebted households constitute 54 per cent among female agricultural laborer households, with 91 per cent having outstanding loans greater than Rs. 1000. These debts have been for various purposes like meeting family expenses, constructing houses and purchase of milch animals etc.

(xiv) Moneylenders charging an average 54 per cent rate of interest are the most preferred source of loan among the female agricultural labour households; only 21 per cent of such loans are for productive purposes. This indicates the urgent need to provide institutional credit to the female labourers (for productive purposes, preferably) and also curtail the role of village money – lenders.

(xv) Not more than 21 per cent households were aware of employment related programmes; 43 per cent households were unaware of Antodaya Scheme, while SSA was known by only 18.5 per cent of sample households. This means that any development programmes of the government have not benefited these female labourers.

(xvi) Employment–related PMGY Programme was able to benefit only 17.5 per cent of female agricultural labour households while IAY had access to only 29 per cent of such families; PDS–related schemes were benefiting only 5 per cent of such households, while social security schemes benefited not more than 7.5 per cent of such sample households.

(xvii) SSA, ARWSP, DPAP, NGO/SHG/Mahila Mandals were benefiting none of the households of female agricultural labourers.

SUGGESTIONS OF THE STUDY

A sympathetic understanding of the socio-economic problems of these female agricultural labourers who contribute substantially to the household economy is required for incorporating them in the planning framework. In the emerging global restructuring, as manual skills and physical strength decline in importance, a country can improve its competitiveness by enhancing and more fully utilizing the cognitive skills of its female labour force. Creating opportunities for women will be a prudent policy, not only on the grounds of equity, but also for economic growth.

Of all facets of women's development, their economic independence or economic empowerment occupies an area of utmost significance for a lasting and sustainable development of society. Women empowerment is a process, which enables women to have access and control of various factors necessary for their economic independence, political participation and social development. A rational and gender friendly attitude towards the needs and requirements of women in the society and a holistic approach to the cause of their upliftment are the pre-requisites for such empowerment.

To address the problems of female agricultural labourers, the following policy suggestions can be forwarded:

(1) Equal pay for all types of unskilled work and schemes for skilled up-gradation for women should be undertaken, through strong endorsement of laws. Steps should be taken to enforce the Minimum Wages Act.

(2) Unless agricultural female labourers are educated and organized, they cannot be freed from socio-economic bondage. To reduce the illiteracy level, adult education programmes should be effectively implemented for all rural women labourers.

(3) The government should provide adequate school facilities in the rural areas. It will improve the status of education in the villages.

(4) To reduce the school dropouts at the primary level, the government should provide high school facility in under developed villages.

(5) A legal literacy programme can enable women labourers to apply that vertical awareness to the law and legal

process. The government and non-government organizations may organize legal literacy campaigns to enable the rural women labourers to understand the various provisions relating to their occupation and to make proper use of them.

(6) Educational reforms required to increase the employability of women are required. Technology choices relevant to employment promotion among women in the light of current trends in modernization in both farm and non-farm sectors are required.

(7) Encouragement of non-farm activities in the study area will help the female labourers to get more employment chances in the non-farm sector as an alternative source of employment within their village area. Further, those labourers can use their unemployed days and enhance their earnings.

(8) There should be re-orientation of self-employment programmes with a view to achieve sustained increase in self-employment at a rapid pace in rural areas, especially in context of female labour force.

(9) Private sector involvement should be ensured in promoting wage employment opportunities for women.

(10) The government and non-government agencies should take necessary steps to organize entrepreneurial and skill development programmes for women labourers, to enhance their earning capacity.

(11) Government should increase the access to institutional finance to landless labourers, particularly to female labourers.

(12) Provision of institutional credit to the women labourers with easy access and without too many formalities will help to reduce the role of village moneylenders.

(13) The government and non-government agencies should take necessary efforts to make the female labourers

aware of the various women development programmes through special awareness camps in rural areas. The NGO's can play a useful role in disseminating such knowledge regarding employment, housing, PDS and education related programmes.

(14) Special programmes to take care of health and stress conditions of female agricultural labourers are needed. The female workers suffer from different types of diseases and discomforts, and also there is dearth of medical facility in rural areas. Such workers should have easy accessibility to medical attention and accident benefit schemes.

(15) Rural housing programmes should be implemented in the rural areas and the benefits should cover the poorest of the poor and needy families. Water, sanitation and power facilities should be ensured in every house by government as well as NGO's efforts.

(16) Fresh impetus must be given to already existing programmes by government intervention so that they could benefit a much larger population base.

(17) There is an urgent need to organize the female labourers to fight against their problems and so collective action is necessary in the form of union/ association to create awareness about their rights and privileges.

(18) Starting of self-help groups in the rural areas will promote the saving habit among the female labourers and also it will strengthen their economic independence. Further, it will promote leadership qualities and ability to make decisions on their own.

In spite of constitutional safeguards, legislative measures, package of programmes by the government, no significant development has taken place in the socio–economic situation of women and they are still lagging behind men in their participation in the process of development. The government has to make effective plans and policies and to take up concrete action for the employment of rural women. The most potentially effective way of empowering women is to enable and encourage their participation in workers' organizations. For this purpose, the administrative machinery should be made more vigilant towards the security of employed women in rural areas. Their involvement should increase in different activities that are taking place in the rural areas in which they are generally ignored. Further, the voluntary organizations should play an important role in implementing government programmes for the promotion of employment opportunities. The government, along with the help of women groups and NGO's should establish vocational training and income generation centers.

The non-performance of the rural development process is due to poor awareness amongst the targeted populace about the schemes being launched for them. It has been found that the awareness level in the rural areas is very low. It is necessary to increase awareness among the female labourers regarding available opportunities, their rights and responsibilities through education from grassroots level in rural areas.

Women are very important segment in development at local to global levels. Unless women have control over their earnings and expenditure decisions, the benefits in terms of empowerment will remain limited. Empowerment of women is a continuous, multi-dimensional process depending to a large extent on the change in the value system; attitude and socio-economic structure prevailing in the country, Experience, awareness, education and competence, willingness, confidence, self-motivation, encouragement from family and society contribute to empowerment of rural women. The movement towards empowerment of women needs to be accelerated. The immense potential concealed within this female labour force is yet to be recognized.

References

A. Balakrishnan, *Rural Landless Women Labourers: Problems and Prospects.*

Agrawal, C. D. (1957), "Employment and Earning of Hired Labour in Agriculture", *Indian Journal of Agricultural Economics,* Vol. XII, April to June.

Ahuja, Kanta (1979), "Women Workers in Rural in Rajasthan", The A.C.M. Sate Institute of Public Administration, Jaipur.

Ghose, M. G. (1974), "The Problems and Prospects of Marginal Farmers and Agricultural Labourers in West Bengal", *Indian Journal of Agricultural Economic,* Vol. XXIX (3).

Goswami, P. C., and Bara, C. K. (1970), "Demand for Labour in Rural Areas", *Indian Journal of Agriculture Economics,* XXV, No. 3.

Government of India (1973), "Economic and Social Status of Woman Worker in India", *Labour Bureau,* Ministry of Labour.

Iyanger, S. Kesva (1951), Rural Economic Survey. Hyderabad State, Government Press, Hyderabad.

Jeemol Unni (2001), 'Gender and Informality in Labour Market in South Asia', *Economic and Political Weekly,* Vol. 3^{6}(2^{6}), pp. 2360-77.

Jeevika Weerahewa and Anoma Ariyawardana, 'Impact of the WTO on Women Workers in Sri Lanka, in Veena Jha (ed.), Trade, Globalization and Gender-Evidence from South Asia, UNIFEM in Collaboration with UNCATED, (New Delhi: UNIFEM, 2003).

Kalpana Bardhan (1986), '*Women; Work, Welfare and Status: Forces of Tradition and Change in India*', South Asia Bulletin, Vol. 6 (1).

Kawadia, Ganesh (1980), "Wages of Weaker Section in M.P.", *Indian Journal of Agriculture Economics.* Vol. XXXV (4).

Mamoria, C. B. (1973), "Rural Unemployment", Agriculture Problems in India, Chapter 17.

Navaneeta Rath, Women *in Rural Society-A Quest for Development.*

Nelly P. Stromquist (ed.) (1998), Women in the third World–An Encyclopedia of Contemporary Issues, New York and London: Gariand Publishing.

Nirmala Buch (2000), '*Women's Experience in New Panchayats: The Emerging Leadership of Rural Women*', Occasional Paper No. 35, New Delhi, Center for Women's Development Studies.

Patricia Alailima (1998), *The Situation of Women: Employment, Unemployment and Underemployment,* in Women in the Economy, Centre for Women's Research, Colombo, Working Paper No. 12.

Rustagi, Preet, Women and Development in South Asia, *South Asian Journal @ southasianmedia.net.*

Rajan, V. Sundra (1957), "Employment and Earnings of Hired Labour in Agriculture", *Indian Journal of Agriculture Economics,* Vol. XII, April to June.

Ram, G. S. and Others (1974), "Wage and Employment of Agricultural Labourers in U. P. and Punjab", *Indian Journal of Agriculture Economics,* Vol. XXIX (3), July to Sept.

R. D. and Others (1972), *Comparative Economic Study on Marginal Farmers and Agricultural Labourers* in Ballia District of U.P. Agriculture University, Pantnagar.

Reddy, Y. V. R. and Rastogi, B. K. "A Study on Employment, Earnings and Standard of Living of Agricultural Labour in Dryland Areas in Hyderabad Region", Agro *–Economic Research in Drought–Prone Areas, Co-ordination Cell. Dry land Agriculture,* (ICAR), Hyderabad.

S. Murty and K. D. Gaur, *Women Work Participation and Empowerment: Problems and Prospects.*

Singh, R. D. and Others (1972), Comparative *Economic Study on Marginal farmers and Landless Agricultural Labourers in Ballia District of U.P.,* Division of Agriculture Economics, U.P. Agriculture University, Pantanagar.

Sharon Y. Nickols and Kamala Srinivasan, *Women and Household Production, Capturing Complexity*, Sage Publications.

Sharma, M. L., Nandal and Bhan Chandra (1974), "Green Revolution and Changing Trends in Wage Structure of Landless Labourers in Rural Hissar (Harayana)", *Indian Journal of Agriculture Economics,* Vol. XXIX (3).

Shahrukh R. Khan (1993), 'South Asia' in Elizabeth M. King and M. Anne Hill (eds.), Women's Education in Developing Countries: Barriers, Benefits and Policies, Baltimore: John Mopking University press for the World Bank, pp. 211-246.

Shah, S. L. and Others (1970), "The Impact of New Agricultural Technology on Rural Employment in North-West U. P.", *Indian Journal of Agriculture Economics,* 25(3).

Shah S. L. and Others (1970), "Impact of New Technology on Rural Employment", *Indian Journal of Agriculture, Economics,* Vol. XXV, July to September.

Sharma, Raj; K. P. Singh and A. C. Ganguwar (1974), "Employment, Wages and Mobility of Rural Labour in Harayana", *Indian Journal of Agriculture Economics,* 29, (3).

Kurukshetra, March 2007.

Yojana, October 2006.

Human Development Report, 2005.

Jehanabad: Ek Mazar Me; from the office of D. M.

www. undp. org. in.

16

AGRICULTURE LABOUR IN BIHAR

Pushpa Sinha & Ratna Mitra

Agriculture is the mainstay of life in India. It is the main source of livelihood to 65 per cent of her population. Most of the states in the country basically depend upon agriculture and Bihar is one of the states which is predominantly an agricultural economy.

The present Bihar constitutes about 3 per cent of the geographical area of the country and constitutes about 8 per cent of total population i.e. 8.29 crore as per 2001 census and is the third most populous state of India. After the division of the state in 2000 by carving out the southern plateau as Jharkhand, it is left with a large stretch of plains with no industry worth the name and no major towns except the state capital of Patna. Bihar has the lowest literacy rate and highest percentage of population living below poverty line except that of Orissa, the state has the lowest per capita income among the major states of India. It is characterized as the most backward state of India. The state ranks among the slowest growing regions of India and the G.D.P growth rate has been low. On the other hand the population growth rate of Bihar which was 23.4 per cent during the 1980s shot up to 28.4 per cent during the 1990s. The overall impact of the demographic situation coupled with slow growth has led to the economic retrogression of Bihar's per capita income, which was about 40 per cent in 1993-94 and further fall to 34 per cent in 1997-98. Presently Bihar is thr least urbanized state of India with just 10 per cent of population living in towns. The agricultural sector employing about 73 per cent of the workforce in the state is very backward with low productivity. The per capita agricultural income of the state is about half of India as a whole and about one fifth that of Punjab. Productive employment in the non- agricultural sector has grown as much as in other states. As far as social scenario is concerned, it presents orthodox, rigid social structure where people are dominated by casteism. Our study is concerned with agricultural labour in Bihar.

We know the agricultural labourers mostly belong to socially and economically backward and poor sections swelling the rank and earn their livelihood mainly by working in agriculture. Agricultural labour may be divided into (a) Landless labour who are attached to the landlords. (b) Landless labourers who are personally independent but who work exclusively for others (c) Petty farmers with tiny bits of land who devote most of their time working for others and (d) farmers who have economic holding but have one or more of their children and dependent working for other prosperous farmers. The first group of agricultural workers has been in the position of serf or slave. They are popularly known as 'bonded labour'. They are not paid wages in cash but in kind. Sometimes they have to offer cash and supply fowls and goats to their masters. Rest group of workers are important but subject of consideration is agricultural labourers as a whole. According to the definition of National Sample Survey Organisation, agricultural labourers are those rural households who work at least 183 days in a year in agriculture and earn a major proportion (i.e. at least more than 50 per cent of their earnings) must be obtained from agricultural wages i.e. the rural households who get their livelihood from agriculture are categorized as agricultural labour.

After defining who are agricultural labour, we here concentrate about the emergence of agriculture labour in the economy. To start our analysis from the time of the Gupta Empire, land grants become increasingly important. Along with the taxes paid to the Rajas, as the empire of the local feudal (samants) began to get an increasing share of surplus. Indian kings made land grants to get the taxes (surplus) collected. In this turn, the granters collected rent from their subject tenants, peasants who could be evicted and even subjected to forced labour. Beside subject tenant peasant, there were also untouchable agricultural labours.

Caste and class on primitive levels of production is not a percales society but within a class society itself. It was a tributary system based on Varna System. The system which determined access to the means of production not only for artisans but even more for tiller of the soil. There were clear categories of those who participate in any labour had a right to a share of the produce. Maliks (owners) did not have a high standard of living but had field labourers to do work for them. There were the subject peasants, kisans who possessed the land and the instrument of production, particularly cattle and gave a share of the produce to the maliks. There were the untouchables or the field labourers 'Mazdoors' who were the ploughmen but had no right to the land. It seems they were often given a plot of land to maintain themselves but had no right of ownership of land. It is not that class developed within castes but that bourgeois classes grew within feudal classes. Some sections of the parasitic classes were pushed down in the ladder and underwent a process of peasantisation. Simultaneously, some section of intermediate peasant classes accumulated land, went upto the ranks to become rich peasant while some other were pushed down to become agricultural labourers.

During the British period, Bihar was one of the regions where permanent settlement was introduced by Lord Cornwallis in 1793. It was a policy adopted by the government to earn fixed revenue through the intermediaries or the so called zamindars who were given task of revenue collection i.e. land revenue or rent from the peasants.

Under the permanent settlement, the revenue demand was fixed at ninth-tenths of the rent that the zamindars were assumed to collect from their tenants. The right of land was vested in the landlords but no protection was given to the class of actual cultivators. It was only through the Act of 1885 that the right of the tenants got some legal recognition.

In course of time, consequent upon the growing demand for land, the Zamindars started extracting exorbitant rent from the tenants, though the land revenue payable by them had been fixed permanently by the zamindars who imposed their own arbitrary assessment as the raiyats. Usually the tenants paying low rents were evicted. After meeting the on crop land revenue demand, the village community was left with bare subsistence if there was little to spare for effecting improvement in land, cultivation and improving living conditions.

On account of small and fragmented holdings, low yields per acre and the limited scope for generating income from subsidiary activities due to the decline of handicrafts that were previously being produced in peasant homes, most of the cultivators had very low incomes. A large proportion of them hardly managed to meet both ends even in good crop years. In bad years with no past saving, they were compelled to borrow for sheer substances. At once the peasant fell into the trap of indebtedness, he found it difficult to extricate himself from the web of very high and mounting debt obligations.

THE AGRARIAN STRUCTURE

The intricately stratified system of relationship of people to land as prevalent in the state during the period of permanent settlement between 1793 and 1950 when the zamnidari system has been captured by Jannuzi in the following order, the state (the 'Super landlord'), the Zamindar and the tenure holder (can intermediary of the state for collation of rents), the occupancy raiyats (a rent paying holder of land having the occupancy on the land held by him), the non-occupancy raiyats (a rent paying holder of land not having the right of occupancy of land temporarily in his possession), the under raiyats (a rent paying holder of land having temporarily possession of holding under raiyats) and Mazdoor (a wage labour having no rights in land).

The permanent settlement was conceived by Lord Cornwallis as a means of providing incentives to Zamindars to promote the development of agriculture and invest accordingly or to lease out land to those who were interested in investing in agriculture. Either possibly would have contributed to the development of agriculture enabling land owners to increase the land revenue to be given to the government unfortunately, these objectives could not be realized. The Indian caste system simply precluded that recreation of English type landlord leading to capitalist agriculture. The hierarchy of land tenure that was stabilized by the permanent settlement simply reinforced the caste hierarchy, which proved inimical to agriculture revolution. This was basically because this hierarchy ascribed to a group, its status according to its distance from the plough as manul work in general. It is thus not surprising that the agrarian structure and its classes had a clear cut dimension also. The four upper castes i.e. Bhumihar, Brahmin, Rajput and Kayastha have heavy stake in land. The upper classes of society Zamindars as well as tenure holders were almost exclusively drown from the upper castes. The upper middle castes were largely peasants, non-occupancy raiyats and to a lesser extent traders and agricultural labourers, while the lower middle castes and the scheduled castes were mainly agricultural labourers. This caste stratification was almost identical to that based on the interests in land. Clearly, the above agrarian structure was inherently exploitative and detrimental to agricultural development. Though the kind of rural scenario described above was not confined to only permanently settled areas but the situation in other areas in Bihar was extremely bad. The Zamindars not only made exorbitant exactions in the form of land rent but also in other forms such as labour rent, produce rent, homage, etc. In short, 'pegging' of land revenue as compared to other taxes was reflected in the inflated value of land, the benefit from which flowed to the limited class of Zamindars, which by and large either purchased more rent receiving land with it or dissipated it in luxury consumption.

The system of produce rent was mainly prevalent in Bihar. It was a vicious aspect of rent exaction from the largest group of peasants the share croppers. Besides the Zamindars, their 'AMLAS' (Subordinate rent collectors) extracted agricultural surplus in various extra legal exactions and an exploitative 'beggar' system climaxing their whole edifice of exploitation was the mal treatment and oppression 'Zulum' of agriculture workers in the exaction of labour rent through the unpaid forced labour was called beggar. Legal provisions notwithstanding the Zamindar had the first claim on tenants labour was exacted ruthlessly.

The exploitative agrarian structure did not lead to the emergence of the agrarian capitalist in the form of rich peasantry independent of landlords. There was almost complete stagnation in agricultural production in Bihar during the British period. The class that acquired the surplus, used it on conspicuous consumption such as luxury good, purchase of more Zamindari, etc. while the class of peasants, which could have invested in land, was hardly in a position to do so because of the prevalent practice of rack-renting.

In view of the policy of the government and partly due to the peasants own monetary needs, the cultivation of some commercial crops like in cone, opium, etc. increased at the expense of food-grain, the per-capita availability of food grains declined. A significant proportion of the tenants were unable to pay rent and consequently they were evicted from their lands, appropriated in compliance with rent decree was the 'BAKASHT' land. There was another class of less tenants, the tenants-at-will (bataidar). Those who lost their land became labourers or resettled on the Zamindars land as share croppers or migrated to other places.

Thus, the permanent settlement produced extremely dangerous agrarian structure in the countryside of Bihar which led to large scale alienation of the peasants from their land which after becoming bakasht lands of the Zamindars come to remain a source of tension often erupting in violent outburst. Apart from bakasht issue, they sometimes took form of movements for conversion of produce rent into cash rent as well as the reduction of rates of rent and at other times, of those for ending the system of illegal exactions like beggar and finally of the movement for the abolition of zamindari itself. Swami Sahajanand Saraswati and others launched this struggle under the banner of the Bihar Paradesh Kisan Shabha. It do not cover raiyat and agricultures labour.

At the dawn of independence, the ruling party hoped for moderate, landlord oriented path of agrarian transition that precluded radical land distribution from this political agenda. This strategy focused on abolition of statutory and land lordism and on providing incentives to ex-landlords and rich peasants for transforming themselves into agrarian entrepreneurs. It led to the abolition of zamindar system in 1950 which encouraged the peasants to buy the land released in the process. Accordingly, only rich tenants could retain land and the smaller peasants simply lost access to it and became either tenants-at-will or landless agricultural labourers. The spurt in the numbers of the agricultural workers in the wake of the first phase of land reforms was a manifestation of this reality.

GROWTH OF AGRICULTURE LABOUR

In Bihar, out of the total population of 82,878,796 (2001 Census) 28, 08,004 persons are workers, out of which 2,163,153 are main workers and 7,026,851 are marginal workers. Thus, of the state's total population the percentage shares of total workers, main workers and marginal workers are 33.88 per cent, 25.40 per cent and 8.48 per cent repectively while the corresponding figure for 1991 census were 30.58 per cent total workers, 29.13 per cent main workers and 1.46 per cent marginal workers. There has been an increase of more than 3 per cent in working force over the decade in the state. The proportion of marginal workers in the total population has shown significant rise during the decade the percentage being more than 7 per cent as the proportion of cultivators are concerned, it has decreased from 43.58 per cent in 1991 to 29.17 per cent in 2001 and the share of agricultural laboures increased from 37.13 per cent in 1991 to 48.18 per cent in 2001.

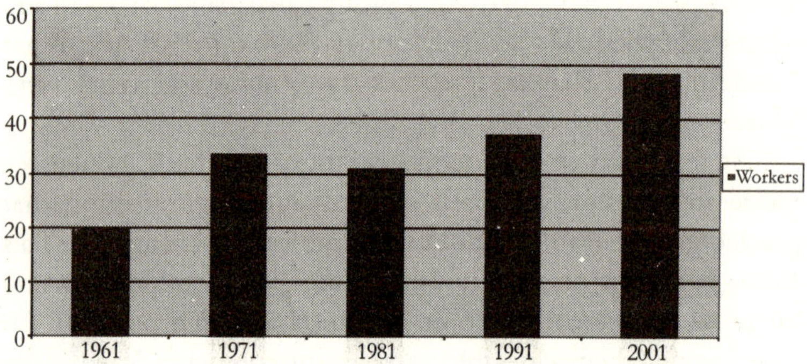

Figure : Agriculture Labour in Bihar

Sources: 1. Census of India 2. National Seminar on Development of Bihar.

The annual increase in population at a rate of 2 to 2.5 per cent over the last fifty years has raised the number of agriculturist by more than 70 per cent while the number of agricultural labour has increased by more than 230 per cent over the same period. As we know that of the total agriculturist, one part is cultivators and other is agricultural labourers. But the rate of growth of cultivators and the agricultural labourers does not generally take place with same pace as the population and agriculturist grow. In case, there exists a tendency of concentration in agrarian economy, the growth of cultivators occurs slowly or even negatively while agricultural labour grows at faster rate. The main reason behind this is the fragmentation of land and consequently poor man land ratio with the increase in population. Further, more gross cropped area per male worker has significantly decreased over the period in the state. In many of the districts, the proportion of cultivators did not increase as fast as the increase of agriculturist while in some other districts, the number of male cultivators remained practically the same or even decreased. The proportion of agricultural labourers on the other hand has increased in every district of the state.

Hence, the main explanation that can be given in support of rising trend of the agricultural labour in Bihar is that as time passes, more and more cultivators are thrown out of their holdings and the concentration of land in few hands has accented for polarization of land.

Table 1
Growth of Agricultural Labourers in Bihar (During 1911-2001)

Year	*Total Workers*	*Percentage of Total Population*	*Agricultural Labour*	*Percentage of Total Workers*
1911	13681740	46.40	3427708	25.05
1921	13928648	47.97	2444401	17.34
1931	12995305	40.14	2628722	20.22
1951	13565176	33.72	3238407	23.87
1961	19234555	41.40	4418475	22.97
1971	17488879	31.03	6808103	38.92
1981	20712215	29.66	7340472	35.44
1991	28111596	32.55	9544444	33.95
2001	28080004	33.88	13527884	48.17

Source: Census of India from 1911-2001.

The above table clearly reveals that during 1911-2001, the number of total workers to the total population has increased by nearly two folds where as, it rose by nearly four folds in case of the number of agricultural labourers to the total workforce. This reflects a paradox of the increased rates of growth in agriculture, the declining proportion of cultivators and the most important is increasing proportion of agricultural labourers suggest a process that indicates a combination of 'de-peasantisation and proletarianisation' in the state of Bihar. This process has been further worsened by the artisans classes that have lost their trade and craft which forced them to join the ranks of the agricultural labourers.

SEX-WISE DISTRIBUTION OF WORKERS IN AGRICULTURE IN BIHAR

Table 2 reveals that total workers in the agricultural sector varied between 80.23 per cent and 84.69 per cent during the decades 1961 to 1971. As per 2001 census, 81.22 per cent of the total workers were engaged in agricultural sector in Bihar. Male participation was found to have varied between 64.28 per cent and 84.56 per cent as per 1961 and 1971 census. Male agricultural workers shared 90.19 per cent of employment opportunities in 2001 as compared to 9.81 per cent of female participation.

A significant transition in the perception of the poor peasants and agricultural laborers with regard to their needs and aspiration can be noticed in the villagers.

Table 2
Sex-wise Distribution of Workers in Agriculture Sector in Bihar

	(1901-2001)		(in percentage)
Census year	*Total workers*	*Male*	*Female*
1961	80.23	64.28	35.72
1671	84.69	84.65	15.44
1981	81.18	79.89	20.11
1997	81.10	76.69	23.31
2001	81.22	90.19	9.81

Source:

PROBLEMS OF AGRICULTURAL LABOURERS IN BIHAR

(1) *Low Wages:* Bihar was one of the first states to implement the enforcement of Minimum Wages Act, 1952. But yet, it has not been fully implemented and quite contradictory Bihar is one the state in the country where the wages of the agricultural labuorers is at the lowest. Agricultural labourers not being organized are even unable to raise voice against their low wage.

(2) *Unemployment and Underemployment:* In Bihar, most of the agricultural labourers remain unemployed in most part of the year except for the peak season in agriculture. Apart from this

labourers who are employed in agriculture are disguisedly employed too.

(3) *Social Exploitation:* In Bihar after 60 years of independence, there is class division in the society as a result of which there is stratification of classes. The richer sector of society exploits the poorer which mainly consist of agricultural labourers.

(4) *Non-implementation of Land Reform Programme:* Land reform laws were passed in Bihar but they lack proper implementation. The lands which are reclaimed are not distributed among the poor people or the agricultural labourers. Bataidari continues and higher revenue continued to be charged.

(5) *Low Consumption:* Due to low level living, these poverty stricken people can easily be imagined because of small income. They are able to meet only their consumption needs to a limited extent. In fact, the incomes are so meagre that they can provide for only a part of the minimum subsistence living and are forced to incur debt to meet a part of their consumption expenditure. Generally, they eat jowar, bajra, maize and other inferior cereals. Such items as fruit, vegetables, milk and other nutritive foods do not at all figure in their diet. The position regarding other essentials is no better. They do not have even the minimum clothing, education and health facilities for them and their houses are no more than places fit for animal which they share with them. In these conditions, many take to gambling, drinking and such other evil activities. They also suffer from many diseases. To meet these expenditures, they take loans and get driven into the clutches of money lenders.

(6) *Heavy Indebtedness:* Low incomes of agricultural labourers had led them into heavy indebtedness. According to one estimate, 44.5 per cent of agricultural labour households were under debt in 1950-51 and such households were 63.9 in 1956-57 taking indebted households the debt on an average was Rs 105. In Bihar, lack of work culture and belief in traditions is one of the causes of indebtedness.

(7) *Socially Deprived Class:* These economically poor workers mostly belong to the socially backward classes like the OBC, SC, ST, etc. As such they belong to the lowest rank of the social hierarchy. They lead a life of social outcastes and are exploited in numerous ways. A majority of these people live below the poverty line. We may describe their deplorable existence by quoting a distinguished agrarian expert, Harsh Dev Malaviya, "unemployment, underemployment and very low wages combined with social oppression make the life of the agricultural workers miserable."

(8) *Unsatisfactory Employment:* The availability of work is much less than needed. A large number of workers are landless who work as casual or temporary workers. They get work only during certain periods of farming operations. These are, for example, sowing and harvesting phases of farming. As such their employment is seasonal, they remain out of work for quite long periods sometimes extending over four to five months. They are paid at market rate and are free to work elsewhere. In other words, they face an insecure employment situation. There are other workers who are attached to particular landlords. They are better ones as they get some regular work on an annual or seasonal basis. Their employment is based on some sort of contract with wages determined largely by custom or tradition. Most of the time, these wages are less.

MEASURES FOR IMPROVEMENT

For ameliorating the conditions of agricultural workers, there is need to adopt various measures simultaneously. Such strategy is called for because the miserable state in which workers find themselves today is the outcome of varied economic social, historical and institutional factors. So, in order to bring about suitable changes in the conditions of agricultural labourers, the several measures can be grouped under two broad types. First, type of measures concerned with improvement in their working conditions and the second pertains to the raising of level of their living conditions.

Improving Working Conditions

For effecting improvement in their working conditions, the following measures should be adopted:

(1) In Bihar, working hours of the labourers are not fixed which need to be fixed. Besides during working hours, provision should be made for such essential things as drinking water, rest and interval of works, etc. Female labour should be engaged as per their physical capacity. Engagement of women during night should be totally prohibited.

(2) Though Bihar was one of the first states to implement Minimum Wages Act but yet the labourers are not able to get minimum wage because of their supply which is very high. They are not in a position to bargain for their hard work.

(3) Formation of unions of agricultural labuorers is also essential for bringing about an improvement in the conditions of these people. It is through such organization that they can effectively bargain for better working conditions with their employers and organize pressure on the authorities for the enforcement of measures like minimum wages etc. There are of course, many difficulties in organizing them in trade unions like industrial labourers.

RAISING STANDARD OF LIVING

(1) In order to raise their standard of living, several measures are needed as social security services like those connected with health facilities, drinking water, necessary consumer goods at cheap rates, etc.

(2) Land made available under reclamation and surplus land required through policy of living should be distributed

among them. This will not only raise their income and economic level but will also improve their social status. It will also help them in formation of co-operatives. Further, necessary production inputs should be made available to them for efficient farming.

(3) Non-agricultural industries should be developed so as to absorb surplus labour and employment in the ban season of agriculture. For this purpose; help in the form of credit, technical training, etc should be provided by the government organizations. Co-operatives are also needed to further attain the objective of promoting such industries in rural areas.

(4) Housing facilities near their place of work should also be provided. They should be allotted land for house and supplied with materials for house building. It will also raise their economic and social status. Improvement in working conditions of these labourers and uplifting their economic and social status are basically linked with economic development of the country. So special efforts should be undertaken to solve their problems.

GOVERNMENTAL MEASURES

After independence, the government has taken several steps to improve the condition of agricultural labour. Some of the steps are as follows:

(1) *Fixation of Minimum Wages:* Minimum Wages Act was passed in 1948. It empowers the legislation to fix the minimum wages for the labourer. The Act has been extended almost throughout the country and accordingly, minimum wages for agricultural laborers have been fixed. At present, legislation have been passed in all the states of the country except Jammu and Kashmir, Sikkim and Nagaland.

(2) *Antodya Programme:* This programme has been started to improve the lot of the poor agricultural labourers in each

village. Poorest families are identified and they are allotted land, equipments, etc. In this way, these families will be able to rise above the poverty line. They are also being provided other facilities to get employment and raising their standards of living.

(3) *Insurance:* Since 15th August 1987, group insurance scheme has been introduced which will cover all the landless agricultural labourers. Under this scheme, life insurance is offered to the bread winner of the family. The premium under the scheme is only 10% per annum for all insurance cover of Rs 1,000. The central government itself pays their premium.

(4) *Abolition of Bonded Labour System:* In 1976, the government has passed the Bonded Labour Abolition Act. According to this Act; no labour can be kept as bonded labour for paying the debt. All bounded labours were freed and discharged from any such obligation. Thus, all contracts for bonded labour and their debt were declared null and void. This Act has really saved labourers from exploitation and inhuman behaviour.

(5) *Rural Employment Programme:* The rural employment programme was launched in 1980. The basic function of this programme is to organize labour intensive works on large scale. The project undertaken under this scheme generally includes road building, minor irrigation, drainage, water conservation, etc.

(6) *Development of Cottage Industries:* In order to minimize the pressure of population on land, the government is making efforts to revive the cottage and small scale industries in the rural areas of the country. Under various plans, different kinds of cottage and small scale industries have been set up in the villages and incentives are given to such units.

(7) *Regional Rural Banks:* The government has established regional rural banks in the villages for providing facilities

to agricultural labourers who want to start their own tiny business.

(8) *Ceiling of Holding:* All states have fixed the maximum limit of agricultural holdings to be cultivated by a single farmer. The excess land of this limit is distributed among the landless labourers.

(9) *Foods for Work Schemes:* This scheme was initiated in April 1977. Under it, the payment of part of the wages is made in food grains. The food grains for such distribution are made available free of charge by central government.

AGRICULTURAL LABOURERS THROUGH PLANS IN BIHAR

The First Five Year Plan: The first five year plan presented free India's first attempt of national reconstruction of its impoverished economy. With the achievement of independence, the demand for all round economic regeneration was universally voiced. In the initial phase of planning, it is difficult to present any spectacular record of achievement.

The economy of Bihar is primarily agricultural. The population dependent on it increased from 78.8% in 1931 to over 86% in 1951 and more than one-third of them are farmers who cultivate lands wholly or mainly unowned or are cultivating labourers .

Bihar is predominantly an agricultural state. Agricultural improvement therefore receives first consideration in the state plan. Agriculture research is undertaken at field level through the national extension service. As an essential prelude to land reform, Zamindari was abolished. Consolidation of holding and the prevention of fragmentation has also been experimented. The Minimum Wages Act came into force in the year 1950. The plan provided Rs. 3.12 lakhs for strengthening of the administrative machinery of labour department for implementation of Minimum Wages Act in agriculture in whole of the state. Minimum wages in agriculture was first fixed at Patna on experimental basis and extended to Gaya and Shahabad in 1953.

Second Five Year Plan 1956-61: The second five year plan in India was aimed at influencing large scale industries and so in second five year plan, the Bihar Government too had the same objective. But the Bihar Government continued with the community development programme as a source of employment to rural landless.

Third Five Year Plan 1961-66: It was the period when Government of India had to face two foreign attacks from China and Pakistan. Hence, the plan of Bihar Government was also adversely affected without starting any new community development programme.

Fourth Five Year Plan: In 1971, 38.9% of the total number of workers were agricultural labourers in Bihar as against 36.3% of all India level. The census figure of 1971 indicated significant increase in the percentage of agricultural labourers to the total population. The fourth plan therefore laid emphasis on the agricultural development programmes irrigation and power sector, community development programme, etc.

Fifth Five Year Plan: A vast majority of the people in Bihar were depending for their livelihood on agriculture. It is therefore proposed to give the highest priority to agriculture production and development programme in areas where assured irrigation is already available or will become wantable shortly. For promoting the agricultural labourers, main emphasis was given on well co-ordinated area development programme, optimum use of the irrigation water available, introduction of multicorppping and the high yielding varieties with other inputs required and development of roads, market and storage facilities .

Sixth Five Year Plan (1980-85): It aims at providing house sites to the landless agricultural labourers, rural artisans and other categories of persons belonging to weaker sections in rural areas. It was introduced under minimum needs programme, financed under the central sector of the plan. This was subsequently transferred to the state. Under this scheme, every family belonging to any one of the categories mentioned above is to be provided a developed house site measuring 200 yards free of cost along with assistance for construction of dwelling unit thereon assisting all workers, agricultural or otherwise in avoiding themselves of employment or self employment with reasonable wage and working condition ensuring at least a minimum standard of living. In concrete terms, 33 rural labour welfare centres were to be set up and 138 agricultural labour inspectors were to be appointed.

Seventh Five Year Plan (1985-1990): Considering that Bihar has 8.5 million marginal and small farmers and 7.37 million agricultural labourers and the state accounts for 57.49% of the total population below the poverty line, the highest priority had been given to the programmes of eradication of poverty and unemployment through centrally sponsored schemes of IRDP, NREP, DPAP in the rural development. The capabilities of two agricultural universities be increased by strengthening the campus facility. Achievement of the plan was that 11 centers benefited 2023 lakh agricultural labourers.

Eighth Five Year Plan (1992- 1997): Agricultural labours constitute a major part of the total labour force in the state. Their living conditions are poor and real wage level is low. Keeping in view the objectives of the eighth five year plan, it is of primary importance that the steps are taken to help the agricultural labourers who are an unorganized sector for this under administrative machinery wages act will have to be strengthened and streamlined. Also steps will be taken to help the agricultural labourers to organize themselves by creating awareness among them regarding their rights by dissemination of information of various labour and welfare enactment through well organized training centers (camps). In the state of Bihar, Directorate of Agricultural Labour had earlier been constituted and posted officials at various supervisory levels.

Ninth Five Year Plan (1997-2002): Ninth five year plan was planned keeping in view the state economy in context of the national economy. Bihar being predominantly an agricultural economy, emphasis has given to this people and problem of this sector. The objective was to check unemployment along with disguise employment which in turn check wages not to rise. Maximum priority was given to rural development.

Tenth Five Year Plan (2002-2007): It has worked nothing much about the agricultural labourers in separate. But there is mention about the labour wing of labour, employment and training department which enforce various labour laws for the welfare of the workers in the state. To ensure better implementation of the labour laws and welfare of the workers, a total sum of Rs. 486.40 lakhs has been proposed for tenth five year plan (2002-2007).

SUGGESTIONS

The agricultural labour constitutes the largest segment in the rural society. They are unorganized and so they are not able to reap many benefits of modernization. They lead a life of object poverty with a very low standard of living representing the most deplorable section of the society. The number of the agricultural labourers is continuously rising over the years resulting in lower wages which are already low due to lack of alternative employment .The rise in the number of agricultural laborers has increased due to sub-division and fragmentation of land and to the social structure of the state. Some of the suggestions that can be put forth for improving their conditions are mentioned below:

(1) The first step should be taken for creating alternative source of employment.

(2) Better infrastructural facilities need to be provided for encouragement of self-employment among female agricultural labourers. Efforts have to be made to bring the development of different skills in line with the social need and give opportunities to rural unemployed women.

(3) There is need for self employment programmes. The role of government is also required for effective self employment programmes, government legislations, etc.

(4) New agricultural technology should be spread over through the information technology to the rural masses.

(5) Once again emphasis should be given to the panchayati raj system by the government.

(6) Creation of social awareness among the agricultural labourers is an important element in the administration of minimum wages. It should be done through rural camps, worker's education and publicity through mass media, etc.

(7) Administration of minimum wages in agriculture is not a regulatory but a developmental process and forms part of longer and integrated efforts for rural development. Employment generating activities outside agriculture particularly in off seasons growth of agriculture sector, raising labour productivity and prices of agricultural products are necessary adjunct to the efforts.

(8) Efficient and adequate official machinery for the implementation of minimum wage regulation is required.

References

Mehta, B. S. and P. K. Mishra (2005), "Rural Non-farm Employment in Jharkhand–Trends and Issues", *Bihar Economic Journal*, Annual Conference Volume 2005, p. 423.

Sharma, Alakh, N. and Mathur Ashok (2007), "Towards Transforming Bihar: Challenges and Opportunities", Global Meet for a Resurgent Bihar, 19-21 January, 2007, Reading Material, p. 1.

Ibid, p. 1.

Kosambi, D. D. (1987), "The Culture and Civilization of Ancient India in Historical Outline, Vikash Publication, p. 50.

Sharma, K. K. and Singh, Paramanand, "Changes in Agrarian Relations in Twentieth Century Bihar", *The Indian Journal of Labour Economics*, Vol. 44, No. 202, p. 933.

Sharma, Alakh N. (2005), "Agrarian Relations of Socio-Economic Changes in Bihar", *Economic and Political Weekly*, March 5, p. 960.

Ahmed, Muzaffar in the first session of Mymen Singh District Krishak Samittee as citied in Chaudhari, Binay Bhusan, "Agrarian Movement in Bengal and

Bihar 1919-1931" in A.R Desai (ed) Peasant Strangles in India, OUP Bombay, 1979, p.361. The session was held in February, 1939 and Ahmad was its President.

Thorner Daniel (1976), "Agrarian Prospects in India", Allied Publishers Ltd., Bombay, p. 11.

Singh, Amrendra Kumar and S. D. Mishra (2003), "Agricultural Labour in Bihar in Socio Economic Perspectives", *Bihar Economic Journal*, p. 158.

Singh, Seema (2005), "Education of Information and Communication Technology as an Aid in Development in Rural Jharkhand", *Bihar Economic Journal*, 9th Annual Volume, 2005, p. 158.

Verma, P. C. Bihar Economy, p. 128.

Ibid., p. 133.

Jha, Bal Krishna and Ranjan Kumar Sinha (2003), "Economic Impact of Occupational Diversification on Agricultural Labour in Bihar", *Bihar Economic Journal*, p. 187.

Ibid, p. 189.

Sinha, Pawan Kumar and Kumari Madhulata (2005), "Rural Non-Farm Employment Scenario in Bihar: Problems and Prospects", *Bihar Economic Journal*, p. 443.

Ibid, 161.

Singh, Amrendra Kumar and S. D. Mishra (2003), "Agricultural Labour in Bihar in Socio Economic Perspectives", *Bihar Economic Journal*, p. 160.

17

AGRICULTURAL LABOUR: A CASE STUDY

Tapan Kumar Shandilya & Md. Reyazuddin

INTRODUCTION

Agriculture labourers are the most marginalized section of the rural economy. They have been benefited least for the last five decades of development of our country. Although the agricultural labour's contribution in the development of agriculture is very high but their share in the gains of development has been the lowest. The proportion of rural population below the poverty line has declined over the years yet the rural poverty of agricultural labour household still persists.

It has been accepted widely that agricultural labourers constitute the lowest strata of the economy and that the incidents of poverty is higher among the agricultural labour households. At all-India level, 49 per cent of the agricultural labourers were found in the lowest range of monthly per capita expenditure (Sarvekshana, 1998). The wage rates of agricultural labourers remained stagnant for a long period of time, nearly till mid-1970s. There are studies to indicate that the wage rates have failed to keep pace with the labour productivity (Nayyar, 1977; Bhalla,1993). The results from the literature studying the trickle down effect of green revolution are rather mixed. It was pointed out that there were several mechanisms at work that counteracted the economic generating forces for the labourers during that period, such as stagnancy in the wages due to the influx of labourers in the second phase of green revolution and increased bargaining power of the rich farmer leading to higher administrated prices of foodgrains (adversely affecting real wages) (Bardhan, 1984). The discussion on the determinants of poverty have gained new dimensions after 1990, in the background of the new economic policy, the structural adjustment programme and the move towards liberalisation of the economy and their likely effects on the employment situation in the labour market. Agricultural labour markets were characterised by declining real wages in the early 1990s.

This segment becomes extremely vulnerable to these adverse effects, if any, of the new policies and effect their real economic status due to their peculiar characteristics-firstly, labourers who are categorized as 'unskilled', face difficulties in mobility towards better employment opportunities. Secondly, labourers are heterogeneous class of workers with differing socio-economic status. As the labour market is fragmented, their bargaining power is weak and hence their organisation becomes difficult. Thirdly, the absence of comprehensive safety nets and imperfection in credit markets increase the risks faced by these labourers.

The history of economic development reveals that with the increase in pace of development, there is a decline in the proportion of agricultural workers as well as the share of agricultural income. Unfortunately, this has not happened in India (Sidhu and Grewal, 1981). On the contrary, the proportion of the population dependent upon agriculture has remained almost constant during the last one century. The agricultural labour is economically the weakest and socially the most handicapped section of rural society. Steeped in age old misery and driven to destitution in times of natural calamity, a vast majority of them continue to live on the verge of poverty (Jit, 1980). Until the conditions of this vital section of the society improve, the economy cannot progress as a whole.

In order to assess them and to identify various functional bottlenecks that frustrate the achievement of goals and objectives and widen the gap between the objective of the schemes and their actual functionality, a small field study has been undertaken. The major objectives of the present study are as follows:

1. To explore the socio-economic status of agricultural labourers and to find out how far these factors have been responsible for a number of occupational and non-occupational risks;
2. To evaluate their actual living and working conditions;
3. To find out their actual wages, total income and debts borrowed from traditional sources and banks and co-operative societies etc.;
4. To explore their awareness regarding various labour laws applicable to them, different governmental programmes launched for their benefits and the also the benefits which they could get out of these.

The universe of the present fieldwork consists of agricultural labourers of some villages of Bakhtiyarpur block of Patna district. The obvious criterion of selecting of these villages has been the investigator's accessibility and acquaintance. The technique of stratified random sampling was adopted for the study. Equal number of cases were included from three categories of agricultural labourers, namely, male, female and child agricultural labourers. Their respondents belonging to all categories who would respond properly to the questions, were included in the sample. The required number of cases were available from four villages. A brief questionnaire was formulated and was given to a very limited number of respondents in the beginning but it did not fetch any proper and meaningful responses or any complete and substantial information. Therefore, an interview schedule was formulated keeping in view the aims of the field study and also the abilities of the interviewees so that their responses may easily be recorded by the investigator himself and the information collected may be classified and analyzed properly.

Process of Data Collection

The investigator visited a few villages interviewing male, female and child agricultural labourers on the lines determined in the interview schedule and recording their responses. Some strictly adhering to the interview schedule would not serve the purpose; so the investigator resorted to some informal questions to elicit the required information. Apart from the interview, for the investigator also jotted down some information by observing the conditions in which these people actually lived and worked. The collected data were edited in order to ensure that all the required information had been gathered and irrelevant information omitted. After editing, the data were classified and analyzed. Two cases from each category was randomly picked up to be discussed in detail.

District Census figures were subjected to various changes during last 50 years. In spite of these variations, the proportion of the depressed and backward section of population-Scheduled Caste, Scheduled Tribes, Backward Classes are in the district. The lower castes have higher participation in agricultural activities than that of others. It may be due to the deep-rooted customs and traditions prevailing in the society since long. The generalizations established regarding socio-economic status working and living conditions and safety and development measures are common even for the agricultural labourer of the district. The increase in the strength of agricultural labourers, inherent weakness of agricultural occupations and existence of exploitative feudal characteristics are explicitly visible in agricultural sector. The agricultural labour households in general are bound to involve majority of their family members to work as agricultural labourers to take out their livelihood. This makes availability of all the three classes-male, female and child, a common trend in labourers give more scope for their easy exploitation. This has necessitated to study their problem keeping them in three different categories in the present field study.

Data Analysis

Data of the labourers constituting the sample reveals the majority of cases belongs to Scheduled Caste and Backward Classes (Table 1). There were 14, 12 and 11 cases belonging to Scheduled Castes in male, female and child labour categories respectively while 13, 11 and 12 cases belonged to Backward Class for the same categories. Only 3, 7 and 7 cases belonged to Scheduled Tribes from male, female and child labourer categories respectively. So far as the educational status of the respondents was concerned, majority of them were illiterate (the number was 14, 20 and 10 for male, female and child labourers). 8 males, 4 females and 16 children were educated upto class V. Only 4 males and 3 children got their education above class V. None of the female labourers had the opportunity to continue her education beyond class V. Only 6

Table 1
General Data

Type of Payment	*Male Total Number of Cases = 30*	*Female Total Number of Cases = 30*	*Child Total Number of Cases = 30*
Caste			
General	Nil	Nil	Nil
S.C.	14	12	11
S.T.	3	7	7
B.C.	13	11	12
Education			
Illiterate	14	20	10
Upto Class V	8	4	16
Above Class V	4	Nil	3
Ownership			
Land	6	1	-
Landless	22	26	

male and 1 female labourer owned some land and remaining 22 male and 26 female labourers were landless.

Table 2 reveals that all labourers whether male, female or child were casual labourers except two male, two female and one child labourers who were attached labourers. The male workers worked for 10 to 12 hours during peak season while during slack season they worked for 6 to 8 hours a day. For females the during of working hours was 8 to 10 hours and 5 to 6 hours daily during peak and slack seasons respectively. For children this length was 8 to 10 hours and 4 to 6 hours during peak and slack seasons respectively. All of them were given break for lunch etc. in between the hours of work. The availability of employment was 160 to 180 mandays for male labourers, 130 to 150 mandays for female labourers and 135 to 150 mandays for child workers in a year in which 130 to 145 mandays were available to men in agriculture and 35 to 45 mandays in other occupations, 105 to 115 mandays to women in agriculture and 20 to 35 in other occupations and 115 to 130 mandays to children in agriculture and 20 and 35 in

Table 2
Working Conditions

Type of Payment	*Male Total Number of Cases = 30*	*Female Total Number of Cases = 30*	*Child Total Number of Cases = 30*
Nature of Employment			
Attached	2	2	1
Casual	28	28	29
Share-cropper	Nil	Nil	Nil
Bonded labourer	Nil	Nil	Nil
Hours of work (in hours)			
During peak season	10-12	8-10	8-10
During slack season	6-8	8-10	4-6
With break	30	30	30
Without break	Nil	Nil	Nil
Total mandays (in a year)	160-180	130-150	135.150
Employment in agriculture	130-145	105-115	140-160
Employment in other occupations	35-45	20-35	20-35
Self-employment	35-45	10-25	15-30

other occupations. The number of mandays in self-employment ranged between 35 to 45 for men, 10 to 25 for women and 15 to 30 child agricultural labourers.

Table 3 shows that 12 men and 8 children were given payment of wages purely in cash while 5 men, 25 women and 20 children were given wages in cash and kind both. No labour received wages. purely in kind and no women labour was paid wages purely in cash. The payment of wages of all the respondents was irregular and on daily basis expect two attached male, two attached female and one attached child labourer who received payment on monthly basis. The amount of wages in agricultural occupation during peak season and during slack season ranged from Rs. 12 to Rs. 18 in case of men, Rs. 9 to Rs. 15 in case of women and Rs. 8 to Rs. 12 in case of child labourers respectively. In other occupations, the men labourers could get Rs. 15-25, female labourers Rs. 15-20 and child labourers Rs. 12-16 respectively. None of the cases had any other income other than their wages from agriculture and non-agricultural occupations.

Table 3
Wages

Type of Payment	*Male Total Number of Cases = 30*	*Female Total Number of Cases = 30*	*Child Total Number of Cases = 30*
Mode of payment			
Cash	12	Nil	8
Kind	Nil	Nil	Nil
Cash and kind both	15	25	20
Regular			
Daily	28	28	29
Weekly	Nil	Nil	Nil
Monthly	2	2	1
Irregular	30	30	30
Per day wages in rupees			
In agricultural occupation (Rs.)	12-18	9-15	8-12
In other occupations (Rs.)	15-25	15-20	12-16
Other income	—	—	—

Table 4 shows the indebtedness of agricultural labour. The amount of debt in cash ranged from Rs. 300 to Rs. 3000 in case of men and Rs. 100 to Rs. 1000 in case of women. The value of debts borrowed in kind ranged from Rs. 150 to 500 in case of men and Rs. 40 to 500 in case of women. Seven men and four women borrowed debts in cash and kind both. 17 men out of 25 and 12 women out of 14 borrowed loans for personal purposes while 4 men and 2 women borrowed it for personal as well as professional purposes. No women took a debt for purely professional purpose whereas 4 men borrowed the loan for such purpose. 17 men and all of the 14 women borrowed loan traditional sources, 4 men from Banks and Co-operatives and 4 men from both kinds of sources. 17 men and 14 women had to pay off their debts with interest while 8 men and 10 women had also mortgaged their property or ornaments, etc. all agreed to the following reasons for borrowing a debt from traditional source-easy availability of the loan without complicated formalities, for all purposes whether personal or professional, limitation of Banks and Co-operatives for providing the loan.

Table 5 shows that 15 male, 15 female and 12 child labourers migrated to some other place for getting employment whereas the remaining did not migrate. The trend of migration was rural to rural in case of 4 men, 2 women and 2 children while it was rural to urban in case of 16 men, 8 women and 10 children. Underemployment was the cause of migration for 12 men and 4 women while unemployment was the reason for 22 men, 6 women and 4 children. 15 men, 10 women and 12 children migrated due to low wages available at their original place while 8 men, 2 women and 3 children migrated for other reasons. The migration resulted into higher wages in case of 15 men, 13 women and 12 children more employment registered 8 men, 8 women and 13 children. Eight men, three women and four children reported various kinds of exploitation due to migration by employers as well as middlemen.

Table 4
Indebtedness

Details	*Male Total Number of Cases = 30*	*Female Total Number of Cases = 30*
Amount		
Cash	8 (Rs. 300 to 3000)	4 (Rs. 100 to 1000)
Kind	10 (Rs. 150 to 500)	6 (Rs. 40 to 500)
Both	7	4
Purpose		
Professional	4	-
Personal	17	12
Both	4	2
Source of loan		
Traditional	17	14
Bank and Co-operatives	4	
Both	4	
Condition		
With interest	17	14
Without interest		
Mortgage		
Others		
Reasons for borrowing from traditional source		
Easy availability	25	14
For all purposes	25	14
Limitation of Bank/co-operatives	25	14
Any other	–	–

Table 6 shows the position of occupational risks. 15 each from men and women and 6 children used dangerous machines in the agricultural tasks assigned to them while all 25 men, 15 women and 12 children made use of fertilizers and chemicals. None of the respondents of any category took special care while using machines or chemicals and fertilizers and received any special training while using the same. Out of 30 men included in the sample, 3 suffered from permanent and partial disability, 2 from temporary total disability and 12 from temporary partial disablement due to accident or occupational disease. Eleven

Table 5
Migration

Details	*Male Total Number of Cases = 30*	*Female Total Number of Cases = 30*	*Child Total Number of Cases = 30*
Availability			
Yes	15	15	12
No	8	22	18
Trend			
Rural to rural	4	2	2
Rural to urban	16	8	10
Causes			
Underemployment	12	4	-
Unemployment	22	6	4
Low wages	15	10	12
Others	8	2	
Consequences			
Higher Wages	15	13	12
More employment	8	8	14
Exploitation	8	3	4

women and 4 children suffered from temporary partial disability and one child labourer suffered from temporary total disability. Only two women labourers suffered from occupational diseases. So far as the provision of relief is concerned, none of the afflicted labourers got any compensation or any other kind of relief except two men and one child who were given some help for medical care.

According to data shown in Table 7 none of the female or child labourers had any knowledge about legal provisions regarding minimum wages while 22 out of 30 men had some knowledge about the same. None of the respondents had any knowledge of amount of minimum wages fixed by the government or legal provisions regarding the payments of legal regarding compensation in case of any eventuality or accident. None except 5 male labourers had any knowledge about the prohibition of bonded labour and no one had any idea about equal remuneration, 22 men and 11 women had some idea of governmental schemes for employment

Table 6
Occupational Hazards

Details	*Male Total Number of Cases = 30*	*Female Total Number of Cases = 30*	*Child Total Number of Cases = 30*
Use of dangerous machines	15	15	6
Use of fertilizers and chemicals	25	15	12
Use of special care	–	–	
Special training	–	–	
Accident/Occupational disease			
Disablement	–	–	-
Permanent and total	–	–	-
Temporary and partial	3	–	-
Temporary and total	2	1	
Temporary and partial	12	1 1	4
Occupational disease	–	2	
Relief			
Medical care	2	–	1
Compensation	–		
Others	–		
Help provided by Employer	-		
Governmental Agency	2	–	1
Non-governmental Agency	–	–	–
Claim of compensation			

generation and rural development while only 15 men, 6 women and 18 children had some knowledge about educational programmes. Only 6 male respondents received some information from Gram Panchayat regarding governmental schemes and regarding governmental schemes and wages etc. No role was played by B.D.O. or voluntary organization at all. None of the respondents except 12 men and 10 women had any knowledge about special measures for Scheduled Tribes, Backward Classes, women and children. These 12 men and 10 women had some idea of special measures for Scheduled Caste.

The overall estimation regarding organisation are given in Table 8 which shows that agricultural labourers are unorganised. Only two of male agricultural labourers had a little idea of organisation and that too due to membership of' local political organisation.

Table 7
Awareness

Details	*Male Total Number of Cases = 30*	*Female Total Number of Cases = 30*	*Child Total Number of Cases = 30*
Regarding constitutional and legal protections			
Minimum wages			
Nil	22	30	30
Some	8	-	-
Wages fixed by the government			
Nil	30	30	30
Some	–	–	-
Compensation			
Nil	30	30	30
Some	–	–	-
Prohibition of Bonded Labour			
Nil	25	30	30
Some	5	–	-
Equal remuneration			
Nil	30	30	30
Some	–	–	
Governmental schemes			
Employment generation	22	11	
Rural development	22	11	
Education	15	6	18
Any other	–	–	
Role of governmental/ non-governmental agencies			
Gram Panchayat	6	–	-
B.D.O.	–	-	
Voluntary organisations	–	–	
Special measures for			
Scheduled Caste	12	10	
Scheduled Tribe	–	-	
Backward classes	–	–	-
Women	–	–	-
Children	–	–	–

All male and female labourers agreed that illiteracy, ignorance and seasonality of employment were the main reason for their not being organised. 10 men and 8 women felt that it was due to frequent changes in employer-employee relationship while 20 men and 14 women attributed this to their lack of consciousness. 11 men and 10 women felt that less demand and more supply was the reason for lack of organisation. None except 2 men respondents told about some efforts made by political parties in this direction. None reported any attempt to organise the agricultural labourers by any voluntary organisation or trade union. The usefulness of organisation was admitted by 18 men and 22 women while 6 men and 12 women pessimistically felt that it will not be useful for their welfare as development.

Table 8
Organisation

Details	*Male Total Number of Cases = 30*	*Female Total Number of Cases = 30*
Membership of organisation/Union		
Yes	2	-
No	28	-
Reasons		
Illiteracy	30	30
Ignorance	30	30
Seasonality of employment	30	30
Frequent change in employer/employee relationship	10	8
Lack of consciousness	20	14
Less demand and more supply	11	10
Attempt to organise by		
Voluntary organisation	-	-
Trade union	-	-
Political party	2	-
Any other	-	-
Importance		
Useful	18	22
Not useful	6	12

CONCLUSION

The present study synthesizes vital informations relating to the socio-economic problems of agricultural labourers. In order to appreciate and eradicate the problems of agricultural labourers, the need is to evaluate the sociological factors, which have resulted into failure of their economic development. These sociological factors may have negative as well as positive character. First group of problems arise out of the persistence of old social institutions like caste, joint family, tribes, traditional religious organisations and serfdom etc. They also emerged out of old forms of social control like supernatural sanctions, authoritarian norms complicated and intricate caste family, tribal religious and other customary sanctions penetrating almost every core of life of the Indian community. Further to emanate from large scale illiteracy, ill-health and unemployment, etc. one of the major sociological factors deciding the fate of agricultural labourers was belief that low castes are born to labour with hands and high castes were to enjoy the fruits of their labour. The social status, economic power and political influence as much as the level of living, which is their consequence. The existence of casteism is an important element which keeps the standard of living of the agricultural labourer at a level more depressed than other rural families. Caste prevents mobility of the people, which is essential for dynamic development. The monopoly of certain castes and groups of certain linguistic zones has generated a peculiar unrest in modern competitive social setting. It is easy to identity now the major aggravating factors that are likely to worsen the problems of agricultural labourers.

SUGGESTIONS

On the basis of the present study and its conclusions, the following suggestions may be made:

1. The upliftment of agricultural labourers is linked with overall development of agriculture itself. It is high time to rethink about the pattern of agriculture to be followed. The majority of fragmented uneconomic holdings are unable to be affected by Green Revolution. Awareness should be developed and encouragement should be given regarding development of cooperative farming so that

modernization of agriculture can be achieved. It will raise agricultural productivity and labour absorption. It is suggested to experiment the extreme methods existing in either conservative Japanese system or revolutionary Chinese/Vietnamese system. To the extent that the rural masses lose the direct control over land and its operation, they also lose their capacity to fulfil their basic consumption needs on the basis of self-provisioning. While there should be command over purchasing power by the rural poor, there also must be expansion of employment opportunities for them, as otherwise the schemes like public distribution system in rural areas have only limited utility.

2. The problem of agricultural labourers in India cannot be overcome by legislative enactments and developmental schemes in isolation. They should be linked with structural-institutional reforms in rural areas.

3. The existing legislations and development schemes have been, by and large, proved to be ineffective in improving the socio-economic conditions of Scheduled Castes, Scheduled Tribes and Backward Class agricultural labourers. More stringent measures are needed to eradicate social inequality of Harijans.

4. Land ownership certainly affects social, economic and political status in rural India. For agricultural workers, it is the perennial source of income. It necessitates restructure of the land reform measures to establish a balance in man-land ratio. Agrarian reforms through legislations will be possible by effective participation of the beneficiaries at policy framing/law making and its implementation to avoid loopholes in legislations, cumbersome judicial process, apathetic administrative attitude of bureaucracy and inefficient and pro-losers implementing machinery. The attitude of State

Governments is an important factor for the achievement of the objectives of agrarian reforms. The State of Kerala is an example where the pro-labour government has helped a lot in this process.

5. Child labour was until recently controlled by the Employment of Children Act, 1938, which was almost on the same lines on Article 24. This has been substituted by the Child Labour (Prohibition and Regulation) Act, 1986. A new National Policy on Child Labour has been formulated in 1987 in which selection of child labour concentration areas was made with an idea of setting up schools for education, vocational training, supplementary nutrition and stipend for children removed from forbidden employments in compensation for the losses in earning. The new Act and new policy, both have tended more towards regulation of employment than its prohibition.
6. The migration is natural consequence of unemployment and variations in wages and job avenues. The Inter-State Migrant Workmen (Regulation of Employment and Conditions of Services) Act, 1979 should be effectively enforced to regulate the working conditions of migrant labourers, particularly the agricultural labourers.
7. It will not be feasible to adopt the western pattern of comprehensive social insurance system available from "cradle to grave" by and large at the cost of the government, estimating the national resources and population explosion. Despite this the special problems of agricultural labourers like unemployment due to seasonality of employment and non-availability of alternative employment, unforeseeable natural or accident causes which destroy the crops or even means of their production in situation like flood, drought, famine, etc., which certainly do fall outside the familiar areas of traditional social security, need special protection.

8. The foremost requirement of effective implementation of governmental policies is the organization of agricultural labourers. It is essential to balance the clashing interests of employers and employees by providing collective bargaining strength to agricultural labourers. Unionisation needs motivation, social or political and consciousness of the labourers reciprocates. The existing model of trade unions in industrial sector should not be followed for agricultural sector because of the differentiations in employer-employee relationship, labour structure and work situation, etc. There is no distinct employer-employee relationship like industry.
9. The awareness amongst agricultural labourers should be developed through legislations and governmental developmental policies so that consciousness may be developed to secure the benefits under various schemes and safeguard their interest. The mass media, various sources of communication, NGOs. and other voluntary organisations, educational media, rural camps and special governmental machinery should be effectively used in this regard with a coordination amongst each other. The lead banks, leading industries and social organisations like Lions, Rotary and Youth Clubs should develop model villages.
10. Government should launch special drive for controlling population. It must be checked through different control methods because it is not possible to increase employment opportunities at once.
11. Government should promote small and cottage industries and agri-based industries.
12. Government should think over and provide better infrastructure facilities. Apart from this, law and order must be taken into consideration with top priority.

References

Bardhan, P. K. (1984), Land, Labour and Rural Poverty,: Essays in Development Economics, Oxford University Press, Delhi.

Bhalla, Sheila (1993), "The Dynamics of Wage Determination and Employment Generation in Indian Agriculture", *Indian Journal of Agricultural Economics*, Vol. 48, No. 3, July-September.

Govt. of India (1998), *Sarvekshana*, Vol. 21, No. 3, National Sample Survey Organisation, January-March.

Grewal, S. S. and M. S. Sidhu (1979), A Study on Migrant Agricultural Labour in Punjab, Department of Economics and Sociology, Punjab Agricultural University, Ludhiana, pp. 1-28.

Jit, Ranjit Singh (1980), A Study of the Economic Profile of Agricultural Labour in Punjab, Ph.D. Dissertation (Unpublished), Department of Economics and Sociology, Punjab Agricultural University, Ludhiana.

Nayyar, Rohini (1977), "Wages, Employment and Standard of Living of Agricultural Labourers in Uttar Pradesh" in ILO, Poverty and Londlessness in Rural Asia, Geneva.

INDEX

C